D0409731

A LIFE TOO SHORT

Also by Ronald Reng

The Keeper of Dreams

Ronald Reng

A LIFE TOO SHORT

The Tragedy of Robert Enke

Translated by Shaun Whiteside

YELLOW JERSEY PRESS
LONDON

Published by Yellow Jersey Press 2011

6 8 10 9 7 5

Copyright © Piper Verlag GmbH, Munich 2010
English translation © Shaun Whiteside, 2011

Ronald Reng has asserted his right under the Copyright, Designs
and Patents Act 1988 to be identified as the author of this work

First published as *Robert Enke: Ein allzu kurzes Leben* in 2010
by Piper Verlag, Germany

First published in Great Britain in 2011 by
Yellow Jersey Press
Random House, 20 Vauxhall Bridge Road,
London SW1V 2SA

www.randomhouse.co.uk

Addresses for companies within The Random House Group Limited can be
found at: www.randomhouse.co.uk/offices.htm

The Random House Group Limited Reg. No. 954009

A CIP catalogue record for this book
is available from the British Library

ISBN 9780224091657

The Random House Group Limited supports The Forest Stewardship
Council (FSC®), the leading international forest certification organisation.
Our books carrying the FSC label are printed on FSC® certified paper. FSC
is the only forest certification scheme endorsed by the leading environmental
organisations, including Greenpeace. Our paper procurement policy can be
found at www.randomhouse.co.uk/environment

Typeset in Sabon LT Std by Palimpsest Book Production Ltd,
Falkirk, Stirlingshire

Printed and bound in Great Britain by
Clays Ltd, St Ives plc

Through these balmy summer days, which seem made for ease and pleasure, the testing continues: what part is being tested he is no longer sure. Sometimes it seems he is being tested simply for testing's sake, to see whether he will endure the test.

Youth, J. M. Coetzee

Contents

Illustrations   ix
The Waning Power of Poetry   1

One: A Child of Fortune   9
Two: The Snap   29
Three: Defeats Are His Victory   51
Four: Fear   71
Five: The City of Light   79
Six: Happiness   90
Seven: Ever Further, Ever Higher   104
Eight: Feet   118
Nine: Novelda   135
Ten: Thoughts by the Pool   151
Eleven: Wrapped in Fog   174
Twelve: No Light, Not Even in the Fridge   192
Thirteen: The Holiday Island   212
Fourteen: There is Robert, There is No Goal   235
Fifteen: Lara   250
Sixteen: Afterwards   270
Seventeen: In the Land of Goalkeepers   290
Eighteen: Leila   305
Nineteen: The Black Dog   329
Twenty: The Cheerfulness of Xylophones Silenced   363

Epilogue: The View of the Palace   386
Notes   389

Illustrations

p.55: picture alliance/Sven Simon
p.85: Getty Images/Martin Rose
p.126: picture alliance/dpa
p.168: Silke Witzel
p.177: ddp images/AP/Murad Sezer
p.278: Getty Images/Vladimir Rys
pp.256, 294, 322, 332: Ulrich zur Nieden
pp.10, 13, 17, 25, 40, 46, 59, 80, 87, 98, 102, 153, 170, 237, 242, 260, 263, 282, 324, 359: private individuals

The Waning Power of Poetry

'I would like a poem,' Teresa says, and for a second that lasts an eternity the house falls silent.

Robert looks quizzically at his wife to see if she really means it. Is he supposed to give her a poem for her birthday? 'It'd be nice,' Teresa adds casually, and thinks no more about it.

But he can't get the idea out of his head.

It's a few years since he last read a poem, let alone wrote one. He tries to remember. A poem, he thinks, has to rhyme; a good poem, he believes, is like a hint of a smile, with delicate humour between the lines. With that idea in his head, Robert starts writing.

Some afternoons he lies to Teresa, saying he's going to his office for a while to go through tax documents or to complete some other paper-work. Then he sits down at his desk with a biro and a note-pad. His gaze drifts to the garden. The rear side of his office is one huge window; it gives him a feeling of wellbeing when the sunbeams fall on him in the spring. But now, in the winter, it's less pleasant at his desk. The heating in the office is unreliable. Their house in Empede, on the flat terrain of Lower Saxony, is a converted farm. His office used to be the stable.

The words he puts down on the paper look bent and rough – he hardly ever uses his valuable goalkeeper's fingers to write. But in his head the words start forming rhymes more and more quickly, and he's filled with joy – not like the flood of happiness he experiences when he steers a difficult shot over the bar, quite gentle, but so intense that Robert has to keep on writing, in the office, in the hotel the evening before a

Bundesliga match, on scraps of note-paper, on the backs of bills. Sometimes, if he has no paper to hand, he taps his ideas into his mobile phone. By the time the big day, 18 February 2009, arrives he has written 104 lines.

He wishes Teresa a happy birthday while they're still in bed. When she goes to the bathroom he creeps into the hall and lets the dogs out. They have nine of them, and two cats. Teresa rescued them from the streets during their years in southern Europe. On her last birthday she'd wished for a pet pig. He'd decided to take it as a joke.

He lights candles in the living-room.

'Let's do the presents this afternoon, when we've got more peace,' says Teresa when she comes in.

He shakes his head; it won't take long. He asks her to sit down at the old farmhouse table, just for a moment. As he presses her gently into the chair by her shoulders he can't help smiling with anticipation. Then he takes his place on the other side of the table.

He sets his poem down in front of him. But he speaks by heart.

For your birthday, what will it be?
A diamond, beautiful to see?
Perhaps a watch from the jeweller's store?
It won't be cheap, of that you can be sure.

And what about having a pig for a pet?
Robbi will put down his foot about that!
Cats, then, or horses, or maybe a dog?
No, please, stop it, my head's in a fog.

So, for her birthday, what's it to be?
Oh no, what she wants is a poem from me!
It isn't too big, or too much, or too dear
Yet the very thought of it fills me with fear.

Teresa is struck dumb with joy. Verse by verse he presents her with her whole life: the move to Empede, her love of animals, even the death of their daughter Lara, who was born with a serious heart defect and died after an operation at the age of two.

> Then Lara came with her imperfect heart –
> That was something that tore us apart.
> But she was strong, and even in pain
> She still lived up to the family name.

When he's finished, Teresa has tears in her eyes. She says only one sentence, 'Please read it to me again.'

He starts again, at the beginning, all twenty-six verses, all 104 lines. At the end he says:

> We can't then help wondering what'll come next
> Along life's long journey – it's got me perplexed.
> Will Grandpa stay, or will he not?
> Are we going to move house? I don't know a jot!
>
> I won't let things become too much of a worry –
> The days soon pass, there is no great hurry.
> Only one thing is certain, and this much is true;
> The one thing is this: that I need and love you.

Robert Enke is thirty-one, the German national football team's goalkeeper, strong, good-natured and happy. It will be the last birthday that Teresa celebrates with him.

On Tuesday, 10 November 2009, he calls 'Hallo Ela!' from the kitchen when the housekeeper arrives at nine o'clock. He gives his second daughter, Leila, ten months old, a kiss on the forehead and says goodbye to Teresa. On the magnetic board in the kitchen he has noted in felt-tip pen all the things that need doing, including a reminder to get four tickets for the Bayern Munich game. Then he's out of the door. He has two individual training sessions today: in the morning with the fitness coach, in the afternoon with the goalkeeping coach of Hannover 96. He'll be back at about half-past six, as always. That was what he said to Teresa.

But there's no training arranged for this Tuesday.

I get through to him on his mobile in the car just after half-past twelve. I'm to pass on two requests: an English journalist friend of mine wants to interview him, and the German Olympic Sport Library wants to invite him as guest speaker to their annual conference in January. Hey, am I your secretary, passing on requests to you like this, I try to joke. But he's abrupt on the phone. Of course, I think, he's in the car between training sessions; he probably wants to get to lunch in the Espada or at Heimweh, as always. 'I'll call you back tonight, Ronnie, OK?' he says. I can't remember how he signed off.

That evening I only get calls from other people.

Robert Enke's suicide on that cool autumn evening brought together people who were close to him and people who had never heard his name before in that state where you feel raw inside, as if you've been torn apart. In the days that followed, the sympathy often bordered on hysteria: the London *Times* devoted half of its front page to Robert Enke; in China, state television included him in the main news; the news agencies announced that the number of guests at his funeral was a record ('more than at any funeral in Germany since Chancellor Konrad Adenauer's'). That Robert's passing had assumed such dimensions could only be explained by the fact that these days everything, even death, becomes an event.

But beyond the headlines, deep down, there was real pain, a profound paralysis. Robert's death reminded most of us how little we understand about the illness that is depression. The rest of us, in shockingly large numbers, were reminded of how difficult it is to speak about depression. Just like Robert, we had always thought we had to keep our illness or the illnesses of our families a secret.

4

The facts are regularly in the newspapers: more people die every day of depression-related suicide than in road accidents. But such figures don't give us anything more than a vague idea that sadness is too hard for some people to bear. And if the headlines were bigger when celebrities like Marilyn Monroe or Ernest Hemingway killed themselves, that seemed somehow – even if people didn't say it out loud – to have its own logic; artists do that kind of thing. Because isn't melancholy, the dark side, an inevitable part of art?

But Robert Enke was Germany's number one goalkeeper. The last bulwark, calm and cool in the tensest situations, able to control his stress and anxieties at the most extreme moments. Every weekend professional sportsmen like him play out the dream that everything is achievable; more than most footballers Robert gave the public the illusion that every obstacle could be overcome. At the age of twenty-nine he'd made it into the national side, having been unemployed after a first depression four years earlier and then stranded in the second division in Spain; after Lara's death in 2006 he and Teresa had managed to find a life in parallel to their pain. And at a time when, outwardly at least, he seemed finally to have rediscovered happiness – a family with a daughter, as well as the prospect of being in goal for his country at the World Cup in South Africa – early in August 2009 the depression returned, worse than ever.

What power must this illness have if it can draw a man like Robert Enke to the mistaken conclusion that death is the only solution? What darkness must have surrounded this sensitive person if he could no longer recognise what pain he would be inflicting on his loved ones with his death, and on the driver whose train he threw himself under that November evening?

How do people live with depression, or even just with the knowledge that it could envelop them at any time? With the fear of fear?

Robert wanted to provide those answers himself.

It was he who wanted to write this book, not me.

We had known each other since 2002. I'd reported on him sometimes for newspapers; then all of a sudden we were living in the same city, Barcelona. We met more and more often. I had the feeling that we thought the same things in life were important: politeness, peace, goalkeeping gloves. At some point he said, 'I read a book of yours, I thought it was great!' I blushed at the praise and gave a panicky answer, just something cheeky to put the conversation on a different course, 'One day we'll write one about you together.' My bashfulness grew when I realised he'd taken my banter as a serious suggestion. After that he reminded me repeatedly about our project. 'I've taken some notes so that I don't forget anything.'

Today I know why the biography was so close to his heart. When his goalkeeping career was over, he would finally be able to talk about his illness. In our achievement-oriented society a goalkeeper, the last bastion in defence, can't be a depressive. So Robert summoned up a huge amount of strength to keep his depression secret. He locked himself away in his illness.

So I will now have to tell his story without him.

It's hard to imagine ever coming across such unreservedly open interviewees as I did on my journey through Robert's life. Friends of his suddenly started talking about their own dark thoughts. His goalkeeping rivals, who were supposed to wear the mask of invulnerability in interviews in accordance with the law of professional sport, suddenly started airing their doubts and anxieties.

In most of us, the death of someone we love prompts the urge to be honest, to do good, to want to change things. But a public death brings one thing to the fore above all: our helplessness as human beings.

We didn't even know how to mourn him appropriately. Debates raged cruelly across Germany about whether the funeral celebration in Hanover was reverent or part of an event. Robert's mother was bothered by the fact that the coffin was laid out in the stadium. 'I thought to myself, for heaven's sake, he's not Lenin!', Gisela Enke said to me as we sat in her kitchen in Jena. Robert, sportily elegant with a velvety blue V-neck sweater under his grey suit jacket, has his arm tightly around her in one of the many photographs above the dining-table. This energetic, cordial woman gave us all a lesson in humility. She has understood that it's ridiculous to argue about how successful a funeral was. She has found her peace in the knowledge that everyone involved in the funeral service wanted the best; that even when we're inspired to do good we get lots of things wrong.

Lots of people misunderstood Robert's death. They thought he killed himself because he could no longer bear his life. There were copycat suicides, committed by people who had succumbed to the lunatic notion that then they would be like him, then they would be close to him. What a tragic misunderstanding. Most depressives who attempt suicide don't want to die, they just want the darkness that defines their thoughts to disappear once and for all. Robert was almost certainly no different. 'If you could just have my head for half an hour, you'd know why I go mad,' he once told Teresa.

But it didn't matter how many such explanations I found, the questions, the recurring, revolving questions, wouldn't be stopped by any answer. Had something happened in his child-hood that made him susceptible to depression? What was going on in his head that Tuesday in November when he spent eight hours driving around in his car before stepping out on to the railway tracks? Such questions return remorselessly, even the day after Teresa's thirty-fourth birthday, which is also her first – the first without him.

We're sitting in the kitchen in Empede. Leila is playing that game so beloved of one-year-old children: clearing out the kitchen cupboards. The previous day had been bearable. (Those are Teresa's new units of measurement – bearable or unbearable.) Lots of neighbours called in with their children and brought home-made cakes, flowers, best wishes, even though Teresa hadn't said anything, no one had. A dozen friends gathered in the kitchen. I'd rather read the birthday cards later, said Teresa. And silence fell for a moment. How hollow some words can sometimes sound; birthday cards . . .

Now, the next morning, the emptiness in the house is tangible once more, and Teresa can't help thinking about her thirty-third birthday, which will in a sense always be her last. When Robert gave her the poem.

Teresa still believed in the power of poetry in the late summer of 2009. 'Write me another poem,' she said to him on the phone at the beginning of September, when he was lying in a hotel room in Cologne, at a training-camp with the national team, and the fear of the new day – the fear that someone would expect something from him – wouldn't allow him to get out of bed. In the evening he put a chair on the balcony of his hotel room and, with Cologne Cathedral glowing in the background, wrote another poem on his mobile.

Sitting on the balcony,
My head is a balloon.
Heavy as lead and stone.
It can't be this way.

He no longer felt the joy that beautiful words can prompt, the contentment that comes from writing down one's thoughts. His poem simply didn't matter to him.

In the diary he kept during his depressive periods the entries also get more concise the more violently the illness afflicts him. On the last page there's a single sentence in huge letters. It was presumably supposed to be a reminder to himself, but today his sentence reads like a challenge to us all:

'Don't forget these days.'

ONE

A Child of Fortune

One Sunday afternoon in December 1995 Robert Enke went to the Western Station in Jena and started waiting. The long-distance train from Nuremberg pulled in, passengers got out, and he showed no sign of disappointment when they all walked past him and left the platform. He carried on waiting. Two hours later the early evening train from the south arrived. Again he let all the passengers drift by as if nothing was the matter. It was not the best time of year to be spending half your Sunday waiting for trains in a draughty station so he decided to go to the cinema until the next train came in. He had turned eighteen four months earlier – an age that excuses almost every kind of wilful behaviour and at which, in your opinion, it's other people who are behaving weirdly.

On Sunday, Teresa always came back to the high school sports college on the last train from Bad Windsheim. Even in her second year in Jena she still went to see her parents almost every weekend.

She was hurrying out of the icy station when she spotted him on the bench. She sat next to Robert at school. When she, a Bavarian outsider, had arrived in Year 12 at the East German sports college a year and a half earlier there had only been two seats free, one on its own at the back and one next to Robert. They got on well, she thought, though if she was him she'd give the haircut a bit of thought. He had already started training with the professional footballers of Carl Zeiss Jena and wore his fair hair the way they did, short at the sides, long at the top – 'like a bird's nest on his head'.

Robert with Teresa and his family after a game between Jena sports college and a Thuringian team.

'Hi, what are you doing here?' she asked him. It was after ten o'clock at night.

'I'm waiting for somebody.'

'Oh, OK. Well, have a nice evening.'

She smiled at him briefly and hurried on.

'Hey!' he cried after her. 'You're the one I'm waiting for, obviously!'

And he'd been waiting for more than five hours, he told her a bit later, when they were having a drink in a bar called the French Pub.

He was still living with his mother in the flats on Liselotte Herrmann Strasse, but he hadn't told her or anyone that he was going to go and wait for Teresa at the station. He kept his feelings, his important decisions, all to himself. For weeks afterwards, while he and Teresa were getting closer, he didn't tell his friends a thing. But they weren't surprised when the two of them became a couple – that Robert Enke could achieve that, too. 'We still often talk about it,' says one of his former school friends, Torsten Ziegner, 'about how Robert was this kid with a really sunny nature who managed to do whatever he put his mind to, who couldn't be thrown off track, who was always in a good mood.' Torsten turns his glass of water around in front of him to keep the short silence from getting too big. And for a moment everyone there in the living-room of Andy Meyer, another friend from those days, thinks the same thing: how strange that sounds today, thinking of Robert as a kid with a sunny nature. 'Although,' Andy says at last, speaking bravely into the silence, 'actually I still think that, in spite of everything, Enkus was a child of joy.'

The daylight, reflected by the snow and given a glaring quality, falls through the window of the single-family house in Zwätzen, an area of newly built houses just outside Jena. It's one in the afternoon and Andy has just got up. There's still a hint of tiredness in his eyes. He's a nurse and was on night-shift. Torsten's jeans fit loosely; the Gallagher brothers would like his jacket with its little diamonds and its stand-up collar. He's a professional footballer, a slender, wiry athlete, and at thirty-two he's back with FC Carl Zeiss Jena in the Third Liga. You see Andy and Torsten, in their early thirties, and you immediately sense the warmth, the humour, of those youthful times. 'We realised immediately that we had the same interests – or rather, the same *dis*interests,' says Torsten.

'More than anything else,' adds Andy, 'we laughed.'

It was always the four of them in those days: Torsten Ziegner, Andy Meyer, Mario Kanopa, who went off to be a teacher on the Dutch border, and Robert Enke, who they called Enkus – who they go on calling Enkus because as far as they're concerned he's still the person he used to be.

Robert grew up among clothes lines. He and his friends met in the courtyards of the flats in the afternoon. 'Over the Line' was the name of the game on the estate. He would stand in goal between two clothes props and lob the ball over to his partner who would then volley the ball at the goal.

From a distance his home, the satellite town of Lobeda, is still the first thing you see of Jena. Some forty thousand people used to live there, more than a third of the inhabitants of Jena;

about seventeen thousand remain. On the side-streets between the fifteen-storey industrialised blocks on the Communist boulevards there are a few lower blocks no different from the ones you might see in a West German suburb like Frankfurt-Schwanheim or Dortmund-Nordstadt. While the two German states were constantly reminding each other of their differences, in the eighties such apartment blocks made boys' lives pretty similar in East and West. Washing props ruled the world, from Jena-Lobeda to Frankfurt-Schwanheim. They only learned about adult concerns, Andy Meyer says, after the collapse of East Germany, though perhaps as children they'd just found them boring and hence ignored them: that Andy's father couldn't become a teacher because he wasn't in the Party; that Robert's father, a 400-metre hurdler, was thrown out of high-performance sports promotion because he received postcards from a brother who had escaped to the West.

They would only interrupt their courtyard games for a special reason – when they had to go to football training. Andy Meyer, who lived a few blocks away, had been spotted by the city's big club, FC Carl Zeiss, early on. He was seven at the time, and he got used to winning with Carl Zeiss. So Andy has a particularly clear memory of one defeat. On the uneven pitch in Am Jenzig, at the foot of Jena's Hausberg mountain, FC Carl Zeiss lost 3–1 to SV Jenapharm. Big clubs have their ways of dealing with such defeats, even in children's teams: Helmut Müller, Carl Zeiss's coach, immediately walked over to the parents of Jenapharm's striker, who had scored all three goals, and told them their son should join Carl Zeiss straight away.

It was Robert Enke.

In every sportsman's biography there's a moment when some people say, 'What luck!' And others, 'So that's what they call fate.' Muhammad Ali's Schwinn bicycle was stolen when he was twelve, and the policeman who took his statement advised him to stop crying and become a boxer. Robert was a decent attacking player in the Under-10 youth team at FC Carl Zeiss Jena when the father of Thomas, the goalkeeper, was moved to Moscow for professional reasons. The side needed a new goalkeeper. 'The

Robert Enke (left) at Carnival.

coach had no idea,' says Andy Meyer, 'so everyone had to have a go in goal. The whole business was sorted out quickly. Our lucky kid saved two shots and from that point on he was number one.'

Without knowing how, Robert did everything right: the powerful jump, holding the hands with thumbs spread when catching, the decision to pluck one cross out of the air and not to risk it with the next one. Although 'most of the time he didn't do a thing', his father says. 'Carl Zeiss was so superior among the children's teams that the goalkeeper got bored. But that suited him.' A gentle smile, for a few seconds free of pain, slips across his father's face as he holds the memory. 'It meant he didn't have to run so much.'

Dirk Enke has the same smile as his son. Unusually slowly, as if he were trying politely to hold it back, it spreads across his face. He was worried about the moment when he would have to talk about Robert; worried that the memories would become too strong. So at first, in his flat on Marktplatz, high above the roofs of Jena, he let the slides do the talking. Someone recently – Dirk Enke says 'afterwards' – gave him a projector so that he could take another look at the old slides from Robert's childhood in East Germany. The three children on a camping holiday on the Baltic – Anja, Gunnar and Robert, the afterthought, who was born nine years after his sister and seven years after his brother. 'You only actually got a pitch permit when you had four children,' says Robert's father, but there were things that weren't followed up all that precisely, even in a surveillance state. 'We always put down four, and no one ever checked.' The projector clicks on – Robert with his third grandma. 'My proper grandma' was what he called Frau Käthe, a pensioner from next door who often looked after him, and with whom he liked to spend time, even as an adolescent. As a child he always used to say, 'I've got a fat grandma, a thin grandma and a proper grandma.'

When Robert was eleven this sequence of lovely pictures took a break. He came back from school to Liselotte Herrmann Strasse to find his father standing by the door with a bag.

'Papi, where are you going?'

His father couldn't bring himself to reply. He walked in silence, with watery eyes, to the car.

His son ran to his mother in the flat. 'What's happened?'

His mother sobbed. 'We had a bit of an argument. Your father's moving into the shack in Cospeda for the time being.'

There was a new woman in his father's life.

Robert asked his mother every day for weeks, 'Mama, how are you?' Gisela could see in his face how much he feared a sad reply.

But his parents refused to believe that their marriage was over. They went on seeing each other, 'and we didn't just do it for the sake of the children. I was with Dirk for thirty years, we'd known each other as adolescents.' That summer they went on holiday together to Lake Balaton. Robert sat in the back of the car and said, loudly but casually, as if he weren't speaking to anyone in particular, 'Well, if it leads to a reconciliation, let's just go on holiday to Lake Balaton.' Rather than joyful, he sounded hopeful.

'The fall of the Wall brought us back together again,' Robert's mother reveals. The intoxication of the demonstrations and the excitement of the big approaching changes reunited the family before the Germanys could do the same. Dirk Enke moved back into the flat. For their silver wedding anniversary they went on a cycling tour on the Rhine near Koblenz.

The Enkes were among those who greeted reunification without a hint of scepticism. Robert's father was able to greet the larger part of his family on the western side of the border. 'My feeling was: at last!' When the Wall came down, the boys amid the washing props were twelve or thirteen – the last generation to have consciously experienced two German states, the first to grow up in both. Andy Meyer can still remember how Robert and he paraded up and down the Löbdergraben with their Carl Zeiss youth team in honour of GDR President Erich Honecker. 'And what we thought was great was that there were food coupons for bockwursts afterwards,' Andy Meyer recalls. They became aware of the new age in a similarly casual manner. In fact they just went on playing, ignoring the changes. They didn't even take a break for reunification. 'There was nothing crucial about it for us kids,' says Andy. He laughs. 'The football training just went on.'

In Lobeda, however, the former socialist dream of a nicer way of living found itself faced with a new proletariat. The children had to come to terms with that. Turks from West Germany sold carpets door to door, believing that they could swindle the naive 'Ossis', as East Germans were known. The young people of the satellite town suddenly started ganging together and saying they were on the far right.

'Don't let anyone in,' Gisela warned her son, who was regularly at home alone after school because both parents worked, she as a teacher of Russian and sport, he as a psycho-therapist at the city hospital.

Robert cautiously opened the door one day when the bell rang. Great-uncle Rudi, a university Latin professor, was paying a visit.

'Hello, are your parents at home?'

The boy looked at him through screwed-up eyes.

'You don't recognise me, do you? I'm Great-uncle Rudi.'

'Anyone could say that!' yelled Robert, pushing the baffled professor away and slamming the door shut.

Another time the right-wing thugs were waiting for him on the way home from school. They grabbed him and started shoving him around, but before he was hit one of them recognised him. 'Stop, it's Robert Enke!' He was twelve. He was clearly already famous as a goalie. They let him go.

But the fear didn't go away. He yearned for a protective skin. He begged his mother to buy him a bomber jacket, then the right-wingers would mistake him for one of their own and leave him alone. 'At first I was horrified that he wanted to give in like that,' says his mother, 'but, OK, I thought, if it means he's not scared. And he only wore the jacket for a few weeks.'

When the first wave of disillusion arrived in the united Germany, even reunification lost its power to hold the Enkes' marriage together.

One Sunday, as the family sat in the living-room, Robert's father took a deep breath.

'I have something to tell you.'

The mother knew already. The other woman in his life had never quite disappeared from the scene.

'Gisela and I are splitting up. I'm moving out.'

Robert leapt up from the sofa and ran out of the door.

'Gunnar, run, bring the boy back!' cried his mother.

Gunnar found his brother in the road. He refused to speak. He didn't want anything to show. He'd got used to dealing with his own sadness.

To his three friends he seemed to have lost nothing of his sunny disposition. 'Enkus chucked a glass of water around, and everyone got wet except him – that's how it always was,' says Andy. A teacher caught Robert cheating during a biology exam, copying the work of the student next to him. He got an E. But when the reports were sent out he got a Satisfactory in biology. He was strikingly helpful, prudent and a gifted goalkeeper, and that combination clearly inclined his teachers

The youth team of CZ Jena on a trip to Tunisia. Robert is on the left, second from the front, and second from the front on the right is his friend Mario Kanopa.

to leniency. Robert knew he would do reasonably well at school without having to try too hard, and didn't strive for more.

Mario Kanopa and Torsten Ziegner had come to the sports college at the age of fourteen, and the names of their home clubs still contained an echo of a villagey world far away from Jena: Mario came from the company sports team Traktor Frauenpriessnitz, Torsten from BSG Mikroelektronik Neuhaus/ Rennweg. They often squabbled in their little dormitory. If anything bothered him, Torsten immediately lost his temper. His impulsiveness infuriated Mario. Enkus got on excellently with both of them. If he was there, they all got along famously.

Newspaper cuttings about them began to be pinned to the wall of the entrance hall at the sports college. In 1993 Robert, Torsten and Mario travelled with the Thuringian state side to the traditional federal states Under-16 Youth Cup where the scouts from the professional clubs would be standing on the sidelines. It's at this annual tournament at the Wedau Sportschule in Duisburg that fifteen-year-olds first become potential professionals in the eyes of the football scene. At first the Thuringian team thought that what happened in Duisburg was a great joke; at the end 'we laughed our heads off about ourselves', Torsten Ziegner remembers. In an absurd repetition, one game was much like another. They regularly looked like the defeated team, but they never lost. 'It was,' Torsten says, 'as if Robert was playing on his own.' With every shot he caught Robert seemed more enormous to the strikers who appeared in front of him. In this tournament he attained the supreme mental state of a goalkeeper: in the midst of all the frantic activity of the game, absolute peace settles upon you. However hard the strikers shoot, you think the ball belongs only to you. An almighty sense of security fills you and makes you ever bigger. Thuringia's results in Duisburg were 0–0, 0–0, 1–0 and 4–0. No one got a shot past him.

In the same year Carl Zeiss Jena reached the final of the German Under-16 youth championship, a feat no club with similarly modest means would emulate over the next fifteen years. The club president invited the team to a bar called Sockenschuss for a round of Coca-Colas. They lost the final 5–1 to Borussia Dortmund. But even the *Frankfurter Allgemeine Zeitung* sent someone to write a report about Jena's sports college. The head teacher went on the record, saying of her footballers, 'They're not particularly tidy, they eat anything, they almost always appear as a team and have a distinct sense of self-confidence.'

Later the four friends will cover the entire spectrum of what may befall a talented footballer: Robert Enke becomes his country's goalkeeper; Torsten becomes a local hero, a captain, a go-to player with Carl Zeiss Jena in the Second Bundesliga and the Third Liga; at the age of twenty-two Mario ends his professional career after a serious injury, his record one Second Bundesliga game, one goal; and at the age of fifteen Andy is told by Carl Zeiss that they're sorry, he's not good enough, from now on he'll have to play in the lower leagues, just for fun.

Unlike Andy, at fifteen Robert Enke, Torsten Ziegner and Mario Kanopa played for the national youth team against

England at Wembley Stadium in front of thirty thousand schoolchildren. The game ended goalless. The *Daily Telegraph* reported, 'A combination of fantastic goalkeeping feats and pathetic shots at the goal prevented England's victory.' They were talking about Robert Enke, perhaps with one incident in particular in mind. He was still on the floor after saving a furious shot from Stephen Clemence when Jay Curtis shaped to hit a follow-up shot. He leapt up and deflected that shot too, his reaction too fast for the spectators to see where his hand had come from.

He had been discovered. German youth footballer of the month, a full page in *Kicker* magazine. In a special edition, 'The Sixteen-Year-Olds', *Stern* portrayed him as the protagonist of his generation. 'Often I don't think about the world,' Robert, very much the teenager, told *Stern*, 'but sometimes I have the feeling the Apocalypse is coming soon.'

In the terraces at Wembley Stadium, Dirk Enke sat with some of the other parents. Football became his bond with his son. After moving out, he tried to go to every game. He studied the other fathers. He saw some of them yelling at their children when they made mistakes, and if their children succeeded in doing something they yelled at them again. Shoot! For heaven's sake, pass the ball! Faster! Shoot! Robert's father sat quietly and attentively at the edge of the pitch. He thought he was doing the right thing. 'Dirk was a great father,' Gisela says. 'But after our separation he had a hard time with the children.'

After the matches father and son would talk.

Good save.

Thanks.

The way you caught that ball from the corner.

I nearly didn't get it. It hit the tips of my fingers, he shot so hard.

And Torsten the Goat (a play on Torsten's surname) back on form – fantastic!

You know what he's like.

At the end I was thinking, Goat, are you crazy? An opponent

tries to get past him and Goat simply knocks him down, runs straight into the opponent. And he does that three times! Normally he'd see three red cards.

Dad, I've got to get back to the changing-rooms.

So many fathers and sons make a laborious effort to use sport as a way of getting close to each other; to use a conversation about football to whitewash the speechlessness between them. 'Dirk and Robert really talked together far too rarely,' says Robert's mother. 'I could never bring myself to argue in the family, to say anything negative. And I don't think Robert could either. There was so much polite reticence in our family.'

Even though words sometimes failed him, Robert's father kept an eye. While his mother benignly believed her older son Gunnar for several days when he said he'd left his guitar at a friend's house, his father noticed the boy's awkwardness. He discovered that Gunnar had sold the guitar. And he recognised Robert's harassed expression when he first had to play in the Under-18 youth team. He was still sixteen. His coaches sent him to the higher age-group so that he would be properly stretched; he was too good to play with those his own age. Even in the Under-18 team he played faultlessly. But that wasn't how he saw it.

To a sixteen-year-old, eighteen-year-olds are the big boys. Most sixteen-year-old goalkeepers who have to play with the older boys get scared. Because in the final analysis a keeper is always measured by his mistakes, and how can he avoid making mistakes when the opposing team's strikers are so big and strong? And how the big, strong players on his own side will despise him if he fails!

Robert cried when he was alone with his father after the game, and told him he didn't want to play on the Under-18 team any more. 'Papa,' he said, 'you wouldn't be cross with me if I gave up football?'

His friends don't recognise this Robert. 'There were always a few nutcases who tore into the weakest players on the youth teams, so Enkus must have put up with the slings and arrows as well,' Torsten says, 'but you couldn't bring him down, quite the contrary. In those days we had the impression that nothing could faze Enkus. Even then he was more confident in goal than other people after ten years as professional players.'

During that time with the Under-18 team, Robert's mother saw a very different Robert from the one his father saw. 'I still remember him getting up after dinner and saying to me, "Mother, there's something I've got to sort out."' He took the tram to the Ernst Abbe sports field and told Ronald Prause, the Under-18 team coach, that he wanted to play in the Under-16 team again. A sixteen-year-old boy, confident and charming enough to tell an authoritarian coach what he wanted.

But Dirk Enke is a psychotherapist. He sees it differently. Over lunch at the Marktplatz, he sets his knife and fork down, rubs his palms over his thighs, then says, 'I thought, what's going on here? Is he having problems with his team-mates? No, it quickly became clear that something was happening to him: his fear of making mistakes was getting to him, that way of thinking "If I'm not the best, I'm the worst". That torment must have started when he was sixteen playing with the eighteen-year-old boys.'

But was it not a one-off, a brief moment of anxiety of the kind that hundreds of youth goalkeepers experience?

'The mind always remembers that sort of liminal experience.'

As a seventeen-year-old schoolboy with a special permit from the German Football Association, Robert signed a professional contract with Carl Zeiss Jena. His mother and father went with him to the Association's office. Ernst Schmidt, the managing director and Hans Meyer, the coach, were waiting for them. His tendency to dominate a conversation with witty opinions later made Meyer a popular figure with the Bundesliga sportswriters. In the office that day he had something to tell the teenage goalkeeper about Jena's mythical goalie from the fifties. 'Harald Fritzsche wasn't to blame for a single goal for over ten years,' Meyer said. 'At least if you asked him for his opinion.'

Dirk Enke pricked up his ears. Did Meyer know about Robert's painful self-reproach after his mistakes? Was the coach trying to send him a message – don't drive yourself nuts?

Before long Robert Enke's life was divided in two. At school he got one-to-one tuition so that he could train as a substitute goalkeeper with the Second Bundesliga team – he was now a professional sportsman with all the seriousness, all the desire to stay on top that that entailed – and at the same time he was starting a happy-go-lucky relationship with Teresa.

They camped at his mother's on a mattress in the living-room and told her they had to study for their leaving exam. Sometimes they went out in the evening; he might have a shandy 'and I danced on the tables', says Teresa. Presumably that's not to be taken literally, but Robert felt she showed her joie de vivre in better ways. She expressed everything so easily, her warmth, her curiosity, her decisiveness. He thought she was much stronger than he was. 'I've never learned to party the way you do,' he said, as if he had to defend her. She immediately liked his reticent, gentle charm. His face was that of the eternally sweet boy.

She had grown up with two elder brothers in rural Bavaria; her father had passed on to them his passion for modern pentathlon: swimming, fencing, riding, shooting and running. At home in the nursery Teresa and her brother secretly fired an airgun at Playmobil figures – 'If you hit them in the chest they explode in a thousand pieces,' her brother said, proud at his discovery. Officially Teresa had come to the high school in Jena for its renowned sports education; unofficially she had been determined to escape the Bavarian school system with its dreaded Latin. 'Don't wear brand-names, or you'll come across as a Wessi snob,' her friends from the West warned her. 'And then on my first day at the new school I saw that they were all wearing brand-name clothes.'

East and West, the opposition that so many people wanted to emphasise at that time, didn't matter to her; it was just a source of amusement for them from time to time. When Robert spent Christmas Eve with Teresa's family he showed gaps in his knowledge of the Christmas story because of his atheist upbringing in the GDR. 'So, who was Joseph?' he asked.

Teresa wasn't very interested in football. For her, football meant disappointing Saturday evenings 'when I'd rather have been watching *Beverly Hills 90210* and couldn't because my brothers had commandeered the television to watch the sports programmes'. Not only for that reason Robert didn't tell her about his first professional games, until eventually, much later, she asked about it. He thought you didn't talk about things like that – it was boasting.

Carl Zeiss Jena did remarkably well in the opening matches of the 1995–96 season in the Second Bundesliga. In midfield a twenty-one-year-old called Bernd Schneider began to attract attention for his elegance; a few years later he would be regarded as Germany's best technical player. The team had levelled out in mid-table when they suffered two heavy defeats in a row in the autumn, 4–1 in Duisburg and 4–0 against VfL Bochum. Carl Zeiss's goalkeeper, Mario Neumann, had had happier times. On 11 November Carl Zeiss played Hannover 96 away. Good keepers, they say, need experience more than anything else, and Robert Enke was eighteen. Coach Eberhard Vogel put him in goal for the first time.

The most striking thing for Robert was how empty the stadium was. The six thousand spectators were lost among the fifty-six thousand seats. And the floodlight masts were even more curious, looming into the sky like gigantic toothbrushes. This was club football in the days before the sport became an event, a national celebration.

The game began, and Robert waited. The battle was being waged in midfield, but he kept his concentration because the opposition could pop up at any time in his penalty area. Then, suddenly, after half an hour, a header from Hannover's Reinhold Daschner. Even an almost empty stadium could suddenly sound incredibly noisy. Robert was already on the spot to which the ball was flying, and he caught it easily.

Less than two minutes after this first noteworthy feat he conceded his first goal in professional football. The *Ostthüringer Zeitung* chose some unusual words to leap to his defence: 'Jena's defender Dejan Raickovic was instrumental in Hannover going 1–0 up, but Robert Enke certainly wasn't.'

He carried on doing the nuts-and-bolts work of a goalkeeper, stopping the odd corner, sending out well-aimed drop-kicks. Once he drew a roar from the stadium, trapping a shot from Kreso Kovacec underneath his belly. The final score was 1–1. It was a game the fans had already started forgetting as they made their way down the stadium steps, but not the young and happy goalkeeper who got the fear again as he walked back to the changing-room. There was a thunderous noise on the Plexiglas roof of the tunnel above him. His father had reached out over the terrace railing and was proudly banging his fist against the roof of the player's entrance to say, well done, son!

The following Saturday his mother drove with a friend into the mountains around Jena, where they turned on the radio. 'I felt ill,' says Gisela.

'Free kick for Lübeck on the left wing,' cried the commentator. 'Behnert crosses, Enke rushes out to collect it, he has the ball – and he lets it slip through his hands! Goal for Lübeck! A terrible goalkeeping error!'

It was at moments like this that Andy Meyer had his view confirmed, that Enkus was a child of fortune. Because when he missed the ball – and it didn't happen that often – his team promptly won and no one talked about his error.

Jena defeated VfB Lübeck 3–1.

The error had been a minor one. But later, many years later, Robert admitted how as a young goalkeeper 'I couldn't forgive myself a mistake.' His team-mates might be saying 'Who cares?', the coach might be saying 'That happens to everybody at some point, things will be better next Saturday, of course you'll stay in goal', but 'for the whole of the next week I had the error in front of my eyes. I couldn't get it out of my head.'

After the Lübeck game Robert didn't go to school all week. He said he was ill.

*Robert in goal for CZ Jena at the German Under-16 youth
championship.*

It's the goalkeeper's torture – the constant demand on him
not to make a single mistake. None of them can forget their
mistakes. But a goalkeeper must be able to repress things.

Otherwise the next game comes along and crashes down on top of him.

Carl Zeiss had to go to Leipzig for the derby. On the terraces his father met a woman he knew from his old athletics days. They sat together. She was supporting VfB Leipzig, but in the third minute of play even she cried out in sympathy, 'Oh, no!' Robert had let a wide shot from twenty yards out, a rather ineffectual and not particularly powerful effort, slip under his body and into the goal.

At such moments a goalkeeper has to act as if nothing has happened.

In the thirty-fourth minute Leipzig's striker Ronny Kujat ran straight at him all on his own. At such moments as these the game suddenly seems to go into slow-motion. The goalkeeper registers each movement of the striker's feet, the fans sit open-mouthed, the keeper waits, frozen. He can't move now. The first one to commit himself – the keeper with his hand or the striker with his foot – usually loses because the other one will see through the manoeuvre. Robert flung himself at the right moment and tipped the ball away. It was the best display of his short professional career so far. But he didn't enjoy it any more for that.

At half-time he said despairingly to his coach, 'Please substitute me.'

Eberhard Vogel told Robert not to talk nonsense, and made him go on playing till the final whistle. After that he never put him back in goal.

His mother noticed that he hardly talked at all at home, that he went to his room after dinner and closed the door behind him. 'But I remembered Dirk being like that after a bad hurdles race.'

A week later Robert hesitantly rediscovered his smile and drove to the Western Station. At the time he didn't even think about it, he saw no connection, but for the remaining six months of the season, when he was the young substitute goalkeeper of whom no one expected anything, he was cheerful again, and even-tempered. If anything, he thought it must have something to do with Teresa.

Jena's coach had talked publicly about what had happened in Leipzig. 'The boy lacks confidence. He wanted me to take him off at half-time. But it's not as easy as that,' Vogel had told sports reporters immediately after the game. Ten years later that could have been the end for a goalkeeper: he made a beginner's mistake and then begged to be able to clear off at half-time. The news would have appeared on the internet, and it would have been broadcast on television and countless other media which now turn Second Bundesliga games into an event. A reputation would have been cemented on the gossipy professional football scene: he's unstable. But in those days the news was hidden away in a sixteen-line story somewhere in the middle of the *Ostthüringer Zeitung*.

The Bundesliga clubs that had spotted him during his remarkable youth career retained an unbroken interest in him. Some of them had called on his parents, including a gentleman from Bayer Leverkusen who said, 'Hello, Reiner Calmund here,' and went on to deliver ten sentences in half a minute without so much as a comma or a full stop. The best impression was left by the envoys from Borussia Mönchengladbach. Because unlike Leverkusen and VfB Stuttgart, Borussia unusually sent not only their manager but also their goalkeeping coach.

Robert wasn't going to leave before his A-levels, his parents said, but the summer of 1996, the end of his school days, was edging ever closer.

Teresa wondered out loud where they could go to university together. She was thinking of training as a teacher or a vet.

'What about Würzburg?'

'Yeah. Don't forget I still play football.'

'Is that so important? Anyway, I'm sure there's a club in Würzburg too.'

'No, I mean professional football. I've had a few offers.'

'And?'

'They're not offering bad money. In Mönchengladbach I could be earning twelve thousand marks a month.'

Oh, Teresa thought, maybe she had sounded a little bit naive.

A few days after Robert and his father first met the big hitters from Borussia Mönchengladbach, Dirk Enke's phone rang. Norbert Pflipsen was on the line. He was a football agent, he said, Günter Netzer, Lothar Matthäus, Stefan Effenberg and Mehmet Scholl had been among his clients. 'I could help your son,' he said. Usually a football agent puts a player under contract and then starts looking for a club. But in those days things were often a bit easier for the handful of agents who ruled the market. Through their informants in the Bundesliga they learned if a club wanted to sign a player who didn't yet have an adviser, and by return of post the agent would offer himself to the player. That was how it was with Pflipsen and Borussia Mönchengladbach in the eighties and nineties.

Pflipsen – Flippi – had one strength: he was one of the first in the business. So for decades he maintained a reputation for being one of the best.

Flippi visited the Enkes in Jena. A man with fleshy lower arms and shirt-sleeve manners, he wasn't short on anecdotes about how he had taken Günter to Real Madrid and Lothar to Inter Milan. It was a time when hardly any youth players had agents, yet here was this man from the highest echelons of football offering himself to Robert. The Enkes felt rather honoured. And in his witty way, Flippi was a likeable guy. They ignored the fact that he could sometimes be a bit crude. 'When we start doing business,' Pflipsen roared at Robert's father, 'I'll give you a combined phone and fax. And,' turning to Robert, 'you'd get a car from me.'

Just before his geography oral (subject: rocks) in May 1996 Robert Enke signed a three-year contract negotiated by Norbert Pflipsen with the Bundesliga club Borussia Mönchengladbach.

Just before that, on the A2 eastbound from Dortmund, the engine of a small Peugeot had thrown up some sparks. Then smoke had started rising from under the bonnet. Driving in a car like that had been perilous, the breakdown services said; there was no oil and no water, and the outlets were blocked.

There was nothing, Flippi remonstrated, he could do about the fact that the second-hand car he had given Robert was in such a state.

TWO

The Snap

Robert was lying on the ground, his head in the grass, now already brown in places. He looked up, and ten feet away, also level with the grass-stalks, two greyish-blue eyes were waiting for him. Come on, the eyes were saying, rigid with concentration, I'll show you.

They lay facing each other in the penalty box on the training pitch, throwing the ball to each other with two hands. Their bodies were like bendy seesaws, swinging rhythmically back and forth, the only sound a brief, muffled clapping noise when the ball sank into the soft foam of their gloves.

That's enough, Robert thought after a few minutes. We're just warming up – why won't he stop?

It took Robert a week to work out that Uwe Kamps would never stop. He wanted to see him, the new substitute goalkeeper, his potential rival, give up; to defeat him, even in the most minor warm-up exercise, every day.

Kamps had already played over three hundred Bundesliga games for Borussia Mönchengladbach. He was thirty-two, the darling of the fans, and in fact, after training, quite genial. Robert was nineteen, a boy, the number three keeper in the squad. In the first few years he would learn from Kamps and sooner or later he would be ready to take over as number one, he had been told by Dirk Heyne, the goalkeeping coach. Heyne was one reason he had chosen Borussia over other Bundesliga teams. He'd struck Robert as likeable and competent.

He looked over at Heyne. The coach said nothing. But he'd seen what Kamps was doing.

'Okay,' said the coach, 'now shoot the ball at each other, at chest height.'

Kamps sent in shot after shot, each one getting harder, firmer and faster. He wanted to see Enke drop the ball.

In the evening, with training behind him, Robert laughed at his experiences, and not without a certain sympathy for Kamps. What a guy. The next morning, on the way to training, the matter would strike him as serious again. He wondered whether a Bundesliga goalkeeper had to be like Kamps, above all whether he could be the same.

Applying pressure was the Bundesliga motto in the nineties. Everybody had to be applying pressure at all times: the coach on the players, the substitute player on the coach via the press, the substitute goalie on the number one, the number one on the substitute goalies, and the manager on everyone. Back in Jena, the only person who had ever put Robert under pressure had been Robert himself.

Sometimes after training in Mönchengladbach he went to the gym, because he was told it was important, and because most of his team-mates did. Before then he had hardly ever gone near fitness equipment; it meant nothing to him. He had enough talent not to have to do any additional training. Kamps usually went there with Jörg Neblung, Borussia's fitness coach. The two of them competed at benchpresses. A long-legged former decathlete, Neblung had no chance of pressing as much weight as the short, bullish Kamps, but the athlete in Neblung was alive and well and he pumped, he pushed, he managed 120 kilos, and Kamps followed suit, wanting to outdo him every time. Robert pretended he wasn't watching.

'So, do you want me to get the weights down for you?' said Kamps when he saw Enke reaching for a dumbbell. 'You'd be better off using only the bar, so you don't strain yourself.' Kamps laughed as if he'd just made a great joke.

That's what a good relationship between goalkeepers ought to be like, Kamps thought: fair in sport, tough in life.

'Uwe enjoyed turning everything into a competition,' says Neblung. 'He had an extremely professional attitude, always last to leave the training-ground. It's only with that view of his job that a professional can be successful, we were sure of that in those days.' With his uncompromising take on training, Kamps had overcome his natural disadvantages: he seemed too small to be a goalkeeper, but in spite of being only five foot ten he had been unshakeable in goal for Borussia for a decade.

Neblung tried to persuade the new goalkeeper to do the same kind of weight training as Kamps. Robert was broad-shouldered, but he had the thin arms and legs of an unformed teenager. 'There was an athlete slumbering in there,' says Neblung. As a former track athlete, Neblung initially had a hard job with the footballers because everyone knew that you didn't become a track athlete unless you were useless with the ball at your feet. Gradually more and more players had come to see him – 'Jörg, we need to stretch'; 'Hey, Neblung, I want to do something about my speed'. In his third year with Borussia he had only half established himself on the team so he didn't push it when Robert dug his heels in over the idea of directed athletics training. He was, after all, only the third-choice goal-keeper. 'I didn't really notice him much,' says Neblung.

As a schoolboy he had made contact with others. As number three goalkeeper he became an observer.

The previous season Mönchengladbach had won the German Cup, its first trophy in sixteen years. The cup-winners had been given hero contracts. Financially, their pay-rises were frighteningly risky, but sporting director Rolf Rüssmann thought about possible future successes first and credit repayment models only after that. An expectation had quickly built that this could be the 1970s all over again, when the club was the epitome of the avant-garde. With its long-haired players and free-spirited football, Borussia had won a whole series of championships. Now, with world-class players like Stefan Effenberg, Martin Dahlin and Christian Hochstätter, Mönchengladbach had some serious figures on the team again. And they liked to demonstrate their status.

On the bus from the training-ground in Rönneter back to the showers in the stadium at Bökelberg, Robert had to stand.

There weren't enough seats. The youngest stayed in the aisle. They had to prove themselves first, the others thought. When the bus turned sharply from Kaldenkirchener Strasse into Bökelbergstrasse, Robert collided with another of the younger players, Marco Villa. Villa was eighteen and lanky. When coach Bernd Krauss put him up front at the start of the season because the established players weren't winning anything, Villa scored three goals in his first seven games. That had never happened in thirty-three years of the Bundesliga. Villa smeared soap in the older players' underpants when they were in the shower. And the older players laughed. Anyone who achieved something, who really applied the pressure, was accepted, even at the age of eighteen Robert understood. Villa didn't do his pranks out of rebelliousness, he just wanted to have some fun. 'I didn't think a lot,' Marco says. 'Basically I just wanted to be accepted by the established players on the team like Effenberg and Kalle Pflipsen. I wanted to be like them.'

When Kamps was giving Villa a top-down lesson one day, Villa said, 'You know, Uwe, there are players who are respected, and others who would like to be respected. You fall into the second category.'

'Have you heard that!' cried Christian Hochstätter, who liked to think of himself, at the age of thirty-three, as the team's tribal elder.

When Villa dared to do what no eighteen-year-old was allowed to do at Borussia, the older players grinned, and Effenberg slapped him on the shoulders. Villa was a goal-scorer. Also, there are people everyone likes straight away without understanding exactly why. Marco Villa is one of those.

Robert never played jokes with soap and underpants. But he felt happy, in a wonderfully weightless way, when other people around him were being silly.

One day Rolf Rüssmann came into the changing-room. 'Has anyone got any face-cream? My skin's so dry.'

'Here,' said defender Stephan Passlack.

Five minutes later Rüssmann's face was frozen in a plastic mask. Passlack had given him hair gel.

After training, Robert went straight home. It was only five minutes from Bökelberg to the flat he shared with Teresa in the Loosenweg. He didn't join in when the other footballers went out for something to eat. He thought he didn't belong there – the newbie, the third-choice goalkeeper.

Three- and four-storey apartment blocks made of ochre-coloured clinker bricks stand side by side on the Loosenweg, where the city of Mönchengladbach peters out. German flags flap in the gardens now. In those days china geese with ribbons round their necks stood on the grass of the communal garden.

Although Robert was already in a high-income bracket, Teresa's parents paid half of the rent every month, as they thought only appropriate, given that their daughter was still studying. Every day Teresa travelled the thirty kilometres to university in Düsseldorf – teacher training, sport and German – and after lectures she drove home again. She wanted to be with Robert, and the other students already seemed to have formed solid circles of friends in their student residences. There were posters up announcing a big student union party, and she decided to go along with Robert. They spent most of the evening standing on their own.

She couldn't help thinking of her old schoolmate Christiane from Bad Windsheim. Sadly, she sent her old girlfriend a text: 'You remember when we used to sit in the Café Ritter when we were thirteen, and imagined how university life would be, having to ask yourself that daily question: shall we go to a lecture, or just to the café?' Only her student job reminded her of this first idea of hers of university life. She worked in a shoe shop. 'Unfortunately I got a thirty per cent discount, so all the money I earned went straight back to the shop,' she confesses.

Robert was amazed at how easily she spent her money on shoes. He found it hard to buy anything expensive for himself. You should, he figured, be careful with your money.

'Forgive me,' said the bank clerk when Teresa withdrew some money from their shared account, 'but I'm just wondering whether you and your boyfriend mightn't possibly want to invest your money in shares or some kind of fund at some point?'

Robert's salary went into his giro account, and he left it there. He had exchanged Flippi's used Peugeot for a little Audi, and he bought himself clothes twice a year – in the summer and winter sales – but otherwise he didn't want much that cost money. He liked to lie on the sofa at home with Teresa. When she was studying, he turned the television on or read the paper, sometimes a thriller, but he didn't go out. He waited for her to finish studying.

The day after her husband's death, when Teresa moved the public by speaking so openly about Robert's depression, lots of people will have seen her as the strong woman who stands behind every strong man. In all the years leading up to that, however, her friends had the feeling that the two of them were simply there for each other. In Mönchengladbach, alone together in a strange city for the first time, they developed a total affinity. 'We'd sometimes go out without our wives,' says Torsten Ziegner, Robert's friend from Jena, 'but Enkus didn't actually do that. If you'd arranged to see Enkus, you'd arranged to see Enkus and Teresa.'

They were happy in their new-found independence, in all the experiences of that stage of life that may seem slightly embarrassing later on, like the limitless loafing or using the clothes horse as a substitute wardrobe. But love and a sense of the freedom of life could only mask their unease; they couldn't eradicate it. 'We were two nineteen-year-olds who should have been in a shared apartment with others, who had been part of a group in Jena only months before,' says Teresa. 'And suddenly we'd been thrown into this little town without a student scene, where we had no friends and didn't make new ones very easily.' Sometimes she wondered: is this what adult life is like?

Every sixth Friday Teresa or Robert cleaned the stairwell; the other five groups of tenants in the block had decided to save the twenty marks needed for a cleaning woman. One Friday Teresa came home early from her lectures. Robert was away at a match with Borussia's reserve team. She would clean the stairs on Saturday, Teresa thought.

On Friday evening the doorbell rang. Corinna, a neat and tidy neighbour of theirs, stood in front of Teresa.

'The stairs haven't been cleaned!'

'I know. Robbi's not here, and I'm a bit tired after university. I'll do it tomorrow, first thing.'

'The stairs must be cleaned on Friday!'

Corinna began to ring the doorbell more often. The stairs hadn't been cleaned properly at the edges. Someone had walked up the stairs in dirty shoes while the floor tiles were still wet. Robert tried hard to go on meeting the woman as he had done before, with shy politeness. For a few weeks, an intimidated Teresa took her shoes off down in the hall and walked up to the third floor in her stockinged feet.

Marco Villa sometimes visited them at Loosenweg. Robert and he had known each other now for three years – they had played together for the national youth team – without knowing anything substantial about each other. Marco came from Neuss, Robert from Jena. Their first coach on the national youth team, Dixie Dörner, had encouraged people to think in terms of East and West. Even when they were warming up there had been an eastern group and a western group.

Once Marco came to lunch. Robert was sitting in a red leather armchair reading a book. Marco glanced at the title: *100 Jobs with a Future*, by Claudia Schumacher and Stefan Schwartz.

'What's that you're reading? Are you looking for a new job, or what?'

'I just wanted to see what you can do apart from football.'

'Are you off your trolley? You're a professional, in the Bundesliga!'

'It's different for you, Marco. You play, you score your goals. But I'm not even a substitute at the matches. I do my training, and I sit at home or in the terraces. I'm useless.'

'You're nineteen, Robbi! It's still your first year here. You'll be playing in a few years. Don't drive yourself mad.'

They left it there. Years later, when Marco reminded Robert of that scene, Robert said, 'What are you on about? I can't remember ever owning a book like that.' But even today the book is still in his office in Empede, a European Championship silver medal dangling next to it. Teresa's father had given him the book. 'Take a look at it,' he had said, 'you might find you're interested in a different profession.' If football's really as bad as that.

He didn't want to go to training any more. It was winter, January 1997, dark at half-past four, and he was sitting in a building where the garden gnomes were treated more kindly than the tenants, in a little town with which he had no connections. And all that to be a third-choice goalkeeper; to play in front of 120 spectators for the reserve team; to put up with the exertion of training every day.

The mood in the changing-rooms was irritable. Every Saturday coach Bernd Krauss had been an hour and a half away from being sacked, and in December 1996 it had happened. The cup-winning team, having been cranked up for an attack on the top spots in the Bundesliga, was wallowing around mid-table.

In a training match against the Second Bundesliga team Fortuna Köln, Robert was allowed to play for the first eleven. Again he felt that hot, hectic thumping inside him. The fear that he had felt on the Under-18 team, the fear that he might disappoint the grown-ups, was back. He was frightened that he might never be like Uwe Kamps, always applying pressure, always putting up with the pressure. He couldn't shake the feeling that no one was interested in what the number three goalkeeper did, that he was invisible – and at the same time he was afraid that in that tense situation he might attract the fury of the senior players. It was a contradiction, but that kind of anxiety is one great paradox.

This was a new Robbi as far as Teresa was concerned. She was confused. Where did this anxiety come from? She didn't know him when he was like this. At the same time she too was feeling disappointed with her anonymous life at university; perhaps he was just as troubled as she was by longing for their carefree life with their friends in Jena. Or else he was just having a bad day or two.

A week passed, and every morning started the same way.

'I don't want to go to training.'

'Robbi, it's not as bad as that.'

'I don't want to go, do you understand? I just don't want to.'

'Marco will be there. You'll see, once you're there, it'll be fine.'

When he was out of the door, she called his father.

Dirk Enke came to visit the following weekend. He knew all about anxiety from his patients. 'But you see,' he says, 'as a therapist I'm simply not responsible – a father can't do that.' He could only say to his son: give your day a fixed structure. While he was there he threw Robert out of bed at seven in the morning, so that the day would get going straight away, and made sure there were solid goals on the horizon, things his son could do, even if that just meant going for a walk. Things that would make him feel that he'd achieved something.

'And go and see a doctor,' his father advised as he left.

Borussia were about to begin their winter training-camp. Anxiety turned to panic. Robert thought there was no way he could go, spend a whole week exclusively as a part of this football team where he thought he wasn't respected, and where he feared his every mistake during training would be precisely recorded.

He went to see Herbert Ditzel, the team doctor.

Medical staff at professional football teams are always under huge pressure from the coaches. Week after week they're urged to send injured players into battle with painkillers, often against their better judgement. But this time the doctor thought only of the person in front of him, not of the club. Ditzel liked this shy young man. He signed him off with a flu virus so that he wouldn't have to go to training-camp.

When the team returned he was given a new nickname. Robert's colleagues now called him Cyrus, after Cyrus the Virus, a character from the movie *Con Air*. No one doubted that he was suffering from a flu virus, and he was able to have a good laugh about his new nickname. The anxiety had faded away after a few weeks.

He made a great effort to study Kamps. If the older man needed to see him as a rival in order to motivate himself, he would secretly learn from him. He watched the veteran keeper out of the corner of his eye during training. He started to jump early, even a split second before the striker hit the ball, speculating where the shot would fly to, and punched away crosses he might have been able to catch. Robert said later, almost shamefacedly, 'I copied Uwe's style a bit.'

After a successful diving save, some German goalkeepers like Kamps would do a double roll on the pitch, to the roar of the crowd, taking their example from eighties idol Toni Schumacher. If the striker advanced on his own, they threw themselves in front of him with all their might. If they tipped the ball over the crossbar, they drew their knees up when jumping, so that even the slowest fan could grasp the drama of the situation. German goalkeepers were the best in the world, the Germans thought.

In the late nineties no German fan was bothered by the fact that even excellent goalkeepers like Andreas Köpke, Stefan Klos and a young man from Karlsruhe called Oliver Kahn played deep in their own box, close to the goal-line, while in Argentina, Spain or the Netherlands the goalkeeper became a substitute sweeper. Advancing far up the pitch, he made it impossible for his oppenent to hit long balls behind the defence. Also he became an extra option for his defenders to pass to, and hence break up the opponent's pressing game. One of the most radical prophets of the new goalkeeper play was Edwin van der Sar of Ajax Amsterdam. Robert watched van der Sar on television, he watched Kamps in training, he compared the two and he took his bearings from the German model of saving spectacularly rather than acting in anticipation.

After nine months in Mönchengladbach he received his first praise. 'Borussia can consider itself lucky to have this young man,' the new coach Hannes Bongartz told the *Rheinische Post*. 'He's the man of the future.' In his first months with Borussia, Robert had learned that football is not a game but a battle, that footballers achieve their aims by applying and taking pressure. But he felt far more inspired by Bongartz's praise than by any such pressure.

At the end-of-season party, at which Borussia wasn't so much celebrating its eleventh-place finish as the fact that the campaign was somehow over, he wanted to go home at around midnight. Teresa wanted to stay. She was curious about this Bundesliga world, and at last here was a party of the kind she'd been hoping for at university. They were sitting in a greenhouse. A garden centre had been rearranged for the party.

'Then you stay, I'm going home,' Robert said, and walked off.

The last handful of players were still hanging on at the party when Stefan Effenberg called out into the night, 'So, where are we going now?'

'We could always go to ours,' said Teresa, as she would have said at university.

'No, let's not,' said Effenberg's wife. It was clearly out of the question.

When Teresa told Robert about that the next morning, he replied, 'If you'd come here I'd have thrown them out. And you too.' She was startled by the serious note in his voice. She found it hard to understand why he usually grew quiet when other people were partying noisily but resolved to think, 'Today I'm proud of him for having such a firm character and saying "I don't like partying, so I'm not going to a party or a disco even if everyone else urges me to."'

Robert liked Effenberg, for the solicitous, big-brother way he treated the young players. If someone like Marco Villa played inspiringly at the age of eighteen, Effenberg didn't just show him respect, he also offered him protection. But unlike Marco, Robert wasn't interested in exploring the world of the Effenbergs and the Kamps away from the Bökelberg. He had an image in his head of nights in neon light with all sorts of cocky behaviour, and he felt he didn't fit in with that.

Robert continued to have the occasional holiday from his anonymous everyday life as the substitute for the substitute goalkeeper. He was still called up as number one for the Under-21 national team. In Belfast he played against Northern Ireland, and shared a room with Marco. They knew about the habit junior national coach Hannes Löhr had of coming into

Robert in the shirt of the Under-21 national side.

their rooms the evening before to get them in the mood for
the game. After a year they also knew Löhr's catch-phrases.

Tomorrow we really have to win. It's a very important game.

'I don't feel like it today,' said Robert. Marco had an idea.
They pushed the television right up against the bedroom door.

As expected, at about half-past eight there was a knock on
the door.

'Who's there?'

'The coach.'

'Oh, Coach. Just a moment, it's not a good time right now.
Careful! Oh no – Coach, please, wait a moment!'

'What's going on with you two?'

'The television's right up against the door, we've got to move
it, I don't know if we can, damn that's heavy!' shouted Marco,
who was sitting contentedly on a chair.

'OK, guys, leave it for now, it was nothing important.' And
Löhr went away.

To the players, it looked as if Marco was messing around

and Robert just happened to be there. Robert felt that he and Marco were playing pranks together.

'Teresa often said, you two together are unbearably silly,' Marco says. 'But the times when we were laughing – that was Robbi at his happiest.'

For a professional footballer who was used to everything in life being secondary to sport, in the summer of 1997 Robert received a piece of bad news. He had to do his military service. He had wanted to do civilian service. But his realism, and to a certain extent his sense of comfort, were stronger than his conviction that he never wanted to serve with the armed forces. Civilian service would have lasted thirteen months; in the army, as a professional sportsman he would have to go through the three-month basic training programme during the summer break but would then be exempted de facto from the remaining seven months of military service, as a member of the Bundeswehr sports promotion section.

Marco Villa was called up at the same time. They ended up in the Köln-Longerich barracks between the A1 Autobahn and the industrial estate of Bilderstöckchen. Radio Operator Enke and Radio Operator Villa.

By way of greeting, the drill sergeant marched up to Robert and hissed, nose to nose, 'Well then, Mr Super-sportsman.'

'What do you earn, what do I earn, what do you earn, what do I earn,' murmured Robert once the sergeant was out of earshot again. Marco burst out laughing.

'What's so funny?' roared the sergeant.

The tone was set.

'Radio Operator Enke!' a voice roared across the parade ground. The drill sergeant was standing at the window. 'Dress code, Radio Operator Enke!'

'Yes, dress code,' Robert muttered down in the parade ground, on his way to the cafeteria. 'Look at yourself!' He had forgotten his glengarry and his Sam Browne belt. He had to write a four-page essay on the purpose of the dress code in the Bundeswehr.

A few days later his shirt slipped out of his trousers when he was doing sit-ups.

'Radio Operator Enke, dress code!'

'What about it?' he hissed back.

By way of punishment, he had to sprint once around the block. He jogged instead of sprinting.

'Sprint, I said, Radio Operator Enke!'

The drill sergeant made him run one more lap, but Robert went on jogging. This time he would be like Uwe Kamps. He would never give up. He was hot with fury. If there was something he couldn't bear, it was the feeling of being treated unfairly.

After eleven laps the sergeant gave up. 'Off you go, Radio Operator Enke.'

Marco Villa had long thought it was inevitable that Robert was prone to mishaps. Once, when they were in a hotel with the Borussia squad, Marco deliberately headed off in the wrong direction to breakfast. Robert toddled politely after him until they found themselves in the storeroom rather than the lift. 'He had the worst sense of direction in the world,' Marco says, 'and he kept making me laugh every time he cried out in panic, "Where have you got me to this time?"' Of course, says Marco, he knows that everyone has some kind of Bundeswehr or football story to tell whose charms are hard for outsiders to understand. But for him and Robert, those three months in Köln-Longerich were a treasure-trove. There Robert found a friend who would stay his friend for ever.

Today Marco lives with his wife and two children as a professional footballer in Italy, his father's homeland. The Italian influence is unmistakable: the tidy Mönchengladbach schoolboy haircut has turned into a fashionably long hairdo. He sits over his breakfast coffee in the Pasticceria Ferretti in Roseto on the Adriatic and talks about the lyrics of the singer Vasco Rossi. 'You're more interested in school,' Rossi sings, 'but who knows how good you are at the rest of life.' There's something in that, Marco says. And he recognises himself, if you replace school with football. When Marco talks, everyone likes to listen. What Robert wanted most from him was the feeling of being understood.

Back in Mönchengladbach after their basic military training for the start of the 1997–98 season, Marco was particularly eager to lob balls over Uwe Kamps in training. He loved the way Kamps got furious every time he did it. 'Don't get me wrong, Uwe was basically a really nice guy,' Marco says. But even though they never talked about it specifically, Marco sensed that Robert was inwardly amused by the raging Kamps, and the idea spurred Marco on. It made him happy.

During that season, his second in the Bundesliga, Robert made the smallest jump possible in a football team, from third- to second-choice goalkeeper. The number two goalkeeper never played either, but for him, this personal promotion meant the world. He was finally a real part of the squad; the second-choice goalkeeper travelled to all the games as a substitute.

Until now his only experience of first-team football had come from Marco's stories – like when the team had travelled by coach to Freiburg the previous year. As usual, Effenberg and Hochstätter sat in the second row right behind the coach, while Marco made himself comfortable at the back, playing cards with Pflipsen and a few others. They started to feel hot.

'Turn on the air-conditioning,' Marco called out to the coach driver.

Just past Karlsruhe the heat became unbearable. By the time they arrived in Freiburg for their game, the card-players were sitting on the back seat wearing only their underpants.

Later they found out what had happened. With the noise of the engine, the coach driver couldn't hear what Marco was shouting from the back seat.

'What do they want?' the driver asked Effenberg.

'They're cold,' said Effenberg, straight-faced.

'What? I've set the air-conditioning back there to twenty-six degrees.'

'Turn it up, then,' said Effenberg.

Now Robert was joining them. He was even cracking jokes with Kamps. Now that he had been recognised by the team as their talented number-two goalkeeper, Kamps's extreme competitiveness was no longer so hard to bear.

Before games he and Marco shared a hotel room. Stefan Effenberg knocked on their door. He wanted to race Marco on his Playstation. In a few minutes Marco had won a thousand marks. Effenberg challenged him to go on playing, even though it must have been clear to him that he would never win.

Robert sat in the background and watched quietly whenever Effenberg was in the room.

At home, Teresa wanted a new tenant. Robert reacted defensively. A dog?

When Teresa had imagined, as a child, what adulthood might be like, she had always pictured a house in the country with a lot of animals. She had asked Robert about his vision of the future. He had always limited his dreams to football.

'A dog would be nice, you know.'

He hesitated. He didn't really want an animal in the house. But neither did he have anything specific against it. What made him happy was making other people happy, Teresa above all. OK, then, a dog.

They called him Bo. On Bo's first day they had to go shopping. The dog was sleeping peacefully. Teresa didn't want to wake him up. 'Come on, we'll just creep out for a minute and he won't even notice,' she said. They would be back in a few minutes, after all.

'When we got back, of course he was traumatised.' Teresa laughs at herself softly. 'We did everything wrong that you can do wrong. After a few weeks we were like concerned parents with their first child. We only went to the cinema separately, so that Bo wouldn't feel alone and bark.'

The dog was another opportunity for the neighbours to get worked up. 'He is always running up the freshly cleaned stairs!' cried Corinna.

For Teresa and Robert, Bo was a further excuse finally to move out. Borussia's coach driver, Markus Breuer, lived fifteen kilometres south of Mönchengladbach. His attic flat was vacant, he told them. So late in 1997, Teresa took one last photograph of Loosenweg, with the china geese in the garden, and they carried their furniture out of the flat. Corinna called out, by way of farewell, 'So much noise at ten o'clock at night, it's outrageous!' Robert shouted back, for the first time. 'Now, give us a break, Corinna, we're moving out. In a few minutes you'll never see us again, so at least leave us in peace right now!'

Drive along the old rural road from Mönchengladbach by way of Wey, through turnip and wheat fields, and in some places the road almost becomes a country lane. After Hoppers you get to Gierath. Over the past thirty years Gierath has changed enormously. The newly built area looms over the heart of the village. It still has only 1,500 inhabitants.

Robert and Teresa Enke were quickly integrated by Markus Breuer and his wife Erika.

On the ground floor of his house on Schulstrasse, Breuer runs a sports shop. One day he had to go out for a while. His wife had taken the child to the doctor, so he rang the bell of the attic flat. 'Robert, could you take over the shop for half an hour?'

Not long after that a customer came in and asked for some goalkeeping gloves. 'Do you know anything about them?'

'A bit,' replied Robert.

He told the local league goalie all about the difference between five- and six-millimetre foam stuffing, titanium foam and natural latex. When Breuer got back, the customer, who was about to leave, asked him, 'Who's that new salesman you've got there? He's really nice. And he even knows what he's talking about.'

Breuer introduced them to Hubert Rosskamp who liked to hunt and who took the dogs off their hands from time to time – they had two of them by now. In the afternoon after training, Robert often went walking through the fields with Hubert and the dogs. 'You couldn't tell what he was, he was dressed so normally,' Hubert recalls.

Robert with Hubert Rosskamp in front of Rosskamp's house in Gierath.

Hubert worked as an industrial buyer at Rheinmetall in Düsseldorf. He has turned his living-room into a personal museum; Robert's football shirts hang all over the place, bearing the inscription 'For my friend Hubert'. On the shelf in Hubert's kitchen Robert and Teresa's wedding photograph is right at the front; the photographs of his family have been placed behind it.

In the afternoons in the fields, Hubert asked Robert questions. Tell me, how do you actually dive as a goalkeeper? Aren't you scared when the strikers come at you? When he dives for a ball a goalkeeper stretches his lower hand out slightly further than his upper hand, and tries to keep both hands parallel, Robert explained. And as for being scared, no, he certainly didn't get scared. A healthy degree of nerves is important, but nothing more than that.

When he celebrated his twenty-first birthday late, a few days after 24 August 1998, Hubert was invited, and neighbours came along too, like Markus and Erike Breuer, and Teresa's friend Christiane, who worked as a bouncer at a disco. The only people there from Borussia were Marco Villa and Jörg Neblung, the athletics coach whose individual training Robert had assiduously avoided in his first year. In July 1998 Borussia hadn't extended Neblung's contract, after four years. He had gone to work for the agency of Robert's adviser, Norbert

Pflipsen. There was sparkling wine, Christiane made pizza, and Hubert brought Robert strawberry tart, as usual. At the time Marco didn't notice that apart from him there was no one there the same age as Robert, no close friends. 'It was a pleasant enough party with just sweet, nice people,' says Marco, 'and Robbi was happy.' Not least because of football.

Just before his twenty-first birthday, Robert Enke had suddenly become a man in the eyes of the public. On 7 August, Borussia were training on the football pitch beside the Bökelberg Stadium. The goalkeepers practised separately from the rest of the team. Dirk Heyne fired in crosses, Robert jumped and Kamps jumped, taking turns. Even the players at the other end of the pitch heard the noise. When an Achilles tendon ruptures, it sounds like the lash of a whip. Kamps was left lying on the ground. At first it was more shock at the sound of the snap that laid him low than the pain in his left heel.

That same day he was operated on at the accident and emergency department in Duisburg. He would be out of the game for four months, the surgeon predicted. The new Bundesliga season began in eight days.

In Jena the following morning, Andy Meyer took a quick glance at the newspaper. Alone in his room, he couldn't help laughing. 'The unchallenged regular goalkeeper had been seriously injured right before the start of the Bundesliga,' recalls Andy, 'and of course our child of fortune took advantage of that.'

For Teresa those eight days passed quickly, and at the same time went on for ever. Over and over again during that time she happily thought, 'At last!' And at the same time, 'What if he lets in a goal?'

Borussia Mönchengladbach had lost a goalkeeper who had 389 Bundesliga games under his belt; only one footballer, Berti Vogts, had played for the club more often than Kamps. In his place there was now a goalkeeper who had never been tested in a Bundesliga game, and who would be the youngest in the league. 'Robert has our complete trust,' announced Friedel Rausch, the fourth coach Borussia had had in Robert's time at the club.

'What else was Rausch supposed to say?' says Jörg Neblung. 'My bet is that the coach felt uneasy. His most experienced player gets injured, and now he's got this greenhorn.'

Marco Villa saw it differently. 'A lot of people on the team thought Robbi was already stronger than Kamps – our sweeper Patrik Andersson, for example. That was why we didn't worry. We really didn't.'

Probably everyone involved shared Jörg's *and* Marco's thoughts. Like Teresa, they vacillated between confidence and unease.

Robert himself was quite calm. He had developed a mechanism for turning inner nerves into outward peace. Only very rarely did the mechanism break down. When it did he'd be gripped with anxiety, as he had been three years earlier in the Second Bundesliga game for Carl Zeiss Jena in Leipzig, and in his first winter in Mönchengladbach. But almost always, unease or excitement was the drug that made him concentrated and calm.

The day before the start of the 1998–99 Bundesliga season the *Westdeutsche Allgemeine Zeitung* wrote, 'This 20-year-old already seems so incredibly mature, so balanced.' He told the newspaper, 'I have no models, or at least not any more.'

His father travelled in from Jena, one of Teresa's brothers from Würzburg. Gisela was on holiday in Slovakia. 'We'll go to Robert's first Bundesliga game together,' she and Dirk had promised each other after their separation. That wasn't going to happen now. Schalke 04 were the opponents at the Bökelberg. 'We drove each other nuts with our nerves up there in the terraces,' recalls Teresa.

The previous season Borussia had only just escaped relegation on the last day, then Big Stefan Effenberg had moved to Bayern Munich for a transfer fee of 8.5 million marks. A bit of steadiness was thus the best thing most people in Mönchengladbach hoped for from the new season – a place in the Bundesliga midfield, just far enough away from the commotion of a relegation battle.

The 34,000-seater stadium was sold out. The sun was shining. The stands directly behind the goals rose more steeply than anywhere else in the Bundesliga. When Borussia's goal-keeper ran towards his goal immediately before kick-off the entire stand behind the goal grew higher with each step he took. By the time he had reached the six-yard box he felt as if he was at the foot of a gorge.

Robert played entirely in black, the colour of great goal-keepers from former days – Lev Yashin, Gyula Grosics, Ricardo Zamora.

The game began. A striker immediately forced his way down the right wing, got past a second opponent and fired a fast, low cross into the goalie's area. The defender stayed clear because he thought his goalkeeper would deal with the cross. But the keeper hesitated. Within a period of time in which no human being can even finish a thought a goalkeeper has to decide whether he's going to run out of the goal or not. It was already too late.

From the other end of the pitch, Robert watched as Borussia's new centre-forward Toni Polster exploited the hesitation of Schalke's goalkeeper Frode Grodås to give his side a 1–0 lead. The second minute of play was just beginning. After ten minutes Mönchengladbach had raised its advantage to 2–0.

The game had already lost its tension when Robert was seriously put to the test for the first time. With the score at 2–0 everything and everyone looked a bit brighter. The economy of his movements, the absence of any haste, gave him the air of an utterly unbeatable goalkeeper.

Borussia had resorted to putting up a concentrated defence and hitting their opponents quickly on the break. Twice Schalke hit the bar, and Robert commandingly saw off a handful of more or less dangerous shots and headers. Ten minutes before the end the scoreline changed again, to 3–0.

'I actually thought I'd be more nervous,' Robert said to the sports reporters in the tunnel after the game. With quiet enthu-siasm he talked about the crosses that had flown in at him, far faster than anything he had ever experienced in training or even in reserve games. As so often when he was in a good mood, he responded to praise with self-deprecation: 'The ball came so fast that I sometimes wasn't sure when I should go out to meet a cross; but somehow the ball always ended up in my hands.'

After the game most people talked about not the goalkeeper but the new striker, Toni Polster. The *Rheinische Post* featured a double-page report under the headline 'Borussia tops the league again for the first time in ten years', which after one game wasn't exactly much of a feat.

At home, Robert cleaned his gloves with shampoo under the shower, laid them out to dry and stroked smooth the soft foam of their surfaces.

THREE

Defeats Are His Victory

In a small, rain-drenched American town, the murderer already had five people on his conscience when he saw the body of a dog lying in the road. 'I didn't do that,' the serial killer said drily.

At this point in the film *Se7en* Robert always burst out laughing. He actually abhorred violence; he was absolutely sure about what he would do if he encountered a threat: run away. Nonetheless, he watched that film, which isn't short of violent scenes, five or six times. *Se7en*, starring Morgan Freeman and Brad Pitt, provided him with something that was getting increasingly difficult to find since he had started playing for Borussia Mönchengladbach. The film was so exciting that for 127 minutes Robert forgot everything else, especially football. Switching off had become his most difficult task.

His internal film ran incessantly. Everything was new, exciting, inspiring, and at the same time professional sport had taken over his life with its constant rhythm. A game every week, without a break. There was no final whistle for him. Scenes from each match swam around repeatedly in his head: the free kick by Kaiserslautern's Martin Wagner, which he didn't see until it was just a blink away; the striking long-range shot by Frankfurt's Chen Yang, right under the bar. For a debutant goalkeeper it doesn't matter much whether a goal is unstoppable or not. After every one Robert brooded on how he could have stopped it.

After only a few weeks he was well known in the video store.

Two months had passed since the start of the season against

Schalke 04. Borussia Mönchengladbach hadn't won a single one of the next eight games. Robert wasn't much more than a footnote in that wretched tale; and the young goalkeeper prevented even worse things happening, it was said regularly in the match reports. After a 2–1 defeat in Bochum, Borussia fell to the bottom of the table.

Marco Villa gave Toni Polster a pair of Mickey Mouse-print silk underpants as a trophy for the worst-dressed man in the team. Polster happily put the pants on. But it wasn't really all that funny any more.

Fewer than three years earlier, when Robert had chosen to go to Borussia, the club was fourth in the Bundesliga, and looked as if they had a chance of getting to the top. Now the two best players on the team, Stefan Effenberg and striker Martin Dahlin, had been sold, at the urging of the banks. Even so, the team Borussia had retained should have been easily strong enough to stay out of the Bundesliga's relegation battle. But football is pure dynamism, and in that sense sport really is like life: dynamics decide things in our life more often than any kind of careful planning; dynamics win more games than tactics. Seconds after Robert had saved a penalty Borussia went 1–0 down against 1860 Munich; they squandered a victory in Duisburg in the last second with an own goal. Before the players had even noticed, the forces that stimulate change were unleashed. Each mishap produced two new ones, and soon the team was looking like one big error. Where Dahlin had pressed the previous season, now Borussia's opponents could calmly get on with building their game from the back because the new striker Toni Polster felt no particular desire to run and press. Where the previous season Jörgen Pettersson had used Dahlin's pressing game to run off his opponent's badly placed passes, now Pettersson was exploding with fury at Polster, that coffee-house footballer. In his irritation Pettersson then forgot to run back, which meant that the midfield was shorthanded. When a club slips away like that, it usually looks inevitable.

Borussia's coach hardly gave an impression of being able to free them from this downward spiral. Friedel Rausch had once won the UEFA Cup with Eintracht Frankfurt. That was eighteen years ago. On one of his first days at the training-ground in Mönchengladbach Rausch had turned to the midfielder Valantis Anagnostou and said, 'Herr Ballandi, yooou' – he pointed at Anagnostou – 'under-stand' – he pointed at his chest – 'me?'

'Yes, Coach,' replied Anagnostou, 'I was born and bred in Düsseldorf. And my name is Anagnostou, not Ballandi.'

'I see,' said Friedel Rausch. 'And who are you?' he asked Marco Villa.

'I'm Marco Villa.'

'Oh yes, Markus.'

For years, Rausch had been an established Bundesliga coach, a passable tactician and a fiery motivator. The players might have grinned about his scatterbrain ways, but they liked him for it. Rausch hadn't changed. But a team that loses too often sees only its coach's shortcomings. Training methods that had seemed innovative for years suddenly looked ridiculous. Rausch liked to train 'all over the pitch', as he put it. On the training-ground in Rönneter there were several pitches in a row, and the practice game covered two of them – over 240 metres. Robert smiled about this even years later, with a mixture of amusement and irritation.

When Borussia slipped to the bottom of the league, Rausch convinced the directors to fire two players, Karlheinz Pflipsen and Marcel Witeczek, without notice. In professional football, that's called setting an example. It's an effort to change the dynamics, somehow. The directors passed the news on to the players in question. When the coach realised that the majority of the team was furious about the measure, he switched sides. The directors had suggested to Pflipsen and Witeczek that they find a new team, Rausch told his team, but he couldn't do without both! He nominated Pflipsen as deputy team captain for the next game against Bayer Leverkusen, on 30 October 1998.

It was the day Robert Enke became nationally famous.

Marco Villa injured his knee in the tenth minute; the ligament was torn. He was lying on the edge of the pitch being examined by the doctor when the first goal was scored. After being substituted, Marco hobbled to the club-room to watch the game on television with an ice pack on his knee. When he turned the set on, he learned that Borussia's central defender Patrik Andersson had had to leave the pitch as well because of injury, and the score stood at 2–0 to Leverkusen. Robert was sitting on the ground – his hands hanging limply over his knees, which were drawn up to his chest – with an expression of profound incomprehension on his face. That was how he became famous, because the footage was repeated as often as if it were a snippet of Chaplin slapstick: Robert Enke sitting uncomprehendingly on the ground after a goal, and then after another.

Mönchengladbach lost 8–2 to Bayer Leverkusen that day. 'Carnival in Gladbach,' the fans sang. The biggest debacle in thirty years, the radio commentators cried. And the young goalkeeper had prevented even worse things happening!

Robert wished next Saturday, the next game, would come quickly, so that he could leave the horror behind him.

A week later, they played in Wolfsburg. Teresa met some of the wives of Borussia's footballers in a bar in Mönchengladbach to watch the match on television. After fifty-three minutes of play Uwe Kamps's girlfriend said to her, 'Oh God, four goals was the most Uwe ever let in, and after that he was always finished.' Brian O'Neil had just made it 5–1 to VfL Wolfsburg. Their fans sang, 'Only three more, only three more!' Goals to top Leverkusen's feat from last week, they meant. The game ended 7–1.

Robert Enke was famous. No goalkeeper in the Bundesliga had ever let in fifteen goals in a week. The reporters outside the changing-room asked how he felt, and put on sympathetic faces. 'Oh,' Robert replied, 'I'd practised getting the ball out of the net the week before.'

The day after the Wolfsburg game he went for a walk in the fields with Teresa and the dogs. Victory or defeat, that was their Sunday routine.

'So, Enke the Aunt Sally,' said Teresa.

And even though every goal had tormented him, for all his

30 October 1998: Robert Enke at the game against Bayer Leverkusen that ended in an 8–2 defeat.

despondency he was suddenly able to explode with laughter.

'We were very easygoing,' Teresa says. 'The important thing was that there was nothing he could have done about the goals. Then we were able to joke about it.'

After unforgettable defeats like these Robert had to resort to little tricks to maintain his composure. 'I convinced myself that the team had let me down. That helped me to calm down.' He had often reproached himself as a goalkeeper – for goals that weren't really his fault, or for disappointing his team-mates even though no one was disappointed in him. He never received as much sympathy and forgiveness as he did after those fifteen goals. 'And God protect this young goalkeeper – he can't help it!' Teresa heard the television commentator saying in the bar, as the camera caught Robert on the ground with his uncomprehending expression for the last time. As he received evidence from all quarters of how impressively calmly he had gone on playing in an intimidated team, he forgot that his own nerves had once been a-flutter, with Carl Zeiss in Leipzig and during that first winter in Mönchengladbach. 'I'm not so psychologically unstable that I'm crapping myself before each game,' he told the sportswriters. 'You don't need to worry about me suffering lasting damage.'

The more people praised him for his calmness and confidence, the more serenely he played, although without noticing the connection. A decade later, when he was with Hannover 96, he took the Reiss profile test that is supposed to establish a player's personality and motivation. He had never thought that recognition was so fundamentally important to him, he remarked with amazement to Teresa as he held the results in his hands. But even in Mönchengladbach she had been struck by the fact that 'if he felt that other people doubted him, he developed self-doubts, and when he was put under pressure by others, he became insecure. But when he received support, he was incredibly strong as a goalkeeper.'

In Hamburg, once again, Borussia were 2–0 down after half an hour. Hamburg's striker Anthony Yeboah was in the zone – that place where movement happens at an incredible pace, with a higher level of coordination – and he was half a step faster than his Mönchengladbach marker Thomas Eichin. Robert was left stranded and Yeboah's shot flew in, between his legs. Such shots are unstoppable – when a goalkeeper has to stand with his legs spread, waiting to dive towards either side, he can't snap his legs shut like that. But a nutmeg always makes a goalkeeper look ridiculous; after an impossible task he lands clumsily on his backside. The only thing he can rely on is the mockery of the fans. When he got back to his feet, rage was pounding through Robert. He felt abandoned, humiliated; it had been Eichin's mistake, and now people were laughing at him. He wanted to start yelling. But he thought a goalkeeper who lost his composure was lost himself. He wrestled with his fury, and he was helped by the knowledge that so many people had praised his serenity. He was the cool guy, so he would stay cool. Seconds after Yeboah's goal the agitation had left his face.

Over the weeks that followed he learned how to turn off the internal film that constantly tried to tell him all about the most recent goals and crosses. In the evenings he and Teresa often went to see Grandma Frida in Rheydt – the fourth grandma in his life. The old farmer's wife had had her farm converted into rented apartments, and Jörg Neblung lived there with his girlfriend Dörthe. The four of them sat together talking easily about God and the world. It was only when a football match was shown on television that he got up to watch it.

Jörg would sit on the sofa next to him. Whenever Jörg perkily commented on some aspect of the game, Robert would reply concisely and analytically. After that he'd fall silent again. When he watched football on television he became withdrawn, studying his colleagues with great concentration, a goalkeeping engineer in search of the mechanisms of the game – on the one hand. On the other, football on television was a most effective anaesthetic. Watching football helped him to forget about playing football.

Sometimes the others wanted to do something else.

'We could always go out,' Teresa said.

'But we could always stay at home,' he countered.

How often had they had that exchange?

But when they visited Dörthe and Jörg, Robert had three people against him, and he went along with it. When they played Bon Jovi at the disco, he even danced. But he didn't want to go out all the time so he soon developed tactics.

'Come on, let's go to the Gebläsehalle,' said Jörg one evening.

'Can't,' said Robert, trying to keep the triumph off his face.

'Why not?'

'Stupidly, I'm wearing tracksuit trousers. The doorman won't let me in.'

Jörg was supposed to be looking after him. 'Can't you do something about that boy? He has no social circle,' Norbert Pflipsen had said to Jörg during Robert's second year with Mönchengladbach, when Jörg was still the team's athletics coach. 'Worrying' can also be a job, Jörg learned when Borussia declined to extend his contract in the summer of 1998. Flippi took him on as a 'worrier', or *Kümmerer* – the slang name given to the staff of an agency that's supposed to look after professional sportspeople in everyday life. 'Fridge-filler is another term,' says Jörg.

He'd really wanted to be an industrial designer. During the entrance exam for technical college in Hanover he had looked out of the window in search of inspiration. He saw the bile-green trams driving past the gardens of the town-houses, drew his next sketches in that colour, and was rejected. After that he wanted to do something completely different. He studied sports science. One of his professors, Karl-Heinz Drygalsky, became chairman of Borussia Mönchengladbach. When Drygalsky took him on as fitness coach in 1994, Bayern Munich was the only team in the Bundesliga with such a post.

Jörg thought professional football would be pretty much the same as athletics. He assumed a Bundesliga team's medical staff would work hand in hand, and the head coach would take an interest in individual training plans. Then he saw his first head coach, Bernd Krauss, forcing the players to run excessively hard endurance races, contrary to all training theory, supposedly as a way of schooling their will. He experienced Borussia's physio-therapist denigrating him to the coaching staff to make sure that injured players came to him first. 'All backroom staff in a Bundesliga side are constantly courting the favour of the coach and the players,' Jörg says. 'And in order to please them, if necessary they sometimes worked against their better judgement.'

A bell rings in the corridor outside his airy office on the third floor of an old factory building. It's a woman with a basket full of sandwiches. She does her rounds every day because the multimedia designers and communication advisers in offices like this on Lichtstrasse in Cologne have no time for lunch. Jörg Neblung, northern German and blond, still looking like a decathlete at the age of forty-three, now runs his own football agency. During our interview he sometimes turns round as if talking to his shelf, where he has set up some goalkeeping gloves and photographs of Robert, and a candle.

There are hundreds of kinds of friendship, and of the one formed in 1998 between Robert Enke and Jörg Neblung the fact will always remain that Jörg was supposed to worry about him. But the will to strive together for goals is more of a bond than most emotions.

Jörg could understand that in his difficult moments Robert wanted to sort things out all by himself. 'I'm like that too,' he says.

In the autumn of 1998, when Borussia Mönchengladbach couldn't stop making mistakes and had a six-week, seven-game run of losses, Robert turned himself into an individual sportsman. The loneliness of the goalkeeper has often been exaggerated and lamented in literature, but for the goalkeeper in a declining team, loneliness is a blessing. He plays his own game and finds his victories in defeat. He conceded two goals to Bayern Munich but thought about the five fine saves he had shown. At least he's still making saves, the experts said. 'While chaos rages, he stays calmly in Gladbach,' wrote the *Düsseldorfer Express*.

Robert in 1998 during his time with Mönchengladbach.

'Calm, serenity, equilibrium, class' – those were the qualities attributed to him by the distinguished coach Jupp Heynckes, who had led Real Madrid to their Champions League victory six months earlier and who now, on a sabbatical in his home town of Mönchengladbach, often attended Borussia's games. 'He had always been more advanced than the rest of us, in his ideas, in his behaviour, in his speech,' said Borussia's midfielder Marcel Ketelaer, who had played with Robert in the national youth team. 'He was always more grown up than we were.'

'Mental strength' was a fashionable expression of the newly psychologised sport. Everyone saw the Borussia goal-keeper as a model of the new sportsman. They gallantly overlooked the fact that he sometimes didn't hurry out of the goal to catch a cross, or allowed Hertha BSC to score a goal when he let a shot ricochet. There is little that moves the football-going public as much as a rookie goalkeeper among hard men; he's celebrated for saves that experienced goalkeepers barely notice. Robert would only fully under-stand this years later when he was an older international goalkeeper among young rivals.

In Mönchengladbach the players tried to deceive themselves about their unparalleled bad run. They kept making jokes in the changing-room. In all the laughter they couldn't hear that some players talked over each other rather than to each other. Jörgen Pettersson used up all his energy in a mute conflict with his fellow striker Toni Polster. No one had anything against Robert. He adopted a listening role during tactical discussions in various corners of the changing-room, he was friendly to almost everyone, he laughed when others railed against the coach – and no one apart from Marco Villa got to know him any better.

The coach had provided an opportunity for mirth when 'Friedel Rausch went off on one', as Jörg Neblung put it. 'If I played Martin Schneider in defence in the form he's in, people would think, is Rausch gay and sleeping with Schneider or what?' the coach teased at a press conference. Then, in September, Rausch was dismissed. Head of the board of directors Michael Viehof said, 'This time it's going to take more than the firing of a coach.' So the club also dismissed its sporting director, Rolf Rüssmann.

In its first twenty-two years in the Bundesliga, Borussia

Mönchengladbach had managed with a total of three coaches. In 1998, Robert experienced four changes of coach in a year.

During the Christmas holiday, Robert and Teresa went to see her family in Bad Windsheim. Robert's father was hurt. Did his son like being with his in-laws more than he liked being with him? He didn't dare talk to Robert about it.

Family gatherings were very important to Dirk Enke. At Christmas, on birthdays, during holidays, he stressed his belief that a divided family belonged together. Robert often forgot birthdays. Sometimes his mother came to his rescue. She would phone him solicitously: it's your father's birthday today, or your niece's. 'I thought it was a real shame that communication between us was so limited,' his father says. He waited constantly for an invitation to Mönchengladbach. When none came, he tried to find excuses to visit his son. He'd like to see the Bayern game, he'd be about to go see his brother in Detmold – so he could just pop in and see Robert, if he did not mind.

Robert didn't think you had to invite your parents or your brothers and sisters. If they wanted to come, they'd come. At Christmas he went to Teresa's parents' for the simple reason that their celebrations were more traditional.

Bad Windsheim is surrounded by fields and woods. On the last day of 1998 Robert wanted to go for a jog.

'I'll come with you and take the dogs for a walk,' Teresa said.

'No, you don't need to, stay with your parents.'

Of course, she went with him.

They drove into the fields behind the Galgenbuck hill, a remote area and ideal for letting the dogs run about. Have fun, she said, before he set off.

Ten minutes later he was back. His eyes were swollen and he kept sneezing. And there was a wheezing noise in his throat.

'I can't breathe!'

They dashed home. In the bathroom Teresa found an old asthma inhaler. Robert pumped away at it like a man possessed.

But the active ingredient wasn't getting into his lungs; his windpipe was too swollen.

Teresa's father took him to the hospital. The wheezing in Robert's throat was the loudest sound in the car. Her father ran ahead and threw the door to the emergency department open. There was no one at reception. Half a minute passed, then three minutes, and at last two nurses appeared. They rolled Robert into the intensive care unit on a gurney. His eyes were shut and he was concentrating hard on breathing in and out through his constricted windpipe, but he heard one nurse saying to the other, 'Isn't that Gladbach's goalie, the one who always packs them in?'

His condition stabilised. He spent the afternoon in bed with an oxygen pipe in his nose, unable to open his swollen eyelids. At one point a nurse asked him, 'Herr Enke, do you want to read something?' At least that made him chuckle.

He celebrated New Year with Teresa in the general ward. It seemed he was allergic to apples and celery, the doctors told him after they'd examined him. He could probably digest each foodstuff on its own without any problems, but he had had celery soup in the evening and an apple tart the next morning, and this had brought on an attack. If Teresa hadn't been there when he went jogging, he would almost certainly have died.

A few weeks later the event had become an anecdote that he liked to tell: guess what the nurse said when my eyes were closed and I was gasping for air! Other than that, Teresa and Robert didn't give any more thought to the kind of chance events that determine whether someone lives or dies.

At the training-camp in January 1999, Marco Villa prepared himself for Robert's usual explosions of fury. By the third day his friend was suddenly bothered by everything. Marco called these phases 'Robbi's days'.

'How loud is that television!'

'Say the word, Robbi, and I'll turn it down.'

Without replying, Robert went to the bathroom.

'You've used my towel!' he called into the room.

'I just used any old towel. There's a fresh one in the drawer.'

'And why's the toilet seat dirty again? I've told you a million times not to pee standing up!'

'Fine, Robbi,' said Marco, still watching the television, waiting for Robbi's days to pass.

News arrived at the training-camp: Uwe Kamps had had another operation on his Achilles heel; he wouldn't be coming back that season. Robert had no competition in the Borussia goal until the summer. But what would happen after that? His contract was due to run out in July. The club management seemed to have forgotten that. Ever since Rüssmann had been fired no one seemed to be worried about the future. The present was already too much for the people in charge. President Wilfried Jacobs summed up his time in office with Borussia with self-righteous concision: 'In twenty months I had the misfortune not to have a single nice hour.'

The second half of the season turned out to be a copy of the first. By April, Borussia Mönchengladbach, still at the bottom of the league, were already talking about their last chance.

On Saturday, in Nuremberg, we've got to win.

Two days before the match coach Rainer Bonhof called Robert into his office. He had to plan the new season: could he count on him?

'I can't exactly say yet.'

'Robert, please. I need clarity.'

Robert wanted to be honest, to do the right thing.

'OK, then, I'll leave,' he said.

He didn't want to play for a disorganised club in the Second Bundesliga. And that was exactly where Borussia was going to be next season. But he gave the coach another reason: he was leaving because he didn't know where he would stand when Kamps came back.

Bonhof said that if Robert was absolutely sure, he ought to announce his decision straight away at a press conference.

Robert was irritated. What was the point? he asked. Now, right before the crucial game in the relegation battle, it would only cause unnecessary trouble.

No, it was better if things were cleared up right now.

Robert didn't understand. Surely Bonhof knowing was enough. He'd be able to start looking for another goalkeeper. 'I think it might be better not to tell the public,' Robert said, carefully and politely.

After training, Bonhof sat down in the press hall at the Bökelberg Stadium, poured himself a glass of water and announced that he had some bad news. Robert Enke would be leaving Borussia at the end of the season.

On Saturday, Teresa's parents went to the Frankenstadion in Nuremberg – Bad Windsheim was only seventy kilometres away. They spotted the bed sheet straight away. It was flapping over an advertising hoarding in front of the away fans end. 'Borussians: Kamps, Frontzeck, Eberl' it said, and beside it, divided by a clean line in the middle, 'Traitors: Enke, Feldhoff'.

Robert Enke had been the darling of the season. Now the Mönchengladbach fans were supporting their team with cries like 'Enke, you Stasi pig!', 'Robert Enke, mercenary and traitor!', or simply 'Uwe Kamps, Uwe Kamps – Uuuuwe Kamps!'

Mönchengladbach lost 2–0 to Nuremberg, who were also threatened with relegation – a team that lately had been in the hands of a new coach called Friedel Rausch. The sportswriters were waiting behind the mobile barriers in the Frankenstadion tunnel. Robert knew what they were going to ask, and he wouldn't let anything show, he had decided.

How painful was the abuse you got, Robert?

'The shouting wasn't nice, certainly, but somehow it was also to be expected.'

Were you annoyed that the coach made your decision to leave Borussia public?

'I told the coach about my concerns. But probably not enough.'

He sounded impressively matter-of-fact. At moments like that, when he made an effort to look relaxed, 'his face divided', his mother says. By way of proof she produces a few photographs. When he wanted to look relaxed, it is clear from the pictures, his mouth smiled and his eyes remained unmoved.

Bochum were their next opponents. Just minutes before kick-off the stewards were frantically clearing the goal where Robert had taken up position. Around him lay toilet paper, lighters, plastic beer mugs. Behind the goal stood the Borussia fans.

'Look, there he is, the mercenary and traitor!'

He wouldn't let anything show.

When he easily deflected a low shot from Bochum's Kai Michalke, the Mönchengladbach fans whistled wildly. A few hundred of them wanted to whistle every time he touched the ball.

In the last minute of play Borussia took a 2–1 lead. In the same minute they promptly conceded a goal that Robert couldn't have saved.

'Stasi-swine, Stasi-swine!'

Teresa walked exhaustedly to the marquee where the players met their friends and families after the game. 'It's madness, what they're doing to you.'

'It's part of the job.'

With calm resolution Robert told Teresa not to go to the stadium for the last home games of the season, to spare her nerves. She was so taken aback by his self-confidence that she didn't contradict him.

'I was just amazed,' says Jörg Neblung. 'How level-headed is he, then?'

Flippi and Jörg were regulars at the marquee. It was about time to find a new employer for Robert. Some clubs were interested in him – AS Roma, Hertha BSC – but there were already two concrete offers, from 1860 Munich and Benfica. In 1999–2000, Portugal's favourite club would be trained by Jupp Heynckes. Norbert Pflipsen's notion of work didn't entail making a special effort to look for better offers if you already had a good one. Apart from that, he was very busy finding a new club for Borussia's nineteen-year-old midfielder Sebastian Deisler. It was said that Germany hadn't seen such a player since Günter Netzer in 1972.

So, to put it briefly, Flippi said, he was in favour of Benfica. They had offered an amazing contract, Robert could play in the Champions League for them, and Jupp was the coach. He'd known Jupp for thirty years – an excellent man.

I'll have to think about it, Robert said.

First of all Borussia had to play in Leverkusen. It's our last chance, they said.

When they pulled up at the Ulrich-Haberland Stadium some Borussia fans formed a guard of honour and applauded. Before the games the fans cheered the professionals, after the games they threatened them. 'How absurd,' Marco said, and suddenly started waving back at the fans, smiling at them and calling out words no one could hear through the double-glazed panes: 'Hallo, you stupid arses, hallo!'

'Of course, he says, 'it wasn't aimed at anyone personally. I just wanted to build a barrier, protect myself from the hatred that would later be spilled over us.'

'Come on, join in, Robbi,' urged Marco.

Robert hesitated.

'Come on, Robbi.'

'Hallo, you silly arses, hallo!'

Once he'd managed to say it, things went quite smoothly. Yes, it was good to rant.

They lost the game 4–1.

'Without Enke we will rise again!' sang the Mönchengladbach fans.

'Without Enke you'll go back down!' answered the Leverkusen supporters.

Half an hour after the final whistle, a thousand Mönchengladbach fans were holding out on the terraces to commiserate. 'I take my hat off to those fans,' said coach Bonhof. He said nothing at all about the tirades against Robert by those same fans.

The reporters were waiting. What do you think of a coach like that, Robert?

'I suppose it wasn't the best idea to announce my departure in the middle of the relegation battle. I should have stated my concerns more firmly. Neither the coach nor me expected such violent attacks.'

He thought he always had to try to see things from other people's points of view. Bonhof had probably just handled things clumsily, without any bad intentions. And it was quite natural for the fans to look for someone to blame after a season like that.

He thought a goalkeeper should always seek the blame in himself first.

Robert told Teresa he couldn't go to Portugal in the middle of the football season, not even for one and a half training-free days – what if it got out? Teresa must look at Lisbon for him. It was decided she'd take her mother with her.

Jupp Heynckes flew to Portugal at the end of April to sort out the last details of his contract with Benfica; Flippi, Jörg Neblung, Teresa and her mother went with him. Heynckes would present Benfica's club president with the signing of Robert Enke as a condition for his signature.

As they walked through the arrivals hall of the Aeroporto da Portela, for the first time in his life Jörg heard Portuguese being spoken. He had thought it would sound like Spanish. Suddenly Portugal seemed a long, long way away.

The translator, sent by Benfica, greeted them in grammatically perfect German. Had they had a good flight? Welcome to Lisbon. On the drive into the city, Teresa asked about residential areas.

'Could you please repeat your question,' the translator said.

Could she recommend a nice area to live in Lisbon?

'What did you say?'

Teresa became aware that she would have to answer her questions all by herself. And she would have to give up her studies if they moved to Portugal.

As she walked with her mother across Praça Rossio and climbed the hills of the Bairro Alto, with its views across the Tagus to the Atlantic, she was seized by the feeling that this city existed in a far-away world. But when they were sitting that evening on the restaurant terrace in the Expo site, the huge sails of the Vasco da Gama Bridge glittering in the night and the waiters serving sea bass baked in salt, all of a sudden it seemed enticing.

So? Robert said when she got back.

'It's a beautiful city. As far as I'm concerned we could go there.'

Aha, he said.

A few days later Flippi rejected 1860 Munich. I'll try my luck in Portugal, Robert had decided after Heynckes had explained the project to him in his sitting-room.

'You should really take a look at the city yourself,' said Teresa.

He had no time at the moment, he replied. They had to win in Freiburg – it was their very last chance.

They lost 2–1. After thirty-four years in the Bundesliga, Borussia Mönchengladbach were relegated for the first time. It felt like a sort of salvation. The team had had to cope with the feeling of just having been relegated every Saturday for weeks. At last they had certainty.

They ended the season with a pitiful four victories out of thirty-four games; since hitting bottom place in early autumn they had stayed there without interruption. The third-from-bottom club, Friedel Rausch's Nuremberg, also going down, were sixteen points ahead of them. Robert had let in seventy-three goals. And after all of them the headlines had read 'Enke outstanding', 'Reliable Enke', 'Enke a great white hope'. He let in the last two of the seventy-three at the Bökelberg against Dortmund, and once again the fans cried, 'Look, there he is, the mercenary and the traitor!'

'It sounds silly, but it was fun playing in the Bundesliga,' he told the sportswriters.

He would let nothing show.

Six years later Robert raised his right hand to greet the fans in Mönchengladbach at Uwe Kamps's testimonial. The mood was solemnly relaxed – an idol was leaving. A lot of fans whistled at Robert's friendly wave. After that he didn't care whether his friends noticed anything. After six years he released his fury over his treatment by the fans. 'It always rains in

Mönchengladbach,' was his curt reply whenever Marco wanted to talk about Borussia again.

'Of course the hostility in Mönchengladbach was deep in his bones,' says Jörg Neblung. 'Here was a man who had been radically misunderstood. He thought he was being fair to the club by saying in good time, "I'm leaving at the end of the season, I'll give you enough time to find a successor." He wanted to do the right thing, and all he got in return was hatred.'

The contract with Benfica was still to be signed. On the plane to Lisbon he sat with a Portuguese language book in his lap and cobbled together his first sentence in the foreign language.

É bom estar aquí.

He wanted to surprise the reporters with that at his presentation.

It's good to be here.

The signing of the contract was planned for the afternoon of 4 June, immediately after his arrival; the official presentation would be carried out the next day at a press conference in the Stadium of Light.

A car was waiting for them at the Aeroporto da Portela. Jörg Neblung wore a light summer suit like Pierce Brosnan in *The Tailor of Panama*. Flippi had said, you do it, and had stayed at home. Robert had chosen a blue shirt with a grey suit, no tie – he was a sportsman, after all. When they set off from the underground car park, Teresa noticed a photographer hiding behind a pillar.

'Look over there,' she said, too surprised to think.

Robert turned his head, and a flash blinded him. He looked furiously at Teresa, as if she'd pressed the button.

'Sorry, how should I know a paparazzo would be lying in wait for us?'

They reached the office of Benfica's president João Vale e Azevedo. Friendly, nervous words were exchanged, then Robert was sitting on a chair with a velvet cushion, the contract in front of him.

He turned around. 'Shall I sign?'

Teresa swallowed. She looked him in the eye and tried to sound relaxed. 'Sign it.'

Hands were shaken. Vale e Azevedo's was fleshy. In profile, the president's face looked like that of a youthful intellectual; from the front, with the gleam of his high forehead and his laughing eyes, he looked like a local politician trying a bit too hard to appear clever.

They stepped outside the door, where the photographers were already waiting. Vale e Azevedo put his arm around Robert, the photographers flashed away, and the next morning the picture was on the front page of the sports newspaper the *Record*. 'Enke signs' read the headline in capital letters.

In the picture Robert looks happy.

An hour after the signing Robert, Teresa and Jörg returned to their hotel rooms on the Praça Marques da Pombal for a quick rest. Jörg was lying on his bed in his summer suit, his arms folded behind his head, when there was a knock at the door. It was Teresa.

'Jörg, Robbi's not staying in Lisbon.'

FOUR

Fear

Jörg didn't move. He lay motionless on the bed, pillows piled all around him, silver and bronze with a pattern of flowers. As always in high-class hotels there were far too many pillows: Jörg never knew what to do with them. He slowly processed the words he had just heard.

'What do you mean Robbi isn't staying in Lisbon?'

'He wants to go back straight away.'

Jörg sat up. He hid his confusion with a smile. His silence challenged Teresa to tell him about that far-off world into which Robert had suddenly plunged after the signing of the contract.

Outside the president's office, immediately after the signing of the contract, Robert hears Teresa saying, 'Let's go to the Expo site and do a spot of shopping.'

The cars on the Avenida da Liberdade are driving slowly in the evening rush-hour. Palms, taller than houses, line the boulevard. The fine cobblestones under his feet are white and smooth, polished by millions of shoes. The summer light in the south, more intense, more brilliant, is still reflected in the shop windows. A few pedestrians look at him out of the corners of their eyes, without slowing their pace; they don't want to look curious, but they'd like to know why the photographers are here. The blackness of their hair is like the sunlight: more intense and brilliant than he knows. He can't say exactly what it is that gives him the feeling of being an outsider.

They take a taxi.

The pavilions of the old World Exposition are now an

entertainment district with boutiques and restaurants. There might be a shoe shop, Teresa says playfully to Robert, and looks at him.

He's holding his head tilted.

He had held his head tilted exactly like that during his first winter in Mönchengladbach, when he was suddenly overwhelmed by fear. He sat at the dining table in the Loosenweg, he said miserably that he didn't want to go to training, then he fell silent, with his head on one side as if to rest it on his shoulder, and he stayed in that posture for minutes at a time. Now all of a sudden he's doing it again, and she can see tears welling up in his eyes.

He feels Teresa's gaze on him. 'I'm going to the toilet for a minute,' he says and turns around abruptly, as if wresting himself free.

'What's up?' asks Jörg.

'I don't think Robbi's feeling very well.'

'Oh, really?'

It's an unusually long time before he comes back from the toilet.

'Shall we go back to the hotel?' Teresa asks immediately, to build a bridge for him.

He tells Jörg he has a headache. Jörg looks at him and doesn't think Robert looks at all unwell.

In the taxi Teresa talks to cover up the fact that Robert isn't saying anything. Jörg is sitting in the front. He can't see Robert sitting motionless, looking out of the window, with his head on one side.

'We'll rest for an hour or so and see how it goes after that,' Teresa says as the lift in the fifteen-storey hotel delivers them to their floor with its wonderful view. 'See you later, Jörg.'

Once she's closed the door he throws himself down on the bed, buries his head in the pillow and weeps so despairingly that it sounds as if he's going to choke on his tears. She strokes the back of his neck to calm him down.

'Robbi.'

'I can't stay here. It's not working.'

'But you signed a contract an hour ago.'

'What am I doing here, in a foreign country?'

At least he's no longer speaking into the pillow.

His weeping subsides.

'OK,' she says at last. 'You stay here, and I'll go and tell Jörg. We've got to tell him.'

There's a knock on the door to Jörg's room. As Teresa comes in, there's still a smile on his lips, as if he's just been having a lovely dream.

Jörg followed Teresa along the deep grey carpet of the hotel corridor, still not quite having shaken off the high of the trouble-free signing of the contract. When they got to his room, Robert was lying on the bed, exactly as he had been before. The earlier dialogue repeated itself.

I can't stay here.

But you signed a contract an hour ago.

This isn't working.

For a moment Jörg could empathise. After his season at Mönchengladbach he had had a clear image of Robert Enke in his head – an extraordinarily unstressed, philosophical, sensible young man. Suddenly, as he looked at Robert, he saw himself, at home at the age of sixteen, when his parents, both teachers, asked him if he wanted to go to the United States as an exchange student for a year. A vague feeling of fear and loneliness had risen up in him. 'America? Oh God, that's far away.' And Jörg had immediately turned down his parents' offer. He thought he could understand Robert's fear. 'He was only twenty-one, a boy going into the unknown, and over-whelmed by foreignness in a foreign country.'

But that insight didn't help him out of this jam.

Why didn't he sleep on it for a night? It might just be nerves – understandable, of course.

Robert shook his head violently. He had to get out of here, he was going to leave. There were red patches on his cheeks.

Jörg rang Flippi. After all, he was just an agency employee, he couldn't make big decisions without consulting his boss. Flippi had an unambiguous piece of advice: 'Give him a slap.'

Jörg understood: he would have to sort out the situation all by himself.

The invitation to Robert Enke's presentation the next morning at the Stadium of Light had already been sent to the media.

Teresa sat on the bed with Robert, and Jörg sat down in a grey armchair. There was a bunch of white roses on the desk.

'What if we say Teresa isn't well and we have to leave at short notice?'

Teresa said she would play along.

Jörg looked at Robert.

Robert waited for them to do something.

'Then I'll sort it out,' said Jörg. But he would have to tell Benfica's coach the truth, at least. Robert owed his contract to Jupp Heynckes, and for that reason alone they should be honest with him. Whatever happened next.

Jörg stepped out into the street. He found difficult conversations easier when he was moving. He marched along Rua Castilho. The traffic roared as he told the office of the Benfica president that they would have to postpone the presentation, the goalkeeper's wife wasn't well, they'd be flying back on the first plane tomorrow – yes, sadly. What a relief that decency requires secretaries not to ask tricky questions.

Jörg turned round and walked back down Rua Castilho, past Sotheby's and the Ritz, which he didn't even notice. The walk took him slightly uphill, which was good, as the greater his physical effort the less he noticed his nervous tension.

Heynckes answered the telephone in a friendly voice.

Jörg wanted to get everything off his chest as quickly as possible and rattled away without giving the coach a chance to interrupt him. Robert was ill, afraid of being abroad all of a sudden, a young guy; in short, they had to leave straight away, no other possibility; everything else they would sort out later but to be honest Robert's switch to Benfica was doubtful.

'Mr Neblung, you are incredibly arrogant.'

'Yes, I'm sorry about that too. But it's the only way.'

He hung up and stopped walking.

'Given the customs of professional football, Heynckes must of course have thought that we'd suddenly found a better offer for Robert and wanted to use excuses to get him out of the Benfica contract. So I could understand the coach assuming the worst at that moment. Agents are partly there to take the blows and spare the player. So it was quite right for me to have to take insults from Heynckes.'

They stayed in the hotel that evening. Jörg changed the booking for the return flights to the following day. Robert went to bed early.

The next morning at the airport Jörg bought Robert a copy of the *Record* with its headline 'Enke signs'. Robert saw how happily he was smiling on the front-page picture. Now he had only one goal: to get away from Lisbon. He was too exhausted with fear to appreciate that someone who flies away has to arrive somewhere and keep going.

He and Teresa went on holiday. The dunes of southern Holland with their windswept scrub began just behind the kilometre-long beach at Domburg. The clouds were so low they seemed to have settled on the sand hills. Robert watched the dogs as they ran around.

Neither of them mentioned their evening in Lisbon, but there was nothing tense about their silence on the subject. It simply didn't seem to matter here.

We have four weeks until training starts at Benfica, Teresa thought. All kinds of things can happen in four weeks.

Meanwhile, at Norbert Pflipsen's agency they were planning the future. Flippi made a call, to Edgar Geenen, the sporting director at 1860 Munich. Would they still be interested in signing Robert? But the prospect of plunging into a legal dispute about a player who hadn't wanted to join them a few weeks earlier and who had now signed for another club didn't strike Geenen as very enticing.

The only way out was to persuade Robert to go to Lisbon after all.

Flippi phoned Jupp Heynckes.

'My dear friend, all this can't be true!' cried the coach.

'Tell me about it! Jupp, I understand you, I'm on your side. The boy's just a bit rattled. The paparazzi in Lisbon intimidated him, the reception was too much for him.'

'Can you actually still see the reality? He's got an excellent contract, because I stood up for him!'

'I know that, Jupp, and I'll tell the boy that too. We'll try and sort it out. Give him a bit of time.'

He had no time, he had a season to plan. Heynckes's tone was close to that of a coach speaking to his team in the changing-room at half-time when they were 4–0 down.

A short time later a report came from Portugal: Heynckes had signed another new goalkeeper. Jörg entered the new man's name in a search engine on the internet, which was then in its infancy. Carlos Bossio. Four years older than Robert, silver medal winner in the 1996 Olympic Games with Argentina, 146 games in the Argentinian top flight for Estudiantes. The accompanying photographs said the rest. 'A huge guy, 1.94 metres, and a chin like Sylvester Stallone,' Jörg recalls. 'That was a goalkeeper with a top-class profile.' Benfica were no longer counting on Robert, no longer trusted him to turn up after his hasty departure. That was the message carried by the report from Portugal.

Jörg told Robert about it as if it couldn't have gone better for them. 'Now you have no pressure in Lisbon – they've fetched a goalkeeper over from Argentina. He might play at the beginning, but that mightn't be all that bad. You can calmly settle in.'

With his skin tanned a deep bronze and his fair hair shining after his summer holiday, Robert said of course he understood that he had to go back to Lisbon, he'd signed a contract.

Teresa organised their move out of Gierath. The day before they set off for Lisbon they watched the removal men carrying the boxes out of the attic flat; the cases and bags for the flight were kept separate, in the kitchen. After the removal van had driven off, Teresa checked the empty flat one last time in case she'd forgotten anything. It was Saturday; the weekend silence of the village matched the emptiness of the flat.

Robert came over and stood in front of Teresa. 'I'm not coming.'

'What?'

'I'm not coming. Where's the car key?'

Teresa was too perplexed even to think, let alone do anything. Once he'd gone, she rang his mobile. He'd turned it off. She called his parents. 'If your son rings, try and come up with some way of calming him down. He's just cleared off.'

She drove to Rheydt to see Jörg and Dörthe. Not far from Grandma Frida's old farm she could see Jörg disappearing into the forest in his tracksuit. Let him run, she thought, let him enjoy his exercise before I shock him with the news.

With the pleasant feeling of exhaustion that you get after doing a bit of exercise, Jörg came back three-quarters of an hour later. He greeted Teresa and asked casually, 'Where's Robbi?'

'He's cleared off.'

'Nonsense.'

'No, really. He's cleared off.'

Teresa, Dörthe and Jörg were aware that laughter was totally inappropriate, so it was the only thing they could do: they laughed.

They rang his mobile every few mintues. The phone remained switched off. They sent him text messages. All they could do was go on waiting.

Darkness gently ousted the glorious day, and soon it was nine o'clock. He'd been missing for seven hours when the doorbell rang. Teresa ran to the door, opened it and saw him standing at the foot of the steep steps. He glanced up then looked away again, as if nothing in this world had anything to do with him.

'God, Robbi, where have you been?'

'Away.'

Teresa never got a concrete answer. Neither did she insist on one. She had the feeling that his inner equilibrium had only just re-established itself, and that she must on no account disturb that fine balance.

'We're off to Lisbon today,' she said the next morning, struggling to ensure that it didn't sound like a question, or an order.

He nodded. It was impossible to tell what he felt.

FIVE

The City of Light

They took a hotel room at the airport, where people stay when they want to get away again quickly. The little park near the hotel was called Valley of Silence. From there it was only five minutes to the old Expo site, the only familiar place from which they could begin to explore this strange city.

The mild evening air after the hot July day settled around them as Teresa looked down on the Tagus from a restaurant terrace at the Expo site. There was a gentle breeze. The lights of Lisbon sparkled on the river, the flags of all nations fluttered on the flagpoles at the foot of the Vasco da Gama Bridge.

'It's beautiful here, isn't it, Robbi?'

He went on cutting at his steak. 'All I can hear is the creaking of the flagpoles,' he said.

Teresa can't be sure he was holding his head at an angle, she can't remember actually dropping her cutlery without a word, but that's how she recalls the scene today.

She went with him to his first daily training at Benfica as if taking him to hospital. She dropped Robert off at the Stadium of Light and went for a coffee in the shopping centre on the other side of the street – a relative waiting outside the operating theatre and trying not to drum her fingers on the table.

An eagle awaited Robert at the entrance to the stadium. He dashed past Benfica's stone emblem and into the changing-room. He couldn't understand what the other players were saying but he understood their laughter: it was the same as the laughter in Mönchengladbach when Marco played his pranks.

Robert in 2000 overlooking the City of Light.

Jupp Heynckes introduced himself to the team, and off they went to Camp Número 3, the training-ground. Robert stayed among the new players, so Heynckes had no opportunity to talk to him person to person. Heynckes's goalkeeping coach Walter Junghans treated Robert as if he knew nothing at all about his panic attack.

There were four goalkeepers – one too many after the last-minute signing of Carlos Bossio. Junghans was careful to treat all them equally. In his time as a player he himself had experienced all the emotional states of a goalkeeper: as the number one at Bayern Munich, as an unemployed outcast, as captain with Schalke, and during a spell stranded in the Second Bundesliga. 'The position involves so much euphoria and pain, a goalkeeper has to expect to be the idiot at any moment,' says Junghans, 'so the goalkeeping coach must be a sympathetic friend to all his goalkeepers.' Accordingly, he didn't like putting Robert in goal first at every training practice, but he found it was the only way. Bossio only spoke Spanish, the third keeper Nuno Santos Portuguese, Sergei Ovchinnikov – who, as fourth choice, had the threat of deportation hanging over his head – Russian and Portuguese. Junghans spoke only German and English. Robert, therefore, always had to demonstrate the exercises so that the others understood. Apart from that they communicated in the language of the voiceless – with smiles and gestures.

The grass was still gloriously damp – it was freshly watered before every training session – and the ball clung with pleasing firmness to the gloves. Robert studied his rivals. Everything about Bossio was enormous – his upper arms, his hands, and, yes, his chin too; and he could do amazing jumps as well. But the most noticeable thing about the Argentinian was his friendly smile.

Robert smiled back. He didn't even think about fear. His urge to be perfect, to rise to every challenge, had instinctively woken up on the training-ground.

When the other pros left after training, he went to the gym. At first, in Mönchengladbach, he had felt uneasy with the weights, under the eyes of Kamps; now he was the only one who sat down willingly with the equipment. Junghans went with him, in the hope – at the age of forty-one – that the machines might do something about the inevitable paunch of a former professional sportsman.

Suddenly Heynckes was standing next to him. He waited until Robert had finished his set of leg-press exercises. Then he started talking about his own first impressions of Lisbon, how pleasing the Portuguese were – at least when they weren't driving – how much clearer the light was down south. Heynckes talked quietly, slowly, convivially, and eventually said, 'Look, Robert, you're not alone here. I know how big a step it is for a twenty-one-year-old to go abroad, but you don't need to be scared. I brought you over here and I'll help you. Walter, you and me, we're here together, and we'll see it through together.'

Neither Junghans nor Heynckes remembers what Robert said in reply.

It was time for the next series of exercises on the leg-press. He clamped his feet in the machine, knees bent, mouth clenched in expectation of the coming exertion. And the weights in the contraption flew up as if no exertion was too much for him.

'I liked Robert from the very beginning,' Heynckes says. 'I'd met him twice in the spring, in my house on the Spielberg in Mönchengladbach, to get him for Benfica. He was incredibly open, likeable, and very confident, and that impression stayed with me, even though at first I was really pissed off when he suddenly said he didn't want to go to Lisbon. But from the moment we talked in the gym at Benfica, his panic attack was forgotten as far as I was concerned. I only thought about it again four years later.'

Robert didn't find it so easy to forget. As soon as he left the training-ground the feeling of being a stranger slowly, paralysingly returned. He knew he had no reason to be afraid, but the hotel by the airport became his fortress. He entrenched himself there, with Teresa.

'Robbi, head straight!' she'd shout, and he'd look away with a start from the television and raise his head. A quarter of an hour later the game was repeated.

One afternoon she received a call from Tina, their mutual friend from Jena. Robert was at training at the time.

'So, what are you up to?'

'Well, nothing, really. I'd like to go out into the old town or something, but Robbi's not in a good way, he just spends all the time moping in our room.'

'Then go out on your own, even if you just sit with your book in a café. You can't spend all your time fitting in with Robbi.'

But Teresa didn't think she could be all right when he wasn't.

Football afforded him a brief respite from the fear. In the middle of Benfica's training-camp near Salzburg he suddenly had to leave for Mexico for the Confederation Cup. He'd been invited join the national team for the first time. It wasn't exactly a cause for celebration. The tournament in Mexico was of dubious value in sporting terms, its timing – at the end of July, just before the start of the club season – a crude joke, which was why the established keepers Oliver Kahn and Hans Jörg Butt had pulled out of the expedition. Robert had slipped in as substitute goalkeeper. No one in German football knew about his inner struggles. Many of them saw his selection as a logical consequence: the future would belong to this young goalkeeper.

Without being played in a single game he spent fourteen

shimmeringly hot days in Mexico. He couldn't sleep at night for heat and jet-lag, and by day he watched a relatively unmotivated German team lose 4–0 to Brazil and 2–0 to the USA. And at the same time he hadn't exactly improved his position with Benfica, because he had missed two weeks of preparation for the season. But he did not see it this way. He felt he had been at home for two weeks, in the familiar world of German football.

On his return to Lisbon he could no longer escape the reality that he lived there now. He went house-hunting with Teresa. The estate agent even showed them a palace, the Palácio dos Marqueses de la Fronteira – the former guest-house behind the palace was available to rent. Aha, said Robert, grinning at the idea of living there. But let's go on, said the estate agent, he had some spectacular houses to show them. It would take them days to make their minds up.

On 10 August 1999 Benfica played a pre-season friendly against Bayern Munich in the Stadium of Light; the Portuguese often just call the stadium A Luz – Light. The new team, Jupp Heynckes's Benfica, introduced themselves to the sixty thousand people who filled the arena that night. There's nothing more tantalising than the promise of a new season: everything will be different, better, now. For the first time the new coach would be playing his starting line-up, with Nuno Gomes as striker, Karel Poborský on the wing, and João Pinto, who stroked the ball with his feet, as midfield maestro. Carlos Bossio was in goal.

Bayern won 2–1. The glaring light pooled on Bossio. Sixty thousand people angrily booed and whistled him. The two Munich goals had left him looking pretty shoddy.

It was just a warm-up, though, and the result was insignificant. No one talks about evenings like that when one looks back over seasons or footballing careers, because no one can believe that careers are decided by such matches.

Ten days later, just before the opening day of the 1999–2000 Portuguese championship, FIFA temporarily withdrew Bossio's right to play for Benfica. His previous club, Estudiantes de la Plata, had reported Benfica to FIFA. His transfer fee hadn't been paid.

The public doesn't know the whole truth even today, Heynckes says. 'Bossio suddenly wasn't good enough for Benfica's directors after his unhappy game against Bayern. Benfica considerably delayed the payments to Estudiantes.'

Bossio was suspended, Nuno Santos was injured, Sergei Ovchinnikov had by now been transferred to FC Alverca. The only one who could play was Robert Enke.

He passed the news on to Teresa casually, the way he always preferred to pass on good news. He took great pleasure in seeing the excitement appear on other people's faces.

'Oh, by the way, I'm playing on Saturday.'

They were sitting under palm-trees by the pool, looking out over a garden laid out in the style of the Italian Renaissance, with decorative trees carved into geometrical shapes. They had moved into the guest-house of Palácio Fronteira.

In a town whose name he forgot even when he was there, in a stadium that had grassy mounds behind the goals rather than terraces, Robert had to prove that he could suppress his anxiety. Benfica were starting the Primeira Liga season against FC Rio Ave, a club from the small town of Vila da Conde in the no-man's-land behind Porto. The stadium only held twelve thousand, which meant there was room for 60 per cent of the inhabitants of the town. The grassy mound behind him was swarming with young people and children; their voices were a constant, unpleasant droning in his ear.

At home in Germany Jörg Neblung was pacing back and forth in his flat. Flippi had decided that no one from the agency had to attend this game on the edge of Europe. 'From today's vantage-point that was simply careless, bearing in mind the state Robert was in,' says Jörg. On satellite television there were snooker tournaments and darts championships, but in those days no Portuguese football matches. He asked Teresa to keep him informed by text from Lisbon.

Game over. 1–1. A solid performance by Robert.

Jörg exhaled.

A week later, after Benfica's first home game, the front pages of the sports newspapers were already full of Robert Enke. *Voa Enke!* (Enke flies!) said Portugal's best-selling *A Bola.*

At one of those moments when a goalkeeper doesn't really know what he's doing, he'd jumped up and saved a firm header from six yards. He experienced such moments in ecstatic slow-motion, all of a sudden reaching a higher level of perception; everything looked pin-sharp – the colours of the shirts, the movements of the striker. Other people have such experiences only in traumatic situations, when they suddenly have to brake their car or when they fall off their bike. A goalkeeper can become addicted to these wonderfully terrifying moments in a match. Towards the end of that first home game Robert tipped another ricocheting ball around the post, ensuring Benfica's 1–0 victory over Salgueiros. A Luz was radiant.

'Enke already darling of the public in Lisbon' reported the German news agencies, for whom nothing can ever happen quickly enough.

The sportswriters wanted to know whether the situation at Benfica – only one seasoned professional goalkeeper available – wasn't detrimental to him; don't you need rivals to push you in training? Applying pressure and taking pressure clearly seemed to be a popular method in Portugal, too. 'I like the situation,' Robert replied. 'I don't need any competition.'

A seventeen-year-old boy from the B-team, José Moreira, was named substi-

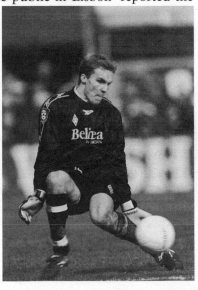

Robert's typical defensive posture, with his knee turned inwards, in a one-on-one situation.

tute goalkeeper and became his new training partner. 'The first thing that struck me was his face,' says Moreira. 'His face during the game was the face of Oliver Kahn! Nothing moved there, not a gesture, not a stirring. Nothing distracted him, nothing broke his concentration.' Robert noticed that the boy was absorbing his every movement, because Moreira started imitating him. 'If you look at me,' Moreira says eleven years later, unable to conceal his pride, 'you'll recognise a few things from Robert.'

In the Cathedral of Beer, as the VIP hospitality area at the Stadium of Light is called, Moreira swings himself down from his bar-stool. In front of him businessmen in suits and ties are eating; Moreira, in loose-fitting jeans and a shabby black T-shirt, ignores the fact that he has an audience. He crouches down, almost doing the splits, his right leg stretched out, left knee bent, torso bolt upright, arms outstretched, all ten fingers spread. 'That's how Robert stood in one-against-one situations, when the striker appeared in front of him.' Moreira's voice is now high and loud with enthusiasm. 'He made himself so wide, and he was so quick and agile he could assume this position from nowhere and immediately jump back from the splits again. No other goalkeeper could master that posture.'

Moreira asked Robert, why do you always do the splits like that? Why don't you run out of the goal for every cross? You've got latex inside your gloves as well – what's that for? And Robert, who had persuaded himself that he didn't care what other people thought of him, blossomed since there was no one putting pressure on him, just one inquisitive pupil who admired him.

On evenings before games they shared a hotel room. They spoke their own brand of Portuguese English together.

'Moreira, in three months I want to be able to speak Portuguese. You're my teacher now. How do you say this: *aipo hortense*?'

'Robert, there's an R in *hortense* – I can't hear your R. You say it as if you had a hot potato in your mouth.'

'OK, I'll learn to do that in three months, Moreira. And you've got to learn German, too. *BRING MIR WASSER!* Bring me water. That's the most important sentence you'll have to understand as my substitute goalkeeper, you understand? *BRING MIR WASSER!*'

Moreira can still say the phrase today, and a few other

things too, as became clear when we first met at the Stadium of Light. '*Gute Nacht!*' Moreira said. It was two o'clock in the afternoon.

'Moreira, let's take a look at the Bundesliga on German television,' Robert said one Saturday evening in the hotel room.

'But we can watch the goals on Eurosport with an English commentary, then I'll understand something.'

'No, it's better if we watch it in German.'

'Better?'

'Yes, yes. Oh, and Moreira, after that there's a good Eddie Murphy movie on ZDF.'

'But it doesn't even have subtitles!' Moreira moaned once the film had started. 'Eddie Murphy's speaking German!'

'Doesn't matter, Moreira, it's fine like this.'

'But Robert, we could watch Portuguese television. They have films in English with Portuguese subtitles.'

'He always had his own way,' Moreira recalls affectionately, 'and I've never slept as well as I did with him in the room, because the German films were so boring.'

Today, at the age of twenty-eight, Moreira wears his hair down to his shoulder. It frames a soft face, though like almost all goalkeepers it is marked by collisions with strikers. There's a big graze under his right eye. He's remained true to Benfica throughout those eleven years, even though the club uses him as an understudy for the more expensive goalkeepers Benfica buy who are wrongly considered more important because of the size of their transfer fee.

Robert with his goalkeeping 'little brother' José Moreira.

'Have you seen Moreira play lately?' Robert would ask every time we fell to talking about great goalkeepers in later years.

'Robbi, I don't even watch Portuguese television.'

'You've *got* to watch Moreira.'

His eyes laughed when he talked about Moreira, the goal-keeper who learned from him, who made him feel unexpectedly jaunty in training, who was his accomplice and not his rival.

In the Palácio Fronteira you could feel like a marquis, even if you were only living in the guest-house. There were more bathrooms than there had been rooms in the flat in Mönchengladbach: six. The garden walls were tiled with blue and white *azulejos*, with motifs of medieval battles and trumpet-playing monkeys.

Phone-calls from Germany were always fun.

'Oh no, it's raining here again.'

'Really? We're sitting in the garden in our T-shirts.'

They explored the city, the fortress of San Jorge and the Gulbenkian Museum, the Eleven bar and the Blues Café; they made their first acquaintances among the Benfica professionals. Sometimes they just sat in the garden and looked at the lights of Lisbon, gold in the afternoon, milky at twilight.

Teresa's pangs of conscience at giving up her studies faded away. 'The truth is that I enjoyed not having to work or study.' When Robert was at training she lay in the garden reading thrillers, irritably skipping over paragraphs with nothing but descriptions of places. Something had to happen in books.

One morning she was sticking photographs of their summer holiday in southern Holland into an album. Robert in his floppy hat in the dunes, smiling. 'We had dark times ahead of us' she wrote underneath. It wrote itself so easily. It seemed so long ago.

'I don't think Robert's going to have any more panic attacks,' she told his father when he visited them in Lisbon.

'Sadly I wouldn't be so sure,' Dirk replied.

Teresa shivered for a second, then shook the thought gently away.

For now, Robert went on flying. When Benfica beat FC Gil Vicente 2–0 at the end of October, the team was unbeaten after seven games. Since the 1–1 against Rio Ave at the start of the season Robert hadn't let in a single goal. 'Enke is an exorcist', the *Record* wrote poetically.

More and more people came to visit from Germany. Teresa's mother was the next one. The autumn light made the garden brighter, milder. Callers from home said that they'd turned on the heating for the first time recently; Robert and Teresa were still swimming in their pool in the palace garden.

'It's wonderful here,' said Teresa's mother.

'And I know someone who didn't even want to go to Lisbon,' Robert called out from the pool. He turned with a cheeky smile to Teresa. 'Remind me, why didn't you want to go to Lisbon?'

SIX

Happiness

At a time of night when the ringing of the phone usually means a call from a lover or bad news, Marco Villa woke with a start. It was 25 November 1999. He looked at the clock: just before midnight. Robert Enke's name flashed up on the screen of his mobile.

After Borussia's relegation, Marco had moved to Austria. The word 'provinces' had assumed a new connotation for him. He was playing for the top-flight team SV Ried. The town, hidden in a dip in the foothills of the Alps between Salzburg and Linz, had eleven thousand inhabitants, and the team had won the Austrian Cup in 1998. The stadium in Ried was called Keine Sorgen Arena – 'No Worries Arena'. Marco could already feel Ried's carefree attitude having an effect on him; he'd scored eight goals for the club in five months.

He answered the phone. 'Robbi?'

'You know what's just happened?'

Marco sensed that he didn't want to know.

'I've let in another seven goals.'

'Oh, shit, Robbi.'

Robert just laughed. As if losing 7–0 in the UEFA Cup to Celta Vigo hadn't left him downcast, just simply seemed unbelievable.

Benfica had gone into the game intent an defending tightly. The coach's vision was for it to be a classic first-leg cup tie, putting everything, decisions and drama, off until the second leg. Then, after a quarter of an hour, Celta Vigo scored. Something broke. Benfica, despite their glorious past and Jupp Heynckes's fresh promise and their great start to the domestic season, were all of a sudden wandering about with their own contradictory thoughts. On the one hand they had only come to defend, on the other they now had to start attacking. Benfica lost their cohesion, and Celta Vigo, who had one of the strongest squads in European club football at the time, found themselves with unexpected room for manoeuvre, especially Claude Makelele in midfield and the Russians Alexander Mostovoi and Valeri Karpin in attack. Their passing game was a whirlwind. Makelele appeared unmarked in front of Robert, then Mario Turdó calmly sent a shot flying in a parabolic curve into the sky over his head. After forty-two minutes the score was 4–0. At half-time Heynckes furiously explained all the things they needed to do to improve. Sixteen minutes of play later, with a third of the game still to go, the score was 7–0. 'The game was basically Robert versus eleven players,' says Moreira. 'And each time a goal was scored he didn't have a chance.'

When Robert walked off the pitch, he looked at the Benficistas, the eight thousand fans who had made the trip across the border into southern Galicia. The sight of them, the overwhelming beauty of their sadness, stayed with him for ever. 'Eight thousand people, and none of them making a sound.'

The club president, João Vale e Azevedo, stormed into the changing-room, ranting and shouting. The three thousand fans waiting for the team at Lisbon airport found their voices too. Robert calmly told reporters, 'Seven goals down is something I'm quite familiar with.'

'A defeat is a different defeat for a goalkeeper if it isn't his fault,' Walter Junghans remarks.

Two days later, before the home game against Campomaiorense, Robert was back with Moreira in his hotel room. In Vigo, Robert's little goalkeeping brother had been absent because of an injury.

'As soon as I'm not there, you let in seven goals.'

'Moreira, *bring mir Wasser*!'

The TV was on – German television.

'Why do only a thousand fans come to some Primeira Liga

games in this country, but three thousand of them get up in the middle of the night to shout at us at the airport? I don't understand this country, Moreira.'

'Robert, it's normal, you're in Portugal.'

'And why does no one here speak English? Are there no schools in Portugal?'

'English is compulsory up to year eight, and then they all forget it. It's perfectly normal, you're in Portugal.'

'Where there are speed limits of 120 km/h on the motorways and everyone drives at 190.'

'Perfectly normal. You're in Portugal, we're all mad here.'

'And why am I so fond of this country?'

'I can't tell you that, Robert.'

In their palace, four months after moving in, Teresa and Robert learned something new about Portugal: nowhere in the world is it as cold as in the warm countries of southern Europe.

Like many flats in southern Italy, Spain or Portugal, the guest-house of the Palácio Fronteira had no heating. Teresa and Robert hadn't noticed that when they moved in on a sunlit day in August. 'There was a fireplace in every room, and in the seventeenth century five members of staff probably went through the rooms making sure the fires were lit,' says Teresa.

The cold crept damply through the walls. In the kitchen they could see their breath. The clothes in the wardrobe began to smell musty. They bought two electric radiators and started living in one room in a house with six bathrooms. Before Hubert Rosskamp, the huntsman from Gierath, came on a visit, Teresa begged him to bring electric blankets. Half an hour before they went to bed she'd switch them on. 'The worst thing was when you'd left something in the bathroom. Then you had to get back out of bed.'

Robert was luckier. He could shower at the stadium. Soon he started brushing his teeth there as well.

Needless to say, the winter visitors to the palace weren't quite as keen as the summer guests. 'This is the world's first walk-in fridge,' said Teresa's brother Florian. One morning Teresa saw him standing motionless in front of the house, arms folded and eyes closed, his head turned towards the sun.

'Flo, what are you doing?' she cried.

'I'm warming myself up!'

During his stay in Lisbon Teresa's brother began to feel a little irritated. He liked Robert, and enjoyed his conversations with him, but why did Robert never ask him what he did? Why did Teresa's boyfriend never ask any questions when he told them about his life as a teacher in Munich?

It was footballer's disease. Professional footballers get used to being constantly asked questions, and gradually they forget how to take an interest in other people.

Unlike Florian, Hubert didn't notice Robert's social short-coming. Hubert didn't wait for people to ask him questions anyway. If he wanted to say something, then Hubert said it. In the Stadium of Light, Robert introduced him to Portugal's legendary player Eusebio. 'Eusebio, this is Hubert.' Eusebio gave him the thumbs up. Teresa and Robert showed Hubert the city, the tower of Belém, the view of the Atlantic, and all the while Hubert couldn't believe how touchingly these people were looking after him.

Marco and Christina came shortly before Christmas. Panathinaikos, one of the twenty-five biggest clubs in Europe, had discovered Marco Villa the goal-scorer in that dip in the Alpine foothills and immediately bought him. After Christmas he would be in Greece.

Without realising it, Robert and Marco were part of the vanguard of a new age. Professional football was leading the way in globalisation. A handful of foreigners played in the English Premier League in 1992; seven years later a third of the five hundred or so premiership professionals came from abroad. Young men like Robert and Marco, who, if they had been born ten years earlier, might have switched from Mönchengladbach to Bremen or Frankfurt, became modern-day migrant labourers. No one had prepared them for it.

In the only warm room in the ice-palace Teresa and Christina sat on the sofa, Robert and Marco on the floor. They were playing the guessing-game of City, Country, River.

'E,' said Marco.

'What river do you have?' Robert asked the ladies.

'The Ems,' said Teresa.

'Oh, we've got that too,' said Robert.

'N,' said Christina.

'What's your river?' asked Robert.

'Neckar,' said Christina.

'Got that one,' said Robert.

Eventually Teresa and Christina realised that the men didn't know any rivers at all, but were just stealing their answers. 'Suspicion naturally fell on me because I was always the one fooling around,' says Marco. But Robert was the one eager not to lose the game.

For breakfast the next day Teresa served scrambled egg without the yolk, as an experiment.

'What's that?' Marco asked, darting a conspiratorial glance at Robert, raising his eyebrows and grinning.

Robert dismissed him with a gruff shake of the head. You didn't make jokes about Teresa.

At lunchtime Robert and Marco went off to their favourite fast-food restaurant. They were standing at the counter when Marco became aware of a buzzing noise behind them. He turned round. Dozens of children were peering through the windows of the restaurant, the first ones were already coming in, and a few minutes later they were surrounded by a hundred or so giggling and laughing Portuguese kids.

'Uenk! Uenk!'

After six months in Lisbon Robert knew who they meant. Enke – O Enke. Pronounced by the Portuguese, it sounded like *Uenk*.

'What's going on, are they mixing you up with someone famous or something?' asked Marco.

Marco recalled that Robert laughed with pride at this. 'It was paradoxical: Robbi was reticent, but he liked all that star stuff.'

For the Portuguese, Robert Enke was more than a good goalkeeper. A country that often thinks sadly of its lost greatness as a colonial power precisely records the small gestures foreigners make. While businessmen and other sportsmen who had moved to the country still expected to be understood when they spoke English or Spanish, after just four months Robert had given his first press conference in Portuguese. 'Of course, not after three months, as you'd planned,' Moreira teased him.

It was Robert's second press conference that became national news. *Fodes!* read the newspaper headlines the following day. The television news bulletins repeated the scene over and over again: Robert on the podium behind the microphones, when he couldn't remember a particular word, putting his forehead in his hands and hissing, '*Fodes!*' – 'Shit!'

People laughed with delight. It was clear-cut for the Portuguese: anyone who could curse as they did was one of them.

Benfica didn't fully process that 7–0 defeat in Vigo; the memory of it held the club prisoner. The public reacted with increasing rage to each new mistake a player made, and naturally the footballers started making more mistakes. The club president, still feeling insulted, made those players who made too many mistakes wait weeks for their wages, and of course that didn't make the footballers play any better either. Dynamics, sometimes the footballer's ally, sometimes his foe, dragged Benfica down. A team that had been flying high for several months won only one out of the five Liga matches they played between December 1999 and January 2000, a wobbly 3–2 against União Leiria. Benfica dropped to third place behind Porto and Sporting Lisbon.

Heynckes found himself under siege. On 3 January, Portuguese journalists lay in wait outside his house in Mönchengladbach and tried to peer through his windows with binoculars. They wanted to check whether he was actually in bed.

Heynckes had been invited to spend New Year's Eve with Bayern Munich's manager Uli Hoeness, but he suddenly went down with a fever and spent that night in a hotel. Then, instead of returning to Lisbon he'd gone home to recuperate. On 4 January Benfica were scheduled to play an eagerly awaited derby against Sporting. The Portuguese media suspected the coach of inventing his flu so that he could spend a bit more time at home. Anyone familiar with Heynckes's work ethic would have been amused by the idea of the coach bunking off work. But things at Benfica weren't all that funny anymore after this episode.

Heynckes flew feverishly back to Lisbon, but on his doctor's advice he didn't go to the stadium, instead watching the match on television. It ended goalless, with Robert as Benfica's man of the match. A coach, however ill, has to be with his team, insisted the outraged sports press. 'Portuguese journalism is even worse than Portuguese football,' Heynckes explained, unasked, as soon as he was better. Benfica's president flew into a rage. He publicly confronted the coach – and stopped paying him his wages.

For months Benfica had been messing around in a similar way with Bossio, the goalkeeper who had fallen into disfavour after that pre-season match. He wasn't needed any more, so they made him wait for his wages. Benfica only sorted out the transfer fee and the paperwork necessary for a playing permit six months after the start of the season. Given how badly he was being mucked about, Bossio remained admirably relaxed. He carried on training with Robert and Moreira without a word of complaint. The public had already forgotten Bossio; he was in the shadow of Robert Enke, who was 'on the way to being an internationally great goalkeeper' in Walter Junghans's estimation. First- and third-choice goalkeeper – that sounded like a definitive, unambiguous qualitative difference. But without Bossio's one bad day in the run-up to the season Robert's and Bossio's roles could have easily been swapped.

There were things that Robert, the public's hero, learned from the outcast Bossio. He noticed how the other keepers at Benfica – Moreira, Bossio and Nuno Santos – positioned themselves further forward, further than Köpke, Kahn and Kamps in Germany. That helped them to cut out more through-passes and crosses. 'I'd rather have a goalkeeper who only goes out for six simple crosses and takes them all than a goalkeeper who runs out for ten crosses and the two hardest ones fly past him,' Robert insisted to Moreira. He really believed that: the best goalkeeper wasn't the one who coped with the most difficult situations, but the one who made the fewest mistakes. Privately, though, he took his bearings from Moreira and Bossio. When a member of the opposing team entered Benfica's half of the pitch, Robert now stood up to eight yards in front of the goal.

Rather than just being a few strides forward, for Robert this represented an expedition into the unknown. The most important thing for a keeper is a feeling of security, and Robert was now standing where he had never stood before. He was giving up the security that he had built up over the years, of knowing exactly how many paces it was back to the goal, and the angles between him and the posts. He kept instinctively retreating to the old conservative position, closer to the goal. Every time he did so he felt impelled to move forward again.

'You didn't need to push Robert, he was self-critical, and he always wanted to learn by himself,' says Jupp Heynckes. 'I've trained loads of players in my career, and as a coach you always get on particularly well with this team member or that one. But if somebody asks me after thirty years in the job who I think my ideal professional is, I always say Fernando Redondo and Robert Enke. Both of them weren't just special footballers, but special people – respectful, sociable, intelligent.'

Every time the team left the stadium after training, freshly showered and damp-haired, Heynckes went to the gym. As usual, Robert and Walter Junghans were there, though now Robert was dragging his 'little brother' Moreira along as well. 'Those were the best times,' says Heynckes. He could shed the tension of work in that gym. After the effort of making himself understood in a foreign language all the time, it was simply wonderful to be able to speak German again. They talked 'about football, politics, everyday stuff', says Heynckes, and then on to subjects like movies, food, dogs. 'These conversations alone in the gym, three Germans abroad,' Heynckes says. 'It was like a prayer.'

In their ice-palace, Teresa and Robert dreamed about the summer. In the autumn they would move out of the Palácio Fronteira, they promised themselves; they couldn't bear another winter there. But for now they were willing to put up with it, so that they could enjoy another summer by the pool.

Robert and Teresa's wedding photograph in 2000.

On 18 February 2000 Teresa unwrapped Robert's present for her twenty-fourth birthday. She'd felt the material through the wrapping-paper.

'Aha, a football shirt,' she said, and struggled to sound pleased rather than confused.

'Try it on,' he said, touchingly on edge, as he so often was off the pitch when things didn't go as planned.

Teresa pulled on the black and yellow Benfica goalkeeper's top.

'OK?' she asked.

The jersey came down to her knees.

'Yes. Stand with your back to the mirror before you complain.'

That meant going to the bathroom – a mini polar expedition.

In the mirror Teresa looked at her back. TERESA ENKE

was printed on the shoulders. Underneath, where the goal-keeper's number was usually displayed, Robert had taped a white question mark.

It didn't take Teresa more than a second to understand what the present meant.

They were married in the summer holidays at a castle near Mönchengladbach. Teresa's friend Christiane, shaking her head, took pictures of her turquoise bridal shoes.

Teresa had found a new pal. With a heavy heart, she had left one of her two dogs in Germany with her parents. Now, whenever she could, she had the palace housekeeper's dog over, so that it could be let off the chain.

'Moreira,' Robert said in the hotel room, 'how come animals are so badly treated here? Everywhere I go I see dogs roaming around, or on chains.'

'I've told you loads of times: you're in Portugal.'

'We've got to help those dogs.'

But he and Teresa were the only ones who thought so.

That autumn they moved out of Palácio Fronteira to a one-storey house with a garden and central heating in Sassoeiros, near the beach, where there were no rules to stop them keeping dogs. Teresa bought the housekeeper's dog from her. In the park she picked up a scrawny mongrel. Word got round that the goalkeeper and his wife liked animals. A dog was thrown over their garden fence, a poodle left tied to a lamp-post outside their front door. A woman who worked in the Benfica office called Robert in after training. A Dobermann that had outgrown its collar which now cut badly into its neck had been dropped off for him.

'My darling, sometimes I hate you for the fact that I can't walk past a needy animal,' Robert said to Teresa.

All of a sudden they had seven dogs.

Joker, however, didn't get on with Alamo. They put Joker in the garden shed. Teresa went in with her mobile phone. When Robert had Alamo under control in the house, he phoned her: 'You can come out with Joker now.'

Eventually, for all their love of animals, it struck them as ridiculous. They put Joker in a dogs' home in Sintra. Robert had sometimes become irritated with Teresa's commitment to animal welfare; after all, she couldn't save every dog in Portugal. But he went to the dogs' home every day to take Joker for a half-hour walk.

'Even I thought, does it have to be every day?' Teresa says.

Robert Enke's second season at Benfica started with a farewell. In September 2000 Jupp Heynckes gave up only four days into the campaign. 'I can't stand this any more,' he said. Benfica had ended its first year with Heynckes and Robert third in the Primeira Liga. With fifteen points more than the previous year, Heynckes stressed; two places behind Sporting and ineligible for the Champions League, the media and fans grumbled. Heynckes hadn't been paid for nine months.

For Robert, his sponsor's step-down didn't seem a watershed moment. In the course of a year in Lisbon he had become more independent, not least as a goalkeeper.

A new coach arrived, and most things at Benfica went on as before. The cheques came in two weeks late, the club president João Vale e Azevedo was arrested on suspicion of embezzlement, the Portuguese parliament debated the club's situation, and the finance minister told MPs about £50 million in debts and 'criminal intrigues'. The public, however, measured Benfica not against these reports but against their glorious past.

After Benfica had lost 1–0 to Boavista, immediately after Heynckes's departure, and then drawn 2–2 with Braga, he sat at home barely capable of conducting a normal conversation with his wife. His thoughts kept taking him back to the goals he wasn't to blame for.

'OK, that's enough, let's go out,' Teresa said, suddenly firmly resolved. 'You can't only ever enjoy life when you've played well.'

They drove to Belém. He went along unenthusiastically.

People stopped him in the street there. 'Uenk, what's up with

Benfica?' 'Uenk, why have you stopped winning?' He smiled, he gave a few vacuous answers, they went for a walk. After that he was more relaxed.

Was he learning to shrug things off? Was it possible to shrug things off?

The new coach was thirty-seven and had never before been responsible for a professional team. His name was José Mourinho. Years later, when he became 'The Special One' at Chelsea and Inter Milan, sports journalists wrote about his fascinating arrogance and his big words. At that time, with Benfica, Robert merely noted – enthusiastically – the tactical precision, the infectious euphoria and his affection for the players. 'He was the best coach in my career.' After less than four months he had gone. Insulted by the club's refusal to extend his contract beyond next summer, even after five wins in a row, including a 3–0 victory in a derby against Sporting, Mourinho handed in his notice. When he said goodbye to the players, his eyes filled up.

It was time to turn the heating on again in Lisbon. Cosy and warm was something else, but with a bit of imagination the stoves in Sassoeiros made them feel it was pleasant enough in the house. When they were invited to dinner by Robert's team-mate Paulo Madeira, they felt better straight away: other people in Lisbon were shivering in badly insulated houses too.

In the changing-room, Robert had found a little group of work-mates: Madeira and Moreira, and Pierre van Hooijdonk and Fernando Meira, too. 'What I remember about Robert is this,' Moreira says. 'He said a friendly *Bom dia!* to all the players, but he only really had contact with a very small group, even when he was made team captain.'

Benfica went on comparing badly with their glorious past and finished that 2000–01 season sixth. The team's undistinguished performances only made the goalkeeper's saves look all the more outstanding. 'Although I was there often, no football moments have lingered in my memory,' says Jörg Neblung.

'It's funny – or perhaps not. The football was okay, but the really lovely thing was life in Lisbon.' For instance, Jörg refused to come out of the shower every morning – 'the loveliest shower in the world with this huge shower-head, as if you were standing under a wonderful, hot cloud'. And he loved the lemon trees in the garden in Sassoeiros. He and Robert spontaneously started playing barefoot football with one that was lying on the ground until the game had to be abandoned because the lemon got stuck on Jörg's big toe. Where are we going? Robert asked in the afternoon. Let's call in on Marc. So they went to see a friend in his record shop, listened to music, stood together until it was evening. Right, come on, let's go to the Blues Café.

Robert's mother visited for the New Year. They celebrated in the Montemar in Cascais, where the blue of the Atlantic merged with the black of night through the wide restaurant windows. The diners wore Prada suits and Gucci dresses and spoke in subdued voices; after midnight, Robert's mother started a conga to see in 2001. Teresa joined in, and after a few minutes the two of them were dragging around half the gaggle of posh guests.

'Come on, join in!' his mother called to Robert, who was still sitting in his chair.

The Portugal years: Robert with Walter Junghans (far left) and Pierre van Hooijdonk (far right).

'Mother, please.'

'What? No one here knows me.'

'But they know me!'

'Those were the small moments that were really big,' says Jörg. 'Times you remember as the best in your life.'

Once Benfica asked Robert to visit a hospital, to cheer up the children in the cancer ward. Teresa went with him. When he stepped through the door, one boy abruptly turned away.

'He's a big Benfica fan,' the nurse whispered to Robert.

Robert tried to talk to the boy, once, twice, three times. Finally he charmed an answer from him, but the boy stubbornly went on looking at the wall. He couldn't bear his idol to see him hairless, suffering, ill.

After the visit the Enkes went for a walk on the beach. The tension fell away from them slowly. At last they broke their silence.

'Those poor children,' said Teresa.

'And their parents,' said Robert.

The idea came to them pretty much at the same time: 'How lucky we are to have the lives we have.'

SEVEN

Ever Further, Ever Higher

On a scrap of paper Robert signed a contract with Teresa.

'I, Robert Enke, hereby declare that I will not henceforth watch *La Ola* except when a) Teresa isn't here, b) Teresa is asleep or c) she expressly gives me permission.'

It was an attempt to use humour to deflate an issue that seemed to be turning into a conflict during their third year in Lisbon. He was watching excessive amounts of football again, even the *La Ola* programme on a Monday, with match reports from the Italian or Greek leagues.

'I never realised that part of the reason he watched football matches was to improve his goalkeeping skills,' says Teresa. 'And I never thought: does watching football help him not to think about his own game? I was just irritated because all of a sudden he spent too many evenings in front of the telly.'

At the end of the season, in June 2002, his contract with Benfica would run out. Robert brooded over which club he should move to; staying in Lisbon, where he was happy, didn't seem like an option. 'It was time for the next step,' says Jörg Neblung.

Manchester United, the superpower of globalised football, had wanted to sign Robert in the summer of 2001. United's coach Alex Ferguson phoned him in person and tried to sound comprehensible in spite of his thick Scottish accent. Benfica indicated to Robert that the club wouldn't mind if he left Lisbon. They needed cash, such as United's offer of about three and a half million pounds, more than they needed a goalkeeping star.

He turned down Ferguson's offer. 'Yes, some players actually do refuse an offer from Manchester United,' Ferguson remarked.

In his first year in Manchester, he would have played between ten and fifteen games as a substitute for the French world champion Fabien Barthez – this was guaranteed, said Ferguson, 'and in two or three years Enke would have replaced Barthez as our number one. That was my plan.' But Robert never wanted to be a substitute goalkeeper anywhere, ever again.

Jupp Heynckes said he had been 'ruled by his head'.

Nine months after that phone call with Ferguson, in La Villa, a Portuguese beach restaurant in Estoril offering Japanese cuisine and a view of the sea, Robert said, 'Perhaps I made a mistake before this season.' He left the sentence floating in the room like a story-teller enjoying the breathlessness of his audience. He meant declining the offer from Manchester. 'When I see Barthez playing rather unhappily these days . . .' He didn't finish the sentence. A moment later he seemed to be talking not to Teresa and me, but to himself. 'What's past is past. Now I have to make the right decision about where to go now.'

It was the day we first met.

He'd sprinted up to me through the reception area of the Estádio da Luz, still wearing Benfica's burgundy training sweater, and shook my hand. I was just thinking that professional footballers didn't usually come storming along to interviews like that when he then ran right past me and out of the stadium. 'Unbelievable!' he called out to me. 'They gave my pay cheque to another player! I'll be right back, but first I have to make sure that I get my money.' Two hours later, over sushi and green tea in La Villa, he still hadn't got his money back, but he was able to laugh about the mistake. Somebody in Benfica's office hadn't been concentrating and had handed Robert's cheque to the first blond who came along, the Swedish midfielder Anders Andersson. He had put the envelope in his pocket and driven home. 'It's nice that even some people here don't recognise me,' Robert joked, 'but does it have to be the man in the office who hands out the cheques? If you see a little Swede with black sunglasses and a big suitcase on your flight home, stop him for me: that's Anders Andersson, taking my money abroad.'

This lunch left me with the impression of a twenty-four-year-old man who reflected on things and was completely uncynical, who felt at home in a foreign city and thought he knew exactly what a happy life was. The strongest image I was left with, however, was that of a professional sportsman inspired by the idea that he has to climb ever further, ever higher.

After lunch we went for a walk on the beach. We talked into the wind.

'It was worth switching to Benfica. Spending three years as a regular goalkeeper with such a big club at my age – who gets a chance like that? But that's enough now.'

'Why?'

'I've been here for two and a half years, and already I'm a senior member of the team. I've seen so many team-mates that I can't remember them all, they change so often here. That's not a way to produce a winning team. This year I'm even the team captain, and of course that's great. But if you're honest, you also have to say to yourself, a foreigner as captain at the age of twenty-four? That only shows that they've sold all the other leading players – it only shows that there's something wrong with the club.'

A man out for a stroll stopped in front of us. At first I took him for a flasher, with his big coat and flailing arms. Then it became clear that he was trying to imitate Benfica's goalkeeper making a save.

I laughed. Robert made a point of looking straight past him.

'I've got a goalkeeping coach here, he's driving me round the bend. I have trouble staying in form with his training.'

At first I thought, where's this coming from? Then Robert told me about Samir Shaker, his new goalkeeping coach at Benfica, and I understood: the flailing man in the big coat had reminded him of Shaker.

Benfica's goalkeepers had thought that their previous mentor, Walter Junghans, had everything a goalkeeping coach needed, and a bit more. 'Once he kicked apart one of the plastic chairs on the terrace behind the goal,' says Moreira. 'He had the hardest kick of all the goalkeeping coaches in my career.' But after two years Junghans had been persuaded to leave, in that special way that Benfica had: all of a sudden his salary was distinctly lower than agreed.

A little while later they were introduced to a beaming white-haired man. Samir Shaker came from Iraq. No one knew how he had come to Portugal; how he had been able to start a career in the country as a goalkeeping coach at Nacional Funchal was no easier to understand. 'Samir spoke no English and about three words of Portuguese,' Moreira reveals. '*Amigo – bola – vamos!*' Friend – ball – come on! 'He was a very sweet, nice man,' Moreira adds.

'Come on, friends!' Samir Shaker called, demonstrating the warm-up exercise for Robert's benefit. He was doing somersaults.

Somersaults!

'Friends!' Samir Shaker called, and showed them the next exercise. One goalkeeper was to stand with his legs spread and his back bent, the other keeper was to run up and somersault over his colleague's back. 'Come on!'

'Moreira, tell me this isn't true,' Robert said.

Moreira laughed and shrugged.

At the next training session Samir Shaker tied the goalkeepers to the goalposts with elastic bands. They were to push off against the resistance of the rubber band.

'Samir, that's dangerous. When we finish the exercise it'll hurl us right back against the goalpost.'

The next time Samir Shaker tied foam mats around the posts.

In the week before the game against Maritimo in Madeira he put a bucket of water on the ground next to him and dipped the ball into it before every shot at goal.

'What's that's supposed to achieve?'

'*Chuva*,' said Shaker. Rain. It rained a lot in Madeira. That was what he was preparing them for.

'Aha,' said Robert. 'In that case wouldn't it be better to put the whole penalty area under water?'

Samir Shaker smiled. He hadn't understood Robert.

That Saturday night Robert and Moreira had their usual conference in the hotel bedroom.

'I can't believe it. He's a nice guy, but he's not a goalkeeping coach. The club's got to sack him.'

'Robert, I have a positive way of looking at it: we can learn new things from him.'

'But I'm not working in a circus.'

'First we had a German goalkeeping school under Walter, and now we've got an Iraqi one with Samir.'

'And have you ever seen a good Iraqi goalkeeper?'

For more than two years Moreira had known Robert as a highly professional sportsman, but also as a cordial, reasonable person. He couldn't imagine the new trainer's quirky methods really putting too much of a strain on him. So when he saw Robert getting angry about Shaker at the training sessions, Moreira thought, Robert's just putting on that rage to keep from bursting out laughing. He doesn't want to be rude and laugh at Samir, so he's pretending to be angry.

Teresa knew better. After he had let in three goals against SC Beira Mar and Benfica failed to win the next two games as well, she saw him entrenching himself in front of the television and brooding.

Under this new trainer his form was draining away.

Nothing, not even the truth, could make Robert shake off the thought. In fact, in that third year at Benfica the outlines of a perfect goalkeeper were beginning to emerge. Since his arrival from Mönchengladbach his body had changed completely: his arms and legs were slowly starting to match his imposing shoulder axis, his reactions were swift and his jump powerful. He was tending to catch crosses now instead of punching them away. When an opponent advanced from midfield he stood waiting a full eight yards in front of the goal and did not retreat into his own six-yard box, which meant his opponent had only a small amount of scope for through-balls. His trained instinct for understanding what was about to happen on the pitch was growing sharper with every game. But, stressed out as he was by Samir Shaker and Benfica's persistently mediocre performances, Robert could no longer draw strength from these improvements.

Teresa was resolved not to yield to the changing moods of a football-player. He had to learn not to let defeats or Samir Shaker silence his laughter.

'Why were you playing for your opponents?' she quipped when a clearance of his landed at the feet of the opposition.

'Do you know your saves off by heart yet?' she asked when he lay slumped on the sofa the evening after a game, until the last sports broadcast devoting itself to repeating his imposing feats in slow-motion had finished.

'Did you see my cool save?'

'Well, I've heard the commentators shouting *Uenk! Uenk!* at least twenty-seven times all over the house for the last hour.'

'But you're a footballer's wife. Read *A Bola*.'

People who were only acquainted with the Enkes were often startled by the rather harsh tone they sometimes used with each other. Teresa simply says, 'We loved teasing each other.'

In the afternoons, walking the dogs on the beach, their ideas about the future began to take shape.

'I'd really like to go back to the Bundesliga,' he often said.

'And somehow,' Teresa says eight years later on a different walk, up the Lange Berg in Empede, 'we managed to convince ourselves that we had to get back to Germany. Even I thought it was the best thing, because it meant I would be close to my friends again.'

The first offer came in January 2002, six months before the end of his contract with Benfica. Robert got a shock: FC Porto wanted him.

There are a few things a professional footballer can't do; switching from FC Barcelona to Real Madrid, from Celtic to

Rangers or from Benfica to FC Porto are among them. The traditional feuding of these clubs represents one of the last remaining opportunities in civilised Europe for people to live out their hatred. And plainly hundreds of thousands of people still sometimes feel the need to hate. In football derbies, clichés aren't ludicrous, they're welcome, as a way of stirring up rivalries. 'Porto works, Lisbon squanders the money' they say in northern Portugal.

'I'm a Benficista, I can't go to Porto,' said Robert.

Even when there's a total of ten million euros on the table for three years, after tax?

Jorge Pinto da Costa loved tormenting Benfica players with irresistible offers. Educated at a Jesuit school, the FC Porto president had ruled the club like the lord of the manor for twenty years. When he split up with his girlfriend, she wrote a book in which she claimed Pinto da Costa spent his money on ladies' jewellery, beating up rivals and bribing referees, but the president was able to repudiate the allegations as 'seriously false'.

FC Porto's coach, who had inspired Pinto da Costa to attempt to lure Enke northwards, was José Mourinho.

'I can't do it,' Robert repeated.

'Ten million euros after tax is so much money that you sign that one contract and you'll never have to do anything ever again,' said Jörg Neblung.

They had to meet Pinto da Costa at least once, they were agreed on that.

The previous summer Alex Ferguson may have phoned Robert to woo him but most player transfers don't involve anything as direct as that. In southern countries in particular, a class of *intermediarios*, or middlemen, has sprung up. Pinto da Costa had his personal *intermediario*, a special agent who didn't have an official post at FC Porto but who was always dispatched to sound out the interest of a potential new recruit.

The president was waiting for them in his summer villa – empty for the winter – in Cascais, the middleman informed them.

The front gate opened slowly when Jörg and Robert reached

the villa in Robert's Opel. You've got to get yourself a bigger car – you're a star, after all, his fans had often told him. Why should he buy himself a car when a sponsor provided one? Robert had always countered. How good it was that he drove such an inconspicuous car, he thought now for the first time. A captain of Benfica who was spotted negotiating with the president of FC Porto wouldn't dare turn up for training the following day.

The middleman opened the door to them. The president, wearing rimless glasses and a dark suit, was inside, sitting in a plush chair. The guests weren't offered anything to drink, not even a glass of water. A lamp was lit. The blinds were down.

Jörg can recall no exchange of pleasantries, no small talk. 'It could be that we spent twenty or thirty minutes in the villa,' he says, 'but in terms of my perception of it, the meeting didn't last longer than five minutes. It felt as if we were doing a drugs deal.'

'We thank you for your interest,' Jörg said to Pinto da Costa, 'and of course it's clear that we must talk, given the sum under discussion. Ten million euros after tax for three years is a handsome offer.'

Robert translated. Pinto da Costa replied in Portuguese, but Jörg didn't need Robert's translation. He could read everything he needed to know in the president's gestures.

Where do you get that figure from, ten million? That was never discussed. We've never mentioned a figure.

The middleman who had aired that supposed offer two weeks earlier sat still next to him, his features frozen.

Robert and Jörg checked with a glance that they were thinking the same thing. A fake offer had been made to Robert to bring him to the negotiating table.

'But we're really very interested in Robert Enke,' Pinto da Costa continued.

'We came here on the assumption that ten million euros were on offer. You know it's actually impossible for a Benficista like Robert to switch to FC Porto. So it seems inevitable that such a risky step would be financially compensated. One might imagine that you'd invited us here under false pretences.'

'Please, let's not argue now. We'll make Robert an extremely satisfactory offer, though it certainly won't be ten million euros post-tax for three years.'

'We're sorry, but we can't negotiate further on that basis.'

Robert and Jörg stood up. They politely shook hands with the president and the middleman. Then Pinto da Costa said something else to Robert in Portuguese: 'If you do switch to FC Porto we'll keep it secret until the start of the season, and on the day of the team presentation you'll suddenly surprise everyone, standing in the Dragon Stadium.'

At crucial moments Robert and Jörg often exchanged a silent glance to reach an agreement.

That's it, the glance said. We can live without Porto.

A few days later a written offer arrived from the club. As expected, there was no mention of ten million euros, but it was the most lucrative offer Robert had ever received in his career.

'But I don't want to betray Benfica for that money, I'd rather play somewhere else for less,' he tried to convince himself.

In her black diary, Teresa recorded the comings and goings of early 2002.

5 February. Balou fought with a strange dog on the beach. Robbi cross with me.
10 February. Porto against Benfica. Bremen comes to watch. Exciting.
11 February. Kaiserslautern want him!

It was an era when the professional clubs were doing everything they could not to have to rely on luck in their search for players. They deployed scouts who looked for talent from Buenos Aires to Belgrade; they set up complex computer files so that when you pressed a button a list of sixteen right-sided defenders appeared with all the details of their skills. In the end, however, many transfers still tended to be based more on chance and personal contacts.

Werder Bremen employed two scouts: Hune Fazlic, the best in the Bundesliga, and Mirko Votava, who had got the job chiefly because he had played for the club in the past. Votava travelled to Porto. Benfica lost 3–2. Votava analysed the goalkeeper he was sent to study in the style of an armchair critic: 'Enke faces three shots and lets three goals in – what do you want me to say?'

Werder Bremen told Jörg that they had no interest in signing Robert Enke.

No one from 1 FC Kaiserslautern came to watch Robert. Coach Andreas Brehme phoned Jupp Heynckes just once to hear his judgement.

25 February. Robbi talked to Brehme. Jörg is meeting Kaiserslautern's sporting director. I hope everything goes well.

In the meantime a few rumours were circulating in Lisbon. Robert Enke was going to leave Benfica! Robert Enke was going to switch to FC Porto! After his bad experiences leaving Mönchengladbach he had hoped he would be able to keep his transfer plans secret until the end of the season.

'I don't get how people I don't know can say on television that I've signed for Porto. It's simply a lie!' Robert said, half-truthfully.

Fica Enke! yelled the fans. *Fica Enke!* The words billowed in the wind on home-made banners in the Stadium of Light. One television channel handed him half a dozen video cassettes. They were full of messages from the fans. *Fica Enke!* Enke, stay!

He was touched. But he had to go ever further, ever higher.

He refused Benfica's offer to extend his contract. Then his plans to move came out in the most surprising and unambiguous way.

4 March. Robbi is taken out of goal. Moreira plays.

When the sportswriters saw him sitting on the substitutes bench again for no good footballing reason three months before the end of his contract it wasn't hard to draw conclusions. Robert had to hold a press conference. 'I'm going to leave Benfica,' he stated. It was reported on the evening news by the state broadcaster, RTP.

He wouldn't be playing in the remaining nine games, coach Jesualdo Ferreira told him.

'After he had sat on the substitutes bench against Gil Vicente, he was suddenly injured for the rest of the season,' says Moreira. 'My suspicion was that he made up that injury to spare himself the humiliation, and I would be the last person not to understand that. Robert was here at a dark time for Benfica, a time when there were many, many problems, and eventually he had enough. But he was always there, helping me with advice and support, even when I was suddenly playing.'

Teresa simply can't remember whether he actually did fake an injury or whether he was injured. At the time it seemed beside the point.

11 March. Kaiserslautern said no to Jörg. Luck isn't on our side. Let's wait for the sun.

'Oh, God!' Teresa shouts and slaps her palm against her forehead when she rereads the entry in her diary in 2010. 'There you can see how spoilt we were by life at the time. If we thought those were the dark days: Kaiserslautern says no.'

After Jörg had told them the bad news from Germany, they drove to the beach with the dogs. 'It promptly started raining,' Robert said, adding – as you might say, without thinking – 'And that made the depression complete.'

Robert's longing for places like Kaiserslautern and Bremen grew with each refusal he got from the Bundesliga. At home in Sassoeiros he watched German football on satellite TV, and felt hurt that German football wasn't watching him. 'It seems peoople in Germany are thinking: Enke has had a great time in Portugal, lying on the beach for three years.' He was wanted by the biggest clubs in the world, like Manchester United, he was a star in Portugal, but in Germany he was just an overlooked world-class goalkeeper. It had little to do with his performances but with Portugal being on the edge of Europe. The Primeira Liga was largely ignored in Germany, and with Benfica he had never qualified for the Champions League – one of the supposed attractions of moving to Lisbon in 1999. In that third season, too, they would finish only fourth in the domestic league. Benfica had been Portuguese champions twenty-seven times, but the last time had been in 1994. Robert only turned up in the German media from time to time as a tour guide to Portugal, when he was able to report that 'they don't drink sparkling water here, it swells the stomach too much', and 'you can't be in too much of a hurry at the cashier in Lisbon supermarkets'. In three years only one German sports reporter had come to see him play for Benfica.

In the garden in Sassoeiros, Robert wore the green Werder Bremen replica jersey his friend Marc had given him.

Jörg Neblung didn't share Teresa and Robert's sudden love of quiet German cities. 'Robert felt like the lost son of the Bundesliga, but I thought, my God, they love you in England and Spain, the countries with the strongest leagues, you don't have to curry favour with Germany.' He'd had offers from Alavés and Espanyol Barcelona from the Spanish Primera División, two ambitious mid-level clubs.

A few months earlier Jörg had gone freelance as a sports agent and persuaded Robert to come with him. At first the only other people on his books were another goalkeeper, Alexander Bade, the number two at 1 FC Cologne, and Olympic long-jump champion Heike Drechsler. 'I knew Robert's transfer was vital for me.' He looked at the top international clubs. FC Barcelona, the guardian of the beautiful game, might have been looking for a goalkeeper: the coach there had recently switched back and forth several times between Roberto Bonano and Pepe Reina – always a sign of latent discontent. 'But Jörg Neblung, a rookie from Cologne, couldn't simply ring up Barça,' Jörg says.

He needed a middleman.

A few days later he had two.

Bernd Schuster, the blond angel of the eighties, whose cross-field passes had shown the footballing public the meaning of beauty, was the only German ever to have played for Barça. One special attraction in those days had been his wife Gaby, who acted as his manager. She was always happy to phone up her old contacts, especially if a commission was likely to come out of it. She told Barça's sporting director Anton Parera that there was a talented goalkeeper in Portugal available on a free transfer, and that Manchester United had been already interested in signing him.

At a club like Barça, with twenty members on the board who all want to push their own agendas, there are no secrets. Someone from Barça's board of directors said to Portuguese agent José Veiga: our sporting director is interested in Benfica's goalkeeper, perhaps you could pick that up. And Jörg immediately had Veiga on the phone. He could open a few doors for him at Barça. Veiga had rushed through the transfer of the decade, Luis Figo from Barça to Real Madrid. Jörg took him on as second middleman.

If the transfer happened, the agents would be able to share more than half a million euros in commission.

Veiga arranged an appointment with Parera for Jörg. They were interested in Enke, Parera said.

'That could mean everything or nothing,' said Jörg.

In the coming weeks he regularly received calls from middlemen who all talked about their really quite extraordinary relationships with Barça's sporting director and board of directors. In professional football there's an army of such men who don't represent a single player but offer the clubs all possible players, chancing their arms. But Jörg heard nothing more from Barça themselves.

In Portugal, the season was coming to an end. Teresa and Robert had terminated their rental contract in Sassoeiros and didn't know where they would go next.

It was reported in the papers that Barcelona planned to sign a new goalkeeper, the Frenchman Ulrich Ramé of Girondins Bordeaux.

Robert travelled with Jörg to Vitoria, to have a look at Alavés. The club was like the northern Spanish town: charming, but small.

Back in Lisbon, Teresa and Robert went on a final drive with a video camera to all the places that meant so much to them – the beach at Estoril, La Villa, Marc's record shop, Monsanto forest park. They stopped at each spot and waved, smiled and cried, 'Adeus Lisboa!'

It wasn't hard for them to leave. After their lovely time in Lisbon they simply thought everything would be fine wherever they went.

The previous summer they had taken a driving holiday – three thousand kilometres in two days – to Germany. They didn't know how else to transport the dogs. This time they left them with Marc in Lisbon and took a plane to Frankfurt. They would just be on holiday for a little while.

Jörg flew to Majorca for a photo-shoot with Heike Drechsler. From there he wanted to go to Catalonia for negotiations with Espanyol Barcelona – 28 May would be ideal.

One or two days before then Jörg received another call from Barcelona. Barça's sporting director Anton Parera wanted to see him.

On 28 May, on his way to the meeting with FC Barcelona, Jörg became aware that he was travelling on a ticket paid for by Barça's city rival Espanyol.

EIGHT

Feet

In Barcelona you can stand a few hundred metres away from Camp Nou and not see the stadium. It's situated in the middle of the city, hidden by apartment blocks; you can't guess its size from outside. If you're sitting inside, the grandeur of Camp Nou suddenly overwhelms you.

Oval and gigantic, it's more like the Colosseum than a football arena. The terraces rise so high that they merge with the sky. When a hundred thousand fans are there they look down on a spectacle of human fragility. The footballers look so small and vulnerable far below. If you sit alone in the empty stadium, the sound of silence brings to life all the battles you never saw but which you can suddenly imagine very clearly – Kubala on the wing, Zubizarreta in the air, Goikoetxea on the ground, in a black fury, having been laid low by a foul by the angel Schuster, to the roaring approval of the hundred thousand, their fists in the air.

In the world of football, Camp Nou is the stronghold of all that is beautiful, good and true. The rest of the world had declared the *juego bonito* – the beautiful game – as finished once and for all after Brazil's heart-breaking failure in the 1982 World Cup; realpolitik football now predominated, sticking to compact defensive formations before switching to attack in a flash. Only in Barcelona did they refuse to admit that reality. Fundamentalist devotees of grace, they bravely went on the attack with an intoxicating short-passing game.

People have their theories about why Barça is so uncompromisingly committed to beauty. Because their eternal rival,

Real Madrid, always won more games, they say, so Barça sought consolation in saying: yes, but our game is more beautiful! Or because the Catalans want to make the point that they are different and independent. The truth is more banal: FC Barcelona had their first great success with the perpetuum mobile of a passing game. In 1992 the club won the Champions League for the first time under Johan Cruyff, and from that point on they became devout followers of the beautiful way.

The reality in 2002 was less grand. Luis Figo, who personified Barça, who dribbled to a melody, had deserted to Real two years earlier, as the most expensive footballer in the world. The trauma lingered. President Joan Gaspart, a man of frantic gestures and pounding heart, tried to inspire the club into action. A neurotic environment wasn't particularly helpful.

But the myth of Barça outshone the reality.

On 28 May, Jörg Neblung left Anton Parera's office with the feeling that he wouldn't be able to keep his joy to himself for long. It was too big for that. Barça wanted to sign Robert Enke.

They might not have heard anything from Barça for weeks, but the club had been making conscientious enquiries about Robert. Barça's goalkeeping coach Frans Hoek dissected his game on video. 'He had incredible reflexes,' says Hoek, 'and that was odd, because at the same time he wasn't your typical muscle-bound German goalkeeper type like Kahn, Köpke or Schumacher, who basically only plays on the goal-line. If he'd been like that he would have been out of the question as far as Barça was concerned. Here the goalkeeper has to be able to join in; he has to act, not only react.' Just to be on the safe side, Hoek rang an acquaintance who knew about Portuguese football. 'I had a word with José Mourinho.' As the coach at FC Porto Mourinho still hoped to sign Enke himself, but he praised the keeper with such honesty in conversation with Hoek that Barça decided to whip Enke away without delay.

Parera had immediately agreed Robert's salary with Jörg. The chief executive would have to take a look at the contract – a formality. He was in Madrid right now, but he was supposed to be back in the office the following day. 'So you could come to Barcelona on Thursday and sign the contract,' Jörg said to Robert on the phone.

'I don't actually want to go to Barcelona,' said Teresa.

Her voice was serious. It still is today, when she talks about this part of her life.

'We'd just managed to learn Portuguese in three years, and I was horrified by the idea of going to another country and starting all over again when, with the offer from Porto, we could have stayed in Portugal, or perhaps even gone back to Germany.'

'Dear Teresa, please forgive me, but I've got to contradict you there,' said Jörg. 'If Barça calls, you run to get there.'

The next day he had another phone conversation with Parera. The contract had been set up. It would be best if Robert came in the following day to sign.

'Enke joins Barça' reported *A Bola* in Lisbon, and the news spread quickly.

A Swiss private bank called Jörg. They would pay Robert and him a lump sum of six million euros. In return, the player and his agent would hand over all rights, the salary, signing on fee and commissions from Barça would go to the bank. 'Think about it: you and the player have six million guaranteed and don't have to worry about any details of the contract. We'll take over negotiations with Barça.'

'Interesting,' said Jörg, thinking: mostly because it'll be a good story later on.

The president of Espanyol, Daniel Sánchez Llibre, who had bought Jörg his plane tickets to Barcelona but never got a chance to negotiate with him, wasn't pleased. 'I'm fed up with this. We do good work here. Our sporting director discovered Enke two months ago, and then along comes this other club and copies our idea. I feel as if I've been taken for a ride by Enke's representatives.'

Teresa and Robert landed in Barcelona. As if they were awaiting a national delegation, waving from grand flagpoles outside Barça's office were the flags of the club, the city and the country – Catalonia, not Spain. In Parera's outer office Jörg hesitated. The middlemen weren't there. They were welcomed not by Gaby Schuster but by a dark-haired young man who was careful only to shave every three days. She had sent her assistant Wim Vogel. José Veiga, the second middleman, rang Jörg's mobile from a noisy room and said he'd got stuck at Rome airport, he was really sorry. Normally middlemen appear punctually at contract-signings, because that's when the money gets divided.

Barça's managing director turned up, and Parera asked them in. Teresa stayed in the outer office. When Parera's office door opened again, she tried in vain to make eye-contact with Robert. He was staring at the floor. She looked at Jörg. He shook his head.

In the contract, net had suddenly turned to gross.

Jörg had stared for a long time at the figures in front of them, and all of a sudden he understood why Gaby Schuster and Veiga weren't present. They would already have guessed that these negotiations wouldn't be concluded in a single morning, without an attempt by the club to bring down the salary.

'That isn't the salary we agreed the day before yesterday,' said Jörg. 'That's illegitimate!'

Parera smiled benignly.

Jörg looked at Robert and knew what he was thinking.

They flew back to Germany the same evening.

'Enke transfer off' wrote *A Bola*.

'Barça wants Fabián Carini of Juventus as its new goalkeeper' reported *Tuttosport*.

'Are Barça doing to Enke what they did to Köpke?' asked *Bild*.

Andreas Köpke, Germany's goalkeeper in the nineties, still has a contract from Barça ready for signing among the files in his house in Nuremberg. When he was about to sign it in 1996, Barça suddenly signed the Portuguese number one Vitor Baía.

On the flight back, Robert and Teresa barely spoke a word.

Two days after the snub at Camp Nou, Robert consoled himself with the thought that there were goalkeepers in much worse situations than his. Back in Bad Windsheim with Teresa's parents, he watched the desperate exploits of Saudi Arabia's Mohammed Al-Deayea on television who conceded eight goals to Germany. The World Cup in Japan and South Korea had started.

He wanted to be at the next World Cup, in Germany in 2006. But at the moment he didn't even know who he'd be playing for come the start of the 2002–03 season. He was nervous, not angry. If Barça played with you, you stayed quiet and hoped things would somehow work out.

Jörg phoned Anton Parera. They were still interested in Robert Enke. They would have to talk to each other again.

Barça wanted to take Carini on loan for the coming season, Juventus said.

Call the coach, Jörg said to Robert.

When the contract negotiations had been under way, they had asked Parera for Louis van Gaal's mobile phone number. The Dutch coach had been taken on by Barça a few weeks earlier and Robert wanted to know whether van Gaal saw him as first-choice goalkeeper or as a substitute. Now the phone-call had assumed a new urgency. Could van Gaal say whether Barça were still taking him seriously?

The coach was on holiday in Aruba. 'Yes, very clever of you to call, Mr Enke, that's good. Because I'm the one who decides who plays for Barça.'

He was just phoning to find out what part he would play in his plans.

'I'm not the one who's going to sign you up. The sporting director wants you. I don't even know you. Each of the three goalkeepers in pre-season gets the same chance to make it as number one, even you, if you sign.'

When he had hung up, Robert told Jörg that it had been a good conversation. Van Gaal seemed at least to accept his obligations, and would treat him fairly.

Years later, when Robert told me about this telephone conversation, he stressed that van Gaal had barked at him straight away: 'I don't even know you.'

Four days after breaking off contractual discussions, Robert was on his way back to Barcelona. He wore jeans and a favourite old torn greyish-blue pullover, the sort of clothes you wear when you don't think you'll be seeing anybody in particular. When he and Teresa landed at seven o'clock, Jörg was waiting for them. They immediately learned a bit about Spanish habits. Seven o'clock is still the afternoon in Spain. They were still working in the Camp Nou office.

Jörg wanted to be prepared for fresh disappointments. He had a contract with him. From FC Porto. He had had the document, already signed by president Pinto da Costa, faxed to him. If Barça wanted to go on playing their little game, Robert would sign for Porto while he was still in Barcelona.

Jörg went alone to Camp Nou. 'My heart was pounding,' he says. Teresa and Robert were to wait in the hotel on Avenida Diagonal until the salary they had originally been promised appeared in the contract; or until Jörg came back empty-handed.

Robert never drank much alcohol, but in their hotel room he and Teresa opened the Cava from the minibar. Then the beer. On television they were showing, over and over again, the 1999 World Footballer of the Year Rivaldo throwing his hands over his face and falling to the ground, screaming. The Turkish player Hakan Ünsal had just hit him in the thigh with the ball, but the referee fell for Rivaldo's melodrama and showed the Turkish player the red card. It was the highlight of that day's play in the World Cup.

Nine o'clock came and went, and ten o'clock. Still nothing was moving apart from Rivaldo.

When his phone eventually rang, after eleven, Robert knew who it would be.

'You can come now,' Jorg said.

In 103 years only two German footballers had been signed by FC Barcelona, Bernd Schuster and now Robert Enke. It was after midnight and he was at Camp Nou surrounded by radio reporters broadcasting the new goalkeeper's words live. He spoke in Portuguese. On Spanish sports radio, where eccentricity is the order of the day, no one minded much. From midnight, a time when they should really be sleeping or doing something else, millions of Spaniards listen to sports broadcasts on the radio. Footballers are expected to take calls for interviews even at that time of night. On Cadena Ser, the most popular channel, the presenters also like to sing the commercials themselves.

Robert was properly introduced in Spain the following day – by Porto's coach José Mourinho. 'Robert's a safe bet for Barça. We wanted him too, but then Barça joined the running,' he wrote in a piece for the Catalan sports newspaper *El Mundo Deportivo*. 'Robert's a great choice, both as a keeper and as a human being.' Since many people in Barcelona drew their image of Germans exclusively from Bernd Schuster, he added, 'Robert isn't your typical German, introverted and a bit ponderous – quite the contrary.'

Robert still had a good month of holiday ahead of him before the adventure with Barça began. He couldn't wait. When he visited Marco Villa, who was now playing for 1 FC Nuremberg, he and his friend went to the club's training-ground.

'Chico, I'm dropping by with Robert Enke, we'd like to do a bit of practice.'

'Robert Enke? Who's that?' asked Nuremberg's groundsman.

All of a sudden it was funny that he wasn't known at home. 'I'm sure there are people in Germany asking: what, Barcelona's signed Enke? For the B-team, or what?' It was when he was happiest that he most liked to make fun of himself.

A few weeks later he was sitting with me for the first time in a pavement café among the gothic buildings in Barcelona's Old Town. He leaned back in his chair to hold his face in the sunlight. 'And a few weeks ago we thought it was the end of the world because Kaiserslautern didn't want me.' He couldn't help laughing at that, too. 'Just imagine if Kaiserslautern had wanted me. I'd probably have said yes straight away. And my face, if Jörg had told me a few weeks later: oh, and by the way, Barcelona would have been another possibility!'

He asked if I could recommend a Spanish teacher. That evening, back in their new home in Sant Cugat, behind the green mountains of the Collserola, he would phone the teacher straight away. After the first lesson he would give him tickets for Barça.

'I don't know why, but somehow I think everything's fantastic at the moment – the city, the club, the life,' Robert continued. The five-storey buildings stood like a rampart around the little square: no cars could be heard. The bright display at the ice-cream parlour opposite us was reflected in the glass door. 'I've only been here for three weeks, but already I have the feeling I'd like to stay for a long time.'

A homeless man made his way through the rows of customers outside the café, asking for money. He was the first person to recognise Robert that afternoon.

'*Enke, el número uno!*'

Robert replied in Portuguese: 'Are you a Benficista?' He couldn't imagine that anyone in Barcelona knew him by sight.

Say a sentence in Catalan, Barça's president Joan Gaspart suggested to Robert before his official presentation. Louis van Gaal accompanied them both into the press room. The walls were hung with small portraits of all the international players who had served Barça. Van Gaal had buttoned up his stiff white shirt under his tie, which made his enormous neck look even more impressive than usual. Robert was wearing a short-sleeved red shirt, his hair freshly clipped by one of those barbers who always cut hair too short. As a result, he looked even younger next to van Gaal.

For his presentation in Lisbon Robert had cobbled together a Portuguese sentence – *É bom estar aquí* – and he had been pleased with that. In Barcelona he spoke English and said only, 'I am going to learn Spanish, and perhaps over time I will learn to speak Catalan as well.' In Catalonia, where politicians used language as a weapon in the fight for independence from Spain, Robert felt it would have sounded subservient, transparent and false if he had said something in Catalan, especially when the club president had prompted him. He didn't want to be used.

2002: Robert with the then Barça coach Louis van Gaal.

'The three goalkeepers, Enke, Bonano and Valdés, are starting at nil, even if the chances are better for the first two,' said van Gaal. 'But everything can change.' His voice boomed. 'Because when I'm in charge no one has a safe place on the team.'

Robert was new in Barcelona, but already used to the fact that the coach thought ruthlessness and honesty were pretty much the same thing. Four years earlier van Gaal had won the championship and the Copa del Rey (the 'King's Cup') with Barça, with a team that was an outstanding combination of free spirit and organisation. Even so, his gruff manner made many players and most fans wish he would go away.

I interviewed van Gaal once, when he was still working for Ajax Amsterdam. He waddled through the old Ajax training complex in his tracksuit; everything about him was enormous – his belly, his neck, his head.

'Good morning, Mr van Gaal, I arranged an interview with you,' I said.

'No!' he roared. 'You arranged an interview with David Endt!' Ajax's press officer had set up the meeting.

Once he had established this to his satisfaction, van Gaal politely invited me into his office.

Ten days later, on the morning of the Champions League semi-final against Bayern Munich, he phoned me at the newspaper office. He was, once again, to the point and slightly annoyed. He had read the piece about Ajax, he told me. 'You've hardly quoted me at all!'

Robert initially fought the duel with Roberto Bonano for the goalkeeper's spot unopposed as Bonano was still on holiday. As Argentina's substitute goalkeeper he had been to the World Cup which meant he was allowed to start training a few weeks later. Frans Hoek, the goalkeeping coach, introduced Robert to the third goalkeeper, a twenty-year-old with a serious expression and thick black hair who was moving up from the B-team. 'Robert's manner was cool, but he had the air of a good person,' recalls Victor Valdés.

The first training session began. Robert's poor Spanish and Victor's broken English gave them a welcome excuse to do hardly any talking. The coach started a lesiurely kickabout to see what state the footballers were in after their holiday. With the eagerness of a boy who's been allowed to join the seniors for the first time, Valdés studied Robert's every movement. He hoped he might recognise a particular German style in him.

Six years earlier, when Robert was learning how to dive

from Uwe Kamps, Bayern Munich played Barcelona in the UEFA Cup semi-final. Standing behind Bayern's goal that night was a fourteen-year-old ball boy, a goalkeeper with the Barcelona youth team. His name was Victor Valdés. He saw Oliver Kahn's powerful jumps and reflexes as he stopped a shot from Kodro and a free kick by Popescu. It had been love at first sight, Valdés said. 'My mouth was hanging open. Whoa! I thought, and I knew: this is my goalkeeper. From that moment on Kahn was my idol.'

Valdés is sitting in the press centre of FC Barcelona's sports city. The room is a curious hybrid, a Portakabin with two brown leather sofas. The fourteen-year-old boy is now a man with huge hands and broad arms. His black T-shirt with a life-sized eagle, its claws extended, emphasises his stature. 'You know,' says Valdés, 'since the day I saw Kahn, I've admired the German school of goalkeeping. German goalkeepers fall much better than Spanish players after a save.'

How exactly?

He starts to explain, then gets up from the leather sofa. 'We Spaniards just drop to the ground like a lump of meat – bump.' Valdés lies down on the press-room floor. 'The Germans roll.' He does the threefold roll with both hands, not with his whole body.

By the time Robert arrived at Barcelona in 2002 he had detached himself from the old German goalkeeping model and had learned to play a much cooler, efficient, rather than spectacular game. Now here was Victor Valdés, who had just come up from the B-team, admiring him for aspects of his play that Robert had left behind.

'Robert rolled so aesthetically.'

That's impossible – he was meticulously careful about not making a show of his saves.

'No, really!' Valdés is beaming with enthusiasm. He can still clearly remember his first training session with Robert. 'Robert was incredible. He made three or four incredible saves. I'd only seen one training match, and already I could see how much quality he had.'

In the changing-room after that first session, midfielder Gerard López came up to Robert and yelled, 'Man of the match, man of the match!' Then he ran out of things to say in English.

Roberto Bonano, Robert's competitor and Barça's number one the previous season, joined the team at its training-camp in Switzerland. Now Robert was doing the watching. Most footballers look bigger on the pitch than they do in their ordinary clothes, and Bonano was no exception. His extra-large torso looked even more enormous in his training sweater. But he was no match for his appearance. It quickly became clear that he wasn't in any sort of form. Disappointed that the coach had only put him on the substitutes bench for the World Cup, and despondent over Argentina's failure at the tournament, Bonano had wanted to forget all about sport in the holidays. He was paying for that now.

The season was due to start in three weeks' time. Robert had a good feeling about it.

'Robert, you're standing too far back!' called the goalkeeping coach.

'Robert, you've got to take the ball with your left foot!'

'Robert, that was another poor pass. Concentrate harder on your feet!'

Frans Hoek, his brown hair neatly parted at the side, shared a tone of voice with his boss, van Gaal, as well as the conviction that a goalkeeper had to be the eleventh outfield player. The attack began with the goalkeeper, so he had to be able to pass, kick or throw the ball precisely and far-sightedly. Barça's defence pushed further forward than anybody else so that the team could play its big-hearted, attacking style of football. This forced the goalkeeper to move up himself, so that the space between him and his defence didn't get too big. During his time at Benfica Robert had gone to great pains to train himself to move his standing position to six or seven yards in front of the goal-line. And now he was supposed to play even further forward? He tried his best, even though he felt uneasy about it, and already Hoek was yelling again: 'Further forward, Robert! I want you to play like van der Sar!'

'The coaches were always telling us about Edwin van der Sar,' Bonano recalls. 'Van der Sar does this, and van der Sar does that.' When the Dutch keeper caught a corner during the European Championship in 1996 in the game against Switzerland and with a precise, long drop-kick seamlessly set up a goal for Dennis Bergkamp, in a few seconds he invented the so-called modern goalkeeper, a man who ironed out the threat of a goal before it could come into being and was the initiator of his team's attacking play.

'I'm not Maradona,' Robert said. 'I have shortcomings when it comes to playing with my feet.' But he wanted to learn. He thought the coaches at Barcelona were well-intentioned towards him. At the time he had trouble seeing the negative in anything. It was just wonderful to be in Barcelona. And given Bonano's struggle to get in shape, he was a virtual certainty to start the season as number one. 'Robert had a fantastic attitude,' Hoek confirms. 'He was very willing. He was open to criticism and instruction.'

At a pre-season tournament in Amsterdam, Bonano and Enke played a game each. Bonano looked uncertain in the 4–3 defeat against Ajax, fumbling several crosses. In the 4–2 victory over AC Parma, Robert clearly came out too late when Marco Di Vaio ran at him and scored. 'In slow-paced training matches he coped well with the big distance between a Barça goalkeeper and the defence,' says Hoek. 'But in matches at competition speed it was clear that he still had difficulties with our very particular form of positional play. It was obvious that he had excellent reflexes on the goal-line, but the question no one could answer was: how long will it take him to get used to the Barça style?'

For the third match, van Gaal announced that Victor Valdés would play.

'Robbi was bewildered,' says Teresa. 'Why Victor all of a sudden?'

* * *

Back home in Sant Cugat just days before the start of the season Robert and Teresa were distracting themselves with the dogs in the garden one afternoon when they heard the doorbell. They weren't expecting any handymen or the language teacher, and they didn't know anyone else who would have a reason to drop by and see them.

Teresa opened the door to a woman, her slim figure emphasised by a short hairdo.

'Hi, I'm Frauke,' she said in German.

The dogs had made more of a name for themselves in their new home than the goalkeeper had. Frauke had heard that they had taken in seven strays. She herself had two mongrels and was involved in animal protection, so as she had just been to see their neighbours she thought she would call in and introduce herself.

Her husband worked at the German consulate. Teresa and Robert were invited to the next reception at their house.

On the terrace during the party a young woman came up to Teresa and asked, 'You're the one with the seven dogs, aren't you?'

'Why, can you smell it?'

That's how friendships are made.

In Mönchengladbach and Lisbon Teresa and Robert had lived in their own world, surrounded only by individual acquaintances. They had accepted this in the belief that that's how things have to be when you're a professional footballer. How was he supposed to make friends, Robert wondered: how could he know whether they valued him or just his status? In an attempt to escape people who simply wanted to get close to a footballer, he had cut himself off from everyone else as well. 'In Barcelona it was completely different from the outset,' says Teresa.

Susanne, the young woman with the direct question from the party at the consulate, took Teresa along to her riding-stables. As a modern pentathlete, Teresa had spent her youth on horseback. Without noticing how, and without Robert having time to wonder about motives, the Enkes soon found themselves part of a little German coterie at the stables. Sant

Cugat is near the German School in Barcelona, which attracts a lot of Germans to the town. People who would never socialise at home become friends, regardless of profession; the feeling of being foreigners abroad is what holds them together. At the riding-stables the goalkeeper for FC Barcelona was just one more member of an ex-pat community.

Again and again Robert found himself looking at one of the horses in particular. The animal's coat was dull, its eyes empty. It was old, fifteen at least, and it was always brought out for the beginners, who tended to bounce hard on its back.

He bought the horse.

Two days before Barcelona's first match, a Champions League qualifier against Legia Warsaw, Robert set off from training for Sant Cugat, taking the scenic route to avoid paying the two euros for the motorway tunnel just before Vallvidrera. 'Do you want to know who's playing?' he said into his mobile. He didn't wait for my answer. 'Victor's in goal on Wednesday.'

He was shaken. Valdés was still a boy with no big-game experience, and athletically he was far from mature.

'Victor seemed, at that moment, to be adapting best of all three goalkeepers to the Barça system's style of play,' Hoek explains.

Robert forced himself to see the decision from the coach's point of view. 'It's very brave of van Gaal, you have to give him that,' he said into his phone. 'He could have made things simple for himself and put Bonano or me in goal. But he opts for an inexperienced young goalkeeper. He must have thought about it very carefully.'

But he could only see it in such rational terms when talking to other people. At home, he brooded. Why Victor?

That afternoon he drove Teresa into town. They had to buy furniture for the house. It was August, and in Spain it isn't just individual shops that close for the holidays, it's whole towns. With mounting irritation they went from one shut-up furniture store to the next. Teresa was happy, because while they were doing this Robert forgot to brood about football.

Teresa went to the match, even though Robert was only sitting on the subs bench. She found the executive box, full of men with gelled hair and frosty women, fascinating, albeit she didn't take the circus too seriously.

She had always managed to find one or two good friends among the other footballers' wives; she just had to make the effort and she would link up with someone at Camp Nou as well. She asked one of the women if they were going out after the match. Of course, said the woman, and didn't ask if Teresa wanted to come too.

At Camp Nou the women behaved as if they themselves were the football team, competing for the starring roles. She was just the substitute goalie's wife.

Down on the pitch, Victor Valdés was demonstrating his huge talent in his first outing. He valiantly stood up to Legia Warsaw's Cesary Kucharski when he broke through the ranks; but then against Atlético Madrid, in the first Primera División game of the season, he ran headlong out of the goal and under a misjudged cross, and the ball landed in the goal.

Robert heard a few rumours. Valdés was preferred because he was Catalan. Van Gaal had a thing about young players; like a man possessed, he was trying to cement his reputation as a discoverer of new stars, and he favoured reckless young talent. Chat, gossip – forget it, Robert said to himself. But it was hard not to think about it. How could it be that Victor remained in goal even after a few mistakes? Why were the fans frantically applauding his every simple save when Robert just got shouted at by the trainers to use his feet, even though everyone could see that he was better with his hands than Valdés? *Hands*, not feet – that was the important thing.

Teresa took him to the riding-stables. Dickens was the name they had given the exhausted horse Robert had bought, more out of love for his wife than for the animal. The riders spoke to him; he found their friendliness refreshing. He shouldn't think about football all the time, he told himself. And a moment later he was thinking about Victor Valdés.

* * *

Next week, in the Copa del Rey, he would use some of his reserve players, van Gaal said. His voice betrayed him. Wound up by all the shouting and raging, it sometimes had an aggressive, barking sound, even when the coach only wanted to convey something in a matter-of-fact way. 'You'll have your chance there.' To Robert it sounded like a threat. In the Copa del Rey you'll be able to show me whether you're really up to the task.

Barça's opponents were FC Novelda, bottom of Segunda División B – the Spanish Third Division. Novelda's La Magdalena sports ground has three entrances; the green iron gate at the back is covered with graffiti: 'Revolution Che!' and 'Ana, you are pretty – a boy tells you that'. FC Barcelona spent the night in Elche, in a hotel with a palm garden, a fifteen-kilometre drive away from Novelda through an area in which the ugliness of cheap warehouses contrasts with the beauty of bare mountains, and where the better restaurants lie outside the town, along the motorways. As always before a game, Robert phoned Teresa. They mechanically reeled off questions and answers – how are you, we went for a walk, now we're having coffee, all fine, okay, we'll see each other tonight. He had forbidden her to wish him luck.

NINE

Novelda

They'd closed off Sergeant Navarro Street in front of the sports ground. Toni Madrigal, who had been too nervous even to read a book all afternoon, left his car at home and walked. It was just ten minutes to the sports ground. Madrigal was early: he wanted to meet a friend from Valencia at the ticket desk before the game.

Novelda – population twenty-seven thousand, reasonable income from marble and wine – is like an onion, with skins of apartment blocks from the fifties and warehouses and mega-stores that you can peel away until you reach the gleaming core with its casino and old town hall. Madrigal, who had lunched on pasta without sauce, just olive oil, walked past the apartment blocks wearing his green and white tracksuit. There were more people in the streets than usual. Some of them waved and held their thumbs in the air. They recognised the tracksuit, not him.

When he reached the roadblock in front of the sports ground, some security men stopped him.

'What do you want?' one of them asked.

'I'm the striker,' said Madrigal. 'I'm playing tonight.'

His tracksuit persuaded the security man to let him through. Otherwise only people with tickets were being granted entry.

Madrigal's first instinct was to look not for his friend from Valencia, but for *them*. They weren't there yet.

In just two hours the referee would blow the whistle and the match would start.

Robert was on the team bus on the way from Elche to Novelda, a police car with a blue light keeping the road clear for them.

Roberto Bonano was next to him. At home Bonano wrote bedtime stories for his two children, he read Borges and Cortázar, his wife worked as a psychologist; Robert felt instinctively close to him. 'But throughout the whole season we never talked about anything personal, even though we often shared a hotel room before the game,' says Bonano, looking for an explanation he can't quite find. 'When you compete as a goalkeeper at a club like Barça, there's always something between you and the other goalkeepers.' Bonano and Robert didn't say anything on the team bus. Some of the players were listening to music on headphones. Robert didn't have a CD player. If you wanted music, you could listen to the radio. But it was quiet on the bus now; they must concentrate, the coach said.

On the country road they passed through villages with names like Tres Hermanas – Three Sisters. The mountains behind them were bare and yellow. It was as if they were entering the realm of Don Quixote.

The bus was air-conditioned, and he was wearing a short-sleeved polo shirt with the Barça emblem over his heart, but Robert felt hot.

He could only lose. Whatever he tried to think about to distract himself, he always ended up with that thought. If everything went as planned, Barça would win 3–0 or 4–0 and no one would mention the goalkeeper. If it went wrong, he would get the blame.

It was a ridiculous way of looking at things, Jörg had told him on the phone. In reality, the game was an opportunity for him to put in a confident performance. Of course no one would say afterwards Enke has to go in goal, just because he had made a decent impression in a cup game against a Third Division team, but he would put himself in the frame with the coaches. Victor Valdés, who had stayed at home this time, would go on to play shakily in the league over the next few weeks, Jörg was sure of that – he wasn't quite ready yet. Robert's day would come. Novelda was the first step.

But however often Robert told himself the same things, he couldn't actually see it that way.

He could only lose.

'Since being surprised on the first day of the season by the news that Valdés was number one, he was in a negative mood,' says Jörg. 'He convinced himself that everything was going against him.'

Minor questions turned into self-doubt, and now, under the pressure of an approaching game, they turned into a fear that had nothing to do with the normal nerves of a goalkeeper. This fear was darker.

If he failed here, not only would he have lost his chance, it would all be over.

Frans Hoek wanted to see Victor in goal anyway. He'd coached him in Barça's youth teams. Hoek wanted to be able to tell everybody, I made this goalkeeper. All goalkeeping coaches dream of discovering their keeper.

God, this damned dry air!

The team bus slowed down. Robert saw a crowd of people in the road, waving and shouting. They must be at the sports ground. The people behind the barriers beamed at him when he got off the bus. His lips were a thin line in his face.

The radio was on in the FC Novelda changing-room, the door open. People stuck their heads in to wish them good luck. Madrigal, who had tried to get some sleep at midday but had just lain awake, heard the noise from the terraces through the walls. 'It sounded as if there was a demonstration going on over our heads.'

There was already a hint of grey in his hair, but he was twenty-six, in the best years of his football career. He had established himself in the Segunda División B. The game gave him enough to live on, 2,000 euros a month, though he still calculated in pesetas – four million a year. He shared a flat on the Avenida de Elche in Novelda with two other players. What he liked to do was study. He had trained to be a teacher part-time. But they were professionals in Novelda – 'we trained like every Primera División player does' – and they were only bottom of the table because of Barça, he thought: with the cup game on their minds they had lost 3–0 to Burgos on Sunday. 'For professionals like us you only get a game like the one against Barça once in a lifetime.'

They had already changed into their kit. The changing-room smelled of massage oil. They were eager to get out there and warm up, but first they had to sit through the tactics talk. Their trainer, Antoni Teixido, wrote on the whiteboard who had to cover who for Barça's corners and told them that this game was a reward for their efforts the previous season, the finest day of their year: they should enjoy it, play as they always did and not injure anybody. The speech lasted only two minutes. The coach didn't outline a single attacking move nor a particular defensive concept, he did not mention a single notion like: Rochemback always goes past on the right, so force him on to his left foot. Teixido knew that his players were already keyed up. More words would only have stressed them.

Robert hurried across the basketball pitch to the away changing-room. Above the main entrance to the sports ground hung the Spanish flag, old and tattered. Children carried the gleaming metal cases containing Barça's equipment back and forth between the gymnasium and the changing-room. 'I kept thinking about the Barça players sitting in that changing-room,' says Aurelio Borghino, Novelda's substitute goalkeeper. 'It's more a shaft than a room. It's just got one tiny window, really cramped, low ceiling, the sweat of many years in the walls.'

Robert tried to listen as the coach dispensed instructions on tactics. Van Gaal's voice was droning about pressing in attack, winning the ball back straight away, being aggressive, passing the ball behind the defence only in the last third of the pitch. A good coach prepared every game with as much care and detail as a Champions League final, thought Louis van Gaal, and he regarded himself as one of the best.

Today, Robert absolutely had to stand eight or nine yards in front of his goal when Novelda got the ball back in midfield. Novelda would immediately go for a long pass, and then he would have to come out like van der Sar, collect the through-ball, even if it was outside the box . . . damn it, now he was thinking exactly the same way as the coaches talked. Bloody van der Sar.

The spectators clapped as if a goal had been scored. FC Novelda had come out of the changing-room tunnel to do their warm-up. 'Then we saw *them* for the first time,' says Madrigal, who had spent hours talking shop with his two flatmates, working out which team Barça were likely to put out. 'It was impossible to concentrate on the warm-up,' says Madrigal. Out of the corners of his eyes he kept seeing the flashes from pocket cameras on the terraces. They did a few sprints and stretched their muscles on the advertising boards. In that position they could take a good look at the Barça players.

Frans Hoek was helping Robert warm up. 'Cup games like this are hardest for a substitute goalkeeper,' says Hoek. 'You haven't got the rhythm, and you're supposed to prove yourself. You're under extreme pressure.'

'You come from a foreign country and you're supposed to play on a crappy pitch in an unpractised team full of substitutes,' observes Victor Valdés. 'Boy, you have doubts, you have a bad feeling!'

'You notice when a goalkeeper's under too much pressure,' says Bonano.

The teams took up position back in the tunnel. The corridor was so narrow that there was barely room for the two sides. Toni Madrigal and Robert Enke could have touched each other. But they never exchanged a word. They stood isolated in their own worlds, far removed from each other in their thoughts.

'I saw the referee, who normally blew his whistle in the Primera División,' says Madrigal. 'I saw the Barça eleven – Riquelme, Frank de Boer, Xavi. I had the feeling: now you're playing in the top flight.'

There are pictures of Robert on the pitch, posing for the photographers with his team before kick-off. It was just before eight o'clock in the evening but still bright daylight. He's on the far left of the second row, Thiago Motta beside him thrusting out his chest and putting his arm firmly around him. Robert's left shoulder and arm dangle limply, his mouth is open and his eyes wide. His fear is frozen in those photographs for ever.

It was 11 September 2002. You can't forget the date – one year after the New York terror attacks, and a Catalan national holiday.

On the narrow terraces, in many places only two rows of green seats, sat Madrigal's parents, brother and uncle.

Teresa was sitting at home alone in front of the television in Sant Cugat. She heard not the commentator's voice but Robbi's, the mounting despair of the previous few days: 'I can only lose.'

When the game began, she wished it would soon be over.

Barça immediately took possession of the ball and wouldn't give it back. They passed and passed, playing in slightly too relaxed a manner. 'They were faster and better, and we were running behind them,' says Madrigal. 'When we got close to the ball, in their minds they were already a pass further on.' Román Riquelme, the most curious footballer in the world – his movements are the embodiment of slowness, but hardly anyone can get the ball away from him because he thinks faster than most – played with the upright back and raised head of a midfield majesty, right at the centre of things.

Four months earlier Real Madrid had won the Champions League with Zidane, Figo and Raúl, and Barça could no longer bear the unfavourable comparisons with the Galácticos. The club felt impelled to win something again, and the Argentinian Riquelme, newly arrived from Buenos Aires, was to be their saviour.

After seven minutes he played a pass, as van Gaal had demanded, in the attacking third, steep and into empty space, and Geovanni converted it. Novelda's fans applauded the goal. From what they'd seen so far they were convinced the only joy of the evening would lie in admiring Barça. Madrigal thought, 'They're going to put ten past us.'

Teresa couldn't see Robert; everything was happening in the

other half of the field. Van Gaal had only put up a three-man defence – a risk hardly a coach took these days, but against a Segunda B side it was plainly fine. So Barça had an extra man in attack – as if they needed one.

Madrigal lurked, he circled. He stood with his back to Barça's goal but kept his shoulder pointing in that direction so that he could strike straight away when it came to it. Whenever Novelda emerged from midfield and danger seemed a possibility, however remote, Robert immediately retreated closer to the goal-line.

Madrigal could feel the goalkeeper behind him, but he never heard him. 'They didn't talk to each other,' Madrigal noticed, which he saw as a strength: Barça's defence knew automatically what their goalkeeper was doing, and vice versa.

Madrigal couldn't entirely concentrate on the game. The atmosphere was so unfamiliar. He looked beyond the goal. Where a few young people normally hung about on the balustrade, extra terraces had been built for the evening; the builders' cranes loomed high over the sports-ground walls. Some fans were sitting in the cabin of the crane, and at the windows of the school on the other side. Some five thousand spectators filled the ground. After half an hour Barça's players were nudging one another on the substitutes bench. Bonano pointed to the sky. Three para-gliders circled there, also trying to catch something of the game.

The Novelda pitch is one of the smallest and narrowest in Spanish professional football, ninety-seven metres long and sixty-three metres wide – eight metres shorter and five metres narrower than Camp Nou. That was an advantage for Robert given his initial difficulties in finding the correct position for a Barça goalkeeper, the sportswriters had written before the game; his defenders would be closer to him. But what do sportswriters know? The ball just came flying much faster out of Novelda's midfield and into his penalty box. All the dimensions were wrong. How was he supposed to come here . . . and now they were turning the floodlights on. They weren't lights, they were just a glow. How was he supposed to see the ball clearly now? How was he supposed to play well under these conditions?

Everyone was glad when the referee blew the whistle for half-time: Barça, because they were easily dominating the game; Novelda, because the score was only 1–0; Robert Enke, because he had survived the first half without being troubled by the opposing team.

Teresa went into the garden to smoke a cigarette. Her temples throbbed.

Novelda's goalkeeper came up to Robert in the tunnel and asked if they could swap shirts after the game.

The second half began as a repetition of the first; few were bothered that Barça's passes remained sterile. People thought: they're controlling the game. In the press seats, Cayetano Ros of *El País* wrote on his laptop, 'Barça thought their opponents had given up: they had made them run after the ball for an hour.'

That hour was almost complete when Novelda were awarded a free kick on the left wing. Miguel Angel Mullor, one of Madrigal's two flatmates, clipped the ball into the box. Robert had to come out of his goal and catch it, but suddenly the ball's trajectory flattened out, right in that damned glowing light. He hesitated. Level with the far post an opposing player was completely unmarked. Robert saw his white shorts out of the corner of his eye – peripheral vision, unconscious perception, one of his great strengths. He had to shout *Hostia, allí, el delantero!*, anything to draw his defenders' attention to the lone man. But he couldn't.

Silent, paralysed, he stayed on the goal-line.

The ball flew on as if it were seeking Madrigal's right foot. He slipped his marker, the Dutch international Michael Reiziger, and took the risk to hit it first time diagonally into Robert's far corner to make it 1–1.

'We'll win this one, we'll win this one!' yelled the Novelda players as they fell on Madrigal.

'Us, win against Barça?' he wondered.

Robert stood frozen in front of his goal.

A goal does what people would love to be able to do: it changes everything in an instant.

For fifty-eight minutes Madrigal had been chafing away at Barça's defenders. One of them, Reiziger, 'ran for every ball at fantastic speed'. Frank de Boer, the Dutch World Cup semi-finalist and Barça's captain that evening, had 'an excellent technique'. The third, Fernando Navarro, a European champion with Spain six years later, hurried over to help his colleagues at the smallest sign of distress. All of a sudden, however, 'Reiziger wasn't playing tightly, Navarro was nervous, and Frank de Boer was starting to criticise everyone and everything. He was no longer part of the game.' Madrigal forgot the significance of the game, the noise, the opposing team. All that existed now was the ball, the pitch, the goal.

When Barça attacked, when the ball was far away from him, things got bad for Robert. He had too much time to think about the equaliser. It had been Reiziger's mistake, but why hadn't he come out? He should have come out and gathered the cross. A shot flew at him and he wasn't prepared for it. He tore himself out of his despair, instinctively threw up his hands and slapped the ball away towards the edge of the box. No harm was done. But everyone could see the state he was in.

Again Novelda slung a free kick high into his penalty area, and again it was deflected but not far enough away this time. Friend and opponent fumbled for the ball twenty yards in front of the goal. When Rochemback finally seemed to have the ball under control, Barça's defence began to move out. Madrigal sensed rather than saw that his flatmate could still get the ball back, which he did. Mullor immediately lobbed it into the box for Madrigal, who was already running towards Barça's goal. He had only a split second's advantage; de Boer was after him, but he wasn't quick like Reiziger. As the cross came in, Robert was stranded in the no-man's-land of a goalkeeper; he knew there was no point running further forward, whatever happened Madrigal would get to the ball before he did. Madrigal buried the ball in the net from twelve yards out, taking the score to 2–1.

'I didn't feel: now you're famous, or: now you've done it,' says Madrigal. 'I was just happy.'

Three minutes later Riquelme equalised with a penalty. The little Argentinian had fought with bravura.

A murmur arose on the terraces. A football crowd often can sense when a game reaches its turning-point, and with Barça wiping out Novelda's lead so quickly, a feeling next to certainty was in the air: The underdog had put up a great fight, but now the big favourite, the twenty-four-times Copa del Rey winners from Barcelona, would dash the hopes of the upstarts with one or two ice-cold masterstrokes. Of course he too was afraid that it would end like this, says Madrigal. But something surprised him. 'Barça weren't reassured by the equaliser. They were talking to each other now, but in very negative terms. De Boer was beside himself, shouting at everyone, Robert included. It sounds wrong for me to say as a Segunda B player, but the truth is that their defence was making enormous mistakes. Reiziger: he didn't grab me by the arm before my first goal, he never used his body as an obstacle.' For a moment Madrigal sounds utterly baffled. 'I don't know whether I'm just used to more violence in Segunda B, but their low level of resistance was very odd.'

The game had long since come apart at the seams. Now the hearts, not the brains, of both teams were driving them back and forth.

The pace of the match left Robert feeling slow. A keeper who blames himself for a goal experiences the remaining minutes of play with an unbearable mixture of indifference and panic. The evening is already over as far as he's concerned: it's unsalvageable, whatever the outcome. At the same time he wants to make everything better again, but immediately he is gripped again by the fear that he'll make everything worse the next time he tries to do anything.

On the left side of midfield, a ricocheting pass fell at the feet of Novelda's captain Cudi, and Madrigal knew exactly what was going to happen. Cudi always crossed to the back post. Madrigal sprinted diagonally towards it, trying to build up enough impetus for a decisive header. Robert saw de Boer going with Madrigal.

There was nothing elegant about Cudi's cross. The ball flew towards Robert's six-yard line. He had to come out. It was an easy take for a goalkeeper like him.

You can spot a frightened goalkeeper by his response to a cross. He always hesitates a moment too long. Robert didn't even take a step forward. De Boer himself just stopped, too. He will never know why; it happened too quickly; perhaps he too was scared of making a mistake, perhaps he wanted to make room for his keeper. He was used to the goalie coming out: he had played for years with Edwin van der Sar at Ajax Amsterdam.

Madrigal suddenly felt calm. He took his time. He didn't head the ball straight at the goal, but placed his header so that it would bounce in front of Robert and spin unpredictably. Madrigal could already see the ball in the back of the net as he met it.

Novelda's subs bench thundered because the fans were thumping the roof. Aurelio Borghino, the substitute keeper, disappeared in a joyous huddle with the other subs. Then, while he still had his arms in the air, something suddenly caught his eye. 'De Boer was standing in the penalty box. He was railing at Enke. I've never seen anything like it. A professional doesn't do something like that, humiliating a team-mate on the pitch. Robert Enke stood there, his face pale, eyes lowered, and didn't say a word.'

There were twelve minutes left, but the game had already found its concluding image.

For Robert Enke it was a long journey to get off that playing-field. Hundreds of fans had stormed on to the pitch, laughing and shouting: We've beaten Barça! They circled Robert; they asked him for autographs, for his gloves; they beamed at him; they shouted: We've beaten Barça 3–2! 'People often have bad manners,' says Madrigal. 'They didn't understand what this defeat meant for Barça's players, like Robert.' The loudspeakers crackled; the stadium announcer had put on the signature tune of the Champions League immediately after the final whistle. Robert fought his way through the crowd without being wholly aware of them. He gave Novelda's goalkeeper his jersey, without feeling the movements as he pulled it from his body.

He phoned Teresa the moment he reached the changing-room, as he always did. After they had put down the phone, neither he nor she could remember what they had said.

He usually loved those moments after a game in the changing-room, when the tension slowly faded away. He had his ritual. He always took his socks off last; often he sat there for a while before showering, his socks up to his knees, but otherwise naked. In Novelda, no other player got showered and out of the changing-room as fast as he did.

He answered only two questions from reporters.

Robert, what happened here?

'I can't find an explanation for what has happened. It's hard to go back in goal and then concede three goals to a Third Division team.'

Do the defenders bear most of the blame for the defeat?

'This isn't the moment to look for people to blame. Each individual should analyse his own performance.'

He pulled himself away, went to sit on the bus, waited for it to drive off, for the darkness to swallow him up.

Toni Madrigal had wanted to swap his shirt with Riquelme, as they had agreed at half-time, but Riquelme ignored him. At the door to the changing-room Madrigal's mother fought the stewards with words and hands to let her in. They relented when someone called to Madrigal and he confirmed that he knew this woman.

A few metres away a boy was asking his father to stop praising the hat-trick scorer to the reporters. 'Otherwise the big teams will take him away from us, Papa,' the boy said to Juan Francisco Sánchez, Novelda's president.

'In three or four weeks no one will remember me,' Madrigal told the sportswriters. He wasn't sure whether or not to believe his own words.

The floodlights were still on; the walls of the ground, with their crumbling whitewash, gleamed. Some of the sportswriters sat on the ground in the gym, which had been converted into a press conference room.

'The old vices were visible again, above all the inexplicable hole in the defence opened up by de Boer and Reiziger in which they buried themselves and Enke in his debut game,' wrote *El Mundo Deportivo*.

'Enke signed his own sentence,' the *Sport* decided.

Frank de Boer, who had been asked to speak for the team as Barça's captain that evening, appeared on the basketball court beside the ground, where the reporters were waiting. He was a veteran of over four hundred top-flight club games and a hundred for his country. 'That first goal didn't make Michael Reiziger look good,' he said, 'but Enke should have come out to take the cross, because he was almost level with the ball.' With regard to Novelda's winning goal, when de Boer had stood beside Madrigal and done nothing, de Boer simply said, 'Enke has to catch the ball.'

It is an unwritten law in professional football: never criticise your team-mates in public.

At Alicante airport the footballers of FC Barcelona waited for their charter plane to take off, each man an island, with no desire to speak and even less of a craving to hear anything. Excited sports journalists were spreading the news. De Boer's behaviour had been incredible, unprecedented; he was the worst of all and he attacks his team-mates, and he does it as the captain? No one dared tell Robert.

It was after one in the morning when he opened his front door in Sant Cugat. He went to the bathroom to wash his gloves with shampoo and lay them carefully out to dry, as he always did.

In Novelda, on the Avenida de Elche, Toni Madrigal sat at the kitchen table with his two flatmates Miguel Angel Mullor, who had set up two goals for him, and Toni Martínez, who couldn't play because of a knee injury – at this of all times.

'It was late when we got back from the stadium, after eleven, and there aren't many restaurants open in Novelda at that time of night,' says Madrigal, so they ordered a pizza at home to celebrate.

The next morning Robert walked into the changing-room in Camp Nou on time for training, with a feeling that he would rather be somewhere else. As always, breakfast had been prepared for the players. If some of them voluntarily sat down for a cappuccino and some fruit and croissants every morning, they were more likely to become a team. Robert ignored the food, and sat down next to the Swede Patrick Andersson, a fellow player of his at Borussia Mönchengladbach. Sitting next to Patrik, talking in German, felt like being home again.

'Did you see what de Boer said about you?' hissed Andersson, who competed with de Boer for a place in defence. 'You can't put up with that, you've got to fire back!'

Robert, too impotent to feel furious, went to see de Boer out of a sense of duty towards Andersson. He quietly asked him what was going on.

He'd been misquoted – you know journalists, replied de Boer.

Robert said nothing more. He thought it wasn't seemly to row with your team-mates. And above all he didn't want anything more to do with de Boer. He just wanted to be on his own.

Luis Enrique, the real captain of Barcelona who, like some of the other senior players, had been rested in Novelda, gave de Boer a good talking-to. Coach van Gaal roared at his fellow Dutchman: a professional didn't behave like that, certainly not one with his experience.

No one paid any attention to Robert. Why would they have? He was a professional, he should be able to get on with things. Van Gaal didn't talk to him; 'he didn't talk to me all year'. No one defended him against the headlines: 'Where was Enke?' 'The German goalkeeper has demonstrated that he's too green for Barça'.

'He was thrown to the lions,' says Victor Valdés.

Robert and Frank de Boer had to go to the press conference. Robert said, 'I've never criticised another player in my life and I'm not going to do it now. The whole team lost.' De Boer said he hadn't intended to criticise anyone, he'd just wanted to explain the goals. 'Enke could have done more to prevent these goals, and me too. I failed over the third goal, but I think I played well.'

'There was one thing I wanted to ask,' Victor Valdés says to me eight years later. 'Did de Boer ever apologise to Robert?'

Never.

A curious noise comes out of Victor's mouth. Is it a gurgle, is it laughter? Is it surprise, is it contempt?

Robert didn't read the newspapers on 12 September. But he did find out what was in them. A professional footballer senses the vibrations of public opinion. Some acquaintance on the phone, some fan at the training-ground, always says, did you see what they wrote about you? In a world where people's destinies are routinely reduced to knee-jerk headlines, all of a sudden he was the goalkeeper who had failed.

He felt numb and at the same time profoundly torn up.

Teresa wrote in her diary – still the Portuguese one, still the same year when she had punctuated her notes with so many euphoric exclamation marks:

12.09: *The game made big waves. The press is in full chase, spurred on by attacks from Frank de Arse. Both nervous wrecks.*
13.09: *Somehow got through the day. Still completely whacked.*

For a few days Toni Madrigal read about what his three goals against Barcelona had started. But he had never bought the sports papers and he soon lost interest in the daily tittle-tattle of the elite of professional football. For most people he will always be the man who knocked Barça out of the cup. He never watched the game on video. 'Why should I watch a football match when I know the outcome?'

He's thirty-four now, his hair all silver-grey. Given that he works in professional football, the job that gives you premature wrinkles, he has a surprisingly smooth, youthful face. He wears his trainers with their laces untied, his khaki shirt hangs casually out of his jeans. He looks very slight for a striker. He is sitting at a pavement café in Elche, where he now lives. There are palm-trees in the plaza. He orders his coffee extra strong.

Since eight that morning he's been studying at home – he's training to be a fitness coach. He's always enjoyed studying. Professional footballers are so lucky to have so much time to study, he feels. Madrigal's career has taken him to teams like Levante B, Sabadell and Villajoyosa, all Segunda B, but now he's back with FC Novelda, who have slipped down to the Tercera División. 'There were rumours that after my three goals against Barça, Elche, in the Segunda División A, wanted me.' He smiles. 'There are always rumours in football.'

Toni Madrigal doesn't believe that one game can transform a football career. But, he adds, thinking about Robert Enke, one evening can mark a life.

TEN

Thoughts by the Pool

He would have loved to destroy his career. The idea became increasingly intense, increasingly enticing: what if I just stopped going to training? Tore up my contract, said goodbye, and gave up football?

But what would he do then? At twenty-five he couldn't just start studying – and what subject would he choose? When he had read the book *100 Jobs with a Future* six years earlier in Mönchengladbach, there was no other profession that had grabbed him. When reporters had asked him during his youth-team days what job he wanted to do if football didn't work out, he had answered, 'Sports journalism.' But now he couldn't be a football reporter either. It would only mean facing up to his failure.

'It was just a game that went wrong. Everyone else on the team was bad. And Valdés has missed the ball a few times too.'

'That's different. The coaches love Victor. I just had that one chance. And I blew it.'

'But you're brilliant as a goalkeeper. Sooner or later things will work out. I firmly believe in you.'

'It's over, Terri. There's no point any more. What I really want to do is tell Parera to tear up my contract.'

Teresa felt he wouldn't do that. But she was still startled. His sadness sounded so definitive.

They were sitting by the pool in their garden, and didn't feel like jumping in. The defeat at Novelda was four days old.

For the other players, everyday life had returned. Just the day before, Barça had won a league game in Bilbao 2–0, with

Valdés in goal and Frank de Boer in central defence. On the way home van Gaal sat in a traffic-jam in the Garraf Tunnel – 'two and a half hours', he said – and the drivers of the other cars gave him the thumbs up. FC Novelda had scored their first point of the season thanks to a 2–2 draw in Palamós, with a goal from Madrigal. Robert alone was left behind. A week later, at the derby with Espanyol Barcelona, he wasn't on the Barça teamsheet.

During those hours of brooding with Teresa he had stuck his feet in the pool and caught a cold.

'Slept late, dogs too,' Teresa wrote in her diary. 'Robbi has depression again.' Today, after having accompanied him through two clinical depressions, she would rather have written: He was in a dark mood again.

The rescue parties arrived. Jörg Neblung hurried to Barcelona; later Dirk Enke did the same. Marco called, and Robert's mother with her unshakeable optimism. Why couldn't he be like her? When Jörg arrived in Sant Cugat, Teresa was ill as well. She had caught the infection from him.

'There was a big difference in Robert's relationship with me and Marco,' says Jörg 'With Marco, it was simple friendship. But I was also his adviser. So there were conflicts. We often rubbed each other up the wrong way, and there were times when I was overbearing.'

'Go to training,' said Jörg. You can also publicly hit back at de Boer, Jörg added when Robert got back from the training-ground.

Robert said, 'What would be the point of that?' He didn't like conflict, and he wanted to be reminded of Novelda even less. 'I simply felt run down. I was so preoccupied with myself that I'd closed myself off to the world.'

Neither Jörg nor Teresa had had any psychological training. They only had their common sense.

Sad people should get busy and cheer up, they thought.

From the Enkes' bedroom you could see Sant Cugat golf course. 'Come on, let's play golf,' said Jörg.

'Golf?' Robert looked at him as if he'd just been invited to fly to the moon.

They weren't sure if they always chose the correct iron from their borrowed golfing bag, and judging by the sceptical looks

Robert with his agent and friend Jörg Neblung.

from the other golfers they were making fools of themselves. So much the better. Jörg didn't have to force himself to be funny, the comedy was there already.

They also went with Teresa to the riding-stables. Dickens was jumping and running around again now; the gleam had returned to his coat, and, she thought, to his eyes. But for half an hour the horse reverted one last time to its terrible old state, with a swaying freight on its back. Robert sat on Dickens like a robot. When he got off, he laughed quite freely.

When people who knew him are asked how they remember him, most of them say without thinking, like the national goalkeeping coach Andreas Köpke, 'How he laughed.'

Minutes later Robert's eyes again had the flat, glassy look of someone who's not really there.

'You've got to go and see a psychologist,' was Jörg's parting shot before he flew back to Cologne.

He found a German specialist in Barcelona, Dr Heinrich Geldschläger, a certified psychologist and psychotherapist.

'Go,' said Jörg.

The practice was in Eixample, where the modernist buildings highlight Barcelona's old beauty, and the masses of cars turn the city into a modern hell. Dr Geldschläger told Robert he'd been thinking about him. After he'd heard about Novelda.

With his steady gaze, his moustache and his combed-back black hair, Geldschläger looked a bit like the England goalkeeper David Seaman, who was at that time developing a reputation for unreliability.

The doctor diagnosed alienation, a deep melancholy of a kind many people experience after a bereavement, after being fired from a job, or after being bullied. They had to try to work through the panic situations Robert had experienced in football. And perhaps some Jacobson muscle relaxation would help, said Geldschläger, because muscle tension often went hand in hand with psychological tension. Robert watched as the doctor showed him the exercises. Clench your fist for five seconds with your eyes closed, then quickly open the fist and concentrate on the change in tension . . .

Robert was sceptical, but he continued to go regularly to Dr Geldschläger for weeks. He didn't dare not to. He felt he had to do something.

When his father came to Barcelona, Robert took him to training. FC Barcelona trained at a football ground most local players would have complained about, distinctly narrower and shorter than the usual size. They couldn't practise corners there. The ground, La Masía, was Barça's trademark. This team didn't need to train for corners.

After the warm-up, the press had to leave the ground so that the players could work undisturbed. 'I was allowed to stay,' his father says proudly. He was fascinated to watch the endless rounds of passing. Like everyone who watches Barça for the first time, his father was overwhelmed by the feeling that he had never experienced anything like it. 'The way they played – chop-chop, boom-boom – and still the coach was shouting away at everybody. I thought van Gaal was awful.'

During a break, the coach called the team together to explain the next exercise. Robert stood outside the circle of players, a few metres behind his colleagues.

'Why don't you join the group, when you're part of it?' his father asked him on the way home.

Robert didn't reply.

'It only makes things harder. The coach will see that and think: he's not integrated, he's not involved.'

Robert didn't take up the subject.

Something tightened inside him when the team stood close together. It was only a vague feeling, but he wanted to show that he felt rejected. He wanted someone in the club to recognise how ill he was. At the same time, he didn't want to show openly how despondent he was.

'He went on joking during training,' says Roberto Bonano.

'Robert was very special,' says Victor Valdés. 'It was hard to tell if he was cheerful or sad. He always looked the same.'

If training went well, he became defiant. He'd show them.

At La Masía, where no one was allowed to watch, there were big holes in the green nylon tarps set up as a privacy shield. The journalists and fans peered through the holes, always ready to run away when the security men came. They watched the centre-forward Patrick Kluivert shoot on the turn, moving sublimely; his shot, as planned landed seven yards in front of the goal and bounced out of the goalkeeper's reach. Robert was already diving, and tensed his body once more. Just before the ball flew into the corner of the net he got to it, no one could really tell how. Afterwards, still on the grass, he was filled once more with the pure joy that only a spectacular save can produce. The fans cheered, his team-mates cheered. And a moment later almost everyone forgot what they had seen.

Barça had concerns that outweighed a substitute goalkeeper's state of mind. After six games the club was eleventh in the championship – an unbearable ranking. The team had been bought in a hurry and it lacked balance: it lacked an outstanding defensive midfield player in particular. Highly regarded internationals like Frank de Boer and Gaizka Mendieta were out of shape, and van Gaal had demoted Riquelme, the saviour, to the status of a bench-warmer. For this team with too many problems, van Gaal's ruthless approach was exactly what they didn't need. 'Things got ugly,' says Bonano. 'The atmosphere was crazy, something different every day. Sometimes the coach was furious and he would insult a player, or else a member of the board would tear into us. Every day I tried to be happy when I went to work. But it was hard.'

In the hope of finally repairing something, at the end of October the coach switched goalkeepers. Valdés had never quite been able to shake off his youthful nervousness. Van Gaal put Roberto Bonano in his place.

Until then Bonano had been third-choice keeper at Barcelona.

'Just three months had passed since Robert's euphoric arrival in Barcelona,' said Jörg Neblung, 'and already people started writing as if it were perfectly natural that Barça would sell him at the next possible opportunity.'

After training Robert would walk the twenty metres from La Masía to the changing-rooms, his studs clicking on the tarmac. That short stretch was usually enough to make him collapse inwardly after the enormous commitment he had put into his training. The fact that he trained so well only reminded him how hopeless his situation was.

Frans Hoek, the goalkeeping coach, sometimes accompanied him. Whenever Hoek said something to him Robert always replied politely, often with a smile. But he no longer spoke first to Hoek. The coach didn't notice. 'After training Hoek always went straight to his computer and worked on his share transactions, or something,' said Robert, almost shouting with rage. It took me a moment to understand what was so bad about that. Hoek couldn't see how much he craved a word of praise, to be asked: how's it going, Robert?

'A goalkeeper has so much pressure, from inside, from outside. The goalkeeping coach should always be the friend of the goalkeeper,' says Walter Junghans, Robert's mentor in Lisbon.

'Robert Enke was a loveable person with good manners,' Hoek says. 'Sometimes, with a goalkeeper like that, you must – figuratively speaking – throw a bucket of cold water over his head so that he wakes up and faces the hard reality of football.'

Esto no! was Hoek's battle-cry. Victor Valdés does a good imitation of his loud Dutch accent: *Esto nooo! Not that!* Still today Hoek is seen as one of the most competent and innovative goalkeeping coaches, but in his school you apparently don't notice if one of your goalkeepers is suffering. 'I sometimes said to Enke and Bonano, "You're too nice,"' says Hoek. 'Football's a hard world. As a player you sometimes have to be brutal. Victor was the only one who had a bit of *mala leche*, as they say in Spain – bad milk in his veins. A bit of the Oliver Kahn mentality, they might say in Germany. I could have wished for more rivalry between the three of them.'

Robert longed for understanding, Hoek shouted *Esto no!* Robert took it personally: Hoek didn't like him, Hoek was treating him unfairly, Hoek bore a grudge against him because he had failed in Novelda. He no longer noticed that Hoek was just as cruelly honest with the other two keepers. 'Hoek often came down on me too, you can be sure of that,' Bonano says.

Hoek remains convinced that his relationship with Robert was impeccably professional. The odd tense moment of course, but it wasn't meant personally.

Robert often rang Walter Junghans during his time in Barcelona.

Jörg, Teresa, Robert's father and Marco complained about Hoek. They moaned about van Gaal, too, wasn't he watching properly during training? For brief moments their fury felt good. But the truth, as Robert saw it, came back all too quickly. He, and he alone, was to blame. He had failed in Novelda. He had blundered, he was sure of it.

Just as Teresa regularly scribbled a few notes in her diary, he once wrote down, bluntly and without further explanation, this quote in his appointments diary: 'It doesn't matter whether what you believe is true. What matters is whether it helps you.'

Why couldn't he bend reality so that it looked nicer to him? Victor Valdés had made mistakes, against Atlético, Betis, Osasuna. But Victor stayed so cool. He had a face like a mask. Nothing seemed to trouble him. Why couldn't he be like that?

'You're playing in Bruges,' Hoek suddenly told him.

After four out of six Champions League group matches Barcelona had qualified for the next stage, so the fifth game against the Belgian champions on 29 October was insignificant.

You have nothing to lose, Robert.

He tried to believe it.

A few hours before kick-off he called Teresa, as usual. 'You could have recorded our conversation on a cassette and then just wiped it again – it was always the same,' she says.

How are you, we went for a walk, now we're having a coffee, right then, okay, see you tonight.

But this time he added, 'Please wish me luck.'

Her stomach did a somersault. He had never let her wish him luck before. That only brought bad luck.

She had never felt more clearly how tormented he was by the fear of failure. And she couldn't do anything more for him than say those few words, which she found she could barely utter. 'I wish you a lot of luck,' she said. She felt as if she weren't saying the words, but spitting them out.

'After that I felt ill.'

In Bruges, FC Barcelona wore jogging pants and tops rather than the custom-made Grisby suits customary on Champions

League trips. Given the irrelevance of the game, the coach had left seven established players at home and instead taken along six young men from the B-team, who had no club suits. 'Baby Barça' was the name the press gave to the team. 'It would be a shame if we couldn't win against a team like that,' said Bruges's captain Gert Verheyen. Bruges were still fighting to make it through to the next stage.

Novelda was two months in the past. Robert Enke hadn't played in public for seven weeks.

The Jan Breydes Stadium is the jewel in Belgian football's crown, rectangular, narrow, the most beautiful stadium in the country. Here France and Spain contested one of the greatest games of the decade, in the European Championship in 2000. When the terraces are full, they pressurise the playing-field. The game was sold out. The fans were wrapped in winter coats and scarves. Most of the Bruges players wore shirts with short sleeves.

The game couldn't find its direction. Baby Barça had the ball, led by an eighteen-year-old beginner with the porcelain skin of an angel and a heavenly touch – what's his name, the fans asked one another; Andrés Iniesta or something. Bruges worked busily and with great concentration to make sure that Barça had no room to manoeuvre. The ball hardly left midfield. Robert had more than enough time to think; to remember. The game was like the one in Novelda.

Then, all of a sudden – and professional football is all about suddenness – Bruges's Sandy Martens had sight of goal. He was still a good distance away from Robert, more than twenty yards, but Bruges wouldn't easily get any closer, Martens felt, and he shot. Before Robert took off, just as the striker was preparing to shoot he did a little hop on the spot, with arms outstretched, as if summoning up some momentum; in truth it was just a nervous reaction, but it helped him to concentrate, to fill his body with tension before discharging it. He leapt and parried Martens's powerful shot. After fifty-eight minutes of play he kept out a similar attempt by Verheyen, aimed at the back corner. For saves like that, goalkeepers are remembered.

In a game that splashed around rather than flowed, Riquelme, the saviour who had been demoted to the status of relief staff, put Baby Barça 1–0 up. There were twenty-five minutes left, twenty-five minutes during which Robert constantly fidgeted, his concentration at its highest level. Bruges were suddenly there again – but he never needed to intervene because there was a defender's leg in the way. The game was nearly over. One more attack, Bruges on the left wing, a fine exchange of passes suddenly leaving two of Baby Barça's defenders running at nothing; Ristic on the ball, free, by the corner of the box; he could shoot, instead he crosses high, fast, towards the six-yard line. The goalkeeper must come out and collect the ball, but ahead of him is a five-man buffalo-herd, three enemies, two friends, and he'll just bounce off them if he tries to take the cross. Robert takes two steps forward, then stops. Martens is the first to get his head to the ball. The fans behind Robert's goal jump into the air with their arms aloft, the ones with the quickest reactions already shouting 'Goal!' The header is firm and well directed. At the last moment Robert tips it over the bar. The fans' hands go to their heads and they forget to shut their mouths.

'Riquelme decided a game in which Iniesta and Enke shone,' it said on the front page of *El Mundo Deportivo* the morning after the 1–0 victory. Francisco Carrasco, known as 'Lobo', the Wolf, European Cup winner in 1979 with Barça and now an analyst with *Mundo Deportivo*, wrote, 'Enke's performance was a message to Louis van Gaal: I'm here if you need me', and the trainer, who was constantly barking, revealed a compassionate side. No one is emotionally one-dimensional, even van Gaal can be sympathetic, it just isn't always so easy to spot it. He never talked in public about individual players, the trainer said at the press conference, 'but a goalkeeper is a lonely player, which is why today he deserves a special mention: Enke was very good, in the end he saved our victory for us'.

Robert, Teresa noted in her diary, 'no longer wanted to admit that he had played a terrific game'.

One game wasn't going to change anything. He would remain a substitute. Bonano was now number one and playing well.

Once a goalkeeper had ended up on the subs bench it was hard for him to come off it again; you didn't switch goalkeeper at the drop of a hat. Three years earlier, at Benfica, Bossio had never been given another chance, just because he had once blown it during the pre-season match against Bayern Munich, and Robert had profited from Bossio's misfortune. But not many people remember the luck they once enjoyed in the past in situations where fortune seems to be favouring others.

Quiet, brief joy such as he'd felt after the game in Bruges only ever made Robert think about how pointless everything was. The day after his magnificent display in Belgium, he devoted himself to his worries. He was the first of the Barça team to call Patrik Andersson to enquire about his health after an operation on his thigh. Robert identified with people who were having a hard time.

After lunch Robert regularly went to Manresa, half an hour to the north, inland, near the gleaming mountain of Montserrat, Catalonia's national symbol. Teresa worked mornings at the animal shelter in Manresa. When he visited they took the shelter's dogs for walks. They had to take most of them out individually so that they didn't squabble and fight; they'd walk a circuit ten times in a row.

With their new friends from the German colony in Sant Cugat they drove to the beach at Sitges, they had barbecues in the garden; Robert went jogging with the men and cheered on Teresa and Dickens at horse-jumping shows – who would have thought that old chestnut horse would jump like that? It was November, and they were living in the sun. He could still forget, at least for a few hours, when he relaxed with friends. If he was suddenly absent for a moment, mid-conversation, mid-laughter, no one said anything. People always treat a professional footballer, a star, with special consideration, even friends, even if they don't intend to.

One Sunday he rang me. 'Have you heard what Victor's done?'

Victor Valdés, twenty years young, a Primera División

professional for only four months, had turned the world upside down. He was mutinying against van Gaal. After Valdés lost his place to Bonano the trainer sent him back to the B-team so that he could keep his hand in. He wasn't having it, Valdés explained. 'My team is the first team.' He didn't turn up for the B-team game against Segunda B side FC Reus. He turned off his phone.

Louis van Gaal, who usually roared all the time, was speechless.

'Victor knows no self-doubt,' said Robert. It sounded admiring, it sounded irritated. 'And of course I sometimes wonder, what if I was like that?'

'I made a lot of youthful mistakes,' says Valdés, and the huge eagle on his black T-shirt flexes its wings. 'But you must understand the situation. A season earlier I got an offer from FC Villarreal. I phoned van Gaal: "I can go to Villarreal." And van Gaal said to me, "No, stay, I'll give you a chance in the first team." When he sent me back to the B-team, I felt betrayed. Today I understand what the coach was aiming for. At the time I felt humiliated.'

Four days after he, a twenty-year-old newcomer, had openly challenged the autocratic coach, Valdés apologised, without really appreciating that he had done anything wrong. He was allowed back in, 'but nothing will be as it was before', warned van Gaal. Valdés would do extra shifts with Frans Hoek. No one mentioned the idea of punitive training; he would have to catch up with what he'd missed, they said. The other substitute goalkeeper was to join in – it couldn't hurt.

Alone with Valdés and Hoek, Robert trained at La Masía. The goalkeeping coach shouted, '*Esto no*, Victor. You're going down too early, you're speculating. I want you to wait a long time before the shot comes, like van der Sar.' After a quarter of an hour Valdés, spitting with fury, called off the training session. 'It ended badly,' he says. 'Hoek and I were throwing footballs at each other.' Robert stood to the side in amazement, doubting himself at least twice as much as he doubted Victor.

But something's wrong. Something does not add up as Victor Valdés sits on the designer sofa in the Portakabin talking about the old days. The Valdés on the sofa seems the exact opposite of the Valdés he's describing. 'At the time I was very withdrawn,' he explains openly. 'I didn't watch football on television because I thought I had to isolate myself from everything to do with the game.'

A baby and a coach transformed him, says Valdés: his son Dylan, now a year old, who has filled him with joy, and Pep Guardiola, a coach who wants more than mere success – his players are supposed to love the sport as fiercely as he does. Victor, said Guardiola, if you go on like this, eventually your career will be over and you won't have enjoyed this wonderful job for a single day because you're always tense, because success is the only thing you want. Watch some football on TV, try to understand the game. 'Pep completely changed my view of football. He taught me to lower the intensity during a game and coldly analyse what was going on rather than just lurking there with grim resolution.'

Victor Valdés became Barça's undisputed goalkeeper, a Champions League winner in 2006, 2009 and 2011, who plays as confidently as van der Sar.

So was Robert right to think that Valdés wasn't affected by anything, that he knew no doubts, no anxieties, on the football field? 'Perhaps Robert thought about blunders more than I did. Certainly at the time I didn't care about anything. I'd ended up in a state where mistakes simply slipped off me.'

Then Valdés smiles, a man so self-contained that he can happily remember even the worst of times. 'You know, between the ages of eight and eighteen there was so much pressure in my life that I couldn't find peace.' Everything revolved around football, and 'the mere thought of next Sunday's game horrified me. Playing in goal was, to put it mildly, a special sort of suffering.' The fear of making mistakes, the fear of disappointing others – we've heard that before.

Robert kept his distance from Valdés. They were friendly, but their conversation remained superficial. Mostly from that distance Robert watched his rival with a mixture of admiration and annoyance. How much good would it have done him to learn that this supposedly invulnerable adolescent had once experienced the same anxieties?

After training Robert and I often met in the lobby outside the Camp Nou changing-rooms, whose walls were hung with oil paintings of dramatic sea-battles. We'd sink into the leather sofas and talk with the passion of philosophers about goal-keeping gloves – about why, for instance, the seam on the thumb had to face outwards. He still loved the gossip of the goalkeeping guild.

'I'm not surprised things aren't going well for the team,' he said to me at the end of 2002, and that was a surprise for a moment, given Barça's quality – until he carried on. 'I'm familiar with that. Teams that I play on always fall short of expectations.' But his face wasn't joining in with any self-irony now. His eyes barely stirred. He seemed to be talking without moving his mouth. 'You have to keep telling yourself there are other things besides football, but . . .' He left the sentence unfinished. 'I've got moody.'

I told him what I had heard from an agent, the South African Rob Moore. At the begnning of December, Barça's managing director Javier Pérez Farguell had given some middlemen with international contacts like Moore a list of seven professionals who were up for sale in the winter break. Robert's name was on it.

He didn't reply. His face was frozen. His eyes were those of a man in search of a lost laugh.

Eike Immel, Christoph Daum's goalkeeping coach at Austria Wien, phoned. They were building an exciting squad with a huge sponsor. They were very interested in Robert.

Austria. Robert was just discovering that things weren't always necessarily wonderful at the biggest clubs, but the placid Austrian league was perhaps going too far the other way.

Immel called again. At first it would just be a loan – six months.

He wasn't thinking about changing clubs at the moment, said Robert.

Barça entered the Christmas holidays tenth in the table. Madrid's Galácticos had collected almost twice as many points. 'You know what happened here again today?' Robert said to Marco Villa on the phone. 'Van Gaal got up on a massage bench in front of the whole team and yelled at us from above.'

The nomadic spirit was driving Robert and Marco further and further apart. To Lisbon, Barcelona, Ried, Athens and Nuremberg they wandered, but however far they ended up from each other they stayed in close contact. They could only see each other once or twice a year, but Robert had got used to this long-distance friendship long ago. He believed 'that you only have three or four real friends in life' and rarely the good fortune to live in the same town as them. Marco and Christina came to Sant Cugat for New Year's Eve. It was a kind of honeymoon. They had got married before Christmas, and football left them no time for a proper honeymoon *and* visiting friends, so they combined the two.

They saw in the New Year at the Plaça de Catalunya. At midnight, with each of the chimes that announced the start of 2003 they swallowed a grape, following the Spanish New Year tradition, *las uvas de suerte* – the grapes of good luck.

'Robbi and I are going home, we're tired,' Marco said a little later.

Teresa gave Robert a critical look. Was he lapsing into melancholy again?

Teresa and Christina went dancing with friends. Robert and Marco went off to their beds. Or so they said. At home in Sant Cugat they opened a bottle of wine. 'Tell me stories from our time in the army again,' said Robert. When Teresa and Christina got home at four in the morning they heard loud laughter coming from the living-room.

At some point over the next few days Teresa had an opportunity to speak to Marco on his own. 'You're one of the few people Robbi will open up to. Please try and help him.'

Marco had always seen clowning around as his forte. 'If you had asked me when I was nineteen about the mind I'd have said, "What's that?"' But he's a dedicated sportsman with a strong urge to achieve goals, so he stubbornly set about pulling his friend out of a life that was lived almost entirely within. You don't sound good today, Robbi; how are things between you and the goalkeeping coach? he asked. Robert usually quickly turned the conversation to other people, events or objects so that he didn't have to talk about himself. Marco went on asking him questions.

It would take years, but eventually Robert would phone him of his own accord if he was in a bad way.

They were only fifteen when Marco, playing for North Rhine, stormed the Thuringian goal on his own during the federal states Youth Cup in Wedau. He saw the goalkeeper in front of him, he knew Robert Enke from the Germany youth team, and the thought ran through his head: you'll never score against him! He shot, Robert saved, Marco heard the cries of disappointment from his team-mates and he lowered his head. The goalkeeper, on the ground, with the ball in his damned hands, smiled at him and said sympathetically to Marco, 'Next time you'll score.'

You don't forget something like that.

At the age of seventeen Villa was bought by Borussia Mönchengladbach from Uerdingen; he was a youth player, but Borussia paid a professional transfer fee, 500,000 German marks. After six months the assistant trainer told him, 'You should be training with the Bundesliga team.'

'But I'm still at school.'

'Then you'll just have to give up school.'

On Saturdays Marco stood as a ball-boy at the edge of the pitch during Borussia's Bundesliga games. He recalls feeling a great rush whenever the stadium announcer said, 'Goal to Borussia! By number nine, Martin Dahlin!', and the cheering of the crowd buzzed like electricity in the air. 'It was the only dream I had: just once to hear the stadium announcer at the

Bökelberg say my name.' He left school a year and a half before his A-levels.

In August 1996 the stadium announcer said, 'Goal to Borussia! By number thirty-two, Marco Villa!' He was eighteen, Borussia's youngest ever Bundesliga striker. After seven games he had scored three goals; nothing like it had ever happened in Germany before. 'Villamania' his team-mate Kalle Pflipsen called it. 'We'll be celebrating – with non-alcoholic beer,' his father told the television reporters who interviewed him as well, because all of a sudden everything about Marco seemed important. 'I had heard the stadium announcer say my name,' says Marco. 'I had no dreams any more.'

He's driving his little Toyota along a country road, right next to the A14 between Giulianova and Resto degli Abruzzi. He's been playing in Italy for seven years, for L'Aquila Calcio right now, and he's unconsciously assumed some of the country's customs, like using rural roads to avoid paying the motorway toll. He recently heard a song on the radio, by Andrea Bocelli, and Marco, who has been listening very closely to song-lyrics lately, recognised himself in the refrain: 'No one taught me how to live life.'

During their time together at Borussia, when Marco and Robert shared a hotel room on away trips, they were in Los Angeles for a training-camp when one evening Marco announced, 'I'm going out again.' Robert rolled his eyes. Marco winked at him and disappeared.

As he crept through the underground car park out of the hotel, big Stefan Effenberg was making his way through the hotel lobby to the door.

'Effe, where are you going?' called the coach.

'Just to get a breath of air.'

'Oh, okay.'

With Effenberg and two other players, Marco stayed in a nightclub until the early hours of the morning. 'In five years' time,' Effenberg said to him, 'either you're going to be a great player or no one will remember you.' Marco took it as a compliment.

Then he tore his cruciate ligament for the first time. After four years with Borussia he had played twenty-four games, only two of them over the whole ninety minutes. To those

Robert with Teresa and his best friend Marco Villa (left).

three goals from his first seven games he had added only one. Marco had a dozen or more images of near misses in his head, and they wouldn't go away. Ried, Athens, Nuremberg – everywhere he went the coaches saw the talent he had revealed in Mönchengladbach, and everywhere injuries got in the way. In Nuremberg he was out of action for fourteen out of twenty months – his knee, his muscles, always something new. After rehab training he sometimes had lunch at the students' canteen with Nuremberg's goalkeeping coach Michael Fuchs. Fuchs had food tokens. 'Eh, Villa? Cheap here, isn't it?' said a student who recognised him, and Marco enjoyed the tease. He was a clown, after all.

At home his wife was crying.

'What's up with you?'

She threw herself on the floor and drummed her fists on the carpet. 'You're only normal when you're injured.'

'Nonsense,' said Marco. He wasn't injured at the time so he was too consumed by an internal pressure to perform to think about what was wrong with him. Instead he thought anxiously for a few minutes about whether the canteen lunches might be damaging his form.

The first time he began to wonder must have been in early spring 2003. He had kept his promise to Teresa not just to talk about what he and Robert were doing, but about how they were. Six months after Novelda, Robert was in a better state. Van Gaal had been fired, but Bonano was still playing under the new coach, Radomir Antić. 'But,' Robert told Marco, 'something I think: I'm almost happier when I'm just a substitute player.'

'What?' said Marco, and only thought about it after he'd put the phone down. He actually felt exactly the same.

Robert's mood had improved, even though his situation at Barça hadn't. Had time healed wounds? Had he discovered a way to deal better with setbacks? Had he actually discovered the happy substitute's secret of being able to watch a game without any stress? 'I think mostly it had something to do with the fact that the end of the season was approaching,' says Jörg Neblung. 'Robbi knew he would have to change clubs then, so he didn't take everything that happened at Barça all that seriously anymore.'

He'd phased out the sessions with Dr Geldschläger. He couldn't have said whether the conversations had helped him or not, but he was sure of one thing: not going any more helped him. It gave him the feeling of having left something behind.

His mother and Teresa's parents visited at the same time. Teresa's parents went to the museums – Miró, Picasso, the Contemporary Art Museum – Gisela took the train to the harbour every day, sat in a little café where the waiter greeted her with a beaming smile, and looked at the sea. 'Teresa's mother knows much more about art than I do,' Gisela says. 'I'd just have felt strange going to museums with her.' As always, Gisela's presence brought out her son's casual humour, as if he was inspired by her panache.

Good luck, then, the combined parents said as Robert waved goodbye before the Champions League match against Bayer Leverkusen.

Robert with Teresa's family.

Teresa dropped him off at the stadium. He went to the changing-room, and right behind the door he looked as usual at the sheet of paper stuck to the wall with sellotape.

His name wasn't on the list.

No one had told him anything, he had just been quietly crossed off, even from the subs bench. In professional football, where people talk a lot about each other but not much with each other, that's a way of forcing a player to resign.

He trotted out of the stadium in a trance. He stood in the

car park, so dumbfounded that he forgot that taxis and trains existed. He thought, how am I going to get home?

He guessed it wasn't just by chance that he had been eliminated from the game against Leverkusen, a club from his homeland. His humiliation was to be as complete as possible. Radomir Antić was a coach who came down on the weakest players when he wanted to demonstrate his strength.

Back home in Sant Cugat the parents fluttered nervously around. How were they to deal with Robert without becoming an additional burden? What could they do to stop him from slipping back into despair? He did what only Teresa usually did in stressful situations. He went to smoke a cigarette on the terrace. He didn't feel much better afterwards, the humiliation hurt, but he could deal with it. 'Why should I get agitated?' he said. His voice faded away, it went blank. 'I've been dead to Barça for ages.'

Eike Immel phoned again. Things in Vienna weren't looking so hot as he had thought. But in the summer he and Christoph Daum were moving to Fenerbahçe. Istanbul was just crazy – the fans, the enthusiasm, enormous potential, absolutely underestimated. They should sit down together. They were very interested in taking him with them.

Turkey. The word sounded strange, far away. It sounded like the end of the football world.

It was too early to make a decision, he managed to say, but many thanks for the offer.

It would be a long summer, Jörg Nebling warned him. So far there had only been offers from Fenerbahçe, FC Carinthia and FC Bruges. 'Not all that exciting if you're coming from Barça,' said Jörg. His contract in Barcelona lasted another two seasons. Jörg had spoken on the phone several times to managing director Pérez Farguell to find out whether Robert was to go or whether he could stay. Pérez used a lot of words to say nothing at all. Barça preferred to pass on its messages symbolically.

Robert was allowed to turn up for training for the new

2003–04 season even though Barça had signed a new goalkeeper and promoted another one from the B-team. Five goalkeepers assembled at La Masía – two too many. Still no one said anything. This was considered respectful; Enke still had a contract, they weren't going to say straight out: just go. Another list was hung up in the changing-room, this one for a summer tour of the United States, and once again Robert wasn't on it, and the same thing happened to Roberto Bonano, who had been a solid shot-stopper in the Champions League quarter-final only weeks before. It was July, a year after Robert's arrival, and the lovely time in Barcelona was over almost before it had begun.

After an hour full of memories of Robert Enke, Victor Valdés's eyes filled up. 'People had written him off after Novelda. That often happened at Barça: a mistake, and the press ticks off the goalkeeper, and the public shouts, "Get rid of him!", as they did particularly in those days. After Zubizarreta's resignation we had a decade when no goalkeeper seemed to be good enough for Barça, and that reflex set in again immediately after Novelda: he's not the one either.' Valdés folds his arms in front of his chest. 'But I saw Robert at training every day, and I'd like to think I'm not mistaken when I see a goalkeeper. He was a great one.'

Robert had only played three and a half games for Barça: two in the Champions League, when there was nothing at stake, twenty minutes against Osasuna, when Bonano was injured, and in Novelda. But was he really any worse than Bonano or Valdés?

'He had problems adjusting to Barça's particular way of playing. But I think in most aspects he was a level above me at the time.' This from Valdés, the man who became Barça's undisputed number one the following season. 'If Novelda hadn't happened, Robert would have become a very good goalkeeper for Barça.'

'Of course,' says Teresa, a life's journey away, up in northern Germany, 'I sometimes wondered how life would have continued if that one game had gone differently.' She has found her own answer. 'Presumably nothing at all would have been different. Presumably he would have blundered in the next game, or the one after that. In those days he wasn't a match for the pressure at Barça.'

We were in the garden in Empede, Barcelona was four years in the past, it was summer, and Robert, equipped like almost all goalkeepers with two left hands when it came to DIY, said, 'Did you see that I've put up this parasol all by myself?' That was when I first dared to ask about Novelda.

'Even now, at the sound of that word everything inside me contracts,' he said. 'When I think about Patrik Andersson's face when he furiously yelled at me the next morning. "You can't put up with that from de Boer!" Or the heat on the air-conditioned team bus before the game.' When he'd been sweating on the inside.

After they left Spain, Teresa went back to Barcelona several times to visit her friends in Sant Cugat. Every time she did, he came up with a reason not to go.

ELEVEN

Wrapped in Fog

La Masía lay deserted in the half-shade of the massive stadium walls. It would take the morning sun another good hour to bathe the whole pitch in harsh light, but the heat of the day was already in the air. The silence screamed at Robert Enke: they have left you behind.

The previous day FC Barcelona had set off for the United States. Robert, Roberto Bonano and striker Dani García had to train by themselves at La Masía. The emptiness reminded the three men of everything that was no longer there: the laughter of team-mates, the rhythmical thunk of the ball when Barça passed it, the eternal hope of summer that this time the season would all turn out fine. The silence of La Masía screamed at them: you're not needed any more, find another club as soon as possible.

It was a Monday; July was almost over. In Germany and England the new season was due to begin in a few days' time. It was unrealistic to think that a suitable offer might reach him now.

'We have no alternative to Fenerbahçe,' said Jörg, 'and if we look at it soberly, it's not the worst club in the world. The salary's okay, and you can become a champion there and put yourself in the shop window again.'

'We'll make it,' said Teresa. 'It's only a year, after all.'

They had been telling him that for days, but Robert said nothing. At the time the Turkish league was seen as a collecting point for players who had had a hiccup in their career. In Robert's eyes, Turkey was synonymous with failure.

*　*　*

Mid-July. Two weeks earlier, on the way back from holiday in Germany to Barcelona, Robert had visited Fenerbahçe's German coaches at a training-camp in Bitburg.

Meet them at least once, Jörg and Teresa had said to him.

He dined with Christoph Daum and Eike Immel in the hotel restaurant. The weather was still nice enough to sit on the terrace. Teresa was by his side. Daum opened his eyes wide and spoke as if auditioning for a part in the theatre, Immel was naturally cordial, and delighted in throwing in anecdotes from the old days. Robert, whom Teresa had only seen drunk once in her life, when he was seventeen, kept generously topping himself up with red wine.

Someone still valued him as a goalkeeper. For an evening, the thought filled him up. He relaxed, he asked a lot of questions: what sort of quality was Fenerbahçe's defence, could you get by with English in Istanbul. How pleasantly natural Teresa and Robert were, what calm determination emanated from them, it occurred to Immel. 'When Daum and I drove away, we were really euphoric. "It's *got* to be him," we said to each other.'

Two weeks later, after that Monday training session at a deserted La Masía, Robert was driving home when he decided to phone Jörg.

'I've talked myself round. German coaching team, good money, let's just try it.'

When Jörg Neblung got to Istanbul he thought he had arived in a biblical scene. 'And he divided the waters' – he couldn't help thinking of that passage in the Old Testament when he stepped out of Ataturk airport next to Christoph Daum. Hundreds of fans received the coach and his retinue, hands and heads stretched towards them, but they could walk quickly because simply by moving forward Daum found he could part the human waves. After many antics and the very public documenting of his cocaine consumption, Daum had ruined his reputation in Germany. In Turkey he was somebody. In the mid-nineties he had turned the Istanbul club Besiktas into champions and cup-winners. The previous season Fenerbahçe had finished sixth – a terrible disappointment for the most popular club in the country; Daum represented a promise that everything would be good again.

For Robert it was the usual scenario. After Mönchengladbach, Benfica and Barça, he had once again ended up with a club whose current performance was no match for past glories.

He arrived in Istanbul shortly after Jörg, on his own. Teresa would stay with friends in Sant Cugat, along with the dogs, and regularly visit him, they had agreed. He was to spend only a season in Turkey, it was just a stop-gap. Maybe after that he would even go back to Barça; his contract there had only been suspended for a year. He himself had insisted that they were on no account to move to Istanbul for good. He wanted to avoid the feeling that the decision was final; he needed the certainty that he could go back to Sant Cugat at any time, even if it was only for a few days off. But now he was alone, for the first time in his life.

The number of fans at the airport had dwindled to a few individual groups. A few then recognised him and shouted something that he didn't understand. To judge by their faces the words were friendly, but how could he be sure? He knew what it said in the papers. Fenerbahçe had sold the Turkish national goalkeeper Rüstü Reçber, a great hero, to Barça. Club president Aziz Yildirim, who was used to making decisions by decree, had dreamed of having France's world champion, Fabien Barthez, as a replacement. And then Daum had insisted on bringing in this German, who Yildirim didn't even know, and who Barça didn't want any more! The Turkish papers had passed judgement before he landed in Istanbul. What business did a substitute goalkeeper have at Fener?

He had to get up on a podium in front of these newspaper reporters. Two buttons of his white shirt were open, his shirt hung casually from his trousers – Istanbul in August. The photographers gestured to him to stand near Fenerbahçe's blue and yellow flag. He put one hand on the club flag, and with his other hand gave the cameras the thumbs-up as a sign meaning 'Brilliant to be here, great to be playing for Fenerbahçe!' His face said the opposite. His cheeks were red, his eyes wide and uneasy.

Jörg decided to pretend not to be aware of Robert's tension. He didn't want to make it any worse by addressing it. Instead he sent a request to Yildirim asking whether he might be prepared to pose for a photograph with Robert. Such a picture might relax the situation a bit, creating the impression that the club president thought highly of the new goalkeeper, or at least tolerated him.

Yildirim ignored the request.

It doesn't matter, Jörg tried to reassure himself. The important thing is for the coach to stand by Robert.

They drove to the hotel the club had booked for Robert – a high-class place, but one of fading charm, amid the sea of houses on the Asian side of the city. Pierre van Hooijdonk, Robert's friend from his Lisbon days, who was signed by chance at the same time as Fenerbahçe's new star striker, was being put up in a luxury hotel on tree-lined slopes on the other side, with a view across the Bosphorus.

Robert didn't want to go out.

Jörg stayed with him there for three days. Once he'd arranged for Robert to move to van Hooijdonk's hotel, he set off cheerfully, because 'the conditions looked

Robert with the Fenerbahçe flag after signing the contract.

good for him to settle in quickly', with his old friend van Hooijdonk nearby, two or three German Turks like Ali Günes from Freiburg on the team, German coaches, and a city which, in districts like Galata and Beyoglu, was as lively as his beloved Lisbon.

He drove to training with van Hooijdonk every day, a simple forty-kilometre journey – and they didn't even have to go as far as the end of the city. The traffic flowed chronically slowly on the Bosphorus Bridge. Robert thought, it's lucky Pierre's here, at least I'll have a bit of fun. Pierre thought, what's up with Robert? He got worked up about everything – about the traffic, about his team-mates' lack of concentration, about everything. After that he wouldn't speak at all for ages.

An estate agent employed by the club showed him some flats. Okay, he'd take that one – just so that the decision was made.

We once spoke on the phone. I mentioned in passing that I was going out for sushi with a friend. That banal word 'sushi' set something off in him. 'And here I am stuck in traffic in Istanbul on this fucking bridge!' He sounded so angry, or perhaps desperate, that I was taken aback.

Effectively he was only alone for three days. Jörg went, then Teresa visited. In the three days in between, Fener played a pre-season match against Kocaelispor. Thirty minutes before kick-off a sheep was sacrificed on the pitch. I'm glad Teresa isn't here yet with her love of animals, he thought. When she arrived at last in Istanbul he was already thinking about how he would cope without her for weeks after she left.

He showed her the flat he had found, and she was horrified. There was hardly any light in the room. It was the afternoon, it was summer, and Teresa had to turn on the lights in the kitchen. Startled by the sudden brightness, cockroaches fled.

'Robbi!'

'When I looked at the flat it seemed fine to me.'

'But now have a think about how we live in Barcelona. What was it that you liked about that so much?'

He shrugged.

'Teresa and I may have made some mistakes,' says Jörg. 'Because he'd been better in Barcelona, we thought he could cope with Istanbul, just as he picked himself up again after escaping from Lisbon, or even after Novelda.' For Teresa and Jörg, Robert was just a sensitive person who sometimes lost his equilibrium in extreme situations, but who then, once he had driven away the melancholy with tremendous self-control, emerged strengthened from the darkness.

Teresa helped him to find another flat in Istanbul and flew back to Barcelona four days later, one day before the start of the season. In a fortnight Jörg was coming out again, and she herself would be back in three weeks. They thought that once he had overcome his initial anxiety things would be fine, as they had been in Lisbon. He only had to convince himself how good he was in the first few games. With any luck nothing would happen until then.

Jörg sent a fax to Robert Enke, Swissotel, room 1296. 'Morning, Robbi, attached the current press cuttings. Spoke briefly on the phone to Eike yesterday; he told me you were making a very good and confident impression . . . nice to hear! There's no doubt about your status and your abilities – I hope you're receptive to statements like that at the moment!!! Otherwise I hope everything's Kebab. Gülegüle, Jörg.'

The night before the start of the 2003–04 Turkish season the teams stayed at Fenerbahçe's training-centre in Samandira, far to the east of the city. Robert had a single room and wanted to watch the Bundesliga – Bremen against Gladbach, Hannover against Bayern – just as he had always done at Benfica with José Moreira the night before a game. In Fenerbahçe he could only get one German channel, and that didn't have broadcasting rights for the Bundesliga.

Moreira hadn't been able to get through to Robert for weeks. After their time in Benfica they spoke regularly on the phone; Robert had always called back when he found the number of his little goalkeeping brother among his missed calls. Now there

179

was silence from Robert. 'This is the last number I had for him,' says Moreira, showing me his phone-book – it's a Spanish number. Later, Moreira talked to van Hooijdonk. 'How's Robert doing? You were with him at Fenerbahçe, weren't you?'

'Robert's not the same,' said van Hooijdonk. 'He doesn't talk any more. He's gone strange.'

Robert sat in his room in Samandira and the hours to kick-off dragged their feet. He looked for a piece of paper, found Jörg's fax, and wrote on the back 'Istanbul Diary'. Then he started writing.

10.08.2003. At the training-camp in Samandira. Tonight's the first league game. It's pretty bleak here.

I'm, as you would expect, not so great. It's a mixture of fear, nerves and homesickness. Homesickness for my life with Terri and the doggies. Terri flew off yesterday.

I often wonder why I did this thing with Fenerbahçe, and long for a time when I still had the decision ahead of me. I probably wouldn't be in a terrific state in Barcelona either, with no prospects, but I would have Terri, my friends and my milieu where I feel safe.

I'm a bit disappointed by the training staff. Daum should put a lot more stress on discipline. I barely have any contact with the team.

In that mood, he drove to the stadium.

It was forty kilometres back to the city centre; another traffic jam on the bridge. Fenerbahçe's stadium wasn't far from the Topkapi Palace, home to the Sultans, the rulers of the Ottoman Empire. The terraces were four yellow and blue walls made up of fifty-two thousand fanatics, their opponents, Istanbulspor, not worth bothering with.

Robert wore a gleaming dark-blue jersey with a hint of a V-neck and a pair of shorts almost as wide as a boxer's. He looked good in his new gear, strong yet agile. His face was only seen in photographs later on.

In Barcelona, Teresa escaped with Dickens. She rode into the forest and let the horse gallop. The speed forced her to concentrate on what she was doing and not think that a football match was happening right now in Istanbul.

Istanbulspor were on the brink of bankruptcy. At the end of the season the team would rescue itself from relegation with a single point's advantage. Fener tried to dominate the game, but Istanbulspor had come to defend – the prerogative of the small team. Fener couldn't get through. They started to get nervous. Then, only eighteen minutes into the game, a long pass was hit from Istanbulspor's half. Robert ran out but realised in a tenth of a second that he would never get to the ball. Istanbulspor's only striker, the Israeli Pini Balili – who had become a Turkish citizen called Atakan Balili – already had it, Fener's defenders far behind him. From nearly thirty yards out he lobbed it over Robert's head with gusto. The keeper, stuck on the eighteen-yard line, ran desperately back, chasing the shot, sensing that he would just be fetching it out of the net.

On the terraces, Eike Immel was convinced 'there was nothing he could do about that goal. It was preceded by an incredibly stupid misplaced pass from Selçuk, and the counter-attack so quickly that Robert didn't have time to correct his position.' Robert, on the other hand, shouted loudly at himself when he booted the ball away towards the centre circle. His foot got caught in some toilet paper that fans had thrown into his area. He thought someone had switched him into slow-motion. In his perception, everything seemed to be moving with extraordinary slowness. Later he remarked to Jörg, 'Everything was wrapped in fog.'

In the second half, the ball came to him after a back-pass. Robert showed no sign of doing anything with it. A murmur in the terraces swelled to a rumble. Immel felt his heart beating faster. Kick the ball away, man! he thought. The Istanbulspor players, who hadn't bothered to trouble the goalkeeper since the goal, hesitated; then the first of them, Balili, began to run at him. And still Robert didn't move. As if he didn't know what to do with the ball; as if he had forgotten how to execute a simple pass. Get rid of the thing, quickly! Immel wanted to shout.

Too late.

Balili swiped the ball away from Robert. There was confusion in Fener's box. Fifty-two thousand people were shouting, shrieking wildly, stunned by the chaos on the pitch. Finally a defender saw off the threat.

Immel needed time to recover from the shock. 'Robert had a complete brainstorm,' he said.

After fifty-seven minutes the score was 3–0 to Istanbulspor. Coins, lighters and bottles flew around Robert's ears. He knew his own fans were standing behind his goal.

When Teresa got back home she knew she could find the result on Teletext but came up with any excuse not to turn on the TV. She would shower first.

A quarter of an hour later, her phone rang.

'Hello, it's Gunnar.'

As children, Robert's friends had found it exciting that Robert had a brother who was six years older. His big brother could tell them something about music and girls. Gunnar had become a father at the age of twenty-one. Ever since Robert had become a travelling professional sportsman they'd only seen each other for a few days in the holidays, and spoken occasionally on the phone.

'Yes, Gunnar?' said Teresa.

'I just wanted to call.'

'Gunnar, if you know anything, then please tell me.'

'Yes. Three-nil.'

'Won or lost?'

'Lost.'

Teresa broke down on the stairs.

She tapped in his phone number again and again. 'It was dark outside by now,' remembers Jörg, who was trying as well. Finally Robert phoned Teresa back. He was on that bridge again, in the traffic jam.

He was coming home, he said. He was giving up.

'For God's sake, Robbi, don't do anything rash. Please sleep on it for a night at least, and let's talk about it again tomorrow.'

No, he had made the decision during the game. There was no more doubt about it.

'I understand how you feel, everyone feels like chucking it all in when things aren't going well. But afterwards it would only get worse. Keep at it for another week or two, one or two games, and you'll get through it, I know. We'll get through this. I love you.'

She was afraid that if he gave up he would collapse completely. And that he would never forgive himself.

Her words did me good, he wrote in his diary. But he'd been adamant on the phone: no, he couldn't do it any more. His career was over.

Robert made one more phone-call before switching off his phone so that no one could reach him.

Marco answered enthusiastically, as always, when he heard his friend's voice. After that he didn't say anything for a long time. 'I'm going to pieces here, I've got to get away, it's not working.' In Marco's memory, his friend's sentences circled constantly in his head, getting faster and faster and making him dizzy.

'Robbi, just relax, try to pull yourself together. And if that doesn't work, leave.'

'But then I'll be unemployed.'

'For six months, and what's that? You'll find another club in the winter transfer market.'

Marco was shocked by his friend's plan to jack everything in but less bemused with the prospect of being without football for six months. He had just switched voluntarily from 1 FC Nuremberg to AC Arezzo in Italy's Serie C. He'd believed that if he restarted his career at a distinctly lower level in a country where no one judged him by the three goals from his first seven Bundesliga games he would finally be rid of the constant pressure on his temples. Three days before his first game in

Italy he heard the coach talking about him on television, saying, 'He's a player you just have to click your tongue at.' Marco's temples immediately tightened again. He dragged himself stiffly, limply, impotently through that first game. 'If all you have is football, and it goes wrong,' Marco says, 'you're left with nothing but doubts.'

The next morning Robert woke up with the feeling that he had gone to sleep only a short time before. He had to get away from Turkey.

First of all, however, he looked for a sheet of paper.

11.08.2003. I'm finished. We lost the game 0–3. Didn't look good from the first goal. After that I was very nervous in the second half. Was mocked by some of the fans. Spoke today to Father, Jörg and Terri. Would like to get away from Istanbul, do a proper course of therapy at last. At any rate, it can't go on. Understood yesterday that I'm simply not up to the demands. Jörg tries to persuade me to have someone fly in or to take some medication. I don't want to do that, I don't want to do that here. Terri just rang and had to put the phone down again to cry. I feel helpless and anxious, I don't leave the hotel room, I'm afraid of people's eyes. I'd just like to live without anxiety and nerves. I know that breaking this contract will have far-reaching consequences, but I can't think about anything else. I don't know how to go on. I want to talk to Daum today, don't know how to put it. Afraid of his reaction. Know that I've missed the opportunity to start a course of therapy several times in the past.

The coach had given the team two days off because of the defeat. Not seeing each other was the best therapy, Daum believed. So Robert would have to call Daum. The red-hot fear of the game was back, building up inside him. What would he say to Daum?

His phone rang.

'Hello?'

'Robert, it's Eike.'

'Eike!'

'I'm sure you didn't sleep any more after that game than I did. I just wanted to say that if you fancy a coffee I'll drop by. We could take a boat-trip on the Bosphorus, too, so that you can see how beautiful the city is. Or, if you feel like it, we could do what Olli Kahn used to do after games like that and go and train till you puke, until you've got rid of all your frustration.'

'Eike, it's great that you've called. I was about to ring you. I've got a huge problem, but we can't talk about it on the phone.'

'I'll drop by at your hotel.'

It was Robert's voice that frightened Eike Immel. Had Teresa split up with him? Had someone in his family died? That would explain the hyper-nervous performance. 'I still see myself knocking on the door of his hotel room half an hour later, thinking: Shit, what happens now? I would never have expected what happened next.'

Thank God, Eike was a good guy, Robert thought. Always talking, always with a positive view of things, even though he had arthritis in his hip – he'd worn it out during twenty years as a professional goalkeeper. Not exactly ideal for a goalkeeping coach, but that wasn't the issue right now.

Light flooded through the wide windows into the hotel room. The Bosphorus glittered in the sun. On the opposite bank lay Asia.

Robert waited until Eike had sat down. The chairs were ochre-coloured rhomboids.

'I have to end my career.'

'Robert, what's up?'

'I can't go on. I'm just scared – scared to leave the hotel room, scared to open the paper, scared to put on my gloves.'

Eike thought back a couple of decades, to when he had been an international goalkeeper, a semi-finalist in the European Championship, and had precipitously announced his resignation from the national team when he thought the coach was suddenly keener on Bodo Illgner. 'I was scared before every season,' Immel says. 'Scared of my rival goalkeepers, scared of a new coach. On some days all it took was for me to discover a tiny hole in the pitch within the six-yard area – oh God, what if a shot lands in that dip? It'll be unsaveable.'

He knew Robert's fear, Eike thought, and he knew how quickly it could evaporate. One or two good games later and Eike had always thought: I hope my defence is really bad today so that I have to deal with fifteen serious shots – I can stop anything!

'Robert, you couldn't have done anything about those goals.' Eike really believed that. 'And the fact that you were nervous . . . how do you think I felt the first time I played for Manchester City, suddenly in a foreign country? In the first half against Tottenham I went flying under two crosses like an absolute beginner, and later on I had a really good time with City. It'll be like that for you, believe me.'

'It's pointless. The anxiety is there all the time. I can't go on. I don't want to go on.'

They talked for two hours before Eike realised that he had lost his goalkeeper. He called Daum, Robert sitting next to him. A short time later the coach came to room 1296. He was ending his career, Robert said, he needed treatment. He never mentioned the word depression, only anxiety. Daum listened, he nodded, he said he understood. He would help him to get out of his contract.

In the meantime, Jörg Neblung had got the number of a respected psychologist via the German Sports University in Cologne. He hoped she would be able to fly with him to Istanbul to examine Robert while he went on playing for Fener. He was the agent who covered his protégé's back, who had to strengthen him whenever he could, Jörg thought. He had left a message on the psychologist's answering machine.

His phone rang. Perhaps that was her. It was Daum. Jorg had to come to Istanbul immediately, he said.

*　　*　　*

Tuesday dawned, the second free day after the game against Istanbulspor. Robert had nothing to do but wait for Jörg. He watched the ships on the Bosphorus from his hotel room, dozens of ferries, oil tankers and steamers. Nowhere is water more alluring than in Istanbul. You can stare at the Bosphorus for ever, and the ships with their leisurely, even movements take you away and bring you back in your dreams. But he was gazing right through the river. His Istanbul consisted entirely of the hotel room.

He picked up the hotel biro with the blue ink and thin nib.

12.08.2003. I've finally got to learn to listen properly to what my belly or my mind says. I don't yet know why I did the thing with Fenerbahçe, probably because I thought I just needed to be needed again, and everything would regain its balance. But unfortunately it's not as easy as that. My year in Barcelona has changed me a lot. All the self-confidence that I built up in three years in Lisbon has been taken away from me. In my current state of mind I'm not properly equipped for football. For a long time I wouldn't admit it although I should have noticed: I was always glad when I didn't have to play, even in training games. When the coach left me out, I presented it as a great injustice (which might have been the case every now and again), but in reality I was always relaxed and happy when I was watching from the sidelines. I'm also really scared of the opinion of the public, the press, and people's eyes. I'm paralysed by fear. I don't know how long ago it is that I've gone into a game excited but relatively unstressed. In future I'll try to write from the soul a bit. I hope that helps.

'Are you already in Istanbul?' Teresa asked Jörg on the phone.

'In principle, yes.'

'What does that mean?'

'I've arrived, but I don't know if I'll ever get to the hotel. The taxi driver thinks it's appropriate to hurtle through the city at eighty miles an hour. And in case you don't believe me, he's got all the windows open, too.'

Teresa couldn't help laughing. As if they'd made a prior arrangement, Teresa and Jörg had been joking with each other since Sunday. Somehow there must be a way through the despair.

The next driver, sent by the club, was already waiting for Jörg at the hotel – windows closed, as he couldn't avoid noticing. Jörg greeted Robert only briefly because he had to get going. They would see each other later. Jörg didn't know where they were off to, so he had the feeling he was being taken to the furthermost corner of the city.

Before long he found himself sitting in a flat with Turkish carpets and lots of armchairs facing five men from the club. The president hadn't come: Yildirim had known straight away that this goalkeeper was beneath him. Jörg knew Daum and his personal assistant Murat Kus but not the other three men with their serious faces. He took them for vice-presidents but they weren't introduced to him. In fact they were already shouting at him. Kus translated in a jovial voice.

What was Jörg thinking of, what had been going on in his head, foisting such a goalkeeper on Fenerbahçe?

Jörg knew the stories about coach dismissals and player sackings in Turkey. In 2000, the president of Bursaspor had taken a gun out of his desk when his German coach Jörg Berger insisted that the terms agreed in his contract were to be honoured.

Jörg acted as if he hadn't heard anything. 'Robert needs a course of therapy, so unfortunately he has to go back to Germany. He's agreed that with the coach. I would therefore ask the club to grant him a few weeks off.'

'What? We're supposed to go on paying him while he takes a rest in Germany? He can have a course of therapy here, too. There are wonderful institutions for therapy like that in Istanbul.'

A servant walked through the room with a silver pot and silently and elegantly poured tea for the men.

'If Enke wants to go, he should go. But in that case the contract is dissolved and that's that!'

It wasn't as easy as that, said Jörg. If the contract was dissolved, Robert would be unemployed until the next transfer window opened in five months' time. The club would have to give him some sort of financial compensation.

'He's not getting any more money! Why do you want money? You won't get the money as far as the airport!'

He could see that they were upset, Christoph Daum said. The best thing would be for Neblung and Enke simply to go.

'I'll have a word with Robert and let you know tomorrow, but I'm sure he won't simply dissolve the contract and give up his salary,' said Jörg.

The conversation went round in circles for an hour, but then the vice-presidents, or whoever they were, stood up and left, without shaking hands. They talked loudly in Turkish and pointed at Jörg.

They made him wait for his driver. Daum stayed in the flat as well. He plainly had nothing more to say to Jörg. Without a word of explanation, Daum picked up his phone and rang the Brazilian middleman Juan Figer. Loudly and without the slightest inhibition, Daum was already negotiating for the next new arrivals. Jörg was still in the flat after midnight, not knowing where it was or who it belonged to. He wondered whether life was perhaps just a soap opera after all.

The next morning Robert had to act as if he was still a perfectly normal Fenerbahçe player. He had to go to training.

Daum took him aside. What on earth was his agent playing at, demanding money on top of everything? People in Turkey were hot-blooded, they could get very angry.

And Robert had only just begun to regard the coach as a friend.

In his diary he tried to get his thoughts in order:

14.08.2003. Fenerbahçe have threatened Jörg and me with open violence if we don't dissolve the contract forthwith.

Daum joined in, and didn't act as middleman in any way.
I was forced to accept that it was a mistake to open
myself up to this man.

'How are you?' Teresa asked on the telephone.

'Good – apart from the fact that they've hung me by my feet from the twelfth-floor window of the hotel,' Jörg said. And for a moment Robert laughed with them. Jörg had moved into Robert's hotel room. There was safety in numbers, he told Robert. Not being alone was better for Robert, he thought. Whenever they left the room, Jörg placed a wet hair across the door and frame so that he could check when he came back whether anyone had been in the room in their absence. It was a joke, to dispel the gloom, but at the same time it was serious. 'We had to be prepared for anything, even for our passports to be stolen, drugs to be smuggled into our suitcases, whatever.'

Robert made it clear that Jörg no longer had to take too much trouble over the negotiations. He wanted only one thing: to get out of Istanbul.

The contract was dissolved the same day. Fenerbahçe under-took to pay Robert's hotel expenses and his return flight. He didn't ask for another cent.

Fifteen days after he had arrived in Istanbul in his summer shirt, Robert set off for home. Fenerbahçe published a state-ment: the contract had been dissolved by mutual agreement. Robert told journalists about 'a feeling', and couldn't explain his decision in the first person: 'If something is simply wrong in a new milieu, and you don't feel right, you can't perform properly. And before you head towards an even unhappier situation, it's better to draw a line under it.' Daum commented, 'He was handicapped, but he only told me after the game.' The journalists concluded that Enke had gone into the game with an injury and had therefore damaged himself with 'his exaggerated ambition'.

Talking openly about his anxieties didn't seem like an option. In the world of football, most people shook their heads anyway. A professional didn't resign. That expectation was encapsulated in the word 'professional'. Being professional means repressing emotions, carrying on. And if things aren't working out on the pitch, then a professional just sits on the subs bench, secretly starts to look for a new club and takes his salary in the meantime. 'Lots of people said Enke has lost his marbles, and fair enough, if you look at it soberly, you could see it like that,' said Robert.

Only Jupp Heynckes, his coach in Lisbon, saw something else. 'For the first time in four years I remembered that at Benfica he'd also wanted to go home straight away. Then it occurred to me that he might have a more serious problem.'

According to FIFA regulations a player couldn't change clubs twice in one transfer window. Robert would indeed be unemployed for at least five months. Was he a lost soul, or was he free? When he thought about it at Ataturk airport, he thought you could be both at the same time, lost and free, defeated and relieved.

In his eagerness to leave Istanbul behind he had arrived at the airport five hours before the flight to Barcelona.

TWELVE

No Light, Not Even in the Fridge

When thoughts became overwhelming at night, Robert went to the loo. He sat on the toilet and waited in vain for weariness to return. Eventually he crept back through the dark house, hoping none of the dogs would start barking. Teresa was breathing evenly in the bedroom. He lay down beside her and closed his eyes, wanting to force sleep to come.

Why did I sign up with Fenerbahçe against my better judgement? And what if I could have stuck it out in Istanbul just a couple of weeks longer, like everybody said? I will never get out of this hole again . . .

When he woke up again one or two hours later, he felt as if he hadn't gone to sleep at all.

How deep can it really go? I pulled my tail in between my legs in Istanbul, and now I'm being punished. But what sort of punishment? Where is it all going to end?

At ten to eight he woke from his non-sleep. He kissed Teresa good morning, told her he was going on the long circuit with the dogs. But even when he was talking there was a heavy silence between them. He could hear it beyond his words. There were so many things he wanted to say to her; he had to tell her how he was. Four times in the night he had tried to flee his thoughts by going to the loo. He noted everything meticulously in his diary, treating himself quite ruthlessly. *The worst night I can remember*, he wrote. But whenever he started talking, the words sounded false, the sentences hollow.

He got dressed in silence, and said once again, just to break the silence, that he was going out with the dogs. He wanted to say something else. So many thoughts raged inside him, but at the same time not a single one came to mind; it was as if he was blocked up. He could still form sentences inside his head – Terri, I know I'm being impossible; please, I don't want to lose you – but the words caught in his throat, they couldn't find their way out. He still had precise ideas of how he wanted to behave, but watched, paralysed, as he got everything wrong.

How was Teresa to go on loving the man he had turned into?

He fled outside. Right behind the house was the nature reserve of Collserola; it was forest all the way to Barcelona. The mild September weather made him feel guilty. On such glorious days you should be happy. On days like this, a Monday in a normal working week during the football season, you shouldn't have time to go walking through the Collserola.

He knew he was sick. Dr Geldschläger had explained it to him. It had nothing to do with the fact that he was letting himself go, that he had to pull himself together. At the moment his brain wasn't sufficiently capable of processing stress. Only negative stimuli registered with his nervous system – fear, anger, despair. Had doctors opened up his head they would have discovered among other things, that the prefrontal cortex – in which, to put it simply, the human impulse arises – was under-active, and that was why he felt so limp. So there was a medical explanation for every facet of the behaviour he was unable to understand.

He suffered from depression.

Depressives are no longer capable of seeing things realistically. They see everything in a black, pessimistic, negative way.

But what good were all the explanations of his current state? Of what use was the fact that the illness reduced many other people around the world, regardless of intelligence or experience of life, to desperate wrecks? What he lacked was an explanation for how he was ever to find his way back out of the darkness.

I can't stand it much longer. Then I just lie there in bed in the morning.

Later, beside him at the breakfast table, separated from him by a thick wall of silence, Teresa was thinking the same thing – I can't stand it much longer – in a quite different way.

The states of anxiety and melancholy that had tormented Robert time and again over the course of the years were indications that he was susceptible to depression. But lots of people were afraid of disappointing themselves and others: Immel, Valdés and other goalkeepers even used that fear to remain concentrated, to tease from their bodies reactions only a person in danger is capable of. Being sad and desperate after shattering experiences, as he had been after Novelda, wasn't depression, it was simply human.

Nothing had prepared him and Teresa for what depressions really are.

He got up before eight every morning. He had to give the day a structure, do things, give his thoughts no chance to go round in circles, Dr Geldschläger had once impressed on him, but yet again his thoughts were starting to go round in circles. Why hadn't he taken the sessions with Dr Geldschläger seriously enough after Novelda? Could he have stopped the depressions then? He wanted to deal with the illness the way other people fought against cancer. But a person suffering from cancer still at least had his reason and, in the best cases, his courage and his will. He had nothing in his head but an oppressive heaviness. Almost every entry in his diary began with the same thought: *I have the feeling it's getting worse every day.*

The important thing wasn't to do anything extraordinary, it was just to do something. Every morning he swooped on the dogs to begin the day in a structured way. Teresa asked him, 'Are you coming with me to the riding-stables?' He sat on the terrace with his head tilted – that tilted head still drove her mad – and he thought, he thought back and forth. There were so many reasons to go to the riding-stables, and so many not to, how was he ever to make his mind up?

'I don't know,' he replied.

For the first days she said, 'Come with me.' But the weeks passed, his head stayed tilted, and Teresa's strength drained away. It plainly didn't make any difference whether or not she spurred him on. Perhaps it was better just to leave him to his own devices for a while. Thrown back on his own resources he might manage at least to make a few decisions.

Dr Geldschläger also asked Teresa along to a session. Life for the relatives of depressives, he said, was at least as difficult as it was for the patients themselves. You have your well-meant, optimistic, rational views, but depressives always know precisely why everything you suggest to them can only go wrong. Bear up, said Dr Geldschläger.

Teresa said to herself: the man by your side is not your Robbi, he's a sick man. It's the sickness that's responsible for all the difficult behaviour. You've got to help him. But patience is a limited resource when your husband's a bundle of neuroses, when he's lost his strength, when everything makes him angry.

'The dogs are driving me nuts!'

'When you came back from Istanbul you said you'd missed me and the dogs terribly.'

'But they're running wild around the flat all the time!'

He needed anti-depressants; he couldn't go on with just one-on-one therapy and muscle relaxation. A doctor friend from the Bundesliga, not a specialist in the field, prescribed some tablets for him. He still felt that he had to keep his sickness secret, without wondering why. He didn't know whether he ever wanted to be a professional footballer again. The only thing that was certain, in his opinion, was that he had already made too many mistakes in a single life ever to make things better, ever to go on living as the word 'life' deserved.

After some toing and froing FC Barcelona allowed him to train again with the other two 'outcasts', Roberto Bonano and Dani García. He had to sign a contract saying that he wouldn't claim any salary. He also committed himself to using the training-grounds only when the professional team wasn't present, when no one could see him. He could not miss the message between the contract's lines. He would never be a part of the club again.

Once he got his training times muddled. All of a sudden

Victor Valdés was standing in front of him in the catacombs of the stadium, on the way to train with the Barça squad. Victor nodded slightly. He couldn't tell whether Robert returned the greeting. Because they were both staring at the ground. 'I didn't dare speak to him,' says Victor. 'I thought the simple question "How are you?" might cause him pain.'

Robert panicked. He couldn't go training when the first team was present. He fled to the physio suite and got some treatment. His foot was sore, he said. Then he drove home. Should he take the tunnel with the toll or the country road? He was still thinking about this, wondering how he was supposed to decide, when he reached the toll-booth and there was no other option but the tunnel.

At home he didn't want to get out of the car.

I don't dare to go home, because then I'll have to face Terri and I won't be able to pull myself together.

He took his anti-depressant, and in the evening his mouth felt dry, however much water he drank. At least the side-effects of the medicine were working well, he said to himself. He didn't know where that irony had suddenly flown in from – his old, quiet sense of humour.

That evening Teresa forced him out to have dinner near the monastery in Sant Cugat. Children frolicked in the square in front of the ancient building. Elderly people sat contentedly on the benches, chewing sunflower seeds; the sinking sun gave the plaza one last tinge of gold. Their friends Susanne and Axel came along, and their presence broke the silence. Even Robert could suddenly talk again – about the taste of apricot ice-cream, about Dickens, even about Barça. But he didn't feel the relaxation he was emanating. Within him there was a double-thick pane of glass that screened him off from the life around him, and only let the conversation, the evening sun and the frolicking children reach him in a muted form.

He and Teresa were in bed by nine.

The question was: why? Why did he suffer from depression? That his ice-cold explusion from Barça had sparked the illness seemed obvious – the feeling of being worthless mixed with despair at having no other choice but Istanbul, where the fans didn't want him and he didn't want to be. Did he have an inherited predisposition to depression? Would he also have fallen ill as a teacher, sports reporter or businessman? Or was it just the extreme experiences of high-performance sport that affected him?

His father is still asking himself that one-word question. The engine of his Volkswagen grumbles as he drives up the mountain to Cospeda. Thick forest surrounds the rural road before a clearing reveals a view of Jena, just a dot in the valley below. The Enkes' dacha is on the left-hand side of a field. They used to come here a lot when the working week was over, when there was something to celebrate. Dirk wants to drive around the places that remind him of Robert: the sports college, Breite Strasse where Grandma Käthe lived – the third grandma. At the dacha he turns the engine off. The car shudders briefly before falling silent.

'Robert had this way of thinking, that if I'm not the best, I must be the worst. And that's a fundamental aberration. That's the thought of someone who's learned I'm only loved for my achievement not because I simply exist.'

The car window mists up from inside. As the windscreen turns milky, the far-away meadows can still be made out as a greenish-brown background. The silence seems absolute.

'That connection must have existed in Robert: if I'm not good, I'm not loved.'

And then, if at one point he really wasn't good as a young goalkeeper, he couldn't cope with it, the self-reproaches went spinning out of control, his brain functions altered, grim brooding took over and he became susceptible to depression?

Robert's father nods, but in his thoughts he's already further on, somewhere else. Perhaps he's even talking to someone else. 'I thought, Robert, you must surely have noticed that we loved you because you existed and not because you were a good goalkeeper.'

Scenarios arise: the father who left his family, who tries to go to every match his son plays so as not to lose the bond. The son who says anxiously, Papa, you'd still like me if I gave up football, wouldn't you?

'I'm more than willing to think about it critically: what did we do wrong? Of course we supported him with his sport, but we certainly didn't drive him into it as some over-ambitious parents do. I think I just said cautiously after every game: what do you think, Robert, did you do well in goal today?' His father would have liked to attend every game, even when his son was a professional. 'I've heard that that turned into a problem for Robert. I asked about tickets so often.'

Without asking a question, Robert's father expects an answer – please, tell me it wasn't a problem. It's time to tell him something else: when someone suffering from depression kills himself, no one else is to blame.

Robert's father wants to move on. He bends down as if the turning of the ignition key requires all his concentration.

One afternoon in Barcelona Robert came home from outlaw training and noticed one of their cats staring at him from the balcony. He stared back and saw only his own failure: that morning he had forgotten to close a window. You can't even do that, he rebuked himself.

'If the cat's got out,' Teresa said, suppressing her impatience, 'then just let it back in again.'

He went on staring at the balcony.

He had the feeling that he was being put to the test. Only the bottom third of the fridge worked these days. The television in the bedroom went on strike. The dishwasher had to be collected four days later. Wherever he looked, challenges awaited him – things that needed to be done, things that were too much for him. All day he thought about fridges, televisions, dishwashers that needed to be fixed, and couldn't get round to calling a repair man.

He treated his life like the fridge. He thought all day about how to fix it but couldn't find any answers because he immediately saw negative consequences. Should he spend a few months in a clinic in Germany? Then he would lose Teresa, if he left her alone. Should he stay in Barcelona and go on placing his hope in Dr Geldschläger and the tablets? Then he would lose Teresa, because he'd get on her nerves. Should he try really hard to find a new club in the winter transfer period? Then he would only fail again. Should he give up football? Then what was he supposed to do?

After lunch I always get tired, I just want to go to bed, but lying down like that only makes things worse.

That was the only logic his brain allowed: in the morning he had no desire to do anything that day, and in the evening he hated himself for not having accomplished anything.

When he went off to training one day, he thought: no one's waiting for you, no one's interested in what you do. Then he simply turned round. At about midday Teresa came back from her work at the animal shelter. The blinds on their house were lowered. He had gone to bed and withdrawn from the world. 'Get up!' said Teresa. 'Robbi, get up!' She had learned that staying in bed is the greatest longing yet at the same time the worst thing for depressives; she knew it was right to drive him out of bed. Yet it was unbearable shouting at him, treating him like that.

He sat down in the sitting-room and looked at old photographs, of Lisbon, of happiness. He found one in which Teresa, he, Jörg and Jörg's new girlfriend were toasting each other with glasses of sparkling wine. They were celebrating his departure from Benfica. He was free, they had believed at the time: he could, without a transfer fee, move to another club – further and higher. He stared at his face in the photograph. How had he ever thought it would be a great idea to leave Lisbon?

When I see that picture, I want to thump myself.

On 14 October 2003, exactly two months to the day since he had left Istanbul, he wrote only four and a half lines in his diary. He started with *About to go mad* and ended with *Often think about . . .*

He couldn't bring himself to write the word 'suicide'.

The next day he decided with Teresa and Jörg that that was enough. He would move in with Jörg in Cologne and go into treatment there.

For depressives, thoughts of suicide are to some extent a relief. The thought that there remains a way out helps them in the short term. The danger comes when the thought itself no longer provides enough comfort. Their irrational view of the world, restricted as it is to the negative, drives them to seek that way out of the darkness.

Robert packed his bags. What should he take? There were so many things he was bound to need in Cologne. Where should he start? How *did* you pack a bag? *There's always the feeling that there's such an incredible amount to do, but if I want to do something concrete, I don't know how to go about it.* He flew to Cologne and moved in with Tanja and Jörg at 29 Krefelder Strasse. They'd set up the guest room for him, and he thought: was it the nursery? Had he not shrunk to that role – the role of a helpless child? He no longer set the alarm clock, simply waited for Jörg to knock on the door. The first morning Jörg stepped into the room and waited. Robert didn't move. 'Robbi?' He touched him cautiously on the shoulder, and finally pulled up the blinds. His friend was lying there with his eyes open, staring rigidly through the ceiling.

From the next day Jörg sent him out every morning to buy the papers and bread, and began to set him some tasks for the day, careful to give him support but not take every decision away from him, or else he would convince himself he wasn't doing anything at all. Over breakfast Robert heard Jörg talking to him as if from the distance – oh, look at this, 1 FC Cologne is throwing Funkel out. He would have liked to answer, but what did he care about any of it? Jörg went on talking as if it were a normal conversation, chatting excitedly with someone who responded next to nothing.

Keep going, Jörg said to himself, even if there is no sign that things will ever move on. Did Robert even notice when his head fell to his chest at the breakfast table?

They visited the psychologist recommended by the German Sport University. A busy woman, she must have helped lots of people. The problem wasn't her, the problem was Robert. He couldn't see how to explain to this woman what it meant to be frightened when a player knocked in a cross. Always those damned crosses. That time in Novelda, all three goals conceded after crosses.

Keep going, Jörg said to himself.

Dr Sun-Hee Lee, senior physician at the University Hospital in Cologne, was described to him as a luminary in the field of psychiatry. Robert sat facing her in the hospital and felt so strange that he didn't know what to say.

'We'll find someone for you,' Jörg assured him as they were leaving the hospital. 'Definitely.'

Robert said nothing. He didn't care whether they found a psychiatrist he could work with, he didn't care about anything. He just wanted to stop thinking back to all his mistakes over the past year. How could he have got so many things wrong – Barcelona, Istanbul . . . Why hadn't he stayed in Lisbon? He kept on taking the anti-depressants, secretly prescribed, and no longer even felt the side-effects.

He continued to train, not because he was working towards something but just for something to do. Jörg saw to it that he was allowed to use the fitness rooms at the Neptunbad for free. Candles on seven-stemmed candlesticks burned by the entrance to the spa. The high halls of the former public baths, a hundred years old, had been given a coat of fresh white paint. He sat down on the barbell bench and thought, as he lifted the weights, that he was already losing muscle-mass. He would have to draw up a plan, remember what regimen he had been following a few months before with Paco in the gym at Barça. But he lacked the nerve, and ended up carrying out a few exercises completely at random. He could only think one thing: the others are at training now, and I'm squatting here. Apart from him, the only people there were housewives and the odd television starlet.

He had to get something to eat. Jörg was in the office, Tanja in the hospital, where she worked as an intern. He went back to Krefelder Strasse, where houses built over two centuries lined up seamlessly side by side. An amusement arcade stood peacefully next to a fine French restaurant; railway bridges running right through the area stressed the place's gritty charm. On the corner of Maybachstrasse he discovered a small pizzeria. The place didn't have much of a connection with Italian cuisine. The owner was an Arab, perhaps a Moroccan, and Robert was the only customer. The cheese on the pizza was tough and fatty. He didn't notice whether it tasted good.

'You ate there?' asked Jörg. 'I wouldn't have dared go in.'

Over the next few days he went back to the pizzeria for lunch several times. He felt sorry for the owner. If he didn't go, there wouldn't be a single customer.

Things went better in the evening. The paralysing fear of the morning, when a whole day lay ahead, a day when so many things had to be done, when there were so many things that he wouldn't get done, made way for relief in the evening, when the day was practically over and no one wanted anything more from him. In the evening he watched films with Jörg, like *Father of the Bride*; they went to Leverkusen to watch football; they even went to a party given by Jörg's friends Verena and Walter. He didn't know anybody but stayed until three in the morning even so, without feeling particularly uneasy. The thoughts didn't come until the following morning: *I have the feeling that I've never really learned to live. For example, why have I never wanted to party, why would I rather stay at home, why have I never taken an interest in other things?*

Keep going, Jörg said to himself; October will soon be over. He had had a Dr Markser at the Rheinische Klinik recommended to him. His practice was nearby, just on the other side of Ebertplatz. Jörg waited outside the house while Robert stepped inside. Half an hour passed, forty-five minutes.

'And?' asked Jörg when the door opened at last.

'We can do it.'

*   *   *

For a man like Dr Valentin Markser, consultant in psychiatry and psychotherapy, it's a great gift that he still speaks with a Croatian accent even after thirty-five years in Germany. The accent softens the harshness of German. Words that would sound stiff and theoretical when spoken by other psychiatrists sound melodic coming from his mouth.

A taste for fine cuisine has left its mark on his figure, but the doctor belongs to that enviable group of men whose paunches fit quite naturally within their bearlike physiques. Dr Markser can look at you, and you know he is listening to you with all the attentiveness a person can muster.

He was a professional handball player before he became a psychiatrist, with VfL Gummersbach in the seventies – German champions, European Cup winners. He was a goalkeeper.

Robert went to see Dr Markser every day, and his days found a structure: things got done. In the morning he went not to weight training at the Neptunbad, but to a rehab centre. He worked with specialist trainers among injured professional basketball and ice-hockey players. He was a part of things again. He told the other sportsmen he had an ankle injury. After a while his foot really hurt.

What he had never learned, his psychiatrist told him, and what he had to learn, was how to cope with making mistakes. The best goalkeeper, perhaps even the happiest person, was the one who came to terms with his mistakes. Robert had to teach himself that a mistake wasn't the whole game, a game was never the whole season, a season wasn't a career. A career isn't a life.

In the afternoons he was sometimes permitted to join in as a guest at 1 FC Cologne's goalkeeper training sessions. Football – and this had already been proved, in Barcelona – was something he could do even when he was depressed. His body, which had been trained for years, made the decisions his benumbed brain couldn't face. He dived, and he reacted to shots with lightning speed, even though slow reactions are one of the most common symptoms of the illness. He saved the shots. He felt nothing as he did so, just emptiness.

That was good today. Peter Greiber, the goalkeeping coach

at 1 FC Cologne, said to him. And he started to get frightened. Did that mean he would soon be able to go back to professional football? That something would soon be expected of him? His telephone conversations with Teresa were painful, too. He had to tell her that he was doing better, so that she knew it had been worth his going to Cologne. But how could he tell her that without her taking it as an insult? I'm doing better, far away from you. And how could he say he was doing better if he still felt bad?

She had visited him for a week, she would be back at the end of November. Dr Markser told him he had to argue with Teresa if something bothered him, like the dogs running round in the house. *Told him that I prefer to avoid conflicts. He doubts whether I take myself, meaning my own thoughts and feelings, seriously at all.*

Have you heard? Jörg asked Teresa, who had arrived in Cologne for her second visit. It was Friday 23 November, midday. Jörg was calling from the office and didn't even stop to ask where Robert was.

Sebastian Deisler had been sent to hospital suffering with depression.

The greatest German talent since Günter Netzer! the sports reporters on the Bökelberg had shouted five years earlier, when Deisler started with Borussia in the Bundesliga. Having only been close to Marco Villa among his team-mates, Robert had only been in superficial contact with Deisler.

The next morning they were able to read detailed articles on depression in the newspapers Robert brought with the bread-rolls.

Depression wasn't a weakness of character but an illness, moreover an indiscriminate illness that afflicted people without regard to their status, success or strength, and regardless of whether these people had all the qualities and possessions we think are necessary for a happy life. One of the most steadfast politicians of the modern era, Winston Churchill, suffered from depression just as much as any unknown secretary; Sebastian

Deisler had been playing electrifyingly for Bayern Munich over the past few weeks. Depression, like cancer, can have a variety of causes and forms, and the doctor treating Deisler called his a 'typical depression' because Deisler had a 'predisposition' that became noticeable under extreme pressure to perform. The huge expectations of the public that he must be 'Basti Fantasti', the new Netzer, had combined oppressively with the even greater demands he made on himself. In five years as a professional player, Deisler had had fifteen injuries and five operations.

Robert wasn't sure what to make of the report. It was good to read that he wasn't the only footballer who suffered from depression, that he wasn't a freak. On the other hand he felt a twinge of envy. Everyone was talking about Deisler, and he was receiving sympathy from all sides.

The Kicker *magazine made an insinuation about me to Jörg, but so far my name hasn't been in the press. I don't know if that's good or bad.*

He went on giving interviews, though not many enquiries came in these days. Sports journalism has only a short-term memory. He was already the forgotten man. Besides, he didn't feel like talking. What would he say? His foot was injured and he just hadn't felt well in Istanbul? But Jörg insisted that he do two or three as a way of working towards a return to football even if it might never happen.

Certainly when he sat facing Dr Markser he was sure he wanted to be a goalkeeper again. The fear he had felt wasn't a fundamental, unchanging fear, only the expression of his illness. If he had his fear of failure treated, the terror would disappear along with the illness. The problems, the thoughts, began when he left Dr Markser's practice.

Keep thinking back to things that happened more than two years ago. When will it suddenly click for me, making me get my butt in gear? I don't think it's going to happen.

For weeks now everyone had wanted him to go to Manchester. Manchester City were interested in him.

'Just draw up a list of pros and cons, the arguments for and the arguments against moving to England,' said Teresa.

'We could all go and have a look at the place,' said Jörg.

Simply look at City's offer as an opportunity, or even just as an exercise, not as all or nothing, as you did in Istanbul and at the game in Novelda, Dr Markser said to him.

'All right then, let's go,' Robert said, and wondered what that decision would bring.

Jörg's business partner in England showed him the city, the stadium and the Citizens training-ground. *I was supposed to decide by last Sunday whether I would say yes to negotiations or not. I did it. I don't need to go into the fact that I have severe doubts.*

Jörg had seen the improvement coming for several days. There would never be a 'click' – that was the dream of a footballer who was used to things changing in a single moment. But since the end of October, since the days of training and Markser had found a fixed rhythm, there had been hope again. Robert sometimes replied to remarks over breakfast. In the evening he came unresistingly along for a beer. The stone mask that his face had once been was showing its first cracks.

He had been taking anti-depressants for three months now.

At the weekend Jörg went jogging with him, down to the Rhine. Jogging was good for depression: the muscles relaxed, stress hormones ebbed away. Robert hated jogging. It was proof of his decay: he was a goalkeeper and he was jogging.

They ran past the old skating-rink where a few Turkish children were playing football. The boys waited until he was past.

'Hey, Enke, bad goalie! Bad goalie!'

Robert just jogged on.

It took Jörg a few paces to process what he had just heard. Then he turned round. 'What did you just say? What? Shall I tell you what sort of a club Fenerbahçe is? The worst! You'll never see a goalkeeper like Robert ever again!'

'Jörg,' Robert said calmly, five paces ahead of him, 'leave them, they're children.'

They jogged on, in silence, Jörg glowing with fury. Only

much later did it occur to Jörg that they were suddenly their old selves again. Not nurse and patient, but adviser and client, in reversed roles. As so often in the past, the protector was being taught good sense by his charge.

Christmas fell in the middle of this phase of cautious hope. Advent lights burned in the streets, people huddled tightly around wooden stalls decorated with fir branches, hot cups of mulled wine in their hands, steaming breath in front of their faces. Robert felt an oppressive expectation that he should be full of festive cheer as well. Why couldn't he be like that any more?

Jörg had made an Advent calendar for Tanja, with a little surprise for her every day. Other people's happiness reminded Teresa how lost she was. She would have liked an Advent calendar herself, she said. He thought he heard sadness in her words: other people got Advent calendars, and she didn't even have her husband by her side in Barcelona.

Suddenly Robert had an idea: he would send her a calendar by text. Every day he sent her a self-penned four-liner on his phone.

Your heart is something you can't define,
It's easier to find a mountain to climb.
Now climbing a mountain's a hard thing to do
When that tiny dwarf down at the bottom is you.

He liked the image. He was a dwarf. He didn't notice himself getting any bigger with each rhyme.

The dwarf says to himself: I can't do that,
I'm just a stupid idiot.
He thinks: for that I'm much too small,
You'd have to be bigger, over all.

One mistake, Dr Markser said, was to wait for something to happen. *Don't yield to passivity!* Robert noted, with an exclamation mark, and drove to Gierath. He wanted to surprise Hubert Rosskamp with a visit.

His old friend was fighting 'to stay ahead of the reaper's scythe'. In Hubert's Rhineland singsong even a phrase like that sounded cheerful. He was struggling to recover from a cancer operation.

Hubert was wearing a pair of jogging pants that didn't exactly bring his ashen face to life. 'For God's sake, Robert,' he yelled, 'I haven't even got any strawberry tart in the house!'

They set off for a walk, along the old path where they'd taken the dogs in his Mönchengladbach days. Alamo, the old hunting dog Teresa had found in the street and left with Hubert, was there. The earth was hard under their feet. He would get some strawberry tart, Hubert said. Robert asked about Hubert's operation, his pain, his progress. He concealed the fact that he was ill too. He had come to help, after all.

'Will you go on giving me an Advent rhyme every day?' asked Teresa before she returned to Cologne on 20 December. She and Robert were planning to fly back to Barcelona together for Christmas.

He didn't think, I'm cured, he just hardly gave his illness any thought. On the radio Michael Jackson sang 'Billie Jean', and he danced the moonwalk with Teresa in Jörg's living-room. They had been invited for a turkey dinner with Jörg's friends. He didn't know anyone, but that didn't bother him; all the better: he would meet some new people. He took along a pile of advertising postcards from a bar. One card showed a black-and-white photograph of a cocktail bar. On the back of it the promised Advent calendar four-liner turned into eight lines:

Today is Saturday, oh so hearty,
We're all going to a party.
Eating turkey, drinking wine,
Going home and feeling fine.
Tanja, Terri, Jörg and Rob,
One of them a real nutjob.
We'll have a laugh, it's really fun,
This one's going to run and run.

Three days later they landed in Barcelona. The ring road from the airport passed the tower blocks of the outer districts – the epitome of hideousness – but he soon spotted the greenness of the Collserola. When they turned into the Calle de Las Tres Plazas in Sant Cugat, he saw their house and knew he was home.

Marco Villa rang that Christmas. He had gone to see a sports psychologist. He couldn't see how she would help him – breathing exercises, staring at the wall – but it didn't matter. He had some news, he would just put Christina on the line. His wife was pregnant.

Having a child of our own would be lovely, thought Teresa, but certainly not in the near future. First they would have to recover from what they had just been through.

Four children were waiting impatiently for the arrival of the Christ child when Teresa and Robert turned up at Axel and Susanne's in Sant Cugat. The hard core of the German expats had been invited for a Christmas party. The presents for the grown-ups were to be funny rather than expensive, they had agreed. Chance decided who received which gift. Teresa drew a man-size pair of turquoise boxer-shorts with Snoopy on the front. She put them on over her jeans. Robert was suddenly sitting on the couch apart from the others. In his hands he held a pile of papers and was going through them with great concentration. Then he got to his feet.

'I've written Teresa a poem for Christmas, and I'd like to read it to her and to you, because I know what you've been through with me over the past few months. I'd like to thank you for that.'

He told them about the dwarf.

But now let's turn to positive things,
Loud the Christmas bell does ring!
The dwarf looks forward to the feast –
A test for him, he knows at least.

A dog for his dwarf-wife, maybe?
Her little smile is fine to see.
Or else a cuddly pussy-cat –
Her little face lights up at that.

What if it's not a pet at all?
Why then, the she-dwarf's face will fall.
And what if she is filled with wrath
Against her loving little dwarf?

When he had finished, silence fell. At last one of the friends remembered that the author was present and started clapping, and the others quickly joined in. Their applause grew louder, the noise driving the shimmer from their eyes.

It's two o'clock in the morning. Teresa is already in bed, and outside the window the golf course of Sant Cugat is just a black wall. Robert sits at his desk and lowers his notes. The pages lie in front of him. The scrawly handwriting with the skewed letters curving from left to right at the top leaves no doubt. He wrote that.

He can't believe he is the same person who wrote that diary over the last five months.

It's January 2004, a new year, and he has just read through his notebooks for the first time. Does that old human dream really exist? You take down the old calendar, you draw a line under everything, and it all starts over?

It almost seems that way.

Most people who are prone only suffer from depression once, and it usually lasts between three and six months. He wouldn't go so far as to say: I belong to that group, it's all behind me. What he feels is that those months already seem incredibly far away. He sees his alien self as a blur, in outline, a person who had nothing to do with him but who for some inexplicable reason slipped into his skin.

He is filled with a quiet urge to act. He will play football again, even if he doesn't yet know where. The offer from

Manchester City fell through, and he doesn't know whether he will ever reach the level of Lisbon again, but it doesn't matter much. He has a very concrete idea of how to achieve happiness. He will stand in some goal somewhere, he will save a shot and he will feel how that makes other people – the fans, his team-mates – happy. He will go for a walk with Teresa and the dogs; on the forest path she will let the dogs off the lead; the dogs will run; he will put his arm around Teresa and sense her smile without looking.

Teresa is pregnant. They've known for nine days. It must have happened during those euphoric Advent days in Cologne. Teresa was shocked by the news: after Robert's depression she would have liked a bit of peace. But he was pleased; she is pleased now.

If it's a girl, they already have a name: Lara.

Under his desk-lamp he looks for a pen, a sheet of paper. He has to finish something.

16.01.2004, 02.00 a.m. At the moment I am happy + content. We had a really lovely New Year's Eve in the Café Delgado. I laughed and danced – incredible!

He looks for a file for his depri-documents. Those are his words: depri-documents, depri-file. He finds a pocket file, bright red, puts his notes in it, along with the dwarf poem, and closes it.

THIRTEEN

The Holiday Island

In the afternoon he had time to take a look at life. He walked to Santa Cruz harbour. After he had stood around idly for a while, he discovered a wall and swung himself up on top of it. From there you could see over the cruise-ship quay and up to the cranes and containers of the freight-yard. Beyond that the jagged mountains of Tenerife grew right out of the Atlantic.

Robert sat on the wall and didn't move. He watched the people in the harbour. 'How contented they are,' he thought to himself, and felt he was one of them again.

On the last day of the winter transfer window he had switched to Deportivo Tenerife. The offers he had on the table told him something about his reputation in professional football: AC Ancona, bottom of the league in Italy; FC Kärnten, bottom of the league in Austria: and ADO Den Haag, second from bottom in the Netherlands. He chose to go to Tenerife, in the Spanish Second Division.

Which meant that he ceased to exist for the German football scene. Only people who knew him personally looked for signs of life from him in the small-print foreign results in *Kicker*. Peter Greiber, Cologne's goalkeeping coach, sent him a text when he read about a 1–0 win for Tenerife: 'Well done, clean sheet.' Robert wrote back: 'Thanks. Unfortunately I wasn't in goal.' Even in the Segunda División he was only a substitute goalkeeper. He wasn't trusted, since he had resigned in Istanbul after only one game and hadn't played a match for six months.

In Cologne, Jörg wondered: substitute goalkeeper in a second division – is this the end? He phoned Robert. 'Come on, man, you've got to put the pressure on the number one keeper!'

Robert replied, calm down, it'll happen.

He sat by the harbour every day and saw things differently from Jörg, from the football scene. 'Football turns you into someone who always wants more, who's never content,' he said. Over the past few months he'd learned to be grateful for what he had.

From the harbour he often went to the pedestrian precinct for a milk-shake. He knew the best ice-cream parlour in town, he said. His pride was impossible to ignore. He alone had explored Santa Cruz, and now he was conducting a guided tour of the town.

Teresa had stayed in Barcelona. She was pregnant, she had the dogs, they thought it wasn't worth moving, he would only be in Tenerife for half a season, until he found something better – with any luck. It was the same situation as the Turkish experiment. But in Istanbul he had felt lost without Teresa. In Santa Cruz he felt inspired.

He was living in a rented four-room flat near García Sanabria Park. The flat was completely furnished, but it still looked empty. Apart from a satellite dish, still unpacked, on the floor, he had brought no personal belongings, and he had changed nothing: he had even left the paintings, still-lifes of oranges and bananas, hanging on the walls. It wasn't worth settling in for those few months, he said. On the bed was a thriller by Henning Mankell. In the dishrack, hand-rinsed, were a plate and a glass.

'It was like being a student for him,' says Teresa.

Every morning he bought two sports newspapers from the kiosk outside his flat. One day as he let his eye slip over the pages he spotted a familiar photograph. It was on the front page, in the top right-hand corner. He wondered why they had used that particular one – the picture was over six months old. He hardly recognised himself in it.

It was the photo of his presentation at Fenerbahçe – his face red, his mouth open, his expression harassed. 'Look at that picture,' he said. 'I'm not even myself.' He pulled the page out to keep it. He didn't want to forget what he had felt like during his depression.

He set the newspapers down on the passenger seat. He had to go to training. The club had put a sports car at his disposal – he had had a clause saying as much added to his contract. On the first day the sporting director Francisco Carrasco had come to him and handed him a car-key. His team-mates laughed. 'What's up?' asked Robert. Carrasco had had to pass his staff car on to him, because it was the only one they had. It crossed his mind that professional football in the Segunda División was only superficially the same job as the one he had been doing for ages. His salary was a tenth of what he had been earning with Barça but he was one of the best-paid professionals in Tenerife's team.

When his first month's salary from Tenerife came in, he looked at his statement for a long time. After seven months, another credit in his account. 'That feeling that money was only ever going out was frightening.' He hesitated. 'As a footballer you don't dare say it, because other people are hit much harder. But the feeling of being out of work is no less bad for a professional footballer than it is for an electrician. You feel worthless.'

Another clause in his contract stated that the club would provide Teresa with tickets for three flights from Barcelona. When he realised how cheap the flight was the first time she came, he was ashamed. A hundred and sixty euros return, and he had made Jörg fight for that stipulation. What must they think of him at the club? CD Tenerife had been fighting for years to be able to pay its professionals a half-decent salary, and he, who was receiving a decent wage, was causing difficulties over less than five hundred euros. After training, when one of his team-mates had to go on some errand, Robert often said 'Here, take it' and threw him the key to his car.

February 2004 passed, then March, and he was still substitute goalkeeper. Jörg phoned him. 'This isn't good, you've got to talk to Carrasco. He brought you in as number one!'

Be patient, Robert replied. He would play eventually.

He never said it out loud, because he thought it was unseemly, but he thought he was better than the number one, Álvaro Iglesias. There were some objective arguments in his favour: his fine saves, his jumping, his anticipation – the difference was apparent every day in training. But he also saw that Álvaro played blamelessly in the matches. Perhaps Álvaro was so convincing precisely because he had a stronger competitor breathing down his neck. A goalkeeper who played his part without any mistakes deserved, in Robert's opinion, to stay on stage. That was true even though he himself was the victim of the situation.

But to do his duty, to be able to say to Jörg 'You see, I've done it', he went to see the sporting director.

The situation was more embarrassing for Carrasco than it was for him. Carrasco had brought him to Tenerife. 'Robert was my personal bet', and now the coach wasn't playing the goalkeeper. At the age of forty-five, Carrasco looked less like a former footballer than an active long-distance runner – slim, tall, ascetic. They both knew what they had to say, and that neither of them could do anything to change the situation.

'You told me you would take me on as number one.'

'I know, but I can't tell the coach which players to play.'

Relieved at having put this behind them, they turned to other subjects.

'Above all I could tell how much in love he was with Teresa,' Carrasco says six years later in the Madrid suburb of Aravaca, where he lives today, still slim and elegant, wearing a suit as he takes his morning coffee. Love doesn't seem like the most obvious of topics when a sporting director and his goalkeeper meet for crisis talks. 'At the time he was about to become a father. I was in my mid-forties, I was already a father, I knew a bit about this – you notice how much in love someone is.' Carrasco played for Barça for eleven years, his hair grey already, which was why they called him 'Lobo' – the Wolf. He won three European Cups, he reached the European Championship with Spain in 1984, and after that he taught himself journalism. After Barça's 1–0 in Bruges it was he who wrote in *El Mundo Deportivo*, 'Enke's performance was a message to van Gaal.'

What stayed in Carrasco's memory about the sportsman was 'the elegance with which Robert endured his difficult situation as a substitute. He was always businesslike with me. He never complained in the press.'

Robert gave Álvaro Iglesias, the goalkeeper he was supposed to be putting pressure on, and whom he had to get out of the way if he was to play again, eight pairs of gloves. He got tailor-made models from his sponsor, gloves that Álvaro, who had long served as a goalkeeper in the lower divisions, couldn't get hold of 'Absolutgrip and Aquasoft, the best latex surfaces from Uhlsport,' Iglesias remembers enthusiastically today, just as other people reel off the names of their children. Robert also gave eight pairs to the third-choice goalkeeper, Adolfo Baines. But Baines didn't wear them to training. The gloves were so posh, he told Robert, that he would save them for special days.

There were now two Robert Enkes at training in the Heliodoro Rodríguez Stadium, according to the personalised Velcro fasteners of the gloves of both goalkeepers. But the original was always easy to spot.

The coach organised a little game, attack versus defence. The striker was through, alone in front of the goalkeeper, and Robert was waiting, one knee bent inwards so that the attacker couldn't shoot through his legs, his torso ramrod straight, his arms outstretched to look wider. The striker went for a shot with the inside of his foot, attempting to curve it round the keeper. Robert pushed himself off the ground with a considerable leap, but what was truly magnificent was the explosiveness of his move. He darted to the left at lightning speed. The pensioners on the terraces clapped when he tipped the ball, which seemed to be on the way into the goal, around the post. 'That was what I missed most,' he said, 'that feeling that what you do is important for somebody.'

Of course the questions still troubled him, that afternoon over the best chocolate milk-shake on the island. What if he had never left Benfica? What was someone like him doing on the subs bench in the Spanish Second Division? 'And then I thought to myself: there must be some point to Enke taking a knock.' And he had already found that meaning: he was enjoying the simple things of life again. 'Belonging to a team, and knowing there's training at ten o' clock. Being needed again.'

It was only another nine and a half hours until the next training session. He sat in the living-room, so full of joy he couldn't sleep. On the shelves, where books and figurines ought to have been, were two dozen pairs of gloves and shin-guards. He was wearing jeans and a T-shirt, and on each hand he had a different model of glove, one Absolutgrip and one Aquasoft.

He fastened the Velcro. He clenched his fists, stretched his fingers, rubbed the gloves together, and stood in the room, concentrating hard. As if he were listening to the gloves on his fingers.

There is no lovelier feeling for a goalkeeper than slipping into his gloves and fastening the Velcro. Then he feels safe and secure, often invulnerable. For that reason most goalkeepers prefer a solid pair – armour for their soul. Robert, on the other hand, wore unusually light gloves. He wanted to restrict the mobility of his fingers as little as possible; he had to feel the ball when he caught it, not only in the foam of the gloves but all the way to his fingertips.

His sponsor wanted him to play with the latest model every year. 'With Robert, it always took us about eight attempts until we found the right glove for him,' says Lothar Bisinger, who looks after professional goalkeepers at Uhlsport. Eight attempts meant that after trying them on for the first time, Robert might say the glove was too tight on the right thumb, and then the glove had to be made again with the thumb a millimetre wider. Then he might notice that with the broad thumb the other fingers now felt too tight. The tailor widened the fingers. 'So we made our way forward, millimetre by millimetre,' says Bisinger. In Tenerife, the Velcro seemed too tight for Robert when he bent his wrist.

The seam on his gloves was always on the outside of the

thumb; on the fingers he insisted on having it inside. Without an outside seam the ball sank better into the foam, while at the thumb he felt the seam on his skin when it was on the inside, and that was irritating. 'He also had latex inside the glove,' says José Moreira, who had naturally tried out Robert's gloves during their time together in Lisbon. 'It was something I didn't know before, it didn't exist in Portugal before him. I immediately ordered some from my manufacturer.'

The foam on Robert's catching surfaces was seven millimetres thick: four millimetres of foam, three millimetres of lining. You can't buy gloves like that. The foam layer in mass-produced gloves is six millimetres thick. When Robert put on normal goalkeeping gloves he noticed the single millimetre's difference straight away.

What exactly the difference was between the natural rubber padding in Absolutgrip and Aquasoft even Bisinger couldn't tell him. There are only three rubber suppliers for goalkeeping gloves in the whole world. 'The recipes are as secret as the recipe for Coca-Cola,' says Bisinger. 'Only the manufacturers know whether the temperature was changed by three degrees in the baking of the rubber dough, or a new chemical was added to produce a new layer with improved clingability.'

Robert needed to test the differences between Absolutgrip and Aquasoft.

Throughout his career he had always worn Absolutgrip, but now, in his living-room, he was trying out Aquasoft. It was after midnight in Santa Cruz. I threw the ball, he caught it, until he was laughing too much to go on.

He hadn't yet decided, he said, suddenly serious, which glove he would wear in his first game for Tenerife. His doubtful words rang with an inexplicable but absolute certainty: eventually, soon, he would have his first game.

His quiet joy made Teresa happy, and at the same time reminded her of her own sadness. She was pregnant and alone in Barcelona. One night she woke up, her whole body shivering. She felt nauseous and she was on her way to the bathroom to drink from the tap when she suddenly felt dizzy. She didn't dare go back to the bedroom, downstairs. She lay down on a towel on the bathroom floor and waited for the dizzy spell to pass. While she was there, she had too much time to think.

Normally a pregnancy wasn't like this. Normally your husband holds your head in such situations.

It was just a few months, such he told her on the phone.

She thought: he's so relaxed, that's just lovely; but how sad that we can't share these moments with each other.

In spite of her pregnancy, she mowed the lawn. She had laid off the gardener during Robert's depression, less because they were pinched for money than out of a vague feeling that they weren't going to earn any more. In the evening she sat exhausted in front of the television.

Suddenly something hit the window. She held her breath. When they'd first started living in Sant Cugat there had been a shooting in her street, she remembered. Again a pebble hit the glass.

She went cautiously to the window. Down by the front door stood her husband, beaming and waving. He had come unannounced from Tenerife, a three-and-a-half-hour flight. He had set off at midday after training and had to get back first thing the next morning. She was knocked out after mowing the lawn. It wasn't even nine in the evening but her eyelids were heavy. She was sorry, but she had to sleep. It doesn't matter, he said, and really meant it. He watched her sleeping.

Back in Tenerife he began to do things that he hadn't done since devoting himself to professional sport as a teenager. He went to the cinema on his own. He read a book for hours. He went to a carnival with the team. He put on a hooped T-shirt, stuck a sheet of A4 paper to his chest, drew a number on it and said he was an escaped safe-breaker. When he saw his team-mates, he wanted to sink into the ground. Álvaro Iglesias was a nurse with a real uniform, including red lipstick, Adolfo Baines was Rambo. Everyone but him had taken a lot of trouble with their fancy dress. He was twenty-six and still learning how other people partied.

After midnight, when the hard core moved on from the

restaurant to a nightclub, he went home tired but happy. He knew more clearly than ever what he wanted to be like. All through his life he had been calm, businesslike, polite to other people, 'not extrovert, but open', says Iglesias. And now, for the first time in ages, he felt inwardly how he seemed outwardly; now he was also considerate and sympathetic to himself. The narrow-minded eagerness of youth had made way for a healthy ambition; the hunger that young sportsmen have, their total focus on being the best, had made way for a certain serenity. He had often wondered what it would be like to go through life with blinkers on, absolutely convinced about himself and his work. Perhaps then he would have been a better goalkeeper. But maybe, he said to himself now, it wasn't that important after all to be the very best goalkeeper.

The ball bounced in the penalty area; the goalkeeper had to come out before any damage was done. And Álvaro Iglesias was already there. He reached resolutely for the ball. Rayo Vallecano's striker jumped into him, even though it was unlikely he would win back the ball. When they do things like that, strikers are usually already thinking about the next goal-scoring opportunity; they want to frighten the goalkeeper, intimidate him so that he will hesitate a moment too long in the next critical situation. Álvaro's forehead was bleeding. It was just a cut, said the doctor, who gave him three stitches on the pitch, and on the game went. Álvaro played the remaining forty-eight minutes, and Tenerife scored in injury time to salvage a draw.

The X-ray the next morning showed that Álvaro's cheekbone had suffered a double fracture near his right eye. The bone was fixed with four pins at one fracture, six at the other. 'Feel that,' Álvaro said to Robert when he looked in on the changing-room for the first time after the operation. 'You can feel the individual pins under the skin with your finger.' Robert shivered as he felt them.

The goalkeeper's spot was free.

He thought about Álvaro, about what it was like to lose your place like that. In four months Álvaro would turn

thirty-two, and he was playing his first proper season in professional football; until then he had spent a decade in the Segunda
B and Tercera divisions expending the effort of a professional
but drawing the salary of a part-time job. Whenever he saw
Álvaro at the stadium he went up to him and asked about his
recovery. In the world of football that was unusually cordial.
'Robert was very close to me in the days after my injury,' says
Álvaro, who would, in spite of this setback, assert himself in
the Second Division until the age of thirty-six.

In the ninth year of Robert's career it still looked as if things
were going to go on like this for ever: his teams had high
expectations which they never lived up to. Mönchengladbach,
Benfica, Barça, Fenerbahçe – wherever he was, his team stumbled. Things were no different in Tenerife. Before the season
they had had an eye on the top of the table. Before their game
against Elche in mid-April they were on the brink of
relegation.

Robert was back where he had started: a half-empty stadium
in a second division, like Hannover versus Jena in November
1995. Sporting director Lobo Carrasco didn't find the comparison at all defamatory. 'Robert had the enthusiasm of a
beginner,' he says.

He strapped on his gloves – he had decided on Absolutgrip,
as always. He hadn't played for nine months.

The game hadn't been going for a minute and he hadn't yet
touched the ball when Elche broke through on the flank. The
cross came over, high but not too hard. Tenerife's centre-half
Miroslav Djukić didn't go for the ball, he waited for Robert
to come out – the ball was easy prey for a goalkeeper. But
Robert stayed on his line. He was lucky. The ball flew past
both friend and foe and trickled out of play.

Robert apologised to Djukić with a raised hand and a faint
smile. It looked as if he was no longer treating his own mistakes
in a doom-laden way. Of course, the fans thought, an experienced goalkeeper like Enke wouldn't be driven mad by
anything.

It was one of those football matches in which the goalkeeper is reminded of his impotence, that sometimes he can do nothing but wait. In the fifty-third minute Elche's Nino finally broke through. He shot, putting some elegant spin on the ball with his instep. Robert saved majestically. Tenerife won 2–1, defender César Belli responsible for the goal against. After hesitating on that first cross, Robert had sorted out the nuts-and-bolts work of a goalkeeper and had caught a few half-dangerous shots. His throws were long and punchy, too. There was nothing more he could do.

The sportswriters in Santa Cruz tried to portray him as the great goalkeeper everyone in Tenerife wanted to see. 'A header from Zárate flew over the goal as if Enke had guided the ball over the bar with a look,' wrote *El Día*.

The day after the game, for the first time in his life, Robert read five newspapers in one go, all of them reporting on his comeback in one way or another.

He rewarded himself with a day in Barcelona – out in the morning, back in the evening. The second ultrasound scan was imminent, in the twentieth week of pregnancy. You'll be able to see the child's hands and head, said friends with children; if you're lucky you'll even be able to tell whether it's a girl or a boy.

A nurse ran the probe over Teresa's belly and a picture appeared on the screen, white outlines on a night-black ground. It was a girl. It was Lara.

They sat down in the waiting-room. Dr Onbargi would discuss the scan with them in a moment.

Teresa felt as if they had to wait for an extraordinarily long time.

'Señora' – Spanish receptionists always pause before they pronounce foreign names – 'Enke?'

Dr Leila Catherine Onbargi-Hunter, trained at the Northwestern University of Chicago, with a diploma from the American Congress of Obstetrics and Gynaecology, was one of the doctors who gave the Teknon Medical Centre in Barcelona the reputation of a superior hospital. But she had no easy answer for the biggest problem all doctors face: how do you pass on bad news?

Teresa was crying when she ran from the room. Robert tried to support her, even though he himself was having trouble maintaining his composure.

Lara had a heart defect. 'There's a high probability that the child will die in the womb, but let's wait another week, then we'll examine it again.'

Teresa's phone rang. Outside the hospital palm-trees stood above hedges trimmed into geometrical shapes. An appointment had been arranged with a heart specialist, immediately, Onbargi's assistant said. Robert's return flight was leaving in eighty minutes. It was his last chance to be on time for training the next day.

'Robbi, get your plane, I'll do this.'

'I'm not leaving you on your own right now.'

'Please, we have enough problems. We don't want to create another one in football because you don't make it to training. I'd like you to get your plane.'

He phoned her from the airport. The specialist had recommended that the child be taken from the womb as quickly as possible and given a heart operation.

A day later, Teresa wanted to have Dr Onbargi's diagnosis calmly explained again. But she was worried that she would be so nervous she would misunderstand certain details. She asked a friend to come along to see the doctor. The child didn't just have a heart defect, said Dr Onbargi, it also had chromosomal damage. They were talking about Turner Syndrome. People with Turner Syndrome are growth-restricted, they have a high risk of deformations of the ear and a short life expectancy.

Teresa flew to Munich to get a second opinion from the German Heart Centre, and, to cover all scenarios, to find out from a gynaecologist how an abortion would be organised. The cardiologist there diagnosed hypoplastic left-heart syndrome. On no account should a premature delivery be induced, as his colleague in Barcelona had suggested – that would be certain death. After the first year of life three heart operations would be necessary, then your child will live. Teresa thought he sounded perfectly calm about it.

Turner Syndrome children are of average intelligence, another friend discovered, and hormone treatment from the age of twelve can regulate their growth. Given the possible damage that had originally been mentioned, these were only the most extreme features of Turner Syndrome, and only a very few patients were badly affected by them.

Teresa's parents and brothers told her she didn't know what it meant to bring up such a seriously ill child. Robert's parents told him they would support whatever decision was made.

Robert was sitting on a holiday island near Africa dealing with all these contradictory opinions being delivered to him from a long way away. How was he to estimate how serious things really were for their child? When Teresa reached a decision about what was to be done before he did, he was glad. Aborting or bringing into the world – he no longer had to make the choice, he realised with relief. Now that she had made her mind up he would of course go along with it, because she was the one carrying the child in her belly. It was only a matter of developing the same solid conviction as Teresa.

This was her child, she said. It should live, with all the consequences.

All of a sudden everything seemed very simple. They knew very well that life with a seriously ill child would be difficult, but the difficulties were abstract so long as the child wasn't there. Still, when they tried to imagine their life, all three of them together, they felt confident that they would manage, somehow.

One sentence sprang back to life, one he had uttered a year and a half earlier, when Kaiserslautern didn't want him and Barça rang up: 'Clearly nothing works normally for me.' We had laughed at the time.

While he was worried about his child's life he was 'reborn as a goalkeeper', says Lobo Carrasco. Club Deportivo Numancia from the little town of Soria, named after the Numantians who bitterly resisted the Romans 150 years before the birth of Christ, came to Santa Cruz as division leaders and went home defeated. Robert made three saves that made the eleven thousand fans in the terraces leap to their feet. 'People fell in love at first sight,' says Carrasco. 'They acknowledged the goalkeeper that Barça had bought, all the more powerfully after everything he had been through. People were gripped by the idea that someone like that was playing for Tenerife.'

Robert was carried by the feeling of being content in goal. Perhaps he would never again turn out for a big club like Benfica or Barça, perhaps he would end his playing days in the Segunda División, but he now knew exactly what he wanted to be like as a goalkeeper, and if he came close to this ideal he would be glad, regardless of which level he was playing at. He had, in the middle of his career, found his style.

He had always taken his bearings from others: in Mönchengladbach from Uwe Kamps, who stuck to the goal-line, who wanted to be spectacular, who dived and punched; in Barcelona he had been driven crazy by Frans Hoek with his cries of *Further forward! Your foot! Van der Sar!* 'That was what annoyed me most, that I let him persuade me that I couldn't do anything.' He had always watched his colleagues very closely. Kamps, Bossio, Bonano, Valdés – he could learn something from all of them, even from Álvaro Iglesias, who had for a long time played only in Segunda B but whose positioning at corners and crosses was excellent. Playing abroad enriched him. Robert had noticed that in Germany, the self-appointed country of goalkeepers, he had grown up in the nineties with a very quirky theory of goalkeeping – lurking on the goal-line, exaggerated punches, holding on to the front post for crosses, storming out when the striker advanced on his own, training that was aimed at power endurance. The new goalkeeper was more influenced by the Argentinian school – standing motionless in front of the striker in one-on-one situations, and kicking out of hand sideways-on instead of chest-on. Argentina's goalkeeper Germán Burgos had even invented an exercise to suppress the human reflex to turn the face away in response to shots from a short distance: the goalkeeping coach tied Burgos's hands behind his back and shot hard at him from close range; all Burgos had to do was parry the ball with his face, again and again. Sometimes his nose broke. Robert learned more from an Argentinian, Roberto Bonano, than from anyone else. He improved his body posture in a duel with a striker after seeing Bonano: he no longer did the splits but, like Bonano, stayed upright, standing frozen in front of the striker, though he kept one knee bent inwards – his trademark – so that the striker couldn't shoot between his legs. Other goalkeepers couldn't spring powerfully off the turf with a knee turned inwards. He became a master in the art of stopping strikers in face-to-face situations. From the groin down his pose was still Enke, from the hips up it was Bonano.

But he didn't want to imitate anyone any more. For the first time he could clearly see what was good for him and what was unsuitable. So in Tenerife he screwed together from all the individual parts he had collected over the years the goalkeeper who would be a model to many others. He placed soberness, calmness, at the heart of his game. He positioned himself clearly further in front of goal than Oliver Kahn, the spectacular saver, but not as far forward as van der Sar, the eleventh outfielder. He wouldn't hurry out at every cross, as Hoek had demanded, as the next generation of goalkeepers was already learning to do, not least in Germany. Even Álvaro placed himself in the middle of the goal for crosses, three or four yards in front of it, while Robert stood closer to the near post and the goal-line. 'Robert, it's too far from there to the back post; when a cross flies over there you won't be able to get to it.' He knew Álvaro was right, but this conservative positional play had been a part of his approach to goalkeeping since childhood; he felt secure with it, so he would keep it and leave some crosses to the back of the box to the defenders. But when he did come out for a cross, he caught it safely.

Robert Enke was the mid-point between Kahn and van der Sar, between reaction and anticipation, between conservative play and risk. The middle way often seems boring and is usually sensible.

CD Tenerife, on the brink of relegation when Robert started with them, no longer lost. 'There are a lot of footballers who have individual significance, and there are a few footballers who have significance for the collective,' says Lobo Carrasco. 'Robert belonged to the second category. Before then we were a featherweight team, with him we developed a different mentality, a different inner conviction.'

It's only two degrees in Madrid and between his fine light-blue shirt and his jacket Carrasco is wearing a kind of polyester tracksuit jacket. On him even that looks fashionable. 'Just one moment, please,' he says, and takes out his laptop. He's writing a book, he says, about a boy who moves into professional football and talks about his experiences. He has a lot of respect for writing, and reads a lot to get better. 'I've built Robert into the book. Because he showed us what a footballer ought to be like.' He runs his index finger over the laptop screen. Suddenly it's no longer clear whether he's speaking freely or reading from a script. 'In Tenerife, Robert, polite, sensitive in his seriousness, showed us that things can be sorted out when someone rebels against a failure, against an injustice. And how he rebelled against what had been done to him at Barça.' Carrasco is moved by his own words. 'If he had had a coach at Barça who had told him after Novelda, "Hang on, you will continue to be my number one, I trust you," in Barcelona he would have become the player we saw in Tenerife.' Carrasco, who has worked in professional football for three decades, folds his hands behind his head. 'In my life I haven't seen ten goalkeepers with Robert's potential. He was like a bull. But our life is determined by who we meet at which point in time. If a goalkeeper happens to work with a coach who eliminates him after just one mistake, the damage is done, and that's psychologically terrible.'

Carrasco hasn't ordered a coffee or a glass of water. He spends his morning break without a drink. 'I can't help remembering that he gave the other goalkeepers gloves – what a magnificent gesture. As if he were saying to his opponents: I'm giving you the same weapons.'

227

The screen of Carrasco's laptop is still glowing. 'It's the Thursday after Robert's death' it says in the middle. 'I haven't been able to write since then.'

In Tenerife Robert developed a new awareness of distance. He wasn't just geographically far away from his previous life, some 2,236 kilometres south of Barcelona, it also felt a long way away. He read the news in the sports papers from the same perspective as the dockers next to him in the café. He had become an outsider. Once he discovered by chance that Timo Hildebrand had mentioned his name in an interview. In 2004 Hildebrand was the rising star among German goalkeepers; he had just set a Bundesliga record: 884 minutes without conceding a goal. You have to think very hard about switching to a big foreign club, said Hildebrand, otherwise you could end up like Robert Enke, who went abroad far too young.

He should have been annoyed about this simplistic way of looking at things. In fact he was glad that Hildebrand remembered him.

When Barça played, he went to a hotel bar to watch the game on satellite TV. The television in the rental flat only received the handful of Spanish terrestrial channels. When she paid a visit, Teresa was pleased to note that he hardly ever watched football on television now. He was proud that he had discovered the hotel bar as a place to do so – a habit, more of a ritual, that he came up with all by himself. The word 'routine' has a bad sound to it, but for him it was vital. Something to cling on to.

He watched Barça in a UEFA Cup match. They quickly took the lead, then made it 2–0. It got boring. He got fixated on the man in front of him, who was forever picking his nose. 'Is that disgusting or what? Look!' What did he feel when he watched Barça on television? 'Nothing at all. I never had the feeling of being a part of it.'

The distance between him and what he saw as real football assumed a new dimension in June 2004. Everywhere people were watching football, everywhere people were talking about football, and he went on playing football, without anyone noticing outside Tenerife. The European Championship in Portugal was beginning. Taking part in that tournament had been his all-surpassing dream only two years earlier, in Lisbon – in another life. Now, in parallel with the European Championship, he had to get through the rest of the Segunda División season.

It didn't occur to anyone to compare Kahn, Buffon and Casillas at the European Championship with Enke against Eibar, Cádiz and Gijón – the comparison sounds ludicrous. But the truth is that at this European Championship where there were no extraordinary goalkeeping achievements and few saves to match Robert's against Eibar's Saizar and Gijón's Bilić.

It would never have occurred to Robert to make the comparison either. As far as he was concerned, during the European Championship he was an excited holiday-maker in front of the television in Tenerife.

Lobo Carrasco asked Robert to visit him at his office. He wanted to contract him to Tenerife for another season. 'With Robert, the whole project had assumed a new orientation: upwards.' Hannover 96 and Albacete Balompié – two top division teams, in Germany and Spain respectively – were also vying for him.

He talked about football to Carrasco for less than ten minutes. They ended up talking about Lara. Teresa was in her seventh month.

She couldn't talk to Marco's wife Christina any more. Christina often tried to ring: Teresa listened to the ringing of the phone and couldn't pick it up. It was unbearable for her to talk to a friend who was having a good pregnancy.

Robert thought the choice of a new club would have something to do with Lara: they should live in a place with good access to a prestigious paediatric cardiologist. But even though the birth was only six or seven weeks away, these big decisions seemed far in the future to him. He had the vague feeling that everything would sort itself out.

❊   ❊   ❊

In Portugal the first big clash was about to kick off, the Czech Republic against the Netherlands, two casually elegant teams fielding two outstanding goalkeepers in Petr Cech and Edwin van der Sar. And Robert couldn't watch the game. That evening he had to play himself, in an insignificant end-of-season game against Getafe in the Heliodoro Rodríguez Stadium. Tenerife were carefree. Twentieth in the table when Robert first played for them in mid-April, the team was now eighth. In their eight games with him they had not lost.

Five days before the match, on the Monday, he got a phone-call. Did he remember him? the caller asked. He was the vice-president of Alavés; they'd been having negotiations two years ago when Robert opted for Barça, which was understandable.

Robert assumed that the vice-president wanted to offer him a contract for the coming season. By now Alavés were in the Segunda División but still had a chance to go up on the last day of play. He tried to remember. He had liked the little town, Vitoria.

He wanted to make him an offer, the vice-president said: he would pay Tenerife 100,000 euros if they beat Getafe.

Alavés would only go up if Getafe lost.

'The Hour of the Briefcases Full of Money' is the name given to the last day of the season in the lower Spanish professional divisions. Some clubs fight desperately for promotion, or to avoid relegation; others are already in the comfort zone – the money-chests are supposed to help them with their motivation.

A hundred thousand euros. That was a good five thousand per player – *limpio*, or clean, as after-tax money is called in Spain.

On Tuesday, four days before the game against Getafe, Robert asked for a moment's peace in the changing-room before training. He had received an interesting phone-call.

Bonuses for victories like the one being offered by Alavés's vice-president were tolerated in Spain. Too many professionals in the lower Spanish divisions aren't paid for months by their chronically stingy clubs. Who would expect them not to have those *maletas de dinero* – briefcases full of money – in the backs of their minds during those final days of play? Robert was still waiting for half of his salary at Tenerife, and he assumed he wasn't the only one.

The same day, after training, Carrasco had a word with the captain of the team, Antonio Hidalgo. 'I don't know what's going on,' he said. 'If Alavés have offered you a bonus to win, that's fine. But there are rumours that we're selling the game to Getafe. It's your responsibility to see that the team doesn't throw the game.' If he heard anything he would step in, Hidalgo promised.

Robert went to have a chocolate milk-shake in the pedestrian precinct, since these would probably be his last days on the island. He had met Ewald Lienen, the coach at Hannover 96, and felt he had found a coach who would not only treat him as a footballer, but as a human being. He drank the milk-shake with a sense of having earned a reward.

On the Wednesday before training one of Robert's closer acquaintances on the team spoke up. 'If you don't mention my name,' this player tells me six years later, 'I'll tell you what happened.'

On Tuesday he had had a phone-call. If he made a few inconspicuous mistakes guaranteeing a victory for Getafe, someone would pay him – he wouldn't say who – twenty-five million pesetas. After the player had turned down the offer, the caller rang back a day later and offered forty million.

Robert first had to convert that into euros – honestly, the Spaniards with their pesetas, three years after the change of currency. It was exactly 240,400 euros.

'I told the caller, leave me out, I don't do things like that,' the player said in Tenerife's changing-room before training on the Thursday. 'If anyone else got a call like that, now's the time to say.'

No one spoke.

Before the last training session of the season, Lobo Carrasco came down to the changing-room. The walls in the stadium catacombs were painted blue and white; you could see the outlines of the bare bricks under the paint. 'If you get a bonus for a win from Alavés, that's fine,' he began calmly. 'But a bonus for a defeat will always be a blot on your career and your conscience. You will never recover from that. If I find out, if I catch anyone, he'll be out. And I will make sure that he never gets another contract anywhere – I'll report him. Do you understand that?'

Some players nodded, some looked at the floor. No one said anything.

When the players in the Heliodoro Rodríguez Stadium looked up, they saw the mountains of Tenerife, soft and green, natural extensions of the terraces. Just after the start of play, Robert heard a murmuring up there. News was spreading from those fans with radios that the Netherlands were winning 2–0 against the Czech Republic after only nineteen minutes.

'There was a holiday mood in the stadium,' Carrasco recalls.

Robert wanted to win at all costs. He wanted to leave Tenerife and be able to say: I never lost a game there. Half an hour later he lost his Spanish while yelling at his centre-halves Corona and César Belli. 'I was so exasperated that I could only shout in German.' They heard and understood Robert's curses on the subs bench, says Álvaro Iglesias, who can still repeat the words today, in flawless German: '*Scheisse! Arschloch!*'

Tenerife were 3–0 down.

Getafe had repeatedly looked for Pachón, their agile striker, 'I felt as if our defenders were opening the way for him,' Robert said. 'Eventually two members of the opposing team were standing freely in front of me. "You're completely crazy!" I roared at our defenders.'

It turned into a rousing game. The eleven thousand fans thought it was the best sort of summer football. Freed from the pressure of having to win, Tenerife played enthusiastically but without concentration. If they lost it wouldn't be so bad: the fans didn't mind allowing Getafe their promotion – they were a team from the Madrid suburbs, the archetypal charming outsiders. Robert thought the Tenerife players were playing against each other. Nine men trying vehemently to win the game and Alavés's briefcase full of money, and one, perhaps two players trying to lose, to fill their own coffers. Carrasco sat in the terraces and saw both versions, the innocent one seen by the crowd and the poisonous one suspected by the honest players. 'I didn't notice anything odd, but then what's odd? Pachón flew, he was all energy, and in their minds our guys were already at the beach.'

In Aveiro in north Portugal, the Czech Republic, in a game that no one would ever forget, turned their 2–0 deficit into a 3–2 victory over the Netherlands. In Santa Cruz, Pachón scored five goals. Getafe won 5–3 and were promoted to the Primera División, and a game that was never to be forgotten was recorded, even in the Spanish sports newspapers, with fifteen lines on page thirty-nine. Only one local Canary Islands newspaper, *La Opinión*, registered some doubts: 'The extreme fragility was something very curious in a defence that was extremely solid until yesterday.'

The lawn-sprinklers came on when Getafe's team were still celebrating their promotion on the pitch. CD Tenerife were in a hurry to bring the season to a close.

In the changing-room the mood was muted. 'Of course we were pissed off,' says Álvaro Iglesias. 'We'll never be able to prove it, but the feeling was that someone out of our own group had messed up our bonus from Alavés. Someone had filled their own pockets at our expense.'

In December 2008 unambiguous evidence emerged that several games in Spanish professional football had been sold. Most of the papers reported the subject for a single day. The Spanish Football Association said they weren't responsible, the Spanish judiciary said neither were they. And the games went on.

Robert opened the roof of his car. He was driving a visitor to the airport, and soon he would be leaving himself. The sky over Tenerife was milky, hazy, a southern wind bringing sand across from Africa. For the German sportswriters it had been his low point, Enke in the Spanish Second Division, on a holiday island. For him it had been a high. None of the aggravation of the last game could spoil that. 'I think I'll have a hamburger today,' he said, and turned up the radio. He hummed along with a song that he didn't know.

FOURTEEN

There is Robert, There is No Goal

For a man who urgently wanted to sell his converted farmhouse in Lower Saxony, Jacques Gassmann set an astonishing condition. For the first few months after the sale he would go on living there. He needed time to find a new place to live and he hadn't started looking for one yet.

He was an artist. That's what artists are like, Robert thought; they saw the world from a different angle, which was how they produced great works.

'Christ, that's not how you buy a house, is it?' Teresa wondered – looking at one and saying yes. They had only ever rented before.

'Why not?' asked Robert, and waited for her bright laughter, certain that it was already on the way.

They'd been back in Germany for a week. Robert had already played his first pre-season match for Hannover 96, a day after the signature of the contract. He was immediately absorbed in the rhythm of professional sport again, training in the morning, warm-up matches, training in the afternoon. Teresa was very pregnant. The sooner they found a house the better.

With sure taste and a love for detail, Jacques had redesigned the farmhouse; the stable had become a kitchen with a French tiled floor, in the hall a chandelier hung over a long farmer's table. He hadn't given much thought to the expense when converting the building; he thought an artist should live unmaterialistically. Now he had to sell the house. But he didn't know where to put all his paintings.

For all his strangeness he seemed to be a nice enough man, and Teresa and Robert bought the farmhouse along with the artist. Jacques was to be allowed to live with them for another three months while he looked for a new home.

Through the big window of the little living-room Robert was able to watch the artist painting in the garden. Once he went outside. He crept over – you don't disturb artists at their work – and stood still behind Jacques's back. The artist's grey hair fell to his shoulders. He gave a start when he suddenly became aware of Robert standing there.

The goalkeeper had a few questions. Where did the darkness in Jacques's paintings come from? Why was everything always black, blurred, overpainted? But how could he, as a footballer, ask these questions? He thought he should feel his way into it with normal questions, questions he was qualified to ask. He asked Jacques how the heating-oil deliveries for the house worked, whether he might be able to recommend a vet for them, since he had a cat, and how he had managed to raise six thousand euros a month in loans and expenses as an artist. If he was lucky, if things went as he hoped, the artist might tell him about his art later on.

In the nineties, Gassmann's cycle *Apocalypse* had created something of a stir. The work had travelled Europe from exhibition to exhibition; some critics detected an evolutionary line: Max Beckmann, Lukas Kramer, Jacques Gassmann. Then, in response to the second Gulf War he painted spiritually screaming, mentally exploding American bomber pilots. *Supersonic* was the name of that series, and he couldn't stop. By the time that well had run dry he had created 160 paintings. 'If I didn't have art, I would explode, Robert,' he said. 'I have to vomit everything out with the paintbrush.' Sentences, bold and heavy, you might expect from an artist. But he couldn't give Robert the real answers. He hadn't even found them for himself.

Robert's death led him to them. 'What have I been painting? I've been painting abysses, people tearing themselves apart,' Gassmann says three months after Robert's death. 'The end of time was a big subject in the nineties, and I went on painting abysses when the nineties were over. It never clicked that I was depicting my own mental state.'

In the garden in Empede – Lake Steinhude starts just beyond the horse-track – Jacques laid his paintings on the lawn to dry.

'Wait, Jacques, I'll just shut Balu in the house so that he doesn't ruin anything,' said Teresa. Balu suffered from distemper, a virus that destroys the brain. He could no longer control himself.

'Don't worry,' said Jacques, 'he can stay out here with me. He's an artist dog!'

'I'd feel better if he wasn't with you.'

'Oh come on. We get on, don't we, Balu, my artist dog?'

Ten minutes later Teresa heard a shout from the garden. 'That's coming out of your insurance! Your dog walked over my paintings!'

Robert with the dogs at his house in Empede.

Robert went to training every day, feeling as if he was coming home. He was in a town he'd never wanted to live in at a club he'd never dreamed of playing for, but the very fact that he was living in Germany again persuaded him that he had finally arrived. For two years he had been at sea. With Hannover he would presumably end up in the bottom third of the Bundesliga, but that didn't bother him; he would come to terms with it. Without any more solid a reason than a newly discovered joie de vivre he was sure he was 'going to feel right here'.

Because the Lower Saxony Stadium was being converted for the 2006 World Cup, the team changed before training in the nearby sport hall. There was only one small changing-room, and the coach got the janitor's office. His new colleagues were startled when Robert walked through the changing-room and introduced himself. He knew nearly all of them by name: 'You must be Frankie – hi'; 'Oh, you're Per.' He had searched for his new team-mates on the internet.

Not everyone in Germany remembered him.

'What number shall we put on his back, twenty-five or thirty?' one of the two team assistants asked the coach.

'Number one,' Ewald Lienen replied.

Lienen, who had as a young man marched with the peace movement for the banning of Pershing missiles and the closure of nuclear power stations, had a mind of his own. If the football scene saw Enke's flight from Istanbul as unprofessional, as weak and cowardly, Lienen saw the step as a sign of strength from a courageous, sensitive man.

No one knew the truth. Robert spoke publicly about his depression without anyone knowing what he was talking about. 'That was a negative experience that had nothing to do with football and everything to do with wellbeing,' he told the *Neue Presse* from Hanover in his first interview after coming home when asked what had happened in Istanbul.

When he thought about depression, he was able to slip out of his own skin and look back with detachment and self-irony at 'Robbi the nutjob', as he called the person who wasn't him. 'Tenerife was my spa cure,' he said. 'But I know it could have gone the other way. I was a has-been. Apart from Lienen it wouldn't have occurred to anyone to bring me back to the Bundesliga. I'm very grateful to him for that.'

What his new colleagues sensed, without being able to put their fingers on it, was an unusual feeling of naturalness that surrounded him like an aura: it was in the matter-of-fact way he went about his job, without drama or pushiness. For the obligatory team photograph at the start of the season the goalkeeper always sits in the middle of the front row, framed by his two substitutes. It's a power ritual: the king on the throne, his subjects at his sides. Robert and the substitute goalkeeper Frank Juric decided to let twenty-one-year-old Daniel Haas, the third-choice goalkeeper, the apprentice, sit on the throne. Robert continued to make such gestures throughout his years with Hannover.

But all this couldn't prevent him from thinking one particular thought when the referee blew the whistle for the start of the 2004–05 season: was he still good enough for this level? It was almost two and a half years since he had last played regularly in a top division.

Hannover 96 were playing Bayer Leverkusen away. The Leverkusen fans remembered who Robert was: the goalkeeper who let in eight goals six years earlier in Mönchengladbach. To the tune of the French children's song 'Frère Jacques' they sang, 'Robert Enke, Robert Enke/Hi there, mate! Hi there, mate!/Do you still remember? Do you still remember?/Two – eight, two – eight.'

He couldn't help laughing. He applauded the fans.

He caught crosses as if it was the most natural thing in the world. He made the fans sigh in amazement when he parried two good shots by Dimitar Berbatov. For the first attempt Berbatov appeared right in front of him but the keeper, with his arms outstretched and his torso straight and his knee bent inwards, suddenly looked like a giant to Berbatov. Hannover lost 2–1 in the last minute but *Kicker* named Robert Enke man of the match. The sportswriters who had in no uncertain terms declared his career over in Istanbul found themselves wondering whether he might find his way back into the Germany squad.

After home games the coach invited the team to dinner at the stadium. One of the cooks who had been serving the guests in the boxes during the game would do the food. Sometimes using knife and fork as pointers, the coach would spend a quarter of an hour analysing the game – ten minutes in German, three in Spanish, two in English – then wish them *bon appétit*. Lienen also organised a visit to the zoo with wives and children. He believed that a team that felt like a family was a better team.

The person Robert immediately took to was one of the assistants. Tommy Westphal had to make sure that the play report form was properly filled out for the referee, that there was soup with and without celery for lunch at the hotel, that the new players had a kindergarten and a mobile phone . . . just name it, Tommy Westphal did it, a hundred things in one day, never forgetting one, while drinking five coffees in an hour and a half – perhaps the one had something to do with the other. 'We immediately found a level because we were both Ossis,' Tommy says with the sort of humour that softens serious subjects. 'We're like the Yugos or the Africans in professional football: we immediately form a clan to defend ourselves.' Tommy noted how much of a presence Robert was within the team from the first match onwards: his easy manner made for a pleasant working environment. Only Robert himself had the feeling that he wasn't putting enough into it, that he wasn't completely fulfilling Lienen's hope of creating a family atmosphere. He had a false self-image of his role in the team because he always disappeared when the others went to lunch after training, and because in general he didn't live professional football as intensely as he'd had in the past.

Because Lara had been born on the last day of August.

Immediately after her birth she had had open-heart surgery. So that her tiny body had a chance of surviving the stress of the operation, she was put into an artificial coma. Her ribcage was opened up as her heart needed room for the swelling to go down. She lay with her arms thrown back in the intensive care ward. The only thing Robert and Teresa could do was hold her little hands and watch her heart beating in her open chest. Lara's pulse rate was 210.

The absolute will to do all they could for their daughter and the throbbing fear of losing her kept Robert and Teresa in a permanent state of high tension. 'When we made the decision to bring Lara into the world we thought we were prepared,' says Teresa. 'Don't misunderstand me, even today I would always decide in favour of Lara, even today – I'm absolutely convinced of it. But I also know that no one can be prepared for life with a sick child. Fear consumes you.'

After four days Lara's ribcage was sewn up again. Progress

was being made, she was getting better, they happily said to themselves. The next morning the nurse told them unfortunately her chest had to be opened up again.

When Robert set off for training at about nine in the morning, Teresa went to the clinic at the University Hospital. During training he would give his mobile phone to Tommy Westphal, in case a call came in from the clinic. After training he'd go straight to Lara and Teresa. The two parents would have lunch in the clinic canteen, then stay until the end of visiting time at eight p.m., every day. Often the door to the intensive care ward was locked and they'd have to stay in the waiting-room with the other parents. Two or three hours might pass, none of them knowing which of the four children currently in the ward was fighting for its life.

Robert thought: 'The one who's really suffering is Teresa. She hasn't got a football match to immerse herself in for ninety minutes.' He recognised how even the most irritating thing about football – the hours on the coach to away games – was becoming a welcome distraction for him. He still didn't have a portable music-player or a laptop to watch films. He was the only one on the bus who listened to the coach radio. 1Live became his favourite station, a mixture of programmes like *Space and Time* and *Cultcomplex* and music, which he couldn't define precisely, it was just different. The coach-driver cursed him affectionately when he had to look for the frequency again every sixty or seventy kilometres.

Meanwhile Teresa was learning all about oxygen saturation. A sensor measured the oxygen saturation in Lara's blood. If it fell below 60 per cent things became critical and the sensor beeped. Teresa couldn't get that beeping sound out of her ears. She even heard it when she was in bed in Empede. Saturation became her fixation, the yardstick of her fear for Lara. In the middle of the night, when she was pumping out breast-milk for Lara in the kitchen, she couldn't help phoning the hospital to find out the percentage of her oxygen saturation.

She had stood by her husband during his five-month

depression, now she spent all day in an intensive care ward sitting beside her daughter, unable even to pick her up.

'Please, go home, have a rest, I'll stay with Lara,' Robert said to her.

But she couldn't go. She had to stay with her daughter and watch the saturation indicator.

Robert and Teresa with their families at Lara's christening.

Every morning they undertook not to let the situation rob them of their happiness. On some days they managed to laugh, even in the waiting-room at the intensive care ward. They discovered cheerfulness where there was none – for example when Robert imitated the sober standard answer doctors gave to the question 'How is Lara?' 'We aren't entirely dissatisfied.' And of course on several occasions during those same days they wondered why the doctors couldn't say something optimistic about the state of Lara's health at least once.

Immersed in his own world, their house-mate had problems understanding the burden they were living under. Jacques had told his assistant to come and start work every day at 8.30.

The young man arrived on time and, equally dependably, Jacques went on sleeping. The half-hour she had over breakfast with Robert had become very valuable to Teresa, almost the only moment of the day that they had to themselves. 'But I'm not the kind of person who can just pretend the assistant isn't there. So I asked him if he would like a coffee too.' And that was the end of her beloved moments alone with Robert.

Jacques would appear at about nine. 'That noise! That coffee machine is driving me round the bend! What's with all this stress, Teresa?'

They had reached an agreement: he would live on the top floor, they would live below. But the communal spaces – the kitchen, the hall, the living-room, access to the garden – were on the ground floor. Effectively the three of them were living on the ground floor. In September a poet friend of Jacques's came for a visit and headquartered himself in the living-room. Once, Teresa and Robert came home from the clinic to find four female violinists standing in the hall. They were setting a verse by Jacques's poet friend to music.

That's just the way Jacques was, Robert tried to bear in mind. When he managed it, he found his artist highly entertaining. But in the evening he generally escaped to watch a football match on television – an excuse not to have to speak, just to have a bit of peace and quiet. Teresa would sit with Jacques in the kitchen. She read biographies of artists – Monet, Picasso, Michelangelo – so their conversations in the kitchen in the evening sometimes began with the great masters. Often they ended with Jacques's views on the world. He was twice divorced, he had become a father at twenty-five, his first wife was a dressage rider, she was the first to show him how to approach art collectors and gallery owners, and he thought he had it all – wife, daughter, dressage horses, house, success – but eventually he found that he didn't dare go into a restaurant, into an aeroplane, that everything he possessed closed him in, oppressed him. Now he had nothing, and he was happy, he tried to convince Teresa and himself.

Jacques considered his hosts in terms of his own story. 'They were a close, good couple. But what was missing from their lives was the tenderness of the everyday.' Isn't that all too understandable when your child is in an intensive care ward? Well, yes, Jacques says bashfully, he hadn't really seen it that way – but anyway: 'I would have said I was exactly the right person for those two. I pulled them out of their five-kilos-of-potatoes, two-kilos-of-rice-and-what-else-do-we-need everyday life.'

Jacques had no interest in football when he met Robert. Later he went regularly to the stadium with Teresa. 'I was interested in Robert. He had a sobriety that was never crude, but always obstinate, alert, curious.' The artist wanted to see him playing, to know whether a game could turn someone into a different person. 'In goal there was something all-encompassing about him. Almost Schwarzenegger-like. He didn't make a fuss, but startled the strikers with his coolness. But when he hugged me to say hello, you felt through his massive body, steely from all that daily training, an amazing warmth and gentleness.'

Jacques gave Robert a portrait for his birthday – a head drawn with quick black lines, and beneath it powerful hands holding something round and pink. At first glance it looks like a ripped-out heart, but it's a football. 'There is Robert, There is No Goal' was the title Jacques gave to the picture. Our friendship isn't about football, it meant. Over the weeks, though, the title became ambiguous: there was Robert, there were astonishingly few goals scored against Hannover.

In a mediocre team, Robert Enke looked almost weirdly good. He was once again the sort of goalkeeper you could imagine in a top team. After their illness, depressives often carry on with their careers as if nothing had happened.

Jörg Neblung paid a visit, and they used the opportunity to go out for the first time since Lara's birth, to the Heimweh. A few of the players often mentioned the bar. It was 20 September. Lara was almost three weeks old. They had something to say to Jörg: they wanted him to be Lara's godfather. They just couldn't say when the christening was going to take place.

They were back in Empede by eleven, no longer used to staying out late. They had just gone to sleep when Teresa's phone rang. It was the clinic. Lara had had a cardiac arrest. They ran off. Jacques's poet friend, sleeping in the living-room, called out, 'What's going on? Oh my God, what's going on?'

By the time they arrived at the clinic the doctors had been trying to bring Lara back to life for an hour. 'If she dies, we'll leave Hanover,' Teresa said. Robert nodded. They stood like that in the intensive care ward until five o'clock in the morning. The doctors had tried over and over again for five hours. Then, suddenly, Lara was alive again.

Robert lay rather than sat on a chair and said blankly, 'What are we actually doing here?' The next day he was supposed to be travelling to Cottbus with Hannover 96 for a German Cup game.

'Robbi, go. Why would you stay here? Lara came through it. We mustn't let fear define our lives.'

In Cottbus the final score was 2–2. It went to penalties. Penalties are football's great duel: the taker's long journey from the halfway line to the penalty spot, the goalkeeper waiting for him. For a moment, in a packed stadium, only those two people exist, the taker and the keeper.

In Lisbon, according to the *Record*, he had been Super-Enke because in the first few months he had parried four out of seven penalties, but since then he had only occasionally saved one. In Cottbus, too, the first four players scored against him. When he saw the fifth, Laurentiu Reghecampf, approaching from the halfway line he suddenly knew he would save his attempt. Every goalkeeper knows that saving a penalty is rarely an art and usually a failure on the part of the taker. But saving a penalty is a keeper's only opportunity to become a hero the way strikers do every Saturday. One single successful action makes everything that has gone before irrelevant. Robert did save Reghecampf's shot. When Thomas Christiansen put the next spot-kick in the back of the net and they had won the game, Robert ran to Christiansen as quickly as he could and hoisted the goal-scorer into the air. That way no one could carry him shoulder high. He didn't feel like having his picture taken as a conquering hero.

Jacques Gassmann, who had decided that he had to bring some life into the life of the Enkes, was a constant source of surprise. He took them to the marksmen's festival at Empede. He didn't want them to end up like him, Jacques explained. He had failed to integrate himself in the village.

In Empede there is no village shop, just a pub, the Ole Deele. For elections it doubles as a polling station. The few houses in the village are made of clinker bricks, the country roads are lanes. In the spring, rape blossoms in the fields. When Robert's dogs were mentioned in passing in a newspaper article about him, the public order office, unrequested, sent him the requisite dog-tags, along with a bill.

In his early days in Empede Jacques had hung pieces of paper from street-lights – Open Studio, Glass of Wine – 'but not a single bastard came'. Jacques felt insulted. At the festival, the artist noted, not without some satisfaction, 'And now they're all staring. What? Here's that lunatic Gassmann with the foot-ball star?'

Soon it was sadly too late to integrate any further with the village. It was just before nine in the evening but they seemed to have been partying, and particularly drinking, for ages; the guests who were still capable of coherent speech were now the minority. A sober man among drunks soon learns the meaning of loneliness. Faced with the choice of getting similarly drunk or retreating, they stayed there politely for another hour and then left. They would go earlier next year, Teresa said.

Jacques, who thought his hosts should live more euphori-cally, more loudly, was now surprised that they didn't think the rough marksmen's festival was all that bad. 'They always stood up for Empede. "It's nice here," they said,' Jacques grum-bles – perhaps he's only pretending. 'But Empede is a dump. When I left, I would have liked to put a sign up in the village: Life just makes you restless.'

* * *

Autumn came, and they learned that even emergencies can become a normal part of everyday life. In theory, Lara should only have been in the intensive care ward for three weeks. In fact it was six weeks before she was brought out of her artificial coma, which was when her parents learned for the first time how her eyes and mouth moved. The fear didn't leave them, even when Lara's monitor showed a high level of oxygen saturation, when the doctor said he wasn't entirely dissatisfied. There was always at least one child in the ward to remind them of the fragility of life. One morning the cot next to Lara's was empty. 'Where's Sandra?' asked Teresa, and didn't get an answer. She can't remember how often she experienced the death of another child – three times, four times? But they still managed to wrest a few beautiful moments from the difficulties of daily life. After three months they went on their first outing with their daughter: they pushed Lara in her buggy on to the balcony of the intensive care ward. The buggy was weighed down with oxygen tanks and heart-rate monitors, there was a feeding tube in Lara's nose, and the saturation indicator beeped – only 64 per cent. 'Is that OK?' Teresa asked the nurse. They were allowed to go out on to the balcony and back again just once. That was happiness, says Teresa, pure happiness.

A few weeks later Lara was able to go back to the cardiac ward, Ward 68b, where they found a picture of a stripy duck, drawn by a child, stuck to the door.

Robert noticed how Lara changed him as a goalkeeper: 'I still get annoyed about bad games but I have no time to go dragging thoughts around with me for weeks.' After a 3–0 win over Bochum he went straight to the clinic; after a 1–0 defeat at the hands of Hertha BSC he hurried straight to Ward 68b. 'The questions are the same, victory or defeat: what are the oxygen levels like, how's her heart-rate?' He had learned something, from the depression, from Markser, from Tenerife, from Lara: 'I know now that mistakes are part of being a goalkeeper. For a long time I couldn't accept that.' Now that he could tolerate mistakes, he hardly ever made any.

Hannover ended the first half of the season a startling seventh in the table; they had been as high as fourth. The coach had created a team that expressed its good mood on the pitch, and their goalkeeper became a symbol of this. The Bundesliga players elected Robert Enke over Oliver Kahn as the best goalkeeper of the first half of the season. It was a reward for his dependability, even though such elections aren't always entirely impartial. His colleagues wanted to grant success to Enke, who made no great show of his virtues, over the toothbaring Kahn.

The national coach rang him. Eight months after Robert had been sitting on the subs bench in the Spanish Second Division Jürgen Klinsmann invited him on a tour of Asia with the national team. Robert declined. He didn't confer with anyone, not even Teresa, he simply told Klinsmann on the phone that sadly he couldn't do it, he couldn't go away for ten days, he had to stay with his daughter. 'I was touched that he didn't even ask me,' says Teresa. 'That he was so serious about being with his daughter.'

Robert felt loved and acknowledged. That made it easier to give love back, even to forgive himself his own mistakes.

But boundless understanding was something else entirely. Where Jacques was concerned, they were finding it more and more difficult to be generous. They felt increasingly that they weren't at home in their own house. They still hadn't been able to move their own furniture in. According to the contract, Jacques had to move out by 1 October at the latest; it was now mid-December. He hadn't even started looking for a new place to live.

'Oh what's all this about contracts? I thought we were friends!' cried the artist when they finally told him one evening that it was really time to move out. Jacques's poet friend had gone, but now his daughter from his first marriage was visiting.

'But Jacques, don't you understand that we can't live together in the long term? And you haven't even started thinking about moving out.'

'OK, then I'll start!' He leapt to his feet and started pulling his crockery out of the kitchen cupboards. 'Look, I'm packing!'

'Jacques, please.'

'I give everything up to live with you and all these animals here, and then you throw something like this at me – if I'd known!'

Teresa was beside herself. Robert, who normally stayed calm when other people got worked up, fought in vain against his rising fury. He couldn't defuse the situation.

Jacques's daughter did that, sixteen years old. 'He's just like that, don't despair,' she said to Teresa and Robert. 'Papa, come on, let's you and me go upstairs now and start packing your things.'

Jacques actually did move out, to a friend's at first – where was he supposed to go at the drop of a hat? But he had one last surprise for them by way of farewell. Teresa's mother called them from Bad Windsheim. 'It's great that there's going to be a vernissage at your house. Are you making the canapés?'

Jacques had sent out invitations to a private Christmas viewing of his paintings. If he sold a lot of them he wouldn't have to take so many away with him. Teresa's mother had been invited because she knew Jacques from her visits to Empede. She was taken with his art and was on his distribution list. Jacques hadn't mentioned the event to Teresa and Robert, which was taking place in his studio, beside their house.

The next evening Teresa and Robert sat in their kitchen watching in silence as a crowd of strangers walked quite matter-of-factly through their house and asked them where the toilet was.

'What is this?' Robert asked Teresa. 'A bad film? Or the normal madness of our life?'

They decided to laugh. It summed up their early days in Hanover, says Teresa. 'It was a lovely time, but a really terrible one.'

FIFTEEN

Lara

In a room for two hundred people, they were the only guests. Red plastic chairs stood at plain wooden tables; a few pot plants between the rows of tables testified to a vain attempt to make the hall more appealing. Teresa and Robert spent Christmas in the hospital canteen. There are some details you never forget: on the menu was salmon with green tagliatelle.

Without intending to, their acquaintances had hurt them over the past few days with simple questions.

'So, where are you going for the Christmas holidays?'

To hospital.

It was raining outside. But the loneliness of the canteen soon gave way to a feeling that they were celebrating a special Christmas. They had Lara, now sleeping peacefully in Ward 68b. They had each other. Teresa took pictures of the canteen food – their curious Christmas dinner.

Robert spent some of his holiday on the phone. His conversations with Marco provided a bit of distraction. Since Lara's birth Teresa was regularly phoning the Villas, who had just had a daughter themselves, Chiara. And while Marco talked to Robert about very different concerns, he thought he understood why it was that his friend played such great football in Hanover. 'He felt more valuable because he was looking after Lara. That feeling of self-worth gave him an incredible amount of strength and pride.'

Experiencing the serenity with which Robert was coping with a difficult situation wasn't just a source of joy for Marco. He was also slightly hurt by it. Because he automatically asked why he couldn't cope with the pressure of professional sport in a similar way. He was only being used every now and then at Arezzo; in the winter break he was going to switch to Ferrara, also in the Italian Third Division. From the very first day Marco had always felt a bit like Robert's protector. Were they switching roles?

When Marco visited them in Empede, Robert said, 'Come with me.' He led his friend to his office. Shelves reached to the ceiling; boxes full of photographs stood next to Spanish textbooks and files marked Business Tax. Robert picked up one of these tomes. 'Here, look. My depri-file.' He showed Marco his diaries, the poem about the dwarf. He thought he could look back over them with a smile.

On St Valentine's Day 2005, Lara came home. Her parents had had a room decorated for her birth five and a half months earlier. Now they were holding in their hands a child with blue lips and had to get straight to work. Every three hours she received liquid nourishment through a tube in her nose. When the saturation indicator beeped, Robert or Teresa had to look at the monitor to check that the oxygen level hadn't fallen below 60 per cent: if it had, Lara would have to go to the clinic straight away. In the first four days Robert didn't sleep much and Teresa not at all. 'I was glad that Lara was home, but my nerves were in pieces,' says Teresa. 'The responsibility, the fear of doing something wrong, drove me mad.' Lara was about to have the last of her three heart operations.

'She's thrown up again!' Teresa cried despairingly after giving Lara the food solution. Now she had to start all over again, and each feed took an hour and a half. Later she was sitting quietly in the kitchen at last when she heard the beep of the saturation sensor; but how could she tell if it was really beeping, or only in her head? She kept walking into Lara's room to check. She had been a passionate sleeper, 'cuddling up in bed at night, and reading had always been the loveliest thing', but since Lara's birth until today Teresa hasn't slept through the night. 'It's embedded so deep within me that I still keep waking up.'

After Robert's death a one-sided impression was created of

a man dependent on Teresa's love and help. But more often than not he helped others, his wife included.

'You don't need to give her the full portion again, she didn't throw everything up,' he said, and led Teresa gently away from Lara's bed.

'I'll go,' he said when she felt compelled to check the oxygen saturation again. 'It's seventy per cent,' he said, when the saturation level was 67 per cent.

On the fourth night of life with Lara at home he said: perhaps there was a meaning to it all, a child with Lara's problems ending up with them, a couple without financial worries. Let's take on a nurse for the nights, even if the health service won't cover the costs.

The night-nurse came for the first time on 18 February. It was Teresa's birthday.

'And what are you doing today?' Jörg asked on the phone, after saying happy birthday.

'I'm going to sleep, at last I'm going to sleep. That's my birthday party.'

With Lara at home, nine months after their return to Germany they were beginning to see the country they had come back to. At the supermarket till in Neustadt, Robert could hardly keep up with the packing. The customer behind him was already giving him sour looks; she couldn't understand why he was smiling. The smile wasn't meant for her, it was a product of his thoughts. He remembered the supermarket in Lisbon, where everyone had waited stoically in the queue until the customer at the front had finished her conversation with the cashier about her raspberry tart recipe.

They hadn't been globetrotters by choice; chance had led them through southern Europe for five years. Even so they felt torn, as people often do when they come home. They missed the light of Lisbon, the sound of the waves, and the feeling of being at home that they had experienced among their friends in Sant Cugat. Robert often read the Portuguese sports papers online for the latest news from Benfica and, although he was reluctant to admit it, *El Mundo Deportivo* for news about Barça. But their memories didn't spoil their feeling of wellbeing in Empede. It was lovely there, with its expanse of fields and the peace of the forest. It would be lovely if you could take your baby for long walks, if you could drop by for a chat with the neighbours, if you could do what normal parents did.

In their life between the intensive care ward and the training-ground they had got to know hardly anyone. Hannover's striker Thomas Christiansen and his wife Nuria had once come to the clinic but Christiansen had left again a few minutes later. He couldn't bear the sight of it.

At training, Robert often spoke in Spanish to Christiansen, a Dane with a Spanish mother, out of sheer love of the language. On Wednesdays, when the team trained twice, a group of players stayed together after the end of the session. They had moved back into the stadium. The refurbishments for the World Cup were done, but the space behind their changing-room looked anything but world-class. Empty drinks crates were stacked in the corners, and the place smelled of shoe polish. It was Mille's realm – Michael Gorgas, who managed the kit, looked after the boots, took care of sportswear in general. On Wednesdays after training he used to cook vacuum-packed bockwursts for the players in his room. In his fridge, he hoarded lemon-flavoured beer. The footballers called his room Cabin Two. This was where the club's success was forged.

Hannover 96 finished Robert's first season back in the Bundesliga in tenth place, which was remarkable for a club that was unused to success. The keen-eyed coach had found the kind of players that made a team better: Robert Enke, Per Mertesacker, Michael Tarnat. He had organised the defence and choreographed the attacks. It wasn't extraordinary football, just clear-headed. But the coach's tactical know-how would have remained purely theoretical if Ewald Lienen hadn't also triggered something with his group initiatives around the lunch table and at the zoo. The hard core of the team now sat in Cabin Two, wearing only towels after their sauna, clutching bockwurst and beer. Michael Tarnat, Frank Juric, Vinicius,

Robert Enke and a few others, eight to ten of them – later on Hanno Balitsch, Szabolcs Husti and Arnold Bruggink too – enjoyed talking shop and acting the fool. And without anyone noticing, a team spirit was produced.

'I bet you can't eat fifteen bockwursts and rolls in half an hour, Mille,' said one of the players.

Mille started eating. The others fetched themselves another beer. After thirteen bockwursts Mille couldn't go on.

'Come on, let's do some track-racing.'

They put up rubbish-bins and crates of water as obstacles, and Mille steered his bicycle along the course. 'Faster, Mille!' the spectators called from behind the bins. He took some bad falls but he joined in with the footballers' laughter. He felt that acting the fool was the most important task of a kit manager.

'It's nice to be successful, but it's even nicer to be successful with friends,' said Robert. 'You don't often find a team as cohesive as ours in professional football.'

In the changing-room he sat next to Michael Tarnat. Tarnat was already thirty-six and had played with Bayern Munich and for Germany in the 1998 World Cup. His ideas on how a professional team should behave came from the far-off days of Stefan Effenberg. When twenty-year-old Jan Rosenthal lost the ball with a back-heel in a training match, Tarnat kicked him viciously a few minutes later. That would teach the lad a lesson. Robert took Rosenthal by the arm and gave him some words of encouragement when he found him, after one bad match, desperate and hyperventilating, bent over the basin in the toilet. Deep down he still found the tough style of the Effenberg generation suspect. But unlike in Mönchengladbach, he was no longer on the receiving end, he was on the side of the ones who set the pace. Tarnat was one of his closest colleagues on the team. His uncompromising and often witty way of addressing shortcomings helped the team, that much was clear to him now. But he also found an answer to a question he had asked himself nine years earlier, during his first weeks in Mönchengladbach: did he have to be like that too? He didn't, and he would never want to be.

In Cabin Two he discovered football. For a long time he hadn't been interested in the game itself, only in the special task of the goalkeeper. Now he listened to Tarnat or Balitsch when they talked tactics. He started thinking about the game the way a coach would. Should one of the defensive midfield players switch to attack more often? Why didn't they hit more cross-field passes from the right-back to the centre-forward to avoid their opponents' pressing? Like almost everyone who becomes strategically aware about football, Robert suddenly felt enriched. At the same time he wondered what a waste it would have been only ever to see football from a superficial point of view.

But football, which seems to divide the world quite clearly, every weekend, into winners and losers, often seduces the most intelligent observers into a simplistic view of the game. Robert was forced to acknowledge this as soon as his second season with Hannover began in August 2005. Hannover 96 soon found themselves clinging on to a mid-table position. Given the club's potential, that was passable enough. But no one outside Cabin Two seemed to be assessing the team in terms of its possibilities; they were all judging it by its impressive tenth place the previous year. They had bought two internationals, Hanno Balitsch and Thomas Brdarić; shouldn't the team be playing even better this season? Instead they lost 4–1 in Bielefeld at the end of October, and a week later they were losing 2–0 to Mainz after sixty-five minutes. The fans shouted, 'We want our money back!' 'Get rid of Lienen!'

The men from Cabin Two knew that their team was going through one of those bad spells most mid-table teams suffer from every now and then. But they had a sense that the club's sporting director Ilja Kaenzig was caught up in the public hysteria, trapped in his own idea that things had to go ever further, ever higher. If the team lost 2–0, the sporting director would sack the coach – their coach.

Lienen, a sympathetic father-figure within the team but publicly thin-skinned, hadn't exactly strengthened his position with some stroppy appearances in the media.

Four minutes before the end of the game Brdarić scored to

make it 2–1. In the last minute of play, which had already lasted 180 seconds, Tarnat got hold of the ball out of a mêlée and fired it into the back of the net. He was the first to run to the sideline, to Lienen. All the players threw themselves jubilantly at their coach. Robert was furthest away so he threw himself on top of the mountain of people. It was a demonstration of their feelings.

Kaenzig vacillated.

It takes a sporting director with strong nerves and an unshakeable belief in cold-blooded analysis, to ignore cries of 'Sack the coach!', when the team is close to relegation. There aren't many around.

Two days after the 2–2 draw against Mainz, Kaenzig spent three hours in a hotel with Lienen. Then he said, OK, let's keep going.

13 May 2006: Robert with Lara after the victory over Bayer Leverkusen in Hanover.

The next morning, Lienen got changed for training. He was already wearing his football boots and his navy-blue windcheater when Kaenzig came in. He was sorry, but he'd decided to dismiss him.

The players were brought into a conference room. The rage that leads to mutiny was throbbing in some of them. 'We don't have a crisis situation, but we have observed a stagnation,' said the sporting director. The players sat in front of him with their arms folded, saying nothing. A professional footballer has to accept the decisions of his superiors without complaint; he needs to serve the club even in defiance of his own opinion. That's an unwritten fundamental principle of football.

All of a sudden a player stood up. Robert Enke spoke clearly. 'As employees, we have to respect the club's decision. But the way you threw the coach out is dishonourable. It's very bad form.'

He still found conflicts disagreeable. But strengthened after his depression, he felt ready to take on an argument calmly and matter-of-factly.

In January 2006, at sixteen months old, Lara survived her third heart operation. 'The life-threatening phase is over,' said Robert. The parents watched their child with pride. She had her father's fair hair, while the eyes took more after her mother. A few months later than usual, Lara learned to sit up. Eventually she picked a chair and tried to pull herself up on her wobbly legs. When her parents talked to her, she moved her mouth as if she wanted to speak. Not a word came out. 'Lara will never be really well,' said Robert, sounding sober, but at the same time like a happy father who thinks his child is capable of anything.

What was striking was how often Lara laughed. When she looked at the dogs, when her father rolled his eyes for her, when her mother wore a baseball cap. Ela, their housekeeper, took it quite naturally that Lara couldn't be fed from a jar or that she wasn't able to walk. Ela treated her without reservations, unafraid that anything might happen to her. She took the little one with her when she went shopping, she took her to see other children. Ela was showing Lara's parents something, without noticing: it was fine. Even for Lara there was such a thing as normality. Or at least an imitation of normality.

That summer she was cheered by thirty-seven thousand people. Teresa had taken her along to the stadium on the day Hannover beat 1 FC Cologne 1–0 and moved up to seventh place in the Bundesliga. Robert took her with him on his lap of honour. He carried her in his goalkeeping gloves.

'That sight brought me a kind of fulfilment,' says Teresa. 'We'd done it: we'd survived both the depression and Lara's heart operations, in terms of sport he was back on top, and we were still happy as a couple. I wish I could have frozen that moment.'

The fairy-tale summer, the Germans called it. The World Cup and the sun were both in the country. Robert was fourth goalkeeper in line for the World Cup squad. As they say in the jargon, he was on stand-by duty. If anything happened to one of the three nominated keepers, he would be called up as an emergency replacement. It was extremely unlikely. Not being able to play but still having to stay at the ready – other people saw it as a humiliation. Schalke's attacker Kevin Kurányi said nobody needed to call him, he was going on holiday. Robert stayed in his garden, proud of his pseudo-nomination, and couldn't get the parasol to go up.

Lara was sitting on my lap in the garden. When Teresa went into the house for a moment, Robert said to me, 'If you think Lara's hands are cold, please don't tell Teresa. She gets so worried about her cold hands.'

Lara had been given a PEG probe. She could now be fed directly through the stomach wall rather than through a tube in her nose. Her parents no longer had to check with a stethoscope to see whether the milk had reached her stomach, instead of inadvertently going into her lungs.

Without the tube in her face she suddenly looked healthier. Her parents packed a suitcase as if they were going off on an expedition – milk, injections, tablets, pulse oximeter – and took her to the zoo. They put Lara in a sling and took her into the fields with the dogs. For several moments they forgot the clock that was constantly ticking in their heads – probe in an hour, bedtime in an hour and a half. One evening they let Lara stay up longer than scheduled. It was only half an hour, but to them it also seemed like a fairy-tale summer.

Robert's phone rang. It was Jörg Neblung, about extending his contract with Hannover, which would run out in a year. Hannover wanted to confirm as quickly as possible that he was staying on. There were temptations. Hamburg SV were possibly interested. Bayer Leverkusen had even sent their chief scout, Norbert Ziegler, to watch him in training. Leverkusen's goalkeeper Hans Jörg Butt was thirty-two and the club's directors were talking about whether they should acquire a successor, even though they were training up an exciting junior international as a substitute, René Adler. But you could never tell, of course, if talents would reach their full potential. 'Of course I could switch to a bigger club, if I applied myself,' Robert said in the garden. 'But if Hannover get the money together I can easily imagine staying.' He didn't want to forget once again that ever further, ever higher wasn't always the right direction to go in. 'I know what I've got here – playing in the Bundesliga, getting good reviews on Monday.'

Lara sat in the grass and watched one of the dogs.

Outside the front door stood a handicapped man from the village, as he did almost every day, waiting for a word or a gesture from his idol. Robert excused himself, he would have to have a serious word with the chap, he couldn't hang around outside the door for hours on end, every day. Robert went outside and then chatted good-naturedly with the man.

Later we went into the house because a World Cup match was about to start. Italy versus the USA. He wanted to study the great Buffon. 'But you never see anything, because he never gets to do anything.'

'He watches all the World Cup matches,' Teresa called out to me.

'Nonsense. I didn't watch South Korea versus Togo.'

In the house, apart from some cheerful colour photographs, they had hung some black paintings. By Jacques Gassmann.

Ever since Jacques had stopped being their squatter Robert had felt a growing affection for the artist who was, somehow, his very own artist. 'I had to revise my image of him,' says Jacques. When he was living with the Enkes he had often spent a long time sitting alone with Teresa at the kitchen table because Robert had clearly had enough of him. Now Robert collected Jacques's post. The police wrote to Jacques more than once: he'd had an altercation with a man at the car-wash, or he'd been caught by a speed trap on the A7 near Fulda. The revenue office had to remind him from time to time that there was such a thing as a tax declaration. Jacques lived some of the time in Hanover and some of the time in Poland, but his post still went to Empede.

'If you go carrying his letters after him, he'll never learn that there are some things in life that you have to do for yourself,' Teresa said to Robert.

Robert and Teresa with Lara during the fairy-tale summer of 2006.

But he had resolved to help his artist get his life in order. Sometimes he rang Jacques; they had to meet so that he could give him his mail. Once he sent the artist a text from Saudi Arabia, where he was playing with the national team. He just wanted to remind him that he had a parking ticket to pay, sixty euros, it had to be paid by Monday, the reference number was . . . He always began his texts to Jacques with the words 'Great Master!'

'In a way I thought his commitment was a bit skewed,' says Jacques. 'Wouldn't it have been easier to pay the sixty euros for my bad parking rather than send texts from Arabia?'

The goalkeeper brushed aside Jacques's insistence that he really didn't need to worry about his mail so conscientiously. 'Jacques, you're a scatterbrain, if you do it yourself it isn't going to work.' Then Jacques seemed to understand what Robert's real concern was. 'The parking-tickets were an umbilical link to me. He always needed an excuse, a pretext, to make contact. And then off he would go with his chattering.'

There was nothing to connect the two of them except for five shared, often painful months under one roof. Now, when they met to hand over the mail, Jacques talked to him about goalkeepers, a topic he hadn't a notion about, and Robert asked about art, which he knew nothing about. Jacques bought a television especially to watch Robert playing. Robert went to the *Apocalypse* exhibition in the St Johannis Kirche in Bemerode. It was precisely because Jacques was so different that he liked seeing him – as long as it wasn't too often. The artist felt much the same. That's why Jacques is vexed that he never told Robert what might have been the most important thing. His own story.

When he got a grant from the Sprengel Museum, the media reported that a new star had risen in the artistic firmament. 'People said, now he's got everything. I thought all I had was pressure.' Eventually he started feeling a pain in his chest, and he was convinced it was lung cancer. What he had was a pulled muscle from wind-surfing. 'Happiness does not consist in being right at the top,' Jacques states.

What is happiness, then?

'Happiness is recognising how much pressure you can take. Happiness means freeing yourself from the people who revere you for something you aren't. Not trying to please those people. Not constantly being preoccupied with making it all look effortless.'

Jacques Gassmann now lives in Würzburg. The Catholic Church has become his major employer. Later that evening he's meeting the cathedral priest. 'He rocks,' says Jacques. His blue trousers are sprinkled with little white dabs of paint; anyone who didn't know what he does for a living might think it was an expensive piece of design. 'That was the other thing I thought was interesting about Robert. Outwardly he was becoming more and more of a classic footballer.' In Hanover he started to wear his shirts wide open, he bought belts with patterns of studs, and for the first time in his life he drove a showy car, a big Mercedes. 'But deep down he had less and less to do with that cliché.' Once, Jacques received a 'very touching letter'. A shame they'd missed each other so often recently, from Teresa and Robert. 'Thanks for the lovely letter,' Jacques said the next time he spoke to Teresa on the phone.

'What letter?'

Robert had written it all by himself.

The Goethe Institute in Lisbon invited Robert and Teresa to an event being staged to coincide with the World Cup. It was the first time they had been back to Portugal in four years. When they saw the city from the plane, Teresa started crying.

'What are you doing?'

'I'm so happy,' she said, and thought of a sentence she thought she had forgotten long ago, his first Portuguese words. *É bom estar aquí.* It's good to be here.

He wanted to go straight to the sea at Cascais, to La Villa in Estoril, to the Palácio Fronteira, to the Blues Café. 'It was lovely to walk beside him and notice that he was at home here,' says Paulo Azevedo, who organised the event. They often had to stop because passers-by kept talking to Robert. They wanted to tell him to come back. 'And the amazing thing was, it didn't matter whether they were fans from Benfica or their great rivals Sporting and Porto. Everybody said, "Hey, come back." If they were Sporting fans, they added, "But come to us this time." That gives you an idea of the impression he made here.'

Events at the Goethe Institute that attract more than fifty people are few and far between. Eight hundred people turned up to see the interview with Robert Enke. A Portuguese television channel broadcast it live.

Lisbon had been great, he realised without a twinge of pain. Life in Hanover had reconciled him to his subsequent path.

Even though Lara had already been with them in Empede for a year and a half, they still felt at home in the clinic at the University Hospital. They had to go there too often for checkups. This time the doctors had some news for them: Lara was deaf. But everything suggested that her acoustic nerve still worked, which made cochlea implants a possibility. Even with

Robert and his new friend Paulo Azevedo at the World Cup event in Lisbon.

a hearing aid it would be a long time before she learned to hear, but it was possible. Teresa and Robert postponed the operation until September so that Lara could celebrate her birthday at home on 31 August.

The 2006–07 Bundesliga season, Robert's third with Hannover 96, was already under way. The previous season they had finished twelfth, but Robert didn't want to admit that the sacking of his mentor Lienen had had a positive effect on the team. 'Our results would have improved with Ewald Lienen as well,' he said defiantly. Where his successor, Peter Neururer, was concerned, he remained sceptical. 'It would be nice if we trained for something other than corners.' After years in the Bundesliga, Neururer had enjoyed some short-lived success with well-practised corners and a halfway decent defence, but in the longer term his plan of action was too limited and his luck soon deserted him. After only three games into the new season he was fired. The team was bottom of the league with three defeats.

The first game with the new coach, Dieter Hecking, coincided with the day of Lara's ear operation. Yet again Robert's focus had to be on two places at once, the football pitch and the operating theatre. But this time the clinic didn't dominate his thoughts, mainly because in comparison with the three heart operations the ear surgery would be less complicated, less frightening. Also, a difficult test awaited them in the stadium. If they didn't win straight away with the new coach they could easily get stuck in the relegation battle.

He was staying in the hotel with the team preparing for the match at VfL Wolfsburg. Teresa was in the waiting-room at the clinic. Lara was on the operating table. Doctors were checking her heartbeat, pulse, oxygen saturation levels; Lara's condition under general anaesthetic was stable, they could operate. After putting in the first cochlea implant they had to decide whether operating on the other ear would be too much for Lara.

In Wolfsburg the new coach announced the team line-up. Thomas Brdarić, capped eight times by his country, and Altin Lala, the captain, were returning to the side. As a result of one of those conflicts so typical of professional football, the kind whose origins no one can ever actually remember, Neururer had left those two out during his last weeks at the club.

Everything's fine, the doctor told Teresa early that evening; both operations had been successful and the little one's circulation was stable. They brought Lara out of the operating theatre. She had a bandage around her head. Visiting hours at the intensive care ward were over, so Teresa drove home.

In Wolfsburg, Robert's game began.

It soon transpired that a coach who articulates his thoughts clearly can change a team in a week. Nothing is harder in football than simplicity, but when Dieter Hecking explained his ideas on defence everything that had seemed like a failure for weeks was suddenly clear and simple. Hannover 96 controlled the game in Wolfsburg. Brdarić put them 1–0 ahead, but Wolfsburg equalised straight away. Teresa had turned on the television at home, and when the other team scored she automatically caught her breath. There was nothing Robert could have done, she persuaded herself as she watched the replay. Brdarić scored again. Hannover had won their first game of the new season. Teresa went to sleep easily that night.

At eight o'clock the next morning Robert went to the clinic. Lara had thrown up a bit but everything was under control, everything was fine, the nurse said. They wanted to keep turns watching over Lara, Teresa in the afternoon, Robert at night. Lara slept, still exhausted from the anaesthetic. Robert read the papers. 'No one in Hanover's interested in Neururer any more,' said the double goal-scorer Brdarić in the *Hannoverische Allgemeine*. Robert wasn't mentioned. It had been the best game for a goalkeeper; he hadn't had much to do all night. Teresa went jogging in the fields. In the afternoon she took over from Robert. He drove to Empede and watched the football. Bayern were actually losing in Bielefeld, Hamburg were also about to be defeated again in Dortmund – what they really lacked was an outstanding goalkeeper. By the winter break he would decide whether he would go or stay in Hanover.

'Everything's fine,' Teresa said to him when he arrived for

his night-watch session, 'but try to give her a bit more food. I didn't get much fluid into her.' Lara was already eating small things like a spoonful of porridge. Solid food like a bit of bread she generally just put in her mouth and then spat out again – she didn't yet know that you could swallow things like that. Sometimes her parents gave her a red lollipop and she sucked away on that for ages. This time Lara only sucked on the lollipop twice before giving it back to Teresa. Was that a sign that her recovery from the operation wasn't going well? Or was it just the normal moods of a child?

That evening in Empede Teresa made herself a pizza. She thought: good, we've got the implants out of the way. What would it be like when Lara could finally talk to them?

In the clinic Robert tried to give her food artificially via the probe, but Lara wasn't ingesting much of it. He wasn't too worried. At least she'd eaten something.

At about ten o'clock Teresa called him. Everything's fine, said Robert. Lara was asleep.

He was allowed to spend the night in his daughter's room. After an hour or so he heard Lara tossing and turning. He put his hand on her to calm her down. Her body was cold. To busy himself, just to do something, he tried to give her some food via the probe again.

At midnight he called night duty. She might be in pain from the operation, the duty doctor said, and gave her a painkiller. Both she and Robert fell asleep. At about five he woke up. A nurse was standing next to Lara's bed fiddling with the pulse oximeter. The gauge was at zero. Presumably the sensor was broken, the nurse said. Her movements were urgent yet calm. They changed the sensor. The new one couldn't find a heartbeat either. The nurse frantically tried to revive Lara. She called the duty doctor. The duty doctor called for the senior physician in charge of the intensive care ward. 'Who is it?' the senior physician asked. Lara Enke. She was perplexed. Lara had been stable that afternoon. The nurse sent Robert on to the balcony. He tried to call Teresa. She had left the phone in the kitchen and didn't hear it ringing in her sleep. He dialled the housekeeper's number and told her, please, drive to Teresa quickly and wake her up. It was a quarter past five in the morning on 17 September 2006. 'Lara's gone,' Robert said repeatedly into the phone, 'Lara's gone.' Then everything went black.

At six, Teresa was about to enter the clinic by the back entrance so that she could get to Lara's room more quickly. She found Robert outside Lara's door, lying on the pavement.

'On the way back from the clinic we immediately said to each other: life goes on. That was our slogan,' says Teresa. That was their attempt.

The car radio was already broadcasting the news: Robert Enke's daughter dies. The cause of death seemed to be sudden heart failure. They called family and friends. Everyone said how composed Robert and Teresa sounded. They told everyone, please, don't come to Empede. They wanted to be alone together.

They laid out Lara at home. The children of the village came to visit her one last time. In the silence one little girl said, 'What will happen to all her lovely toys?' Teresa was pulled up short by the innocent cruelty of childhood. It was so easy for children, they just carried on playing. Robert stood next to her as if under anaesthetic, as if he were no longer there.

At the funeral service the day after Lara's death, for which they asked everyone to wear white, Teresa noticed that something was gnawing away at him.

'So, training tomorrow – better not?' he asked, his voice still too fragile to form a whole sentence.

'Of course, Robbi!'

'You think?'

'Of course, if it helps. Football is part of our life. Make sure you go back to everyday life.'

'And the weekend?'

'Play.'

'Yes?'

'Robbi, whether you play this Saturday or next, it doesn't

change anything. It'll be harder for you to come back the longer you wait.'

On Tuesday, two days later, Robert turned up for training. He dragged a silence behind him: wherever he went conversations dropped away; a mute bubble formed around him. He didn't sit down in the changing-room. He had something to say to them, he said. Most of the players stared at the floor. 'As you know, Lara has died. Please, don't be stand-offish, talk to me openly if you have any questions. Just be perfectly natural about her death.' He seemed commanding, grounded.

'It was a moving performance,' says Tommy Westphal, his friend, the team assistant. 'But no one asked him about Lara. No one from the team could say a thing to him that went beyond normal sympathy. I had the feeling his team-mates found it harder to deal with the situation than he did.' How were they to go on talking to each other when Robert was among them? Were they even allowed to go on laughing on the training-ground?

It was no easier for their parents and friends. How were they to express their sympathy and support if Teresa and Robert didn't want to see anybody?

Robert's mother escaped to the mountains around Jena. It was a beautiful day, the day after Lara's death, the third-last day of that fairy-tale summer of 2006. Gisela Enke remembered to drink a large amount of water before she set off. She marched more than she walked, as if she could outpace the news. At some point she tripped on the mountain path. She didn't try to get up; she felt she wouldn't be able to do it anyway. Just lie where you are, Robert's mother said to herself, no one will come by anyway.

Back at home she wrote a letter to Robert and Teresa. She pretended it was Lara who was writing. 'You remember, Papa, when I spat out my food and covered you from head to toe? You couldn't bring yourself to laugh that time.' When Robert and Teresa read the letter they couldn't help crying, and that did them good.

The next Saturday his father was suddenly standing in front

of him. Robert was lining up in the changing-room corridor before the game against Bayer Leverkusen. His father threw his arms around him. Robert shivered, touched and embarrassed at the same time. He wasn't keen on the idea that his father had battled his way past all the stewards to the sanctum of the stadium: 'I'm Robert Enke's father, please let me through, I've got to get to my son.'

The referee blew his whistle. Six days after Lara's death, Robert performed strongly in a Bundesliga match against Leverkusen that ended 1–1. He alone registered that he had made a few small mistakes.

It didn't occur to anyone that Lara's death might topple him back into a depression. In his grief there was hardly any time or room for the idea. And besides, he seemed so composed.

Marco Villa hadn't been able to attend Lara's funeral. He was a professional, he had to play football, now for a Serie D club based in a suburb of Naples where a local meat wholesaler had promised amazing salaries. That day Marco played unemotionally. He thought about Lara and scored a goal without noticing what he was doing. Three thousand people in the stadium applauded him. His team-mates came running over to congratulate him and couldn't understand why he wasn't throwing his arms up in the air, why he wasn't beaming from ear to ear. Before half-time, Marco scored another goal. Then he pretended he'd sprained a muscle and got himself substituted. He sat alone in the dark changing-room while the second half carried on outside. He was a striker, and he had just scored for the first time in seven years.

SIXTEEN

Afterwards

Teresa had some photographs stored on her camera that she still hadn't printed. They were a few weeks old. They showed Robert with Lara by the Maschsee – their last outing together, by the big lake in Hanover. What would they do with those photos now? How could they do anything with those photos?

'Let's put them on the wall,' said Teresa.

He nodded, so that he didn't have to speak.

They didn't want to avoid their daughter's death, they wanted to remember the beautiful moments. But of course that didn't work every day.

Teresa stopped eating. She helplessly watched herself getting thinner and thinner, feeling no desire for food. He was pursued by questions. Could Lara's death have been prevented? What if the doctors had operated on only one of her ears? Would her little heart have stood the strain then? 'We all overestimated her strength,' he said, without noticing how loudly he was suddenly talking.

The high chair still stood at the kitchen table. They couldn't simply clear it away. But how, when they saw that chair, could they keep from thinking how empty it was?

But the countless inner breakdowns, most of which lasted no more than a few minutes, led to an unimaginably beautiful insight: pain brought them together. 'There are moments in life when you feel very powerfully: I'd like to grow old with this person. That's how it was with Robbi and Terri after Lara's death,' says Marco Villa.

They went together to Lara's nursery. Her name was still on the door in bright magnetic letters, her toys still lay on the carpet. They sat down on the floor. Do you remember, they said to each other. Lara wanting the nurse to put on the same sort of baseball cap as Teresa. Lara eating a whole jar of food on her last day.

They didn't want to avoid their daughter's death, they wanted to remember the beautiful moments. And on some days they actually could.

Lara's death was less than two weeks in the past when Robert got some news. For the first time in seven years he had been included in the Germany squad. Could he only ever experience extremes of sorrow and joy? He persuaded himself that he could be proud of his selection: he didn't need to be ashamed if he felt something like joy. He felt like a robot issuing orders to itself: be glad.

In early October the national team met in Berlin for a training-camp. At the end of the week they would play a friendly against Georgia, and he was to be substitute goalkeeper. The director of media at the German Football Association cautiously asked him how he felt about a press conference. His inclusion after such a long time was obviously newsworthy.

Of course he would do it, said Robert.

But he would have to expect questions about Lara.

He was prepared for that, said Robert.

He hadn't talked to reporters since her death, which hadn't been very hard: journalists, even from the tabloids, had reverently kept their distance. Now here he was in Berlin sitting on a podium in front of a hundred of them. He asked if he could say something before the first question. 'First of all I would like to take the opportunity, in my wife's name as well as my own, to say thank you to all the incredible numbers of people who have expressed their sympathy to us over the last few weeks. Each individual letter was very welcome, and helped us go on a little further. Please publish that. It's really important to my wife and me.'

The questions that followed were asked in muted voices. He kept interrupting his answers with a little cough.

'Lara's illness forced me to confront life and death,' he said, which is why even before her death he had been preoccupied with the question of what would happen if she died. 'Things have to go on. Grief can't defeat you.'

Robert's performance was one of the most impressive ever experienced at a football press conference, the sportswriters wrote afterwards. Testimony to his enormous strength. Robert himself didn't feel enormously strong. He had simply pulled himself together. 'I was just scared that people would avoid me because they didn't know how to respond to me. That's why I tried from the outset to be as natural as possible.'

After two or three months he sometimes spoke about Lara on the phone of his own accord. He had been looking at photographs of her only yesterday, he might say, and 'in every other picture she was laughing'. But once when we talked about her for a newspaper article – publicly, so to speak – he said, 'Come on, let's leave the television on' (there was a football match on at the time). That way he wouldn't hear his own words so much. 'I can't run away from her death,' he said. 'I know I have to come to terms with it.' Coming to terms, he then said, that sounds wrong now, but he couldn't think of a better phrase. I knew what he meant, didn't I? I nodded, and we stared at the television.

Shortly before Christmas their dead daughter put them to the test again. Should they go on living in Empede to be close to her grave, or should they move on? Perhaps they could only really leave the horror behind them by moving away from it. Robert's contract with Hannover 96 was due to run out in six months. The moment to make the decision had come: stay or go? The options of Hamburg and Leverkusen had fallen through. Through a happy chance, Hamburg SV had suddenly been able to sign up an excellent goalkeeper in the form of Frank Rost. Bayer Leverkusen wanted to try their hand with Butt and the talented Adler in the background. 'If my goal-keeping coach hadn't had me, presumably he would have brought in Robert,' says René Adler. 'He was always taken with Robert.' That left VfB Stuttgart, who were on their way to the German championship and were wooing Robert.

'Let's go,' said Teresa. 'Let's have a new start in Stuttgart.'

'I don't know. I owe so much to Hannover. If they hadn't saved me from Tenerife that time I might still be playing in the Second Division.'

'But in a new place we'd be free of that depressing memory that clings to every object, every place.'

'Going away would only mean running away from the memory.'

'OK then, stay with Hannover, then at least we won't have to think about it any more,' Teresa said abruptly.

But it wasn't as simple as that. Of course he went on thinking about it. He would be playing Champions League matches with Stuttgart; he might even win a title. Maybe he should meet Stuttgart's coach Armin Veh during the winter break. But Veh avoided making any firm commitment to see him. In all likelihood Stuttgart would lose their goalkeeper in six months' time. Timo Hildebrand wanted to go abroad. In that case Veh wanted Enke. But the coach was still fighting for Hildebrand, and before that battle was won or lost he didn't want to be seen with another goalkeeper.

So Jörg Neblung negotiated with Hannover first. He met the club president Martin Kind the day before Christmas at his company headquarters in Grossburgwedel. Kind employed almost two thousand people making hearing aids and distributing them around the world. He wasn't a particular fan of football so many people wondered what possessed him to use his millions to put Hannover 96 back in the Bundesliga. On the other hand it could hardly have harmed sales of hearing aids when the name of the company was made more famous by the boss's commitment to football.

Robert was one of the few footballers at the club with whom Kind had anything like a personal relationship. Kind liked the analytical, lofty perspective from which Robert viewed football. He knew that losing him would strip the club of its optimism. Robert gave life to the dream that Hannover 96 could be something bigger than a local favourite. Professional footballers are adored after only three good games, and Robert Enke, a top-ranker in a mid-ranking club, benefited from an excess of esteem at Hannover.

To keep the keeper, Kind assembled an extraordinary sum of money for Hannover 96, some of it from external backers – over six million euros. But it soon became clear during the negotiations that there was a problem. Kind thought the six million would be enough for a four-year contract, Jörg argued that Robert should receive the same amount of money over three years. He would still be earning less than he would with Stuttgart.

Kind had brought along Gregor Baum, a member of the board of directors who deals in real estate and racehorses. With his harsh tone, Baum ensured that the meeting was over quickly, but that it also finished without an agreement being reached.

Robert and Teresa waited for Jörg in the Hotel Kokenhof, right next to the hearing-aid company. There were Christmas decorations up in reception. After he had described to them what had happened at the negotiations, Jörg said he thought Robert should say no to Hannover for the time being. That didn't mean they couldn't do business in a few weeks' time. 'And then,' says Jörg, 'the decision was made against 96.' Hannover knew what a goalkeeper in his category earned elsewhere, Robert thought out loud, and he had been prepared to stay even though he had worse prospects with 96 and would receive a smaller salary than in Stuttgart. If the club was then half-hearted in its financial treatment of him, that might be a sign for him to go.

Jörg's phone rang.

'Mr Neblung, we've talked again. We're willing to raise the offer. It's important to us that Robert stays with 96.' Kind asked the agent to come to his office straight away.

That evening a press photographer was called to the Kokenhof to take a picture of Robert Enke and Martin Kind shaking hands. Enke had signed a three-year contract, until July 2010.

In Hanover the fans and local media celebrated as if Robert had given them a present by deciding to stay. He started to get a bit frightened. The fulsome commentaries read as if he were a romantic who had pegged back his personal ambition out of gratitude to Hannover 96. But what if he wanted to leave in two years' time? Would he be denounced as a hypocrite? 'I stayed not least because 96 stretched themselves financially for me to an incredible extent,' he stressed, 'and because I expect things to go forward here in a sporting sense.'

In the end he was a professional, not an idealist. But at the same time he unconsciously derived a new source of joy from the devotion of the fans. Immersed in cries of thank you and bravo, he no longer doubted his decision to stay. He sat with Teresa by Lara's grave and suddenly he was sure he couldn't have gone away. He was slowly coming to believe what Teresa and he had been saying to each other like a mantra since 17 September 2006. 'You can't grieve every minute. It's not reprehensible to be able to eat again, to laugh again.'

Two months later it was announced that Timo Hildebrand of VfB Stuttgart was switching to FC Valencia. Now Stuttgart's coach Armin Veh would have loved to talk to Robert Enke.

When a session was over at the winter training-camp in Jerez de la Frontera in January 2007, the men from Cabin Two didn't leave the pitch. Midfielder Hanno Balitsch put on Robert's gloves and went and stood in goal and Michael Tarnat fired in free kicks. Robert lurked in the box, and Tarnat sometimes directed the ball not at the goal but deliberately at Robert's backside. 'I can't work like this!' shouted Robert, and laughed with the others.

There seemed to be an area in his body that was untouched by fun, that laughter couldn't penetrate. But increasingly often he found that he was able to cut himself off from that part. He could be thinking of Lara one minute, filled with despair, and the next laughing at Tarnat. Even during Bundesliga games 'my thoughts strayed repeatedly to her'. He smiled again. 'But with a goalkeeper that's not so dramatic.'

Teresa had no team. She started jogging in the fields around Empede. She ran every day, at least ten kilometres, until her feet started hurting. A fatigue fracture, the doctor diagnosed.

'Perhaps I should go to a psychologist this time,' she said to Robert one evening.

'You?'

'I think it would help me.'

'*You* don't need a psychologist!' He said it to cheer her up. They would find their life without Lara together. But did he say it partly because it would have destroyed his view of the world? His wife, the stronger one in his eyes, seeing a psychologist?

In the weeks that followed Teresa found herself thinking the same thought on a number of occasions: perhaps she did need professional help. His rejection of the idea became more vehement the more often she expressed it. Eventually she herself believed that she would get better without a psychologist. But she often wondered why he had protested so strongly against the idea.

Suddenly they had time. The afternoons that had been subject to the severe rhythm of Lara's needs now lay ahead of them. Would they manage to do something and enjoy them without a guilty conscience?

They drove to Hamburg, they went to Lake Steinhuder. One afternoon Robert rang their neighbours' doorbell. His internet was down, could he quickly use his neighbour's computer? Uli Wilke had been the best footballer in the village before Robert moved to Empede. He had played for TSV Havelse in the Third Liga. In his early forties, he was now working as a car salesman. After Robert had used the internet, they fell into conversation.

Uli came over to watch football on the television with him, and he and Teresa helped the Wilkes build a stone wall in the garden. The Wilkes had two little girls – that was the test the others couldn't even see: bearing the fact that other couples had wonderful children.

Would they ever try for another child? Robert told himself it was too soon to ask the question. But the question kept coming back.

A doctor they had met at the clinic asked if they could look after her little daughter Laura. Teresa and Robert didn't like to say no. Laura came to see them more and more often. Finally they realised why the doctor was entrusting her daughter to them. It wasn't so much to do with the child needing to be minded; they were to get used to being around children again. They were to stop seeing the lack of Lara in every child they came across.

Teresa can't say when, whether it was after four or five months – there wasn't *a* moment – but eventually they were glad when someone called out 'Hello?' in a bright voice outside their door. The children from the village began to call on them unannounced. The garden gate was always open.

At around that time an eight-page fax arrived for Robert at the Hannover 96 office. The national coach was inviting him to play in the international against Denmark in Duisburg on 27 March 2007 (and also reminding him that for his submission to the referee he would need to produce a valid passport or ID card).

It was no longer possible to ignore the fact that the Germany coach Joachim Löw was serious about him. At an age when careers on the global stage are usually coming to an end, Robert was to play his first international. 'I wouldn't have thought that I was going to be selected again – I'm nearly thirty after all.'

'Don't make yourself any older than you are – you're only twenty-nine,' said Germany's goalkeeping coach Andreas Köpke.

After the 2006 World Cup, Oliver Kahn had stepped down. At the age of thirty-seven Jens Lehmann only had a limited future ahead of him as Germany's number one. The goal was open, and Robert was the most likely applicant after Timo Hildebrand.

When Denmark's coach Morten Olsen learned about Löw's line-up, he grumbled. They were too weak an opposition. It was a friendly but Olsen wanted his team to be put to the test. Seven players in the German team, from Robert Enke to Jan

'Enke flies': one of Robert's phenomenal saves in goal.

Schlaudraff, didn't even have experience of ten internationals between them. But the future was supposed to belong to them. In fact the steepest career curve of all the newcomers in Duisburg that night would be that of the referee. Howard Webb, another international beginner, would go on to oversee the 2010 World Cup Final.

In the tunnel outside the changing-rooms, before they went out, Robert's hair stood straight up in the air. He had been tousling it with his gloves. His lips were narrow. There was nervousness in his eyes, not fear.

The game left him no time to brood. Only a minute had passed when a free kick flew in from the left wing and the Dane Daniel Agger soared high seven yards in front of goal, unencumbered. It was an outstanding header, solid, aimed at the right-hand corner. Robert hadn't yet touched the ball. He dived, and as he flew in the air parallel to the bar, his back arching with physical tension, he steered the ball around the post. People who have never been goalkeepers themselves see saves like that as a goalkeeper's greatest feats.

Shortly before half-time Thomas Kahlenberg ran towards him on his own with the ball. Robert just stood there. To the unpractised eye he was doing nothing. He didn't even touch the ball when Kahlenberg ran past him. 'Kahlenberg dribbled round Enke,' the sportswriters wrote. In fact Robert had just executed the greatest feat of the evening. He had blocked the Dane's line of fire so skilfully and for so long that all Kahlenberg could do was move past him on the left, where he found no space and inevitably ran out of play.

'A lot of charisma and excellent reactions,' the coach said of him after the game. Robert called his debut 'quite decent'. Germany had lost 1–2, but the sports journalists wanted to make a winner out of him. Now he could lay claim to being Germany's number two goalkeeper, couldn't he?

'You know you're not going to get an answer to that one from me.'

Didn't he at least see himself fighting Timo Hildebrand for the number two position after that game?

'You mustn't forget that this is only the third time I've been named in the squad. Timo has been included many times before.'

Germany defined itself as the promised land of the goalkeeper, the home of Sepp Maier, Toni Schumacher, Oliver Kahn. Even the most mundane question was enough for an extended debate, in this case: who would be the country's substitute goalkeeper?

'I'll never be able to say publicly this colleague or that one is worse than me, I should be ahead of him. I know what respect is.'

The journalists were disappointed. What had happened to German goalkeepers? Didn't they like stirring up trouble any more? At least they still had Lehmann for a while longer – Mad Jens.

In the summer of 2007, after Robert's third summer in Hanover ended on familiar terrain – eleventh position in the Bundesliga – he and Teresa went to Lisbon for their holidays, as they had done the previous year.

The comparison couldn't be ignored: a year ago they had spent their time in Portugal in a state of euphoria, not least because Lara had made such good progress. And now? They were enthusiastic again, even if the excitement could no longer capture them completely. 'The loss of a child is terrible, that never goes away,' says Teresa. 'But we had spent two years living with Lara in a state of emergency, with the constant fear that she might die. On holiday in Lisbon I noticed for the first time, unbearable though her death was, it was also to some extent a liberation. We could live without fear again.'

They were sitting in La Villa on the beach at Estoril. It was half-past nine in the evening and still broad daylight. Even the sea was moving with the lethargy of a fading summer day.

'I'd like to live here for ever,' Robert said.

'We could move back here when your football career's over.'

'Why don't we buy a house? Then we could come to Lisbon for a few days all the time, not just in the summer holidays.'

The next day the fantasy seemed to be taking shape.

He met Paulo Azevedo. They had stayed in contact since the event at the Goethe Institute the previous year and Robert had discovered that they had something in common: almost ten years earlier Paulo had once scored two goals against him. Having grown up in Freiburg, Paulo had played as a professional for Carl Zeiss Jena in 1999. In one training session he had scored twice against Robert, who was there working out with his old club during a summer visit.

'What would you say to me playing for Benfica again at the end of my career, at thirty-five?' Robert asked.

'Let me do the sums. You'll be thirty-five in August 2012. That works perfectly: then you would have played the 2010 World Cup and the 2012 European Championship for Germany, and you can let your career fade away here in grand style.'

'And what sort of smaller Primeira Liga clubs are there around Lisbon?'

'Belenenses.'

'Of course, Belenenses! I could play there from thirty-six to thirty-eight. I'm sure I could manage that.'

It sounded like a joke, but as he was coming out with those words they turned into serious ideas in his head. He had dreams again.

He went with Paulo to the German Embassy, where Paulo was now working. A reception was being held in the garden for the national deaf team, who were taking part in their European Championship in Lisbon. Robert Enke was the surprise guest.

The deaf footballers shouted with joy when they recognised him. He tried not to let his uncertainty show. Could he talk to them, could they read his lips? He stuck with their coach, Frank Zürn, who wasn't deaf but who had learned sign language from his deaf parents.

Zürn was pleasantly surprised at how many questions the goalkeeper had. How did deaf people manage in their professional lives? How did they communicate on the pitch? Could they play in a normal football team? When Robert said at some point 'Perhaps you know that I had a deaf daughter', it was Zürn who didn't want to let anything show. He was overwhelmed by the natural way Robert talked about her.

Encouraged by the coach, who told him the deaf footballers would understand him if he talked slowly, Robert mingled among them. They kidded each other, as footballers do. He wasn't as muscular as Kahn; why didn't he come and play with them; why didn't he switch to Werder Bremen. Two days later the deaf players were amazed. He was standing with them on the training pitch in Cascais and changing into his kit.

That's right, he was training with them. That was what they wanted, wasn't it?

A few months after this holiday, Robert rang up Zürn. He had thought about what Zürn had told him that evening at the embassy in Lisbon, that the deaf players had problems funding the running of their team. He had had a word with his glove sponsor. Frank Zürn could buy the team's equipment from them at cost price.

Lara's death had given Robert a deeper sensitivity to the needs of others and a sure sense of how he could bring joy into their lives.

He sat in his neighbours' garden in Empede and heard about how Uli Wilke's brother-in-law, a roofer, suffered from chronic back pain. He took the roofer along to training and walked him into the team changing-room. 'See that you make this guy fit again, he's my handyman,' Robert said to the physiotherapist.

Robert in the pool at his holiday home in Lisbon.

He asked the clinic at the University Hospital to set up a room so that parents could be alone with their child as his or her life came to an end. He collected donations to finance the conversion. He went to Göttingen to play football with children with cardiac problems, children who had to be connected to oxygen-bottles after the strain of shooting at goal. 'Shoot low – I can't reach the high ones at my age,' he told the children.

But he didn't want to help everyone. In his obituaries it often said he never turned down requests for autographs – as if that was the highest level of niceness for a footballer, as if that showed human greatness. In reality he always wondered why he should give rude people autographs.

'That's unreadable,' a woman once said when Robert had signed something for her.

'Oh really?' asked Robert. He took the card back and wrote his name in childish capitals underneath. 'That better?'

'Hey, Enke, got an autograph?' a boy asked another time.

'For someone who says Robert or Mr Enke and then please, then yes, I would have one,' he replied, and walked on.

But he still found it hard to say unpleasant things to people. In January 2008 he had to talk to an office clerk at Hannover 96. The woman who cleaned the changing-rooms had come to see Robert: the clerk, who was always very polite to the players, talked down to her. Robert took him aside and explained the principles of courteous behaviour. He could speak quietly and still sound thunderous; he had learned that from giving orders to the defenders and the dogs. But when it was over he felt relief, not contentment.

All the disputes in the team now came straight to him. He had been club captain since August 2007. He was Hannover 96's figurehead. 'I also thought he'd grown up since coming to Hanover,' says Tommy Westphal. 'From an introverted player who was grateful to be back in the Bundesliga, he had turned into a professional who was interested in the club as a whole. But making Roba the captain – I don't know. To my way of thinking that wasn't his natural role. He wasn't someone who naturally took a position on everything, who settled all kinds of conflicts.'

He had been a captain once before, in his last year in Lisbon. Once, the Brazilian Roger Flores had taken a free kick quickly, just because he felt like it, even though as Benfica's free-kick specialist Pierre van Hooijdonk should have done it. Roger's shot flew high over the goal. After the game Robert went up to him with his index finger raised. 'You never do that again, do you hear me?'

When he was angry, he often stumbled unexpectedly into arguments. But when Hannover's coach Dieter Hecking and Michael Tarnat fought out a quiet little war, he understood both sides and chose to stay out of it. 'There were situations when the whole changing-room was arguing noisily – about whether we should play in diamond formation in midfield, for example – then Robs would say something from the back corner of the room, and everything would calm down,' Hanno Balitsch remembers. 'But I think he felt better when Altin Lala was captain.'

The captain of Hannover 96 had countless duties, Robert

discovered during Advent in 2007. He even had to write the team's Christmas cards to the attendants.

During the holidays, Marco rang him. Robert thought he was going to wish him a happy Christmas. Instead Marco told him he wanted to go into treatment with Dr Markser.

Robert was amazed – almost angry, Marco thought. Marco, after all, was blessed with a cheerful demeanour, he was always up for a silly joke, always at the centre of any group; Robert had often taken his lead from Marco's good mood. So what made Marco think he had problems like his own? 'Well, yeah, you often had worries about injuries,' Robert conceded at last, as if he was still thinking about what to make of this turnaround.

Marco didn't suffer from depression; he had no idea what was wrong with him, he just knew he had to do something. He was playing in Serie D now and at that level he was without doubt an outstanding footballer, but even that certainty didn't free him from a self-inflicted tormenting pressure. On the contrary, he just felt a new pressure: didn't they now expect him to be the best every Sunday?

He often thought back to the moments in his career when everything could have gone differently. At the age of twenty, still the talent with those three Bundesliga goals in his first seven games, Hertha BSC were desperate to sign him. In a hotel in Essen he'd actually shaken hands on a deal with Hertha's sporting director Dieter Hoeness. Ten days later his agent Norbert Pflipsen suddenly said to him: you know what, son, you'd be better off staying in Mönchengladbach. Marco didn't understand: he would get a bigger salary at Hertha, the coach there envisaged him as a regular player. But he was twenty and he didn't dare contradict his agent. Flippi knew what he was doing. 'Don't you know why Flippi didn't want you to go to Hertha?' his older team-mates told him later. 'Because Mönchengladbach threatened him: if Villa goes, you won't earn anything from any other transfer here.'

Memories in an endless loop . . . How Liberopoulos, his

strike partner at Panathinaikos, played his passes too hard and inaccurately, so that Marco missed out on a goal – because Liberopoulos really saw him as his rival. How the newspapers in Nuremberg called him a 'non-starter' who should be 'mucked out'. Memories that turned into eternal questions . . . Did a professional footballer have to put up with cruelty like that? Should a professional have stood up to Flippi and insisted on switching to Hertha? Should a professional have kicked Liberopoulos on the ankle the next day at training? (An unfortunate tackle, not even a foul – you could easily fake something like that with a bit of skill.) Shouldn't a professional have shrugged when he was treated at Nuremberg like a 'piece of meat, a piece of pizza, a piece of cheese that you have to get rid of'? His parents and teachers had always taught him that sensitivity and good manners were among the most important things in life.

But was it perhaps simply a question of being strong? And if so, could Dr Markser make him strong?

'I went to Valentin Markser with the goal of freeing up my head,' Marco says.

What he initially got from his conversations with the doctor was just more and harder questions. What did he consider to be a successful life? Was it just a clever move in front of goal? Did he actually know what he wanted to achieve? What sort of things did he notice in life generally – was he even enjoying the coffee he was drinking, for example? Marco Villa needed time to come up with answers to such questions. And he slowly came to see not just himself but his friend more clearly. Robert now seemed to know exactly what he wanted to be: a goalkeeper with a healthy detachment from the excitements of the professional footballing business.

But Marco could also see how much more difficult it was becoming for Robert to maintain his composure.

Even though thirty to forty thousand spectators still came to Hannover 96 games, Robert suddenly felt far more eyes than that weighing down on him. The country wanted to know whether he was really good enough for the national team. The 2008 European Championship was fast approaching, and the question of which goalkeeper was the right one for Germany was becoming a national pastime. Could Jens Lehmann stay as number one even though he had been on the subs bench at Arsenal for weeks? Shouldn't one of the talented young players like René Adler or Manuel Neuer be appointed rather than Timo Hildebrand and Robert Enke? The internet surveys, interviews with experts, newspaper campaigns and general lobbying were endless. 'You can forget about Enke and whatever all those other people are called,' said Bayern Munich's manager Uli Hoeness – Bayern's Michael Rensing was going to be the next national goalkeeper. Nobody except Hoeness thought that. So Robert told himself it was a lot of fuss about nothing; the only important thing was the objective assessment of the Germany coaches. 'If Hoeness wants to push his player, then let him get on with it, but he still has to behave with decency – and he's lost that,' he replied. It sounded level-headed. He himself had thought that he was past letting such skirmishes drive him mad. He had to admit to himself that he had been wrong. Criticism wound him up.

Hannover's coach Dieter Hecking criticised him just once in public. In a friendly against Grasshopper Club Zurich Robert had missed a corner and slipped during a goal-kick. 'He wasn't concentrating as much as he needed to,' Hecking said to the journalists. It was just a friendly, it was just a casual remark, it was forgotten by everyone two days later. Only Robert was still talking about it three weeks later, his hand clenched with fury on the steering wheel. What had made Hecking think he hadn't been concentrating? What had made him pillory him in public?

In April 2008, with two months to go to the European Championship, Hannover 96 beat Eintracht Frankfurt 2–1. At home at night Robert watched the Bundesliga highlights on television in his sitting-room. The camera moved with slow relish when Stuttgart's goalkeeper Sven Ulreich punched a cross away only for Leverkusen's Simon Rolfes to trap the ball and slot it home. Minutes later, Ulreich couldn't hold on to a shot, Leverkusen's striker Stefan Kiessling was quick to convert the rebound. 'Football is sometimes very simple,' the Stuttgart coach Armin Veh told the television reporter: 'We lost as the result of two goalkeeping errors. Everyone saw that. It's no good protecting the goalkeeper.' Robert was furious. How could a coach say that about his goalkeeper! Particularly when the first goal hadn't been a mistake, just a decent punch that had unfortunately been picked up by an opponent. He was used to television reporters overlooking something like that, but a coach! Robert yelled at the television: 'That's completely out of order!'

Sven Ulreich was nineteen and still living at the family home. He had played in the Bundesliga only ten times and was wondering dejectedly the next day whether that was it, whether he'd blown his chances, when his phone rang. He looked at the caller's number and didn't recognise it. He thought for a moment, then picked it up.

'When I heard the voice, I was startled,' says Ulreich.

Robert didn't really know Ulreich. Two weeks earlier, after a Hannover–Stuttgart game, they had talked to each other for three minutes. He'd got his mobile number off his glove manufacturer. Robert thought he knew the situation Ulreich was currently in.

They talked for over half an hour. Robert analysed the goals scored against Ulreich. What was important, Robert told him, was decisions. You punched the first ball – fine. For the second goal Ulreich actually executed a perfectly good dive; the rest was bad luck. He mustn't despair, even if the coach now wanted to take him off the team. That public criticism from Armin Veh was really the worst. He'd had exactly the same thing at Barcelona – one stupid match and he was out of the team. He'd gone into a very deep trough but – this was the important thing he wanted to say to Ulreich – he'd come out of it again. Ulreich would do the same. He had a huge talent.

'When I hung up,' says Sven Ulreich, 'I had goosebumps.'

He turned to his mother. 'That was Robert Enke.' His mother waited for an explanation, but Sven didn't really have one. 'I don't think there'd ever been anything like that in professional football before, a national goalkeeper spontaneously ringing an unknown nineteen-year-old to help him.'

In the afternoons in Empede his route still led him, as before, to the cemetery – up the Lange Berg with Teresa and the dogs, through the fields to Lara. When they were all walking back from the grave along the country road to the village he realised that he could now imagine standing by the graveside with a child and saying to that child quite naturally: that was your sister.

A second child wouldn't be an attempt to replace Lara. It would just be their second child. He saw no reason now why they couldn't love a second child just as much as all parents love their children.

What Teresa could no longer contemplate was pregnancy. She didn't think she'd be able to bear the risk, the fear of having another sick child.

They knew a couple in Hanover who had adopted. They'd found out about the procedure – examination by the youth-welfare office, waiting periods. Why didn't they start looking into it after the summer?

The summer lay like a big block of stone in front of their future. For the time being, the question of whether Robert would be selected for the European Championship in June was putting everything on hold. Jörg and Teresa worked themselves up into a rage when the sportswriters, with open affection, called for the inclusion of René Adler, because he was a nice high-flyer who made sensational saves. It did Robert good when Jörg and Teresa got worked up on his behalf. When they lost their temper he felt forced to keep his. Then he had to calm them down: don't panic, the national goalkeeping coach values me, and anyway three keepers go to the European Championship. After his performances over the last years he felt quite honestly that he was second-best. When he argued as calmly as that in front of them, he usually ended up convincing himself.

A year and a half after Lara's death it was the normal anxieties, the usual doubts of a goalkeeper, that were bothering him again. 'It's all coming back,' said Teresa. 'Fury at letting in a goal, irritation because they don't have the jeans you fancy in a size thirty-four, all the everyday nuisances. It just doesn't go so deep.'

They had gone to Hamburg for two days again, to be a normal, happy couple. Teresa wanted to buy some jeans in a boutique. While she was slipping into a pair in the changing-room, he started flicking through *Kicker*.

'How do you like these?'

'Yes, fine.' He'd barely looked up.

Teresa tried on five different pairs. Each time she came out of the changing-room so that he could pass judgement. Every time he said, with one eye still on the magazine, 'Yes, fine.'

She had had enough. She went back into the changing-room and put on another pair.

'Or shall I take these?'

'Yes, they're fine too.'

'Robbi, can you not even look?'

She had put her own jeans back on.

SEVENTEEN

In the Land of Goalkeepers

Joachim Löw came to Königsallee to see nothing and not to be seen. In a place where other people admire the latest fashions and put themselves on display, the national coach had come in search of seclusion. He booked into a hotel suite on the Düsseldorf boulevard for three days from 5 May 2008. He wanted to confer undisturbed with his coaching staff on the squad for the European Championship. The position of goalkeeper wasn't the most urgent topic, but it was the most sensitive. There were three places. And four candidates.

Jens Lehmann had to be number one – Löw had decided that months ago when he left Lehmann in goal even though he remained Arsenal's substitute goalkeeper. The memory of what Lehmann achieved during the 2006 World Cup carried more weight than thoughts of what the other three might be able to achieve.

That left Timo Hildebrand, Robert Enke and René Adler. Hildebrand and Robert had been permanent members of the squad, as substitute goalkeepers, for a year. Throughout that period Adler had been the most outstanding goalkeeper in the Bundesliga.

It was easier to make the decision if they chose the third goalkeeper first. Germany had never fielded their third-choice goalkeeper in a World Cup or European Championship match, so it had become a tradition to take as third keeper a young man who could gain valuable experience of tournament life. The twenty-three-year-old Adler, who had appeared like a revelation in the Bundesliga, was the ideal candidate for the post.

'That left us with the question, whether we hurt Timo or Robert,' recalls Germany's goalkeeping coach Andreas Köpke. Over five years, Hildebrand had been built up as the logical successor to Kahn and Lehmann, he had been number three at the 2004 European Championship and the 2006 World Cup; the lad with a future. Robert had slipped into the national squad at the age of twenty-nine and had only played a single international. Hildebrand had just had a hard year, however. In his first season with FC Valencia he had clashed with his fellow keeper Santiago Cañizares, who wasn't going to give up his place in goal without a fight. He treated Hildebrand with cold contempt, exchanging not a single word with him. It was nothing personal, it was just a weapon. Two changes of coach in one season didn't improve the working atmosphere at Valencia. 'There's always something going on here,' said Hildebrand.

The tension was apparent in his game. If you analysed the season in Spain unsentimentally, one of Löw's colleagues at the hotel on the Königsallee observed, 'Timo made mistakes in almost every match.' Sometimes Hildebrand wasn't sure-handed enough to gather a shot first time, sometimes he collided with his defenders when trying to catch a cross. These mistakes rarely had serious consequences, but Timo's playing didn't exactly exude a sense of security. For Germany, too, Hildebrand had wobbled under genuine pressure in his one game, a qualifier against Cyprus. Robert, on the other hand, had been playing with great consistency for four years in Hanover. 'With someone like that the guys know for sure: he's there. And that gives the defence the security they need,' said Köpke.

But Hildebrand had had great moments in Valencia too. Once the fans were treated to a *mano de milagro* – a 'miraculous hand' – when he parried a header from Levantes Álvaro de Aquino while his momentum was taking him in the opposite direction. For five years they had been inviting Hildebrand on to the national team because they saw him as a possible number one. Shouldn't they overlook a bumpy season in extremely difficult conditions?

Or was the question precisely this: which goalkeeper could best cope under extreme conditions? Wasn't that the crucial point in the search for a substitute goalkeeper? 'What if Jens Lehmann gets injured in the European Championship semi-final?' Köpke asked, and answered himself: 'Then you can put Robert in goal for the final without any problem. His nerves are so strong that he'd go calmly even into a game like that. After his daughter's death he knows that there are more important things in the world.' The other people in the room – Löw, his assistant coach Hansi Flick and chief scout Urs Siegenthaler – saw things exactly the same way. Löw would have to make the final decision on his own.

On 16 May, three weeks before the European Championship, the time came to reveal the squad. Seven television channels were going to broadcast it live. Köpke called the four goal-keepers before the announcement so that the unlucky one wouldn't learn the sad news from the media.

At about nine o'clock in the morning Timo Hildebrand was already on the way to the suburb of Paterna for FC Valencia's last training session that season. He had sprained his hip. He wanted to sit out Valencia's final league match two days later against Atlético Madrid to spare the joint for the European Championship. He had spent five years waiting patiently behind Kahn and Lehmann: this was to be his last tournament as a substitute goalkeeper, and then Lehmann would step down. The way to the top would finally be free.

Köpke's call reached Hildebrand in his car. He listened to the coach for a good minute, then tried to say something in reply, but the words wouldn't come together into sentences. Hildebrand simply hung up.

It took him a quarter of an hour even to begin to regain his composure. He parked at the training-ground and phoned Köpke back again.

'But why, Andy?' he asked. 'Why?'

As the public learned about Löw's squad on one of the seven television channels, Robert called a friend.

'Jacques,' he said, 'where are you?'

'Hey, Robert, fantastic! Fantastic! I just heard on the radio. I'm delighted for you – incredible! You're going to the European Championship!'

'Yes, thanks.'

'This calls for a party. You must be over the moon, Robert!'

'I've known since yesterday evening. Listen, Jacques, I just wanted to know where you are. I'll call round with your mail.'

He took a detour on the way home from training to the other side of Hanover to take Jacques his letters and have a bit of a chat. Then he rang Timo Hildebrand.

Their relationship had been reticently professional. He had watched Hildebrand more than he had talked to him, but he had noticed one thing: the switch to Valencia, which had rather put him off his sporting stride, had done Hildebrand good in other ways. 'It seems to me that he's become more sympathetic, more affable,' said Robert. The fact that Hildebrand had experienced powerlessness alone in a foreign team in a foreign country had made him more sensitive to others, Robert thought. It seemed all the more important to him to show sympathy to Hildebrand now. However difficult the phone-call was.

He actually didn't know what to say to his competitor, whose place he had taken. 'And I don't know whether there's such a thing as the right words in a situation like that,' he said when we talked about it later. He simply rattled on. He was sorry. He could understand how Timo felt. In three months a new season would start and there was still a lot to win in football, even for Timo. The conversation was short. 'But I had the feeling Timo was glad of my call.'

The European Championship began as a nice boat trip. A yacht took the national team into the open sea near Majorca where they could dive and swim and believe for a while that they were actually in a rejuvenation training-camp, as the coaches had called the first part of preparation in Palma de Mallorca.

In his year with the national team Robert had found himself part of a clique along with centre-backs Per Mertesacker and

Christoph Metzelder. He didn't find it as easy to get close to his natural friends, the other goalkeepers.

'He doesn't talk,' he said with a shrug about Jens Lehmann.

Lehmann cultivated the role of the goalkeeper as a lonesome cowboy who must grimly and recklessly go his own way. When he did open up, he tended to become didactic. One of his favourite topics at the time was that everything was better at his club, Arsenal, and in England generally, than anywhere else. Rather mysteriously, however, Lehmann failed to pick up on the two most important English virtues – politeness and irony – during his five years in London.

Where the other goalkeeper was concerned, Robert had certain reservations. The fact that there would be a time after the European Championship, after Lehmann, could not be ignored; then René Adler and he would fight it out for the

Robert with his goalkeeping rival Jens Lehmann.

number one spot, according to the recent squad selection. But that didn't seem to worry the lad too much. Robert noticed with surprise that Adler was trying to make contact with him. While Lehmann went ahead with his training programme in complete silence, Adler called out 'Super, Robert!' after a save, or wanted to know whether he should stand a bit further back to take a cross. After a few days he offered Robert the ultimate fraternisation ritual between goalkeepers: he asked if he could try on Robert's gloves. 'He had a really wide hand,' says René. 'I slipped about in his gloves.'

Robert didn't know what to make of it. Adler received much better treatment in the newspapers than he did; unconsciously, Robert had transferred his resentment over this to Adler himself before the European Championship. Now Adler was revealing himself as a likeable guy.

René Adler was seven years younger than Robert, and in football seven years was a generation gap. When Robert made his debut in the Bundesliga in 1999, René was a fourteen-year-old boy sitting in front of the television in Leipzig who believed that the road Robert had followed was the path he himself had in front of him. Like Robert, René went from the East to the West to triumph in football. At the age of fifteen he went on his own to Leverkusen. Bayer's goalkeeping coach Rüdiger Vollborn and his wife took him into their home as a foster-son. It was a unique bond, the coach not just training his goalkeeper but bringing him up as well. While René lived far from his parents and his childhood, under the roof of a former professional goalkeeper whom he looked up to, whom he on no account wanted to disappoint, his natural characteristics were reinforced. Almost everyone who met him was won over by his sense of tact and his openness. In national youth teams at all ages he stood out as a unique talent; 'he *had* to go to the European Championship after his outstanding season', said Köpke. René himself hadn't been able to believe that. 'I had only been in the Bundesliga for a year and a half, and I thought: you must have achieved more than that to go to a European Championship,' he says. 'And then they make this odd decision to take me with them.'

He wouldn't have known how to be anything but friendly and respectful to Robert 'I didn't see myself on the same level as Robbi,' he says. Learn something from Lehmann and Enke, the greats, he had said to himself before the European Championship, and 'Get a move on, and have fun.'

But having fun wasn't as simple as that. Part of the training-camp, the team soon discovered, was a very demanding fitness course, in the guise of a 'supporting programme'. René had to do exercises he had never done in his life, such as resistance runs on which they pulled little metal sleds behind them. On the first evening his legs hurt, on the second his back was stiff. He had to stop training and go to the physiotherapist. Robert couldn't quite escape his suspicions about the darling of the media and noted this weakness with interest. Could it be that his rival wasn't yet physically mature enough for international football?

The players' wives had come along as well. The German Football Association had found them a hotel in Ascona, the same town on Lake Maggiore where the team was staying during the tournament. On his evenings off Robert met up with Teresa. She had made friends with one of the other women, a very nice young lady, she told him. The four of them could go out together.

'What?' Robert asked. 'Now you want me to go out with René Adler?'

They had a good laugh with the women that evening, René said, 'mostly at the expense of the men. We were both bungling great oafs when it came to DIY, so there were a few stories to tell.'

René began to spend more time at team meals with the clique of Mertesacker, Metzelder and Enke. Whenever Teresa and Robert did something with other people, it was with René and his girlfriend. And they met another nice woman with whom Teresa would always stay in contact: René's mother.

For Robert, playing for Germany was the peak. But wasn't substitute goalkeeper the best job of all? He was a valued part of the team, he experienced all the excitement in Switzerland, the victories and the fun, just like every other player, and he didn't have to expose himself to the pressure of the games. 'He was in a dazzlingly brilliant mood during the European Championship,' Teresa recalls.

After the 2–0 win against Poland a man spoke to him in the changing-room corridor. Frans Hoek, the goalkeeping coach who had, in Robert's view, run him ragged in Barcelona, greeted him with a smile. Hoek was now the goalkeeping coach for the Polish national team. 'You see, you found justice after all. Now you're the goalkeeper I saw when I brought you to Barça. I'm happy for you.' Robert was perplexed. Hoek went on talking as if they had had a close relationship in Barcelona. According to Hoek's internal clock they talked for three-quarters of an hour. Then he asked if he could have Robert's shirt. Robert gave it to him, too startled to do anything else.

Four days later their lovely world was thrown into chaos when Germany lost 2–1 to Croatia. Getting thrown out at the group stage had become a possibility. Arguments flared in the team, and the debate among the players rapidly descended to tabloid level. The older players were scandalized that the younger ones had been by the pool sipping cocktails after the defeat. The leadership debate came out into the open, as it did so often during those years. Did it lead to success if a team was dominated by a few players in the authoritarian, often crude manner of the Effenberg generation, as Germany's captain Michael Ballack believed? Or did a successful team need a flat hierarchy in which the footballers saw themselves as servants of an overarching game plan, as the younger professionals in particular saw it? Robert was glad that as a substitute goalkeeper he could remain outside the dispute. He wouldn't have known which side he was on anyway. In principle he shared the idea of a team in which everyone helped each other rather than followed one or two leading players. On the other hand, at the age of thirty he often caught himself thinking that the older players sometimes needed to use a firm hand to ensure order.

With the best of both models – an outstanding Ballack as pack leader, and a solid team sticking to a painstakingly elaborated plan of action – Germany progressed, beating Portugal 3–2 in the quarter-final with their most impressive performance in years. They went on to reach the final in Vienna where they lost 1–0 to a superior Spanish side.

After the defeat in the Ernst Happel Stadium Robert lay with his legs spread on the pitch, still wearing his bile-green substitute's jersey, and with his silver medal around his neck. In the floodlights it was no longer possible to ignore the physical changes he had undergone over the previous few years. He had become angular. Lara's death had taken the boyish look from his face. The fact that he had recently shaved his head because he was starting to go bald at the temples reinforced the hardness of his facial expression. His body was now extremely muscular. Two years earlier he had said, 'I was never as obsessive as Olli Kahn, I never had to work as hard as he did, because I had the talent,' but since the prospect of playing for his country had come into view he'd trained religiously in the gym, because the not exactly innovative goalkeeping training he got with Hannover 96 wasn't enough. As he lay on the grass, all alone among his defeated team-mates, he looked straight ahead. Lehmann's career had been over for several minutes now. It was just up to him whether he would be Germany's number one.

He flew to Lisbon with Teresa on holiday. They had recently bought a house there.

'The question is, are you still coming back to Benfica when you're thirty-five?' asked Paulo Azevedo.

'Of course,' said Robert.

After a decade with Oliver Kahn and Jens Lehmann, Germany had got used to having a national goalkeeper who was a ruthless individual fighter. When the post-Kahn/Lehmann era began in August 2008 there was still a firm belief in the country that a goalkeeper had to be like those two, extremely resolute in total isolation.

At international level Robert noticed with irritation how

everything that had been valued at club level was suddenly being turned against him: his objective style of play, his reticent, respectful manner in public. Now people were comparing him with Kahn, who had once bitten an opponent's neck on the pitch; with Lehmann, who had tried to defeat Kahn in every interview he gave; and of course with René Adler, who daringly caught even difficult crosses, the sort Robert remained in goal for. 'Enke has no charisma,' Ottmar Hitzfeld concluded from these comparisons. Hitzfeld was at the time the most successful German club coach.

Robert thought he was prepared for such populist criticism. What the columnists said was of no importance in the end; what counted was the view of the national goalkeeping coach. And Köpke saw the simplicity of Robert's game as elegance. 'His calm manner on the playing-field impressed me. He had an incredible presence and authority, precisely because he wasn't fidgety like the others, but objective and determined in all his moves. Once he had brilliantly resolved a situation with a striker all by himself, he went back in goal as if a save like that was the most normal thing in the world. No dramatics, nothing.'

In the first international after the European Championship, against Belgium in Nuremberg, Robert played in goal for Germany. It was a sign that the national coaches saw him as the first among three or four equals to succeed Lehmann. Germany won 2–0; Robert effortlessly accomplished the little work he had to do. When I rang him to congratulate him, the first thing he said was, 'Unfortunately I had no opportunity to really shine.' He was in a hurry to demonstrate his class. He could tell himself ten times that he wasn't affected by public scepticism, but even so he felt the pressure to convince the country of his ability as quickly as possible.

But how was he to convince a public that mistook grand-standing for charisma?

'Right,' says Jörg, 'but you can't dismiss it as empty chatter if someone like Hitzfeld talks about a lack of charisma. You have to wonder: where did Hitzfeld get that from?'

Jörg reached the conclusion that it was also a question of image. With his sober goalkeeping style Robert produced fewer spectacular scenes than other goalkeepers who either took more risks to catch crosses or saved more dramatically on the goalline. And when he gave dry, hard-faced interviews, the mass media inevitably preferred to run after René Adler with his blond surfer hair and youthful smile.

Robert listened to Jörg on the phone and got grumpy. Surely the national coach could tell without the help of smiley interviews whether or not a goalkeeper made his defenders feel secure? That was achieved with clear and objective instructions that no one could hear off the pitch.

'Of course, Robbi,' said Jörg. 'But if you had a better public image you'd shake off some of the pressure you get from the media needling away at you.'

They talked about other goalkeepers with more exciting images, and Jörg tried to explain to Robert in technical terms that great saves often occurred only because at the last minute the keeper speculatively threw himself at a shot. There was nothing contemptible about that. Then in the heat of the debate a sentence slipped out that Jörg still regrets today: 'Just try to throw yourself speculatively at a shot the way Tim Wiese does.'

Robert didn't feel angry any more. He felt insulted.

After the European Championship, Tim Wiese of Werder Bremen had been made third-choice goalkeeper in the national team. He was a good keeper with a powerful jump that even Lehmann could only envy. The other top keepers, however, saw Wiese as a thorn in their side. He was a tabloid goalkeeper. He dived even for shots half a yard away from him; shots he could have parried standing up. But then the fans wouldn't have marvelled at his exploits. If a solitary striker ran at Wiese, he slid like a kung fu fighter with his leg stretched out at his attacker, and the commentators cried with great excitement 'Wiese takes the most amazing risks!' The other keepers seethed with fury in front of the television: didn't the media understand that it was simply a mistake to throw yourself so frantically at a striker? Anyone who looked carefully would notice that Wiese even turned his head away as he threw himself forward. It was easy for any striker simply to go around him.

After his thoughtless suggestion that he imitate Wiese, Jörg didn't address the subject of image with Robert again. But he did notice that from that day onwards Robert made an effort to smile in every television interview.

But basically he remained what the British call a 'goalkeeper's goalkeeper' – one who is revered by his colleagues but whose value the masses don't fully appreciate. Against the trend, against the modern model of the 'radical goalkeeper' who tried to intercept every through-pass and catch every cross, Robert clung stubbornly to his idea of the 'reasonable goalkeeper'. What use was it if a keeper only caught eighteen out of twenty long balls by audaciously running out? 'I think it's overstating the case for people to say a modern goalkeeper has to run to collect every through-pass. What a good keeper needs is an infallible sense for which through-ball he's going to go out for and which one he isn't.'

He was pretty much alone in thinking like this at a time when the next generation, the 'radical' players like René Adler and Manuel Neuer, were thwarting opponents' manoeuvres far in front of goal and the last 'traditionalists', like Tim Wiese, were making breathtaking saves on the goal-line.

But the very fact that in autumn 2008 Adler, Enke and Wiese, three goalkeepers with very different styles, were in the national team shows how theoretical the idea is that one style is fundamentally better than another. Among strikers, the public sees it as the most natural thing in the world that there should be different types, all of whom can reach world-class status in their different ways. It's much the same with goalkeepers. The only important thing is that a goalkeeper should act surely and consistently. In the closing months of that year, Robert Enke was the German goalkeeper who had perfected his style more than any other.

'He never made serious mistakes, that was what marked

him out,' says Köpke. So in September Robert was in goal again for the World Cup qualifiers against Liechtenstein and Finland. 'If you go through all his games in the national team, you won't find a single goal where you could say: he should have been able to stop that ball, not even the 3–3 in Finland.'

The most important test of the year came after that game in Helsinki. The adoption agent from the youth welfare office came to Empede. She never made the Enkes feel they were being put to the test, though. The house visit was the last hurdle of the suitability procedure.

They showed the agent the nursery. Lara's name was still on the wooden door in magnetic letters. Teresa and Robert wanted to put their adopted child's name up next to it. They wanted their second child to learn in the most natural way possible that it had a dead sister.

In October they received confirmation that their application for adoption had been accepted. Now they had to wait, and they didn't know whether it would be four weeks or fourteen months until they got their child.

Time flew, it seemed to Robert. His newfound status as Germany's goalkeeper had given his life a new pace. Everything seemed faster, more sudden, particularly his excitement. He travelled to training with the national team in Düsseldorf as the climax of the World Cup qualifiers was imminent – the game against European Championship semi-finalists Russia. Since Lehmann's departure he had been in goal for all the internationals, and his performance had been faultless. But four days before the game against Russia, Germany's biggest selling tabloid *Bild* carried a headline about him and Joachim Löw that sounded like a threat: 'Enke: Jogi's number one – until the first mistake'.

He tried not to take it personally. He knew that what looked like a campaign against him was basically only a personal prejudice: the *Bild* correspondent covering the national team usually reported on René Adler and Bayer Leverkusen, and he liked René so much that he fought for the lad in every headline. But his fury didn't subside. Why did the *Bild* man have to attack him just because he was René's competitor? Hannover had lost 2–0 in Leverkusen once – an everyday result in the Bundesliga. In *Bild* the man had as his headline 'Enke in the shooting-range'.

It's not important, Robert tried to reassure himself.

In other media, too, he and René were turned into great rivals in the days leading up to the Russia game. Lehmann v. Kahn was yesterday; now the battle of the goalkeepers was between Enke and Adler. In fact they were becoming increasingly close. There was an awkward awareness that they were fighting for the same place but they didn't talk about it. They were cordial rivals. 'Robert and René tended to need harmony,' says Köpke. 'They were different from Olli Kahn and Jens Lehmann. They didn't need that kick to wind each other up, to turn each other into enemies. Those days are over anyway. These days life in a football team is more about companionship.'

'I always had the feeling that there was no competition between us,' says René. 'And I think that did us both good. It helps if you don't have that pressure in training – if he saves that ball, I have to save a better one.'

In Düsseldorf, three days before the big match, the coach organised a four-a-side practice game on a small pitch. At one point Philipp Lahm shot from a short distance away. Robert threw his fists up and deflected the ball. In the other goal René was concentrating on the game because the next shot could come straight at him. The game was going back and forth on the little playing-field, the players learning to make the right decisions in the tightest space in the shortest time.

At the next drinks break Robert went up to Andy Köpke and said, 'I've pulled my wrist back punching, something's gone. I might have dislocated my hand.'

'Put some ice on it and go and see the doctor straight away.'

René was standing a few feet away, his thoughts still on the practice game, which resumed within minutes. Out of the corner of his eye he saw that Robert wasn't coming back on to the pitch, and that Tim Wiese was coming on in his place.

The doctor carefully moved Robert's left hand. Then he said, 'We've got to go to hospital.'

EIGHTEEN

Leila

His scaphoid bone was fractured. While the national team were having one last practice at corners in Düsseldorf, Robert was in the hand surgery department in a Hamburg hospital.

Dr Klaus-Dieter Rudolf had put a screw in Robert's wrist – a 'Herbert screw' – to stabilise the carpal bones at the spot where the hand was broken. The operation had been successful, Rudolf told him, which suggested that the break was going to heal smoothly; the method had been applied successfully many times before. But the doctor wanted to be honest with him. Robert Enke was a goalkeeper. His wrist was subject to extreme movements and strains. The healing process was a complicated one and there was a risk that he would never be able to stretch his hand out fully again.

Teresa collected him. His hand was in a red plaster-cast with Velcro fastenings as he was supposed to take it off for a few hours every day and keep the wrist moving. In three months he could expect to be back in goal. But it wasn't so easy for Robert to look forward to that day. Why did things like that always have to happen to him? 'It was a normal shot, the kind of shot I'd saved a thousand times.'

He called on his neighbour Uli. Did he want his two tickets for the game against Russia in Dortmund? Uli told him his brother-in-law Jürgen had once fractured his scaphoid bone, in both hands. He had fallen while doing his job as a roofer.

'Can you stretch your hands all the way out?' Robert asked Jürgen when he met him.

'I can hardly stretch them out at all,' said Jürgen, and showed him.

Robert stared at him.

He watched the match that was supposed to have been his on television. Teresa sat down with him. Germany played energetically, they were quick on their feet, and after half an hour they were leading 2–0 with goals from Lukas Podolski and Michael Ballack. Shortly before half-time Philipp Lahm on the left wing lost the ball to Aleksandr Anyukov who immediately cut into the German penalty area. René Adler came out a long way towards him, following the theory of the 'radicals', dashing out of his six-yard box to keep Anyukov's angle of fire as small as possible. René's feeling was that the Russian, so close to the byline, would pass back into space. So when Anyukov made a move to put in a low cross the keeper sidestepped to the right. But René was out of luck. Anyukov knocked the ball straight through his legs. In the six-yard box Andrei Arshavin connected with it and made it 2–1. It hadn't been a goalkeeping error; it was a situation in which there was hardly anything a goalkeeper could have done. Robert alone was thinking, 'There was a different way of resolving that.' He was sure that with his technique of bending his right knee inwards he could have prevented that pass between the legs.

There was still half a match left, and that goal changed the game's dynamic. The Russians suddenly charged. René tipped a lovely header over the bar, then successfully threw himself at Sergei Semak at the last moment, and, surrounded by seven players, took a fabulous catch off a cross Robert wouldn't have gone for. Robert sat in his living-room and heard the television commentator shouting: 'Great stuff from Adler! . . . I repeat my compliment: that is truly great stuff from Adler . . . and Adler again!' It was twenty past ten in the evening, with ten minutes still to go in Dortmund. The excitement was palpable. Could the Germans hold on for victory?

Robert got up and said to Teresa, 'I'm going to bed.'

He didn't want to read the papers over the next few days. But his colleagues talked to him during rehab training at the Hannover stadium. 'That's just impossible. Have you seen what the papers are saying, even the supposedly serious ones? "The age of Adler has begun, the battle of the goalies is decided." Are they all bonkers?' His colleagues meant well. They were trying to say these were absurd celebrations, he shouldn't let himself be put off by all this media hubbub. But by referring to the headlines they had really disconcerted him.

Two days after the game against Russia he called me. He didn't give me time to ask about his scaphoid bone. He wanted to get to the point: 'You're a journalist.'

'Yes.'

'What do you think about what your colleagues did with René's game?'

'You mustn't forget that it was René's first international. Considering this he did really well. And unfortunately sportswriters always tend to predict a brilliant career for young footballers when they've had a good game. You were just as hyped as a nineteen-year-old in Gladbach. Try to ignore it.'

'Sure. I don't even care. I just wanted to know how you saw things.'

In November 2008 Robert agreed to speak to the magazine *11 Freunde*. It turned out to be his most open interview, although the readers couldn't have known it. He said of his time after Istanbul, 'It wasn't the kind of crisis that any goalkeeper experiences when he misses the ball five or six times in the Bundesliga. There was something existential about it.' But one passage was never published. Robert had it deleted because it struck him as too honest and bitter in retrospect. He was asked what he thought about the fact that the media had declared René Adler to be number one after a single international, and he replied, 'This hype about René didn't just start over the past few weeks. The subject has been being stirred up for ages. I sometimes wonder what's going on. It was a completely normal game that he played against Russia, nothing sensational. It's not easy for me to deal with it . . . In the public perception I've been left standing by the Adler and Neuer generation, and I've got to accept that that's the case.'

One man in Germany shared Robert's opinion that he unfairly came off worst in comparison with René Adler: René himself. 'I could understand Robbi being disturbed by the reports after the Russia game. It was a good match of mine, but it wasn't a stunner. What the media made of it was pretty extreme. I found it embarrassing.'

In the weeks that followed René often wondered whether he should ring Robert or send him a text. He had stored Teresa's phone number since the European Championship. In his head René was already formulating the words he wanted to write. 'But I was worried about coming across as hypocritical,' he says, 'Because quite honestly I had the feeling of having taken something away from him, of having exploited his suffering. The thought was there: it should have been his game.'

Ever since his comeback in Tenerife Robert had effortlessly dealt with pressure, putting stress and sadness in perspective. After this double blow, the fracture of the scaphoid bone and the public coronation of René Adler, his view of the world narrowed again. Wherever he turned, everything looked black.

The autumn days in Lower Saxony started grey and ended grey. 'This darkness is wearing me out,' he said to Teresa. He went to rehab training every day, always anxiously wondering whether his hand would ever again be fit for goalkeeping play at the highest level. What if he ended up like his friend the roofer? Once he admitted those questions, more and more came flooding in. Did he have the slightest chance of being Germany's first-choice keeper again when he was fit? Wasn't he standing there on his own against René Adler and the media – against the whole country? His anxieties fed on those questions and spiralled into irrationality.

At the end of November he was being treated by Hannover's physiotherapist Markus Witkop. He had something to confess to him, Robert said. Then he started crying. He had suffered from depression in the past, and he was afraid it was coming back. He hadn't had any notable psychological problems for five years, not even after Lara's death.

For Witkop, the sight of the team captain weeping was difficult to deal with. Robert had been carrying the flag at the club for four years; now all of a sudden he looked as vulnerable as a child. It was a heavy burden for the physiotherapist to have been let in on the truth. It's the most difficult job a professional team's physio has to do: keep all the players' confidences to himself. 'So many things work away inside you and eat you up because you can't on any account let them out,' says Tommy Westphal.

Robert saw his depression as a striker attacking him – someone he could still stop if he acted correctly. The overwhelming darkness hadn't yet come – he had no difficulty getting up in the morning, he wasn't short of drive – but the dejection, the first harbinger of the illness, had taken hold of him. He thought he could marshal his defence mechanisms, to give the day a structure, get things done. He decided to go for a few weeks to a rehab clinic for professional athletes in Lower Bavaria. There, among like-minded people who were suffering in a similar way to himself, he might overcome his fear of being left behind. When he came back in December he would try to find a psychiatrist for himself in Hanover.

The plan was fixed. But it didn't make him optimistic.

'I should have done it the way you did,' he said despairingly to Marco on the phone. 'Why on earth didn't I go on working preventatively with a psychiatrist after my depression in Barcelona?'

'Robbi, it's not too late. Do what I do, and phone Valentin regularly.'

'Oh, phone-calls are no use.'

'It helped me a lot.'

For a good year now Marco Villa had been talking to Valentin Markser regularly on the phone. He just felt as if he was talking to a good friend. And then Markser's bill came in at the end of the month.

Marco had started to make some key decisions. He lived with his wife and, by now, two children in Roseto degli Abruzzi, a little town on the Adriatic, and he planned to stay there for the time being. He wouldn't move around Europe for football every six months. He was enjoying life with his family by the sea, and they could live reasonably well on the money he made in amateur football. In the mornings he was doing a correspondence course in business management. He wasn't wild about the subject, but he did it partly to prove that he could do something other than play football. He actually had professional dreams beyond football for the first time: after business management he wanted to study homeopathy and acupressure. He was fascinated by the way people could ease pain with their hands alone.

Things hadn't suddenly got better just because he was no longer letting himself be pushed around by the life of a professional footballer. He trained with L' Aquila Calcio, a Serie D team, at a sports ground that was more soil than grass. The local players who trained after them once stole his football boots from the changing-room. And in the evenings Serie A football was often on television. Deep inside he still belonged to that world of professional football, and the question still came to him, the question still hurt the way it did before: how come you've ended up in the Italian Fifth Division? But he had learned to live with it.

Sometimes, even at the age of thirty-two, he enjoyed practical joking the way he had in Mönchengladbach. For his birthday he served his team-mates at L'Aquila doughnuts filled not with custard but with shampoo.

He had found a fundamental contentment in his life.

'Robbi,' he said on the phone, 'I know it's hard, sometimes I can't do it myself, but try not to get too fixated on football.'

'But I can't do anything apart from football. I've only ever seen myself as a footballer.'

'Then let me tell you that you're much more than a footballer. You're a special friend to me.'

'But I've always neglected my friends and my family. I even forget my parents' birthdays all the time.'

'Yeah, whatever. What does it matter if you forget a birthday? It doesn't matter at all! It's just a formality. What counts is that you've also got a life outside football, with friends who value you. You have got to realise that it isn't the end of the world if you can't play for three months.'

'*Jawohl*, Herr Markser,' said Robert.

Marco couldn't help laughing. His friend seemed to be a bit better already.

In the rehab clinic in Donaustauf Robert discovered a new team spirit. About a dozen footballers were working away in the gym. Vinicius, his team-mate from Hannover 96, was trying to strengthen his back after a slipped disc; Roland Benschneider, a Second Bundesliga player from Augsburg, was working on stamina after a cruciate ligament rupture. At first sight they had nothing in common, they carried out their exercises on their own, but the feeling of working towards the same goal turned them into a community. And Robert was able to see himself as captain of this FC Walking Wounded. He was the international among Bundesliga professionals, Second Bundesliga starlets and Third Liga substitutes; he sensed a certain respect in the tone of their questions, in the way they tried to approach him. This acknowledgement – at last, some kind of acknowledgement – allowed him to relax. The gloom and the inexplicable sadness, the first signs of a depression, dragged him down only for very brief moments.

'You feel like Rocky in a rehab clinic like that,' says Marco Villa. 'Weeks in the bone-mill to prepare yourself for a single day: your comeback.'

Robert was still Rocky when he returned to the club in mid-December: he could barely rein in his ambition. At the winter training-camp in the new year he would be back in goal. He would be playing again at the start of the Bundesliga's second round of matches on 31 January 2009, he decided as resolutely as if he could compel it to happen.

He was no longer ruled by fear. But neither did fear quite go away.

He sat at the kitchen table, stretching his left hand back to see how far he could move it. He did it maybe twenty times during dinner. He no longer even seemed to be aware of doing it. He went to the Pius in Neustadt for a glass of wine and his friends spotted him. What was that thing he was always doing with his hand? A few minutes later everyone else was busy seeing how far back they could stretch their own hands. He could get even further than Jürgen's wife Ines, with her healthy scaphoid bone.

The physios bought him a machine. He put his hand in it and the machine stretched his hand back. He was to leave his hand in the machine for ten minutes. Afterwards he immediately tried to see if his hand could be stretched further. He was determined to do everything properly. Which is why in January 2009 he went to see Dr Johannes Stroscher, a psychiatrist and psychotherapist recommended by a doctor friend. Even if he was only suffering from a depressive alienation and the worst seemed to have been prevented, he would exhaust all possibilities. He never wanted to let things go as far as they had in Istanbul.

Dr Stroscher's practice was in a residential street not far from the zoo. Robert pulled a baseball cap low over his face so that no one would recognise him whenever he went into the doctor's house. Over the next few weeks he would always have to have the cap ready in the car, he reminded himself.

What would have done him good at this time was the old solidarity at Hannover 96. But Cabin Two was now the relaxation room, with loungers and massage chairs. After his treatment with the physio Robert walked past the renovated cabin. Sadly it lived up to its new name: there was nothing but relaxation in the relaxation room, and he couldn't avoid thinking about how much had changed in six months.

Hannover 96 had ended the 2007–08 season in eighth place – their best position in forty-three years. It had been the day after his selection for the European Championship squad,

17 May, when they beat Cottbus 4–0 in the last game of the campaign and the coach grabbed the microphone and yelled cockily, 'Dear fans! I promise you, next season we'll get the five points we lacked this year to qualify for the Uefa Cup.' Forty-seven thousand people cheered. Robert and his team-mate Hanno Balitsch had looked at each other aghast.

Eighth in the Bundesliga is the best of the mid-table; ahead of it is the prestige of the top group. But no leap is more difficult than from place eight to seven. The eighth-place team has to be a decent side and will have done all the simple things properly – played solidly in defence and counter-attacked purposefully. But to get to the top group a team must be able to do something special – actively shape a game, let the ball run, vary their attacks.

In the autumn of 2008 Hannover 96 overtaxed themselves with their ambition to be special. Coach Dieter Hecking now wanted 'always to play a dominant attacking game' with two strikers rather than their previous one. And this team that was supposed to attack conceded more goals than ever before.

The relaxation room became a symbol of the good intentions that just made everything worse. Jens Rasiejweski, the sporting director's assistant, had visited some of the biggest clubs in the world – Manchester United, Chelsea and the American football team Baltimore Ravens – to see what the very best training facilities looked like. So Hannover 96 got a relaxation room, and no one in management realised that the best thing about the club, shabby old Cabin Two, the cradle of the team's special solidarity, was being lost. Who went to a relaxation room to laugh with his team-mates?

Robert certainly suffered from the feeling that the footballers around him were becoming less and less *his* team. The players he had met up with in Cabin Two to eat bockwurst or shave Mille's head out of sheer high spirits were growing fewer in number. Frank Juric, Silvio Schröter, Dariusz Zuraw – more than a dozen of his former team-mates had left the club during the previous three years. A club with aspirations, Hannover 96 thought it had to keep buying better players. Players such as Valérien Ismaël and Jan Schlaudraff, who had been thrown out of better clubs and were therefore preoccupied with themselves, were signed. There were also Bulgarians and Danes who had never learned to put down roots because they had been passed on like commodities by their clubs every year or two. Robert and the shrunken clique from Cabin Two thought that these newcomers weren't integrating themselves. 'They always said, we're bringing in new players with individual quality, but in fact all they brought in was individualism,' says Hanno Balitsch, who had become Robert's closest confidant in the team. For their part, many of the newcomers thought that the old players had formed a closed circle of power. And there was no longer a Cabin Two where each side could learn that the other lot weren't that bad.

The coach tried to build a sense of community. Training finished at 4.30 in the afternoon on Wednesdays. Hecking told them: everyone stays until at least five p.m. A year or two earlier ten or twelve men would have sat together for hours. Now many of the players showered in five minutes, sat down in silence in the outer office, stared at the television and kept looking at their watches until five o'clock finally came round. Robert stayed at the training-ground and practised until five p.m. exactly. All that united them was the opinion that this was an idiotic edict by the coach.

The pressure the club had foisted on itself with its high ambitions was omnipresent in the autumn of 2008. Many players, such as Robert, Hanno and Steve Cherundolo, were sceptical about the coach's attacking philosophy. In his first year and a half Hecking had turned them into a team that knew exactly what it was capable of doing: excellent defence, simple attack. Why was he changing something that had worked before? Hecking, in turn, was irritated because he thought the players simply weren't doing what was being asked of them.

'So, I'm going to draw a rucksack on the black board here,' Hecking said one afternoon in the changing-room, 'and we'll throw into it all the things that have bothered us lately.'

It was an offer of reconciliation. But by the end of the

discussion emotions were stirred up again. Michael Tarnat, one of the old keepers of the team spirit, targeted one of the newcomers. Schlaudraff had repeatedly lost the ball with reckless dribbling and put the team in jeopardy. 'I'm going to hunt you down and kick you!' said Tarnat.

Robert was too preoccupied with his own troubles to be driven mad by the irritable mood in the club. But subconsciously it bothered him – another dark stain, further proof that everyone was conspiring against him. Even he had let himself get carried away by the charged atmosphere, to the point of publicly criticising Schlaudraff for foolishly losing the ball. Afterwards he was startled by what he had done. How could he forget his supreme iron rule – never admonish a colleague in public? He thought what a great team they had been, and found himself thinking about the team in the past tense.

He was nervous when he felt his second skin on his fingers for the first time in three and a half months. He fastened the Velcro of his goalkeeping gloves and waited for the first shot from the goalkeeping coach. When he caught it, he pressed his fingers into the ball to reassure himself that these were his old hands, that nothing, not even an odd feeling, was left in his wrist. The ball felt exactly the same. He rolled it back to the coach with gusto, and already the next shot was coming at him.

What seemed to have changed when Robert returned to team training in January 2009 was not his hand, but his sense of territory. He knew exactly where he had to stand in every situation, but he felt as if he was moving on unfamiliar terrain. His distance from the defenders and the strikers on the other side of them seemed sometimes too big, sometimes too small; even the goal behind him seemed to be growing and shrinking. 'I lack a sense of space', he said.

He was still completely preoccupied with regaining his sense of territory when the Bundesliga resumed after the winter break. In the last four months he had had only two weeks of football training.

Before his comeback he pulled his baseball cap low over his face again and went to see his new psychiatrist. He liked Dr Stroscher, and after each conversation he felt better.

He went through his rituals before the match against Schalke 04, to regain the feeling that this was just a game like hundreds of others before. He ate his rice pudding with apple puree and cinnamon the evening before the game. He watched the Friday evening Bundesliga match downstairs in the hotel bar with a few of the other players. Before kick-off Tommy Westphal slipped the match report form Robert had to sign as captain under his door, while he was on the toilet.

The day after the game Teresa was going to go skiing with her friends, he remembered. Then he would be alone. He sent Teresa a text. 'Sorry for my behaviour over the past few days. I'm so tense at the moment.'

Schalke started as if something had thrown the team into a rage. They overran Hannover. After two minutes Jefferson Farfán stood clear in front of Robert. He still felt raw and didn't notice that his body was already unleashing the old automatic reflexes, making him stand tall, for a long time. Farfán played around him, but he was pushed so far out that his shot hit the post. Robert was still lying on the ground when the rebound came towards him, and went over the goal. Before long another shot whistled just over the goal, and then he stopped a firm header by Heiko Westermann. Not even six minutes had passed.

The first goal came only two minutes later. Hannover finally got hold of the ball in midfield. Pinto saw that Schalke's goal-keeper Manuel Neuer was standing far in front of his goal, in line with the radicals' theory, and punted the ball over him and into the net from nearly thirty yards out.

Until the final whistle Robert barely had a moment's peace. Thousands of fists punched the air when he deflected a shot from Halil Altintop over the bar with an incredible reflex, and a minute later he was lucky when the next shot hit the post. Hannover won 1–0. Robert had played one of his best games ever.

When he collected Teresa in the stadium lounge, she immediately saw the red patches on his face.

'Robbi, is everything all right?'

'I feel really hot.'

He had a temperature. His body was reacting to the tension.

'Would you rather I didn't go skiing?' She only said it to calm him down.

'Would you really do that?'

That night, even though it was past eleven, he called Sabine Wilke. 'When things were unpleasant, it was always Robbi who rang, not Teresa,' says Sabine, 'even if their hot water wasn't working and Teresa wanted to ask if she could shower at ours.' Unfortunately Teresa couldn't go on the skiing trip, he said. He was ill, flu – who would look after the dogs if Teresa went away?

Two days later he called Sabine again. She was sitting outside an alpine hut near Kufstein.

'I'm feeling much better already,' he told her. 'I told Terri she should go on the skiing trip after all, but she doesn't want to now. Could you have a word with her?'

He passed the phone to his wife.

'Teresa, won't you come? You said you'd been looking forward to the trip for months.'

'I don't know. Robbi's not that well.'

'I said go!' he called out in the background.

'Do you really want to blow your holiday because your husband's got a cold?' asked Sabine.

'I'll have to answer that when we have some peace and quiet,' said Teresa.

In the background Robert said he was going to book the flight for her.

The next afternoon, during après-ski in Austria, Teresa told Sabine that Robert suffered from depression.

'He suffers from what?' cried Sabine. She had worked for almost twenty years as a doctor's receptionist in neurology and psychiatry. That long stint had left her with a picture of people who suffered from depression very different from that of the balanced goalkeeper she had come to know over the past few years.

He hadn't had an attack in years, Teresa told her, but when he broke his scaphoid bone he had started slipping again, even though the illness hadn't really broken out this time.

Robert had agreed with Teresa that she should tell their friends in Empede. It was wearing him out, always having to play the person everyone thought he was.

Gradually he forgot the screw in his wrist. Steadied by the unbroken rhythm of training and Bundesliga games his thoughts resumed their old pattern: don't go down too early, talk to the defenders, move two paces forward, what's my mark in *Kicker*, how did René Adler play.

He often made notes on pieces of paper now, in the office at home and in the hotel before Bundesliga games. He was busy writing Teresa a poem for her thirty-third birthday. She had just said in passing that he should give her a poem. She would be amazed if he really wrote one.

In the spring, seven months after Robert broke his scaphoid bone, Dr Stroscher told him that he thought the therapy was finished. Robert was looking at life with quiet optimism once again.

He thought about the advice Marco and Jörg had given him. Shouldn't he stay in therapy, just as he did back exercises every day – by way of prevention? Stroscher had told him that simply meeting wouldn't do any good, Robert told Teresa. Only if Robert had the feeling that he had to heal old, deeper-rooted mental wounds should he seek to work them out. But there was nothing there, Robert assured his wife. His hand had healed, and so had his head.

He was doing better than Hannover 96. The victory over Schalke was just an illusion. They were dragging themselves through the Bundesliga season, hovering at the bottom of the mid-table grouping, close to the relegation rankings. They were conceding goals with alarming frequency: three against Cottbus, Stuttgart and Mönchengladbach, five against Bayern Munich, four against Dortmund. At an away game in Wolfsburg the coach had raged once again at half-time, when they were 1–0 down. He expected them to show a more positive attitude. 'Why don't you look at yourself first,' Balitsch hissed back, 'is there anything positive in your pep talk?' Most of the players felt that Balitsch had been talking for the team. Hecking substituted the midfielder and suspended him from training for a week.

'Hecking was a really good coach, a competent trainer with clear ideas,' says Balitsch, 'but in the third year the relationship between him and the team was completely in shreds. We no longer enjoyed the training, or hearing his remarks – and he probably felt exactly the same about us.' The players now called their coach the Cat because he seemed to have nine lives; he wasn't fired even after the heaviest defeat. 'Miaow, miaow,' some of the footballers said in the changing-room, and Hecking's assistant Dirk Bremser innocently joined in.

The press were counting the goals conceded – already more than fifty. Could Germany's goalkeeper play for Hannover 96? they asked every week. Didn't a national goalkeeper need the week-in-week-out experience of standing behind a confident defence? Didn't a national goalkeeper need the hard competition of the Champions League? 'He was repeatedly confronted with the same arguments,' says Jörg. 'Every day he was called into question as the national goalkeeper because his club team wasn't playing well. So the question became unavoidable: perhaps I really should go?'

But one person was analysing those conceded goals instead of just counting them. National goalkeeping coach Andreas Köpke found Robert's suffering at club level not unusual, but all too familiar. When he was his country's keeper in the 1990s Köpke had twice been relegated, with 1 FC Nuremberg and Eintracht Frankfurt. 'I recognised myself in him a bit and was able to empathise with him.' Köpke combed through the goals; he watched closely as Cottbus's striker Rangelov headed unopposed, as two Dortmunders appeared unguarded in front of Robert. He saw a goalkeeper who stopped what he could, and

Robert was once again invited to the World Cup qualifiers, against Liechtenstein and Wales at the end of March.

The goalkeeper was not usually a focus of attention before a game against Liechtenstein, but yet again the sportswriters scented their quarry. Who was the number one? René Adler, who had performed so thrillingly against Russia, and later respectably against Norway, or Robert Enke, who had lost the job through injury? Again there was no definitive answer.

As it was, René couldn't even train because of an injury to his elbow.

René and Robert were sitting at the hotel bar in Leipzig, where the team was staying. Robert knew how hurt the younger man must be to miss an international in Leipzig, his home town. Yet René had a cheerful, friendly conversation with him, showing no sadness or envy. For one brief moment Robert was ashamed of himself. How unfair his initial suspicion of the boy had been.

Sometimes he wondered what the game was doing to him. Why did professional football sometimes awaken in him a trait he hadn't previously noticed in himself – resentment? Even now, seven years later, he didn't want to hear that Victor Valdés had become an excellent goalkeeper. 'I can't be objective about Victor,' he admitted. He was glad that René had come over to him. Perhaps their good relationship would help protect him against the bitterness that lurked within.

Germany beat Liechtenstein 4–0. In ninety minutes one shot came Robert's way.

In Cardiff four days later he was the only one to throw his hands in the air after the final whistle against Wales. Outfield players like Michael Ballack and Mario Gómez registered the 2–0 victory coolly and casually; Robert, on the other hand, believed that he had proved something. With fine reflex saves he had twice abruptly silenced the singing of the Welsh fans. Surely everyone must see now that he was Germany's number one?

Indeed the nagging question of whether the Hannover 96 goalkeeper could also be Germany's had been growing quieter for a few weeks, perhaps because the sportswriters were exhausted by endless repetition, perhaps also because Robert had now dampened the critics' ardour by performing well. But the question still echoed in his head. Only three days after his clean sheet in Cardiff, Hannover 96 suffered its annual embarrassing defeat at Werder Bremen. In his nine Bundesliga apperances for Hannover against Bremen Robert had conceded forty goals. 'I'm not going to the next match against Bremen,' he had once said after a 4–2 defeat. This time the score was 4–1. 'Same procedure as every year, James!' he wrote in his diary, using a line from a popular comedy film. But he quickly became aware that this defeat couldn't just be ticked off as Bremen's annual target practice.

The smouldering conflict between the coach and the team was escalating. With the score at 1–1 and with only sixteen minutes to go Hecking had brought on the defensive midfielder Altin Lala for striker Mikael Forssell. It was a tactical switch dozens of trainers would also have made in his position. But Hannover conceded three goals after the substitution. The players were fuming. How could the coach have brought on Altin at such a critical moment in the game? Altin had just come back after a long lay-off through injury!

The point had come where the players held the coach personally responsible for every setback. Club president Martin Kind could no longer ignore the fact that something was wrong. But he had just fired sporting director Christian Hochstätter for his unsuccessful signings, and he resisted the idea of firing the coach as well. Hecking had proved himself the previous season; the president had even been the one who suggested to him that he aspire for higher things.

Kind rang Robert.

'The president has called me in,' Robert told his closest colleagues. 'He's going to want to know what's going on. What shall I tell him?'

The seven or eight players on the team who carried weight met in an Italian restaurant that they never normally went to for lunch. Even over the antipasti it was clear that there was

Every year Robert and Hannover 96 suffered serious defeats at the hands of Werder Bremen. The Bremen players Miroslav Klose (left) and Hugo Almeida celebrate their latest coup.

basically only one thing to discuss: should Robert tell the president on behalf of the team that things just couldn't carry on under Hecking?

Robert listened attentively and said very little. By the time the main course was served there was no longer any doubt. Robert was to tell Kind that the team would approve a change of coach.

He went quiet. His features barely moved.

'It was hard for him to go to the president with a message like that,' says Hanno Balitsch. 'Robs wasn't the type to ditch a coach. He was aware that things couldn't go on the way they were, but he also saw the coach's side.'

He would do it, Robert said at last.

'So?' asked Hanno when Robert called him early that evening.

'I didn't go and see Kind.'

'What, did your car break down?'

'Break down' was a pretty good description of what had happened.

On his way to Grossburgwedel Jörg Neblung had called him.

'Where are you?'

'On my way to see Kind.'

'Then turn round.'

'What?'

'Turn round. I've just had a tip-off. The press have got wind of the meeting. A photographer's waiting for you outside Kind's company headquarters. If you go, you'll be in the papers tomorrow as the man who wants to topple the coach.'

Robert took the next turn-off. He called the president and told him he was sorry, but the tabloids were in the know about their meeting, so he'd rather not show up as it would only lead to nasty speculation. The bigger portion of the truth – that the team wanted to get rid of the coach – he never passed on to the president. One of the eight conspirators must have betrayed him to the newspaper. The suspicion lay deep. During training the next day, Robert withdrew into himself.

Dieter Hecking stayed as coach.

The papers reported that Robert Enke was clearly moving to Bayern Munich at the end of the season. It was just a rumour that the sportswriters copied from each other until they believed it themselves. Robert knew that the Bayern bosses Uli Hoeness and Karl-Heinz Rummenigge weren't really interested in him. But against his better judgement he became preoccupied with the idea that the German champions might sign him.

He didn't want to leave Hanover for anything in the world and, he'd ruled out a switch to a foreign club – he didn't need any more adventures. But if one of the leading Bundesliga clubs were to tempt him he would go at the end of the season, he had decided.

Tommy Westphal thought back to when Robert had asked him three years earlier, 'What do you think, then, Tommy, should I go or stay?' 'You *must* stay!' Tommy had said back then, with devotion and conviction. Now, in April 2009, he thought of all the reasons he had given to Robert: the team's unique bonding, the feeling of being at home, the belief that the team could only go forward. And when he thought about what had happened to all those hopes he knew that Robert wouldn't even ask him his advice this time.

On 28 April, a Tuesday, the woman from the youth welfare office paid a visit. She had something to tell the Enkes. They had become parents again.

The adoption official then told them everything that was known about their daughter and her biological mother.

'When can we see her?'

'Tomorrow.'

'Tomorrow!'

Robert felt exclamation marks pounding in his temples.

They visited their new daughter at her foster family's home and stayed there for two days to give themselves and the girl a little time to get used to each other. He barely knew what to do with all those exclamation marks in his head and wrote a few lines in his diary:

Robert and Teresa with their adopted daughter Leila.

29 April 2009: Leila entered our life at about half-past four! She is a ray of sunshine, and there was a sense of intimacy straight away!
30 April 2009: Leila is at home! Lara has a sister! We're a family again!

The Bundesliga paid no heed to his paternal joy. The same day he had to set off again, to a hotel in Bochum, to play football the next day. He called Teresa from the hotel at least ten times that afternoon. What was Leila doing? Were her eyes open, those penetrating blue eyes? Had she had anything to drink?

That was a blessing they hadn't had before: just watching their daughter drink quite normally from a bottle.

He amazed the fans in Bochum. While stretched horizontally in the air he stopped a header by Wahid Haschemian, shots from Mimoun Azaouagh, and more besides. Hannover won 2–0. At their fifteenth attempt they had finally won an away game. *Kicker* raved about 'Enke in a brilliant mood' and didn't realise how precisely the description applied to him.

He got home at half-past two in the morning. His heart was still beating quickly from the exertion of the Bundesliga game. He sat down on the bed beside Teresa and Leila and looked at them for an eternity. *I even got some sleep myself!* he noted in his diary.

Over the next few weeks Hannover drew 1–1 with Frankfurt and beat Karlsruhe 3–2. *Leila remains undefeated*, he concluded.

He called his friends to tell them that he had become a father again. The conversation inevitably turned to his future. 'The market for goalkeepers in the Bundesliga is closed, nothing's moving,' he said. 'Perhaps the job at VfL Wolfsburg will come up. That would be ideal, then I could stay in Empede and commute. If not, I'll just stay with Hannover, and I'll be happy there too.'

Leila changed his view of life. The fuss at the club wasn't actually all that bad, it suddenly seemed to him. They had a new sporting director in the form of Jörg Schmadtke – 'I hope he can become a balancing element between the team and the coach'.

People valued him at the club, he felt at home, and whether they were eighth or eleventh it wasn't the end of the world. It was just football.

Since his comeback Robert had played perhaps the best half-season of his career, and he rounded it off in May with a brilliant performance for his country against China.

The season came to an end, and Robert was right: none of the Bundesliga clubs higher up the table was looking for a new keeper. His daydreams about Bayern Munich had been shattered in the strangest way: Bayern's new coach was Louis van Gaal, his tormentor from Barcelona. He certainly wouldn't be buying him any time soon. The only one who made Robert an offer was Tim Wiese.

'Maybe you'll join Werder after all,' Bremen's goalkeeper said to him at a national team training-camp. Robert looked at him and waited for the punchline. 'If Manchester United sign me.'

Robert smiled, then did a double-take when he saw Wiese's face: he plainly believed that United were interested in him.

It was summer again. The pressure that had weighed down on him even on training-free days fell away. During the holidays he would start up a conversation with a stranger next to him on a plane, or pose like a fan with a cardboard Benfica player at a shopping centre in Lisbon.

Before visiting Portugal he planned to meet up with Marco in the Rhineland and go to the wedding of Simon Rolfes, a colleague from the national team. At the wedding in Eschweiler near Aachen he spotted René Adler. They immediately started talking, and he didn't notice as they moved a few metres away from everyone else in the castle garden. They talked about injuries, pressure and Tim Wiese, and at some point – Robert didn't know how much time had passed – they were entirely free of the feeling that as competitors for the same role they were supposed to keep aloof from each other.

Everyone stressed passionately that he absolutely had to move to a big club abroad, René said, but he was unsure whether he should really go away – whether he was mature enough for that. Robert told him about Frank de Boer, Frans Hoek and Novelda, about his great humiliation. He encouraged René not to let anyone – agents, team-mates or newspapers – force him into a state of mind where he thought he had to go further and higher as quickly as possible. All this desire for the next step obscured for most professionals how well they were currently doing. Perhaps the time would come when René himself felt it was time to go, but until then it was better to enjoy what he had rather than focus on a more prestigious club that might never come in for him.

For René it was the most honest conversation he had ever had with a team-mate. 'Among Bundesliga professionals you're always showing off about how strong you are. It was really good to talk to someone about anxieties, about the problems involved in dealing with pressure; problems that torment everyone.'

Afterwards René thought about their conversation, and as he did so he didn't just become aware that he would have to be certain before he risked the leap to a world-class club. As Robert had advised him, he also called to mind everything he had achieved already. After all he was, at the age of twenty-four, already in the Germany squad. Of course he wanted more – he wanted to be the German number one. And of course he would make a huge effort to ensure he was first-choice keeper for the 2010 World Cup. But there was something else that was equally important: not wearing himself out for the dream. He said to his goalkeeping coach and foster father Rüdiger Vollborn, 'If Robbi plays the 2010 World Cup, I'll have no problem with that. The world won't come to an end. I'll sit down on the subs bench and watch what happens next.'

At Simon Rolfes's wedding Robert went back into the banqueting hall in Haus Kambach and loudly drew in a breath, as he always did when he wanted to say something important. Then he said to Teresa, 'René's a really sound guy.'

* * *

On holiday in Portugal, after thirsting for action for a few days he started training for the 2009–10 campaign. It was to be the season of his life, involving a friendly duel for the number one position at the World Cup in South Africa. Like René he was confident that he could live with whatever decision Germany's coaches made. But he was sure in a strange way that he would be in goal in South Africa.

The Portuguese sun had left him tanned. Leila was on a blanket on the terrace. Bare-chested, he was doing press-ups over his daughter, and every time he lowered his body he gave her a kiss.

NINETEEN

The Black Dog

Robert Enke invented the kissing machine. He was sitting on the parquet floor in Jörg Neblung's house in Cologne, lifting Jörg's one-year-old daughter Milla gradually into the air with the jerky movements of a robot. 'I am the kissing machine,' he said to his godchild and went on bumpily working away until he had hoisted the child up in front of his face. There the machine concluded its programme with a smacker on the chops.

Jörg watched them and thought how great Robert looked. He was wearing a white summer shirt, and his skin was bronze against it. He had interrupted his holiday in Lisbon to play a benefit game in Germany.

'Again?' he asked Milla, and the kissing machine started whirring into action.

A month later Jörg saw Robert again. In July he travelled, with the image of the kissing machine in his head, to Carinthia where Hannover 96 were training for the new season. He found a sober-looking goalkeeper.

'I don't know what's up. I've been feeling limp all day.'

'That's normal, Robbi, you're getting old.'

He would turn thirty-two in a few weeks.

Jörg tried his best, but they couldn't really get a decent conversation under way. They got stuck on the usual professional topics: disability insurance, René Adler, and the evergreen question of whether Hannover should play with one or two strikers. 'This season we're battling against relegation,' Robert prophesied. Over the last few years the club had spent millions on players who hadn't raised the team's quality or lifted its mood. Now there was no money left for reinforcement, and

Michael Tarnat, one of the founding fathers of Cabin Two, had ended his career.

Jörg thought that Hannover's bleak outlook programme might be oppressing Robert.

'I'm always so tired,' Robert said to Teresa on the phone.

'You're always tired at training-camp.'

Hanno Balitsch noticed that Robert often withdrew to his room in the afternoon while the others stayed on the hotel terrace telling the old stories, like the one about how they'd covered Mille with eggs and feathers two years earlier. The jokes and the shop-talk with his team-mates had always been Robert's favourite time of day. Often he'd imitated the well-known German television comedy character Stromberg.

Even at training Robert now no longer really seemed to belong to the team. He practised alone a lot with goalkeeping coach Jörg Sievers. The World Cup season had begun and he was working hard on his game. But he still couldn't understand why he always found it so hard to get out of bed in the morning.

'The holidays were really stressful as well,' he said when he rang Marco from his hotel room.

Marco wondered for a moment: how could they have been stressful? When they'd seen each other on holiday in the Rhineland, Robert had told him how wonderful everything was.

'In the last two weeks in Lisbon I was never properly able to rest. My brother was there, and there were arguments. Sick street dogs were running around the property and we had to take them to the vet, so that was another day gone, and because of the house we were constantly dealing with workmen of various kinds. But I'll tell you about that in greater detail one day.'

The exhaustion was still with him when he got back from Carinthia. He tried to ignore it.

Andreas Köpke visited him at training in Hanover. The day before, Köpke had been with Tim Wiese in Bremen. A year before the World Cup Köpke wanted to give his keepers a few pointers on how they could improve their game. He had put together a DVD of scenes from matches to demonstrate his concept of the ideal goalkeeper. For Robert, one sequence featuring Chelsea's goalkeeper Petr Cech was particularly interesting. For crosses, Cech stood in the middle of the goal, often a few yards in front of the goal-line; Robert stood much closer to the near post, and to the goal-line. 'When you're standing in the middle you can take down crosses aimed behind the goalkeeper or far into the penalty area, where you'd never get to otherwise,' Köpke explained to him. Álvaro Iglesias, the second division keeper from Tenerife, had said exactly the same thing to him already five years earlier. Now that Germany's goalkeeping coach had said it to him he tried out Cech's approach during training.

When he started the season on 2 August with a cup match against the Regionalliga West side Eintracht Trier, Robert was tense. He thought it was normal. But it was starting again.

The Mosel Stadium in Trier had low terraces with light-blue corrugated-iron roofs, and wasn't even sold out. At half-time Hannover were leading 1–0 and could have had two or three more goals. Trier drew strength from the narrow deficit – everything was still to play for. Excited by playing in the spotlight, the Regionalliga side went for it. A cross flew in towards the edge of the six-yard box in front of Robert. He saw Trier's Martin Wagner sprinting for the ball and dashed out, spreading his arms to make the goal small. But Wagner had already equalised. No one holds a goalkeeper responsible for a goal like that – just the goalkeeper himself. He had got there too late. Four minutes later the score was 2–1. His defence, confused by the equaliser, had left Robert on his own against two Trier attackers.

There was no getting around it: Trier, a team from the Fourth Division of the German league, was another Novelda. The course of the game was exactly the same, even down to the timing of the first two goals. The fact that Trier won 3–1 rather than 3–2 was neither here nor there.

Robert between Hanno Balitsch (rear) and Mikael Forssell (front) at a Hannover 96 training-camp.

The season was just one game old and Hannover 96 had already lost faith that things could end well for them. For a whole summer the players and Dieter Hecking had made a great effort to persuade themselves that things could work out between them. But this defeat brought out all the destructive thoughts in the team: the playing system with one defensive midfield player and two strikers wasn't working; they weren't a real team any more; when would the club finally release them from their coach? Working with them must have been a source of torment for Hecking.

Thoughts raged in Robert's head, too, and again and again he reached the same conclusion: nothing was going to work out. The black thoughts multiplied, his head grew leaden under their weight, and suddenly it became clear to him just what he had been incubating since July.

He had a moleskin diary in which he recorded his appointments. For Wednesday, 5 August 2009 he wrote *10 and 3.30 pm training*. Immediately after that he now added: *At the moment it's incredibly hard to be positive. It hit me quite quickly and unexpectedly. Talked to Terri and told her about my need to open up. I know myself that it's impossible.*

He was wondering: why now? The first clinical depression had hit him in 2003 when he felt worthless with FC Barcelona as a misunderstood goalkeeper. But this time he could see no similar trigger. He never did find a clear answer to the question of why the black thoughts returned that summer, and no one will ever be able to give him an answer.

There were things weighing upon him at that time, of course. He felt the pressure, self-created but multiplied by the media, not to allow himself a single mistake from now on, in the season of his life, if he wanted to be Germany's number one. The tense situation at Hannover 96, in which as captain he was caught in the middle, was also tearing at his nerves. Lara's death was ever-present, even though he had come to terms with it as best he could over a period of almost two years – but one can never forget the death of a child. It could be that that burden alone brought the darkness back. But it's equally possible that his second clinical depression was triggered by something else, perhaps a minor factor that neither Robert nor his psychiatrist nor anyone else could have recognised. Depressions don't arise according to a pattern. If someone is susceptible to the illness it's quite possible that he will regularly cope with extremely stressful situations without any difficulty, but at a particular moment will be thrown off the rails by what might appear from the outside to be a trivial or mundane matter.

He thought he knew what needed to be done. He would

have to get up early in the morning, ideally change Leila's nappy, not spend long over breakfast, and then get off to training. If he started the day in a structured way, if he did one thing after another, the fear wouldn't find so much room inside his head. The crucial thing was the morning. He woke up with a fear of the day, and if he stayed in bed even for a minute that fear would take him prisoner.

Hanno Balitsch couldn't understand it. Robert was constantly biting his lips, and he hardly spoke these days. Even when he was with the other players trotting down the beaten path from the training-ground back to the changing-rooms he seemed strangely stand-offish. His gaze wasn't focused on anything any more. He looked right through his team-mates.

After training the outfield players kept on their boots, which had short plastic studs, as they jogged the few hundred metres back to the changing-rooms. The goalkeepers, who used long aluminium studs, swapped their boots for trainers, for reasons of comfort. Hanno exploited the opportunity when Robert knelt down on the pitch on his own for a moment to change his footwear.

'Are you leaving the sinking ship, Robs?'

'What do you mean?'

Hanno had been wondering about what might be troubling his friend and he had remembered something Robert had recently confided in him: he could be joining Schalke before the start of the Bundesliga if Bayern Munich managed to winkle away Schalke's goalkeeper Manuel Neuer. Schalke's coach Felix Magath had once sounded out Robert over such an eventuality.

'No, nothing happening there,' Robert said.

'But something's bringing you down.'

'Yes, but I can't tell you right now.'

'OK.'

Hanno didn't ask any more questions. He and Robert had a friendship with clear boundaries. They didn't talk about private concerns. Hanno had the feeling that 'Robs wasn't the type who could cope if you told him private things like, "I'm having problems at home at the moment". He would have felt uncomfortable about that.'

They walked to the changing-rooms together, the only sound Hanno's football boots clattering on the tarmac of the car park.

At home, Robert said to Teresa, 'Shit, Hanno's noticed something.'

In the afternoon he looked for something he could do to prove that he was still in control of things. He cleaned the jacuzzi. He didn't feel any improvement. Then he got furious: why should cleaning the jacuzzi make anything better? How were things *ever* to get better?

Over dinner, Teresa thought out loud. Perhaps they should tell somebody, at least their best friends, so that he didn't have to live in a cloak-and-dagger way all the time?

Before training the next morning he asked Hanno if he had a moment.

'Have you ever had any experiences with depression?'

'No,' Hanno replied cautiously, thinking that someone in Robert's family must suffer from it.

'I have serious problems with it.'

The term 'depression' meant something to Hanno Balitsch, as it does to most people. But on the way home, when he thought about what sort of an illness it was, he realised he couldn't put his finger on anything concrete at all.

Hanno bought the book *My Black Dog* by Matthew Johnstone. It's a little picture book in which a young man with a magnificent quiff is pursued by a black dog. When the black dog appears, the man can't enjoy anything any more; he can't concentrate on anything, or eat anything, he's just frightened of the black dog. And he's so ashamed of his fear that he doesn't tell anyone about the black dog – which only makes everything worse. 'Keeping an emotional lie takes an incredible amount of energy,' says the man in the picture book. 'How I put my depression on a leash' is the book's subtitle.

'Now I can understand a little bit what Robs goes through,' Hanno said to Teresa.

She asked him to keep an eye on her husband. It was important that he didn't stray during training, that he didn't slip into dark thoughts. 'If you notice that he's letting things slide, give him a kick in the backside.'

'Teresa, much as I'd love to, I can't have a go at the team captain in front of everybody.'

'OK, then just push him in a positive direction.'

Hanno Balitsch gazes steadily with clear eyes. He's convinced that things in life are always best solved straightforwardly, even though this has caused him a few problems in his career. He stopped talking to the *Bild* reporters after he felt they had treated him unfairly; since then he could be sure of a devastating review if he delivered a below-average game. Robert admired Hanno's openness while at the same time being startled by it. 'Hanno can be very aggravating for the coach and his team-mates, but also for our opponents,' he once said. They had immediately got on. 'Where football was concerned, Robs and I were often of the same opinion,' Hanno says and smiles, 'although we usually expressed it differently. I was perhaps often too blunt. I said things to the coach or the sporting director that as a player I shouldn't have said. Robs could say the same thing and all of a sudden it sounded diplomatic, acceptable.'

It struck Hanno as a little bit strange that he was now giving Robert encouragement and praise for saves in training he had thought were perfectly everyday for four years. But if there's one thing Hanno can do it's take things as they are with a shrug. He persuaded Robert to play table tennis with him after training; he took him along to lunch. Once Robert's mobile rang when he was on his way to the restaurant with Hanno. It was Teresa.

'I'm going to lunch,' Robert said to her.

'Are you alone?'

'Don't worry. I've got your pit-bull with me.'

* * *

A week after the defeat in Trier, Robert travelled to Berlin with the team on the InterCity Express for the first Bundesliga game of the season. As always on train journeys he sat next to Tommy Westphal and went through his club mail. 'He's a creature of habit,' Tommy thought to himself. Robert thought the letters were going to fall out of his hand. He felt so incredibly tired.

Hannover lost 1–0 to Hertha BSC. He had guessed, he had known, that nothing was going to work out any more. Jörg Neblung was watching the game on television in Cologne and thinking the opposite. 'Amazing how Robbi can play, even in his state!' His defenders had obstructed Robert's view a quarter of an hour before the end of the game and he only saw Raffael de Araújo's long-distance shot when it came flying over their heads straight at his goal, and still he managed to deflect the ball around the post with his fingertips. If he could stop shots like that, his depression couldn't be all that advanced, Jörg thought to himself. He wanted to tell Robert, 'Your save was sensational.'

Robert phoned him first. 'I can't feel anything any more,' he said blankly. 'No nerves, no joy, nothing. I stood out there on the pitch and didn't care about anything.'

What Robert did still feel was the presence of the black dog. He put his baseball cap back on and went to see Dr Stroscher. For the second time in his life he needed anti-depressants. He was adamant that he wanted the same medicine that had helped him in 2003. By now the drug existed in an advanced version, which was supposed to mean it was more effective. He couldn't wait too long for it to take effect, he felt.

On 16 August he and Teresa were invited to the Wilkes' as their younger daughter was turning six. The weather was good enough to have a party in the garden. He felt battered. Everyone was bound to expect him to talk to them, but how could he do that? He didn't think he could conduct a sensible conversation. He lay down on a lounger and pretended to go to sleep.

Uli Wilke thought, 'How lovely. He feels so much at home here that he can just lie down and have a nap.'

Teresa, however, was getting impatient. She knew that afterwards he would be racked with self-reproach because he couldn't even behave normally at a children's party. That was the trap of depression: it stripped him of the power to do the most normal things, and then the impression that he couldn't accomplish anything any more dragged him all the more deeply into the illness.

She rested her hand on his shoulder. He stretched on the lounger and pretended to wake up.

'Come on, let's play some tennis.'

She pressed a racquet into his hand. He was to hit the ball, and she would try to catch it. She held Leila in one arm as she didn't want the child to start crying as soon as she set her down, on top of everything else.

Sabine Wilke wondered why Teresa was always answering on Robert's behalf, why she talked to him as if he were a little child: 'Come on, Robbi, have a piece of cake, you like cake.' It was a great effort for him to decide all by himself whether he wanted plum cake or cheesecake. He felt chronically overtaxed by the minimal demands of everyday life. But he manoeuvred himself through the day: he trained, he smiled at the birthday party, he played his part. Doing something, however much energy it took, was still better than giving in to fatigue and having a rest. Because then the thoughts came.

Then he saw three unopened letters in his office and felt that the place was subsiding into chaos. He thought, I just can't get my papers in order, I can't do anything any more. He thought, it's all too late anyway, I've done everything wrong already.

There was just a slim margin between the need to be pushed and the danger of being overstretched. And his work at Hannover 96 became an extraordinary strain on his nerves; even for a healthy professional it would have been. President Martin Kind and sporting director Jörg Schmadtke persuaded Hecking that it was best for everyone if he stepped down. The pious wish to start over again after the tensions of the previous year had proved illusory after only two Bundesliga matches of the new season. It was 19 August – the same week in which Robert wasn't capable of making his mind up between two types of cake at a children's party. Now he was supposed to respond to Hecking's departure in front of the television cameras, and as captain he was supposed to help the new coach Andreas Bergmann settle in – and he had to deal with the pangs of conscience he felt because they were partly responsible as a team for the fate of their coach.

When Hannover won their first game under Bergmann 2–0, the players in the changing-room at Nuremberg celebrated as if they had avoided relegation. Robert wasn't there. He had to give one television interview after the other. Nearly half an hour after the final whistle he at last reached the changing-room.

Hanno Balitsch knew what an effort it had been for Robert to face all those reporters. 'Herr Kuhnt,' he said to Hannover's press spokesman, 'it's not right for Robs to have to give all the interviews, which means he's not here when the team celebrates. We've got to share out the interviews.'

No one suspected anything. The press spokesman thought what Hanno said was quite understandable: it was important for team spirit that they all celebrate together.

There always seemed to be a logical explanation for Robert's altered behaviour. Tommy Westphal was struck by the fact that Robert was suddenly turning down all the charity benefits to which he had previously always given so much time. Well, all right, of course he's going to want to be at home with his little daughter, Tommy said to himself.

On the long bus journeys to away games, Robert gradually told Hanno everything about his black dog. They could chat without fear of being overheard because at least three-quarters of the players had headphones on. Robert told him about his flight from Lisbon, about Novelda, Frank de Boer and Istanbul. Depression kills all positive feelings, he explained to Hanno, 'suddenly everything strikes you as pointless, hopeless'. It was as if access to his brain had been reduced to a tiny crack through which only negative impulses could slip. Non-depressives could rarely grasp the power of depression because they didn't understand that it was an illness. People wondered why he saw everything in such a negative way, why he couldn't pull himself together. They didn't understand that he was powerless in the face of it. He could no longer control it. His brain functions were altered; synapses inside his head seemed to be blocked. He found it hard to concentrate from day to day, but he could talk lucidly and in great detail about his illness.

He wasn't getting better. On 24 August, his thirty-second birthday, he started crying when his sister Anja rang. For other well-wishers, like Torsten Ziegner, his boyhood friend from Jena, he effortlessly played the part of the cool goalkeeper – 'I just need to keep on playing well then I'll be number one in the World Cup'. When his mother wished him a happy birthday, he asked straight out, 'Mum, have you ever suffered from depression?'

'No, I haven't. I've been profoundly sad, but not depressive, no.'

Today Gisela wonders whether he expected her to ask him a question back, whether he wanted to talk about his experiences of the abyss. Or had he simply wanted to know if he had inherited the illness? But she didn't dare go into the subject further at the time.

After that she only spoke to Teresa on the phone. He didn't want to talk to anyone; he needed peace and his routines in order to regain his equilibrium, he said. The family complied with his request. They wanted to help him, after all.

The Wilkes had bought him a patio heater as a birthday present since he liked to sit in the garden late into the evening. It was better if they didn't bring the present for the time being, said Teresa. 'Otherwise it'll just be another thing standing around. He already gets quite worked up enough about things standing around the place.'

She had now told all their friends from the neighbourhood. 'Act quite normally,' she'd said to the Wilkes. 'But I didn't,' Uli

340

confesses. 'I didn't know how to deal with him. I was completely uptight.'

On Lara's birthday, a week after his own, he went with Teresa to the grave in the morning and released a white balloon. He was sweating with nerves. The InterCity to Cologne left at 3.31p.m. He would be going on a training-camp with the national team for ten days. How was he going to get through that? How could he spend ten days in close proximity to his team-mates without giving himself away? If his depression got out, it was all over.

'Robbi felt walled in,' says Marco Villa. 'He had these two great dreams: to play the World Cup and to out himself as a depressive. And he knew that both weren't possible: one definitively excluded the other. He felt that regardless of what he did he couldn't get over the wall around him.'

Robert wrote a single sentence in his moleskin book that day:

31 August 2009. It was a struggle, but Terri has persuaded me to go to Cologne.

The players were just sitting around in the hotel as they hadn't been given any responsibilities yet, but for Robert, that evening was his first test. The professional footballers union, VdV, had chosen him for their team of the 2008–09 season and invited him to an awards ceremony. In order to get through the proceedings he took some mood-enhancing drugs a doctor friend had prescribed.

A minibus took him and two other members of the national team to the Brauhaus by the main station, where the ceremony was taking place. They were greeted at the front door by Tim Jürgens, deputy editor-in-chief of *11 Freunde*, which was hosting the event with the union. Jürgens knew Robert liked his magazine: the goalkeeper had given *11 Freunde* two open interviews. So why did he return his greeting so coldly? Jürgens wondered. Robert didn't even seem to notice him.

The high ceiling of the Brauhaus bounced the guests' voices back into the hall. The footballing scene was in its element; a few Bundesliga players from Bochum and Cologne were chatting with ex-players and agents. Jörg Neblung switched off mid-conversation a few times to see whether Robert was coping. Luckily he was a goalkeeper, so he received his award first. He was wearing a brown corduroy jacket and jeans, and his face looked gaunt, a lot of people in the hall thought. There was still a hum of conversation from the rear of the hall as he stepped up on to the stage. The business manager of the German football league delivered a dry eulogy. When he passed the microphone to Robert, Jörg stiffened.

Some members of the audience thought Robert looked embarrassed. Others thought it was rather an aloof thank-you because his speech was so sober. Jörg thought his friend was putting in an Oscar-winning performance. He was even smiling! Jörg quickly took a photograph with his mobile phone and sent it to Teresa. 'You can't believe how well your husband is presenting himself here,' he wrote.

An hour later the bus picked up the players again. Tim Jürgens hurried to the exit. 'Once again, many thanks for coming, it would have been a sad event without you,' he said to Robert. The goalkeeper shook his hand and walked on, without looking at Jürgens, without saying a word. 'Christ, they're obviously flying through the world on special flying saucers as soon as they're on the national team,' Jürgens thought to himself, 'if even a man like Robert Enke can behave like that.'

The moment he'd stepped down from the stage Robert had lost all his strength again. He was no longer capable of reacting by the time he left the Brauhaus.

Later, he lay in his hotel bed. The mood lifter kept him from sleeping. He tossed and turned, he was exhausted and wide awake, alone in the darkness. He was easy prey for his thoughts. How could he train tomorrow? There was a jump test on the schedule; the national coaches would have the results in front of them in black and white and see that he was just a wreck. But how could he ever get fit again if he didn't train tomorrow? When he woke up the next morning he hadn't even had two hours' sleep. He had to get up, that was the most important thing. But outside all that awaited him were challenges, demands, expectations he couldn't fulfil. He was only safe in his bed, in the darkness of his room, sealed off by blinds and curtains.

His mobile rang. Teresa.

'I didn't get a wink. And now I'm lying here, just staring at the alarm-clock, and can't even get out of bed.'

'Robbi, get up right now. I'll call again in five minutes, by then you'll have drawn the curtains and showered.'

Five minutes later: 'So?'

'I've done it. Thanks!'

Teresa told Jörg. 'Oh God, and all this while he is with the national team!' He drove straight to the hotel.

Teresa had told him the room number so he took the lift without asking at reception and knocked on the door. Robert wouldn't let him in. Jörg couldn't shout 'Robbi, open up!' as the rooms of the other players were on the same corridor. He went back downstairs and asked the receptionist to put him through. Robert picked up the phone because he saw the in-house number and was afraid it was someone from the German Football Association on the line.

'I'll come down,' he promised Jörg.

Jörg waited in vain. He called again.

'There's no way I can do the jump test today. Everyone will see that my legs are like matchsticks.'

Jörg knew that Robert was in decent physical shape, but he realised that it wasn't the time or the place to talk to the black wall in Robert's brain.

'OK,' he said. 'Go to the team doctor and tell him you've been shivering, that you had cold sweats all night and that you're feeling terrible.'

It was all true.

The team doctor said he'd better skip training. He would give him a blood test to see if he'd caught a virus.

Robert went back to bed.

He kept a diary, as he had done with his first depression;

writing his thoughts down helped him to put them in order. But he usually managed no more than one or two sentences.

1 September 2009. Spent half the day in bed before Terri persuaded me to get up. Don't give up!

The national coach still believed that Robert Enke would start in the World Cup qualifier against Azerbaijan at the end of the training-camp. That summer, Joachim Löw had surprisingly decided that Robert would be in goal for the remaining three qualifiers. 'At a time when no one expected it, we said publicly: he's our number one in the crucial games in the autumn,' says Andreas Köpke. 'You can't give a goalkeeper greater proof of your confidence than that.' Robert, who had shown no signs of waywardness, seemed like the safest choice. But Löw and Köpke hadn't just been watching their goalkeepers playing, they'd also been studying their behaviour. Löw thought it would do both Robert and René Adler good to take the heat out of the competition between the two players by making a clear statement. The fact that both keepers yearned for a life free of conflict was the most important reason to resolve the issue as soon as possible.

The blood test was negative. There was no medical reason why Robert shouldn't stand in goal in a week. And the match against Azerbaijan was in Hanover, Robert's city. He wouldn't let that one slip away.

But he still felt limp, Robert said. On the third day of the course he only managed two light sessions outside of team training. In the hotel he saw some of the Under-21 national players who were in Cologne for a performance test. Among them he recognised a tall, slim boy with a high-cut fringe, and immediately walked over to him.

German footballers usually greeted each other with a loud clapping handshake; Robert had preserved his Portuguese habit of hugging people he liked. The urge to hug Sven Ulreich in the hotel in Cologne came over him spontaneously. A year and a half had passed since he had comforted the young man. Now, Ulreich had established himself as the Under-21 national goalkeeper and was to take over from Jens Lehmann in goal at VfB Stuttgart in the summer of 2010. They talked for a few minutes, and in the end Ulreich said, 'If we don't see each other before, the best of luck in the World Cup.'

And all of a sudden Robert, who had momentarily forgotten his depression, seemed to disappear into his thoughts. 'Yes,' he said at last, absently, 'let's see if we ever see each other again.'

A strange farewell, Sven Ulreich thought once they had gone their separate ways.

3 September 2009. Didn't sleep. Everything seems pointless. It's hard for me to concentrate. Thinking about S.

He felt he could no longer control the black dog. He'd sat down at the dinner table that evening with René Adler and Per Mertesacker; the fourth member of their clique, Christoph Metzelder, was no longer in the squad. René and Per started a conversation, but 'getting Robbi to talk was like pulling teeth', says René. 'He sat there quite mechanically. That wasn't Robbi.'

He no longer had the concentration to take part fluently in a conversation. He just wanted to get back to his hotel room, his shelter, as quickly as possible.

But his commitments weren't yet over. They were due to do some advertising for Mercedes. He was assigned a convertible for the film shoot. 'How long is this going to take?' he asked René. 'What's it all about?' René waited until he could catch Per Mertesacker at a quiet moment. 'What's up with Robbi?' he said. 'He's drifting around like a ghost.' They thought he was still suffering with the virus. 'He must be in a really bad way, with his cold sweats or whatever they are.'

That was how he lived through those days. And with every passing day his distress deepened. The game against Azerbaijan in Hanover was getting closer and closer, along with the expectation that he would play in it.

On Saturday, four days before the match, the team had the

evening off. Jörg organised an appointment with Valentin Markser.

They hadn't seen each other for a long time. After Lara's death, when he had visited Jörg in Cologne, Robert had looked in on Markser. This time it wasn't going to be a session in the usual sense: Markser needed to prepare him for his decision. The next day or the day after that he would have to tell Löw whether he was going to play in Hanover or whether he was going to leave the squad.

The psychiatrist ran through Plan A with him. Robert would tell the team doctor about his persistent complaints, the cold sweats and the sleeplessness. He wanted to have himself checked by his doctor in Hanover, he was to say, so he had to abandon the training-camp. Markser tried to give Robert a sense of what it would mean for his psyche if he cried off the game in Hanover. Then they discussed Plan B. How Robert would go on behaving with the squad, how he could get through the match.

That evening he wrote,

6 September 2009. In the session with Valentin, I'm not honest with him.

He had tried to play down his illness to the psychiatrist. He'd unconsciously felt he had to maintain the lie that everything was all right, even to the man who was supposed to be helping him. Even he didn't understand why.

After the session with Markser he got into the car he'd borrowed from the German Football Association and drove into the night.

Teresa tried to get through to him several times. At half-past eleven he finally answered the phone.

'I'm on my way to the underground car park at the hotel.'

'Oh. I'm glad the conversation with Valentin went on for so long.'

'It didn't.'

'Then where have you been all this time?'

'I drove through the city.'

'Robbi, why did you drive through the city?'

'I just did.'

'Tell me why you drove through the city.'

'I was seeing where I could kill myself.'

'Robbi, are you crazy?'

He managed to calm her down after saying that. It had just been an impulse, it had gone away. Then he took the lift to his room, opened the door to the balcony, went right up to the balustrade and imagined what it would be like to jump.

On Sunday morning he went to the team doctor, Tim Meyer, and put Plan A into effect. Joachin Löw told the press that 'because of a general infection' Robert Enke would not be taking part in the game against Azerbaijan. The team doctor couldn't put it any more specifically than that. Meyer hadn't found any viral or bacterial illness.

The vagueness of the explanation stirred up speculation. Swine flu was the topic of the day – had Robert Enke caught it? The sportswriters opened their reports with lines like, 'The story of Robert Enke is a never-ending drama.' Every time he seemed to be establishing himself as number one with the national team some mishap stopped him in his tracks.

The national coaches were aware of this too. 'We were talking about it: first the scaphoid bone, now the virus – whenever there was a major game on the horizon Robert had some piece of bad luck,' says Andreas Köpke. 'And when Tim Meyer said his blood profile was normal, we wondered: has he got a problem with his head?' Köpke himself had hardly ever been injured in his playing career, but once, when an international against Georgia was taking place in his footballing home town, Nuremberg, he pulled a muscle in his calf. He's convinced that his body took a time-out because of the unusual level of stress. 'But a scaphoid bone fracture when punching – that can't be caused by what's going on in your head. We couldn't imagine that.'

Still, the virus remained a strange thing. The coaches asked the advice of Hans-Dieter Hermann, the Germany team's sports psychologist. He spoke with Robert. With the symptoms he was showing, exhaustion and sleeplessness without an infection, one would have to wonder whether he wasn't suffering from depression, Hermann said to the goalkeeper. Depression, for heaven's sake? He'd just become a father! He was happy, Robert replied convivially. He couldn't detect anything particularly unusual, Hermann told the coaches.

And that was that as far as the coaches were concerned. Robert Enke was just unlucky.

A chauffeur drove him back to Empede. He hadn't shaved – he had neither the strength nor the desire. He looked down at himself. He had dropped out. He had failed.

'Robbi, you've got to promise me something,' said Teresa when they were alone in the house.

He looked at her reluctantly.

'I know depression is making everything look black at the moment, but you've got to fight against that. We're all fighting with you here. You can't just stand on a balcony and jump.'

'Everything's pointless anyway.'

'Robbi, promise me you won't kill yourself!'

'I promise.'

She looked him in the eye, and he held her gaze. 'If you could just have my head for half an hour, you'd know why I go mad,' he said. It sounded like an offer of reconciliation.

A death-wish, to a greater or lesser degree, is part of the illness. For Robert it had never been as intense as it was that Saturday night in Cologne. He had assumed that by stepping down from the game in Hanover he would free himself from one source of pressure. But the fact that he had stepped down exerted an even greater pressure on him. He had failed.

Jörg Neblung interrupted his holiday in Majorca to go and see Robert and Teresa. They sat, as they'd done many times before, on the orange chairs in the kitchen, and ran through Robert's options. Should he feign an injury and secretly undergo a course of therapy? Should he make his illness public and go to a clinic for treatment? For every possible solution Robert saw a reason why it would never work. Seeing only pointlessness was also in the nature of the illness. And Teresa and Jörg found it hard to contradict him. Every possible solution only seemed to raise new problems.

When he had resigned from Fenerbahçe six years ago he was a half-forgotten talent; he could disappear for days and no one asked what he was up to. Now he was number one in the country of goalkeepers. If he took a break for a course of therapy or went to a clinic he wouldn't be able to keep it quiet. Then the World Cup would be out of the question. And what would happen after the therapy, after the clinic? Would he be strong enough to stage a comeback as the Depressive in the full glare of the media? Would he grow bitter if he had to give up football entirely?

At the end of the conversation they seemed to have come back to the beginning: the best option was that Robert should go on playing hide and seek and continue with his treatment with Dr Stroscher. The anti-depressants would have to kick in eventually!

Once they'd seen Robert off to bed, Jörg and Teresa stopped in the hall for a moment.

'What are you doing?' asked Teresa.

Jörg was putting a large porcelain candlestick in front of the bedroom door.

'In case he wants to run off and do something silly tonight. He'll trip over the candlestick and we'll hear him.'

Valentin Markser had told them that suicidal thoughts on their own weren't grounds for panic, but they would have to be alert, and at the same time make sure they didn't control him too tightly. Otherwise he would feel helpless, which would only drive him more deeply into depression.

On the second morning the porcelain candlestick got broken. Teresa had forgotten it was there and had fallen over it.

Valentin Markser was used to being lied to. Depressives often tended to play down their illness, in a kind of false

349

self-protection. Robert Enke had been no exception that Saturday evening in Cologne. That very fact had enabled Markser to recognise the seriousness of the illness. But Robert was being treated by a colleague, so he couldn't get involved. He could only warn him.

When Marco Villa spoke on the phone to Markser, as he did every Monday evening, he thought he heard between the lines that something urgently needed to be done. Marco rang Jörg.

'Jörg, we can't let things go on like this. If football is such a burden for Robbi, we've got to take him out of it.'

'Teresa and I have already talked to him about that several times. But he really doesn't want to go to a clinic because he doesn't want to lose football.'

'If he has to give up being a footballer he'll get over it. He'll find something else. He'll go into hotel management or I don't know what. The important thing now isn't his career, it's about finding his way out of the depression.'

'But if he drops out of football, that's going to make him really ill.'

Robert's best friends were arguing over him for the first time.

Marco was in Italy, and he wasn't to call Robert because it would only wind him up. Jörg had left his wife alone in Cologne with their little daughter and moved in to the house in Empede to support Teresa. But the despair that Marco and Jörg felt at that moment was the same. They were neither competent nor authorised to make decisions about Robert's life. Yet that was precisely what the situation seemed to require from them and Teresa.

He was sitting in the garden, crying.

Teresa ran over to him. 'Robbi, what's up?'

'I don't want to die. I want to go back to Lisbon.'

LISBOA! he wrote in his black book that evening.

One afternoon Jörg asked him to come to the laundry room. Jörg turned the light off. The room had no windows, so it was dark. 'This is your condition at the moment,' said Jörg. 'Now try to feel your way along the walls to the door. That's the path you've got to take. We'll build the walls for you, but you have to walk by yourself.' If Robert found the door and opened it he would see the light – that had been Jörg's intention. Dr Stroscher thought it was an excellent idea when Jörg told him about it later. However, Robert walked not to the door but to the light switch. He clicked it on and shouted like a ghost: 'Boo!' Then he walked to the door, opened it and said, 'And what do I see behind the door? My office. That's what really makes me depressed.'

For brief periods, sometimes for hours in the evening, he seemed to be freed from the illness for no discernible reason. Then just as abruptly he fell back into the darkness.

He even managed some light training on his own. By now Germany had beaten Azerbaijan, 4–0, and the Bundesliga season had resumed. Every day reporters stood at the Hannover training-ground meticulously jotting down which players were missing. And the players who were missing had to have a good reason, like a torn cruciate ligament. Robert may have turned up but there was still no explanation, no justification, for his withdrawal from the national side. In the papers the 'general infection' had turned into a 'puzzling viral illness', and finally into a 'mysterious virus'. There was now a new pressure on Robert: when would he finally be able to explain what was going on?

He had told Tim Meyer that he would have himself checked by a doctor in Hanover. That meant he would have to be able to show that he had undergone some medical tests, otherwise he would lose credibility. And it wasn't impossible that he was actually carrying a virus. Fatigue in the summer had troubled him before the depression had settled in. Perhaps one had influenced the other; perhaps his physical exhaustion had weakened him so much that his psychological weakness was able to return.

Hannover's team doctor sent him for a heart examination at the stadium's sports centre. The examiner was surprised to find that Robert's heartbeat reacted to stress with a slight hesitation. That wasn't normal. The doctor didn't know that Robert was taking psychotropic drugs for his depression, which delayed his reactions.

He was referred to a cardiac specialist at the Agnes Karll Hospital. Jörg went with him. The specialist said that he wanted to give him a urine and a blood test. But what if they found traces of the drugs he was taking in his blood? When the specialist went off to see another patient for a moment, Robert turned to Jörg and said, 'We've got to get out of here.'

When the cardiac specialist returned, Jörg told him that Robert wasn't going to have another blood test, they kept tapping his blood at every hospital he went to, he couldn't lose that much blood, he was an athlete, they were going now. The specialist watched them leave with a bemused expression on his face.

'Mystery surrounds Enke' the papers wrote. There was still no explanation for his strange viral illness.

Without being aware of it, Robert had allowed the dynamics of events to propel him into his next vicious circle. He absolutely had to show evidence of a virus that possibly didn't exist.

'I'm not going along with this any more!' he yelled at home. When Teresa asked him cautiously if it mightn't be better to make his illness public and undergo a course of therapy, he shouted: 'I'm not going to the clinic!'

Instead he went to see a tick-bite specialist in Langenhagen and visited the Institute of Tropical Medicine in Hamburg. Again some blood was taken, for the fourth time in ten days. And the doctors actually found something: he was suffering from a campylobacter infection of the intestine, the club doctor told him. The bacteria weakened the body and caused diarrhoea. It wasn't the sort of infection that made a footballer take a break of several weeks, but he hoped no one would ask too many questions.

Jörg was as pleased about the bacteria as he would have been about a Bundesliga victory for Hannover 96. At last Robert had a reason to disappear from the public eye for a period of time without destroying his World Cup dream once and for all.

On 18 September, the papers reported: 'Enke out of the qualifiers!' The goalkeeper who was always so unlucky was now having to take a break of at least two weeks because of an intestinal infection that had just been diagnosed. In the remaining qualifiers René Adler would play in goal, and was therefore a clear favourite for the job in the World Cup.

Over the past few weeks it had all been too much for Robert, what with stepping down from the World Cup qualifier in Hanover and the anniversary of Lara's death, Jörg told Hannover 96's sporting director Jörg Schmadtke. Robert needed a break. 'If it helps, he can even go to Portugal for a few weeks,' Schmadtke replied.

That same day, Robert travelled to Cologne with Jörg. He wanted to be treated by Valentin Markser again. He was hoping everything would work out as it had in 2003.

That evening he watched the Friday Bundesliga game on television with Markser and Jörg, Schalke v. Wolfsburg. They ate pizza and drank beer. *Couldn't enjoy it*, Robert wrote in his black book.

He went to see Markser every day. He told him to go jogging, it was good for the head. Robert went running and told himself that he hated it. Jörg came up with a programme to occupy him – fetching the papers and bread in the morning, going to the woods with Milla in the afternoon. On the way up the hill he made Robert push the buggy so that he would have to make an effort, so that he would finally have the feeling of having achieved something.

Around this time I suddenly got a text from Robert. He normally replied to texts almost compulsively, but over the past few weeks he hadn't even managed that. Now he apologised for his silence and wrote about his illness: 'I should say this'll be another good chapter for our book. All the best, Robinho.'

Ronninho and Robinho we called ourselves if we were in a good mood, in memory of the time we spent together in

Barcelona, after Barça's idol Ronaldinho. Where, in the middle of a depression, had the good mood come from, the detachment to think of his illness as a chapter of a book? He and Jörg had cut the hedge in the garden. *After that I felt a bit better*, it says in the black book.

But there was no getting over the fact that this depression had a different power from the one in 2003. After a week in Cologne he absolutely had to get back to Empede, to Teresa. 'In Cologne I always have to walk around in a baseball cap. I don't want to have to hide any more.' After a day in Empede he thought the same thing as he had in Cologne: he couldn't stay there. He really didn't want to be anywhere.

24 September 2009. Decided to go back to Cologne. Madness!

Four days later he drove back to Empede. He wanted to train again, he had to play football again. He got upsurges like that quite often. Suddenly his fighting spirit returned, all of a sudden he wanted to make up in seconds for what he thought he had missed in months. But on this occasion his vigour didn't fade after a few minutes the way it usually did.

Valentin Markser had changed his anti-depressants.

Robert arranged with the psychiatrist to continue the conversation therapy on the phone from Empede, at a higher frequency – three times a day.

On 29 September, a Tuesday, he went back into training with Hannover 96. Hanno Balitsch hugged him, Tommy Westphal said, great that you're back. And he no longer felt the fear. The fear of being found out, of not being good enough as a goalkeeper, of having to have a perfectly ordinary conversation with his colleagues.

'I think I'm a bit better,' he said to Teresa when he got home.

The next morning he woke up, got out of bed and paused. Was it really that easy now, just getting out of bed? How had he managed that?

When he got home from training he phoned Andreas Köpke.

He was training again, he just wanted to say. He still didn't feel a hundred per cent, of course, and it would be a while before he was back in goal, he didn't know how long, but he was back. That was all he wanted to say. Then he went to the nursery and played with Leila. The next morning he brought Teresa coffee in bed.

30 September 2009. It's lightening up! Joining in with life again.

He had done it. They had done it. Teresa couldn't quite believe it, but she was ecstatic. She had had to live with his gloominess for two months, all the moods and injustices of a depressive. She had made an effort to react patiently to his endless complaints, even when she thought her patience was exhausted. Scientific studies showed that divorce rates in marriages with a depressed partner were nine times as high as non-depressive marriages. And they were about to survive again.

On the third day after returning to training he was still well. On the fourth he came back from training with three roses. Before he gave her the flowers, he recited a poem he had written himself. It was about the two Robbis: one Robbi loved her very much, the other one could no longer show it.

The act of buying the roses had reminded him, however, that the illness was still slumbering within him. When the florist had asked him how many roses he wanted he hadn't been able to answer. Three or six? It hammered away in his head. Three or six? He didn't know how long it was before he said in a panic, 'Three, please.'

On the morning of the fifth day he didn't feel like training. He had an appointment with the fitness trainer in the gym. The team were at the hotel; they were playing SC Freiburg that afternoon. He called Edward Kowalzuk and said he would rather skip training today, he wasn't feeling so good. Not a problem, said the fitness trainer. You didn't contradict Robert Enke at Hannover.

It's a test, Robert said to himself, to see how he was if he didn't compulsively structure his day from start to finish.

That afternoon, on the way to the stadium, he wondered, why didn't I go to training? How am I ever supposed to be a good goalkeeper again if I don't train? It's too late – I haven't trained now and I'll never be able to catch up.

At the stadium he went to the changing-room to wish the team luck. He also looked in on the treatment room. Something had changed. His photograph on the wall had disappeared. One of the physiotherapists had stuck a poster of the substitute goalkeeper Florian Fromlowitz over it – just a small gesture, to give the young man a boost before the difficult task that lay ahead of him. Robert said nothing and left the room.

He sat down in the terraces. It was a while before kick-off and he didn't want anyone to talk to him, so he picked up the match programme to use it as a shield. He flicked through it and stopped at the cartoon. Fromlowitz was shown as a human brick wall standing in front of a goal.

What was this? Had they totally written him off here? Did everyone suddenly think Fromlowitz was the number one goalkeeper?

Hannover won 5–2. Fromlowitz played decently, and Robert took the cheers of the fans as an insult to him. Did no one need him here any more? Had they already forgotten him? Was he a face from history that you could just stick a different face over?

In Empede, Teresa tried to catch him out with logic. It was understandable enough that the physios should try to build up the substitute goalkeeper: it wasn't aimed at Robert. And it wouldn't occur to anyone that Fromlowitz was a rival. As soon as he came back he would be playing again.

'You're right,' he said, but the abrupt movement with which he turned away told Teresa that she could no longer reach him with logic.

She hoped things would be better the following morning. Maybe it had just been a bad day.

In the past, when she woke up on a Sunday morning Teresa

had often experienced a feeling of dread in the second or so it took her to get her bearings: 'What happened yesterday, did they win or lose?' She knew the answer would determine how nice Sunday was. Now that same dread ran through her again, but with a slightly different question: what mood would Robert be in when he woke up?

He didn't feel bad, but he didn't feel good either.

Over the next few days he didn't want to get up again in the morning. Teresa would lie just to get him out of bed: 'I have such stomach pains, could you please look after Leila for ten minutes?'

He fought his way through the days, but a fear had returned, the original fear: the fear that all fears would return.

The following Saturday he went to Cologne to see Valentin Markser, as he did on almost all his free days. Russia versus Germany was on TV, the second leg of the World Cup qualifier. It was almost exactly a year since the first leg, before which he had fractured his scaphoid bone. Again he sat in front of the television, again René Adler played outstandingly, again the commentator hyped René. With the 1–0 victory Germany qualified for the World Cup in South Africa, which was to be the highlight of his career. The television pictures showed a jubilant German team triumphantly thrusting their fists into the air. Robert felt as if the fists of his happy team-mates were punching him in the face.

Four days later he pulled out of a training session.

He slipped back into the past. He couldn't stop thinking about those four or five bright days in late September. Why had he suddenly been alive again then, and why, above all, had the illness come back after that? What had he done wrong to allow the darkness to take him by surprise again?

'It's over, Terri. I had the chance to get out of it and I missed it.'

'Robbi, imagine for example that you're moving to Lisbon and you haven't done a language course first. You don't say, it's too late, I'll never be able to learn Portuguese.'

'Brilliant example.'

'It's not over yet! You got better for a while. That only suggests that you will soon be really better.'

She often went with him to training now. The important thing was that he didn't feel lonely. Above all he was to be left unsupervised as little as possible.

The goalkeeping coach put each of his three keepers through the wringer in turn. Teresa went and stood on the sideline, virtually level with the goal; the pensioners who came every day stood closer to the halfway line. The coach volleyed the ball at the left-hand corner of the goal, and as soon as Robert had stopped the ball he had to get up again and jump across to save a shot into the right-hand corner. Three repetitions, then it was Fromlowitz's turn. When she noticed that Robert was losing his concentration as he waited, and hanging his head, she gave the advertising hoardings a quick kick. He felt the sound rather than heard it, and looked over at her. She clenched her fist. Concentrate. Fight.

After two such visits the sports journalists were on the phone to Jörg. Why was Frau Enke always coming to training?

She didn't dare go after that. But because she couldn't leave him alone with his thoughts for that half-hour car journey every day she continued to drive in with him. Sometimes she went to the museum, sometimes she waited in the car, for maybe two hours.

That wasn't the end of it. In the afternoon he also had to be kept busy; he must have no time to brood. She persuaded him to go to the zoo with her and Leila. There he saw a ten-year-old child arguing with its parents, and had a sudden fear of the future. 'How are we going to manage, with the house, with the dogs, and when Leila's bigger?' In the evening she gave him a picture-book about the Hanover region. 'Choose a place where we can all go for an outing,' she said. One of the dogs chewed up the book after it had lain unused for days beside Robert's bed.

16 October 2009. The team is going to Frankfurt, and I don't think I'll ever go with them again.

It was in that mood that he received a message from Teresa to say his mother was coming.

Gisela Enke had, like the other members of the family, stuck to Robert's request to leave him in peace. In her family, this kind of reservation was considered simple good manners. But his mother had had enough. She hadn't spoken to or seen her

Gisela Enke with her son Robert on her back.

sick son for almost two months. She simply told Teresa to say that she was coming, not for him but for Leila. 'I want to see my grandchild.'

Robert's mother was already sitting in the kitchen in Empede when he returned from training the next evening. One impulse within him still worked: his mother's presence relaxed him, as it had done in the past, even if he wasn't enthusiastic about her visit. She opened a bottle of red wine and he even had a glass with her. There was a certain formality to their conversation because his mother sensed that there was something there she wasn't allowed to touch. But he made the effort to speak to her, which was more than he did for most people. He even told her a bit about the depths of his illness. When they got up from the table at last it was half-past ten. He hadn't stayed up as late as that in weeks.

The next morning his mother hugged him. 'Lovely to have you here,' he said, and set off for training. When he came back it was as if the previous evening had never happened.

'Would you like an espresso?' Teresa asked after lunch.

'No.'

'But you always have an espresso.'

'But not now.'

He wanted to punish himself. He didn't deserve any beautiful moments, and the day before he had had a glass of red wine, so he had to punish himself all the more.

His mother told his father about her visit.

'I can't get through to him,' said Dirk Enke.

'Well, then do what I did and just go there.'

'No, I don't want to impose. He's an adult. If he doesn't want to see me, I have to respect that.'

But in the end his father found a way of getting round his own reticence. His son-in-law had bought himself a new car and it needed to be collected from the Volkswagen factory in Hanover. He could do that, said Dirk Enke. He was in the area so could he drop by? he asked Teresa on the phone. She collected him from the station. When Robert opened the door, by way of greeting he said, 'You're lucky to find me alive.' He made no attempt to hide his irritation about the visit.

'Have you actually read *Black Dog*?' his father asked him at the kitchen table.

'Of course.'

'How often?'

'I'm not enjoying this conversation, I'm going to bed,' said Robert, and got to his feet. It was just before half-past nine.

'So we'll talk again tomorrow?'

'We won't talk tomorrow.' He was already on his way out of the kitchen.

Dirk Enke didn't need to be a psychotherapist to recognise that depression hadn't left his son with much of his true personality.

Sometimes Robert startled his team-mates at Hannover 96. Tommy Westphal got curious text messages from him. 'What time's training tomorrow?' 'When is bed-rest before the game?' Why did he ask that? Robert knew all those things. Someone like Robert didn't forget things like that.

Arnold Bruggink, who had played with him now for over three years, was struck that Robert showed hardly any emotions in training.

'Everything all right, Robert?'

'Yes, fine, it's all great.'

When Westphal and Bruggink didn't get answers from Robert, they started providing their own. Maybe Robert wasn't getting much sleep because his daughter was keeping him up at night. Perhaps it was nagging away at him that he had lost his position as Germany's number one.

Autumn rain had softened the pitch, and Robert had blades of grass stuck to his face. Goalkeeping coach Jörg Sievers told him, 'That was great today, you'll soon be ready.' Sievers meant well. Robert panicked. There was no way he could play with his head, and not with his body either. Was he the only one who had noticed how his muscles were wasting away?

'He wasn't in perfect physical shape, but he was good enough for the Bundesliga,' says Jörg. 'He just couldn't see it any more.'

He was sitting at the kitchen table with a mountain of sweet-papers in front of him. It was his pudding. He had already had an extra-large pizza and a bowl of ice-cream. The new drugs Markser had prescribed for him made him ravenous.

Jörg was sitting opposite him at the table. He couldn't remember how many times he'd made the trip from Cologne now; he was there for Robert more than for his family. 'You'll manage to get off the game against Stuttgart on Saturday,' said Jörg, 'but then you'll have missed five weeks since the bacteria were discovered. The journalists can see how well you are playing every day in training.'

Jörg didn't say it straight out, but next week Robert would either have to play or reveal the truth.

TWENTY

The Cheerfulness of Xylophones Silenced

The car radio came on automatically when he turned the key in the ignition. He let the music play; he wouldn't hear it anyway. The B6 was free, it was a Sunday morning – nothing to be seen that could prevent the situation he was heading towards. The day before, Hannover had beaten VfB Stuttgart 1–0. The last game in what could credibly be seen as his period of grace had been and gone.

He was on the way to the stadium. Ideally, he would perform really badly at training and then everyone would recognise that he couldn't play yet. But if he trained badly everyone would ask what was up with him, and then someone was bound to see through him.

And what good would it do him if he managed to get out of the next match? The game after that still awaited him. As far as his fear allowed him to look into the future, Robert saw nothing but tests that he would fail, that he had to fail.

There was no training on Monday – one less test, but one day more when he had too much time to think. Teresa helped him get up. Sometimes she had to return several times until he did it. When Jörg was there he pulled open the window, took Robert's pillow and shouted, 'Come on, Robbi, you can't just lie there all day! It's just your head, not you!' Usually Robert lay there motionless and said nothing. Once Teresa had got so desperate that she kicked the bed. His room only had two narrow windows: if only they had a brighter house so that he'd find it harder to hide away from the day! He lay in bed and pretended he couldn't see her.

All of a sudden, however, he said with despair in his voice, 'I don't want to play on Saturday.' He lay there all morning after that.

Over the next few days the fears competed. The fear of having to play was chased by the fear of being discovered, so he went to training every day. On Thursday the reporters asked him if he was going to be in goal against 1 FC Cologne. 'I'll have to discuss that with the coach.' They had seen the training session and wrote that it could be assumed Robert Enke was returning to the team.

On Friday the team was due to set off for Cologne after morning training. Teresa was playing with Leila in the nursery when Robert came downstairs.

'How are you today?'

'I can't play. Take a look at my thigh. There's nothing there now, all the muscle mass has gone.'

She had already heard this line thirty times, and thirty times she had answered, 'Robbi, you've been training all the time, your legs are as strong as ever. It's not over!' This time she answered, 'Look, there's no point in any of it any more. Let's go to the clinic.'

For a moment he said nothing. Then he just said, 'OK,' and sat down with Leila on the fluffy carpet.

He wanted to check in at the private clinic in Bad Zwischenahn Valentin Markser had recommended. Teresa fetched the clinic's brochure and phoned Markser.

'We're doing it,' she said.

Markser asked how Robert was. Then he said he would call senior consultant Friedrich Ingwersen at the clinic, and call her back.

Meanwhile, she rang Jörg.

'We're going to the clinic.'

Jörg was surprised by his reaction: he was relieved. 'OK, but make sure that you've left the house when it goes public.'

Teresa had to go to the bathroom before they left. She managed to hold back the tears until she had closed the door behind her. That was the end of the dream that they would get their lovely former life back. It was over.

And a moment later – or was it the same one? – she thought: at last it's over.

Valentin Markser rang back. Dr Ingwersen wasn't at the clinic today but he'd made some enquiries and another doctor would welcome them: he was waiting for their phone-call. Teresa jotted down the doctor's name.

Then she wondered out loud: 'But we should also call the youth welfare office before they find out from the newspaper.' What would they say if it was discovered that Leila's adoptive father had to be treated for depression? Could they take his daughter away from him? He had too many other anxieties to have to worry about that as well. Robert dialled the number of the youth welfare office without hesitating. Teresa had insisted on him making the phone-call because she knew there'd be no going back as soon as the lady from the adoption agency was informed. Then he couldn't suddenly turn round on the way to Bad Zwischenahn.

Her colleague wasn't there, an unfamiliar woman's voice said on the phone, did he want to leave a message?

'No, thanks.'

After he had put the phone down, an acrid smell hit Teresa's nose.

'What's that?'

'I'm sweating so much.'

'Shall I call them?' she asked, and waited for him to hand her the clinic's telephone number.

'Not quite yet.' He wanted to go to the bathroom first, to wash.

Two minutes later he came charging back into Leila's nursery, stripped to the waist. 'I'm going to the stadium now! I'm playing tomorrow!'

'Robbi, look at yourself, you can't possibly play.'

'I'm playing!'

'At least let's call Valentin and Jörg again.'

Dr Markser wanted to talk to him. Immediately Robert's

voice was calm, his reasoning sensible. He wanted to try again. He would keep the clinic option open. Markser couldn't force a man who said clearly that he wanted to play football, and who denied having any suicidal thoughts, to go to a clinic.

'You still have the option of Robbi dropping out before the game,' said Jörg. 'In that case he should just pretend he's pulled a muscle during the warm-up.'

Robert got dressed.

'I'm off then.'

'What? On your own? You can't do that, Robbi.'

Teresa rang Markser again. He couldn't go on his own, under any circumstances, Dr Markser agreed.

They left Leila with the housekeeper and were soon on their way. Teresa phoned Markus Witkop, the physiotherapist, from the car. Robert could pull a muscle whenever he liked, at the final training session today, during the warm-up tomorrow, during the game or, as far as he was concerned, even in the hotel, said Witkop. He would do his bit to make sure the truth didn't come out.

Teresa waited in the car during training so that the reporters didn't get suspicious. She didn't dare go into town, because what if he dropped out during training and she wasn't nearby?

Hannover 96 practised their corner-and free-kick variations, and at the end the coach let the team play freely for ten minutes so that they could let off a bit of steam. On the way back to the changing-rooms Robert trotted along with Hanno Balitsch, some distance behind the rest of the team.

'Hanno, I can't play tomorrow.'

'What do you mean you can't play tomorrow?'

'My legs are tired. I can't lift myself off the ground.'

'Robs, you've just saved three balls in training that no one else in Germany could have saved, and you're trying to tell me you have no strength in your legs?'

'I can't feel myself jumping. I can't feel anything at all.'

'Then just play tomorrow without feeling in front of fifty thousand people. You'll do brilliantly in spite of everything.'

From the car, Teresa saw him coming towards her.

'I'm going with the team,' he said.

The players were travelling by train to Cologne. They walked through the main station with their headphones on. Robert grabbed himself a single seat by the window.

Tommy Westphal was startled. 'Have you forgotten me?'

Robert always sat beside Hanno on the bus and beside Tommy on the train.

'Oh, right, no,' Robert replied, with no intention of moving to a pair of seats.

He looks tired, Westphal thought, I expect he wants a bit of peace. For a moment he recalled something that had surprised him during the week. A third of the way through the season, Robert had given fifteen or twenty pairs of his gloves to his fans. He usually did that only in the winter or summer break, when he knew a new delivery was coming in. He could have asked Robert what lay behind this action, but now he had to find another seat. Well, OK, Tommy thought to himself, perhaps he got a new delivery of gloves in October for some reason.

Once Robert had left, Teresa wondered what she should do.

'You don't need to go to Cologne especially,' Jörg said to her. He would call in at the hotel later; until then Hanno and Witti were by Robert's side.

'But I think it's worse for me if I'm not in Cologne,' Teresa said.

That evening in the hotel, Tommy saw Robert sitting in the lobby with Teresa, Jörg and Markus Witkop. Of course, he thought to himself, Jörg lived in Cologne and Teresa was probably using the game as an opportunity to visit Jörg and his wife Tina. They'd recently had a child as well, if he remembered correctly. Tommy tried in vain to make eye contact with someone in the group, then walked on. They seemed to be deep in a serious conversation.

'Look, I'm really sorry to drag you into this too,' Robert said to Witkop.

'No problem.'

'But you'll get into trouble if it comes out.'

'I'd like to do it for you.'

Anyone in the football business with a hint of sensitivity is tormented by a bad conscience because he doesn't see his wife and children for so many evenings and weekends. For Jörg Neblung, that Saturday, 31 October, was one of the days when he really didn't want to leave Tina on her own under any circumstances. He had planned for them to move house that day.

While Jörg was unpacking boxes in his new home, Sebastian Schmidt, a colleague from his agency, went to the football with Teresa. An hour before kick-off they had no idea whether Robert was about to run out on to the pitch or whether he would be overwhelmed by fear in the changing-room.

'I need a glass of sparkling wine,' said Teresa.

He appeared on the pitch for the warm-up. He looked concentrated and powerful in his tight black tracksuit. His face was fuller again, from all those pizzas and sweets. Anyone who knew him, and who looked carefully, wondered why he apathetically let some of Sievers's balls go straight past him.

A quarter of an hour before the whistle the teams went back to the changing-rooms to put on their shirts. The coach said another few words – pass the ball calmly back and forth in defence, better to pass it back rather than riskily forward. Under their new coach, Andreas Bergmann, Hannover had climbed to eleventh place in the Bundesliga. They were back where they belonged.

The players took up position in the corridor outside the changing-rooms. Outside on the pitch a row of red-skirted cheerleaders waited for them. The stadium announcer had put on the club song. There were Cologne fans 'in Rio, in Rome, in Gladbach, Prüm and Habbelrath' sang De Höhner, 'the chickens', a popular local band. The fans waved their red and white scarves, and when it grew quieter the referee marched out.

As captain, Robert stood directly behind him. In his right hand he carried his gloves, in his left he held the hand of a black-haired boy who had been chosen as mascot for the game. Just as the referee started moving, Robert jerkily twisted his head to the right as if to rest it on his shoulder. It was the same movement that had told Teresa ten years ago in that shopping-centre in Lisbon that the fear was inside him.

The captains had to go to the centre circle.

'White or yellow, Herr Enke?' asked the referee, Helmut Fleischer.

'White.'

The referee threw the coin in the air and caught it again.

'White!'

Team captains have normally thought for a long time before hand about which half they would like to start in. Robert looked frantically behind him at one goal, looked ahead to the other goal, grabbed his nose and said, 'Ermmm . . .'

Five seconds later Fleischer was looking at him in amazement.

'We'll stay where we are,' Robert said at last.

'Fine!' said the referee cheerfully.

Helmut Fleischer, an orthopaedist with the army in Fürstenfeldbruck, blew his whistle and two completely different games began. Forty-five thousand people watched Robert Enke in goal again in an ordinary Bundesliga clash after some sort of infection. Teresa and Sebastian watched Robert starting the riskiest game of his career.

One of the side-effects of his anti-depressants was that they slowed down his reactions. How could a man under the influence of these drugs play in goal in a Bundesliga game? Could a man who found the question 'Three or six roses?' overtaxing at a florist's stall decide, when a cross came into his area at speed, whether to run out or not? Could a patient who no longer has enough concentration to form complex sentences stay on high alert for ninety minutes of top-flight football?

Less than half a minute had passed, without a single Hannover player having got anywhere near the ball, when Lukas Podolski abruptly launched the ball long and low into the Hannover penalty area from over forty yards out. Robert ran towards the ball. A split-second later forty-five thousand people muttered with disappointment because Enke had blocked the through-ball without a Cologne striker getting anywhere near it. Teresa and Sebastian yelled with enthusiasm. It was an everyday feat for a goalkeeper, but it was impossible to ignore how quickly and resolutely he had run out to collect that pass. He'd hardly had time to think, which was his good fortune. A goalkeeper's instinct, trained over twenty years, had made his decision for him.

But could he keep his concentration?

Slowly and carefully, Hannover moved the ball around their defence, and when Cologne had the ball they did exactly the same. As soon as the game took off in midfield both teams made crude mistakes. Sometimes Hannover showed a bit of spirit. Cologne, on the other hand, were revealed as a team without an even vaguely passable concept of attack. In the most banal way they kept trying to pass the ball through into the free space behind Hannover's defence. Robert had to run out several times to intercept harmless through-balls. Teresa and Sebastian cheered every time he collected the ball. What's up with them? said the expressions of their neighbours on the terraces.

At last Podolski energetically broke through on the left wing; Robert came out again and safely gathered the ball. Forty-five thousand people were watching a goalkeeper putting in a solid performance.

Anyone who knew about his illness, though, could tell that he wasn't quite right. He had been standing by the near post waiting for Podolski's cross – not, as he had recently started doing, more in the middle of the goal. His instinct was unspooling movements he had made his own since boyhood; for more complicated manoeuvres he lacked both attention and strength. Teresa saw him repeatedly tensing his body when the ball was far away in the other half of the pitch. He was using up an incredible amount of energy just to guard against losing his concentration.

After thirty-seven minutes Jan Rosenthal put Hannover 1–0 up. The goal changed nothing. Cologne continued to pass the ball long and badly. They couldn't think of anything else to do. One corner for Cologne, and then it would be half-time.

Podolski took it. The ball flew into the area six yards out. Robert was standing in the middle of his goal and should have been able to intercept it easily. But as the ball came over he nudged Rosenthal away with his right hand to gain more room for his jump and this made him lose his balance for a fraction of a second. He jumped too late to take the ball, and this time the forty-five thousand shouted along with Teresa and Sebastian.

He had dropped the ball. Cologne's Pedro Geromel kicked at it just a few yards in front of goal. He caught the ball with the tip of his toe so it flew high into the air rather than straight towards the goal and Robert, quite calm once again, caught it and immediately tried to throw it straight to a team-mate so that the game could go on.

That never happened to Robert Enke, the sportswriters murmured. It was his first game after that infection of his – that was how they explained this little mishap.

The television camera caught his face. It seemed frozen with concentration; there was no annoyance, no nerves. It would look exactly the same for the whole ninety minutes. Only one thing seemed strange: he was breathing heavily for a goalkeeper.

Teresa worried at her fingernails. It was half-time. There were still forty-five minutes in which the dread of the corner could return.

But his team protected him in the second half. They carried on defending emphatically in midfield, and Cologne barely bothered him. With a thrilling reflex he punched one long shot from Petit away from goal – in the eyes of the forty-five thousand his only serious test. But it was impressive, perhaps even unbelievable, how alert he was. He was playing very aggressively, taking every available chance to collect a through-ball, even outside the penalty area. When Fleischer confirmed the 1–0 victory with a blast of his whistle, Hanno Balitsch immediately ran over to Robert.

'That was the first step back,' said Robert as his friend hugged him.

On the terraces a fan asked Teresa, 'What's up with you?' She was crying.

The team, with their shirts hanging out of their shorts, marched towards the Hannover end. Robert walked behind them, and high-fived the fans. On the way back, Hanno gave him a high-spirited nudge with his chest.

He saw Teresa standing behind an advertising hoarding on the main terrace. She hugged him, her tears still flowing. 'I'm so proud of you, Robbi.'

He smiled.

'I felt something again,' he said to Markus Witkop.

On the way back, on the bus this time, Hanno Balitsch put on a film on his laptop. He had bought a double plug for two sets of headphones so that Robert could watch with him. Every now and again Robert sent Teresa text messages. 'Don't drive too quickly' and 'Are you drunk already?'

Empathy and humour, two devourers of depression, were shimmering into action again.

Teresa was already waiting at the stadium in Hanover when the team bus arrived that evening. Perhaps they could go and get something to eat, she hoped, maybe even – the word seemed appropriate – celebrate a bit.

'So, how are you?' she asked as he fastened his seat-belt beside her.

'Bad.'

The word was like a blow to the stomach.

'Not even a little bit better?' Her voice was gentle, as if she were begging for a positive answer.

'No.'

He wanted to go home.

When he got there he put his gloves out to dry in the bathroom, took a sleeping tablet and went to bed.

Teresa sat in the kitchen and remembered all the great moments of the afternoon in Cologne: the through-ball collected in the first minute of play, his warm hug with Hanno, his smile when he came over to her after the match. When she saw that smile she had been sure that the game had helped him.

'Today, the words from his farewell letter come to mind,' says Hanno Balitsch. 'He wrote that he had been tricking us all over his last few weeks; that he was only pretending to be better. So I'm afraid he was just saying what we wanted to hear when he came over to me right after the game and said, "That was the first step back."'

Sunday lay before them like a desert. The crushing realisation that the game had failed to change his mood paralysed Robert. For a moment Teresa thought she would never be able to deal with the situation on her own.

She called the Wilkes.

'Sabine, we need a plan. We've got to do something. Isn't there anything we can do together?'

Sabine Wilke talked to her husband, she phoned her sister Ines. All of a sudden they were aware of an incredible feeling of pressure. What were they supposed to do?

Cheesecake, it occurred to Ines. Robert had always loved her cheesecake. She started baking.

That afternoon everyone was sitting at the table at Ines and Jürgen's – Robert and Teresa, Uli and Sabine and the children. Before Ines could cut the cake, Robert leapt to his feet. He had to go to the bathroom.

'Where is he?' Ines asked several minutes later.

'I'll go and get him.' Teresa pushed her chair back. She knocked on the bathroom door and didn't go away until he came out.

He sat down, he praised the cheesecake, but after a few minutes he got up again.

'What do you need, Robbi?'

'I'm just getting myself a wheat beer from the fridge.'

'Stay there, I'll bring it to you.'

'No, no.'

He stayed in the kitchen until Jürgen came to get him.

A little while later he went back to the toilet. As soon as he came back he announced that he was going to have a look around the flat. He wandered through the rooms for a quarter of an hour. He had seen Ines and Jürgen's flat many times.

He simply couldn't bring himself to sit down at the table and chat while thoughts were flying through his head at the same time. Why hadn't his comeback brought him contentment? How could things ever get better if nothing was better even after a game like that? Why didn't he just put a stop to this madness?

He walked through the flat. His body required movement to shake off the thoughts.

The others stayed in the living-room and tried not to s how how unsettling they found his behaviour. It was a natural response to depressed people. His friends believed they had to treat him as if everything was normal out of consideration for him. They didn't want him to remember his suffering. So not only is a depressive an actor, he turns most of the people around him into extras.

He hadn't written any whole sentences in his black book for a long time. *Nothing but self-reproach* was the sole entry for 2 November. He had been sick for nearly three months now. When he had had his first depression, by this point he had been watching comedies with Jörg again and noticing that he sometimes felt a feeling of joy. Six years later he only felt one thing: that it was getting worse.

One sound had not been heard at their farmhouse for several weeks: the cheerfulness of xylophones, the enthusiastic beating of drums and a smoky, powerful woman's voice singing '*Como la rabia de amor, como un asalto de felicidad*' ('Like the fury of love, like an attack of happiness'). In good times he had made the song 'Alegría' by Cirque du Soleil his ring-tone. Now he had set his mobile to silent.

The mobile's display was lighting up on the kitchen table.

He hardly ever took calls any more. The flashing of the phone scared him. What was he supposed to say? What did someone want from him?

'Who is it?' Teresa asked him. If she could at least persuade him to go to the phone, perhaps it might bring him a bit of contentment.

He looked at the display. 'Alex Bade.'

'He's tried to get you five times. Please go and talk to him, Robbi.'

He steeled himself.

Alex Bade, the goalkeeping coach at 1 FC Cologne, wanted to know if there was a chance of enticing Robert to Cologne for 2010–11. Robert's current contract ended in eight months – end of June 2010.

'I can't say what I'll be doing,' he told Bade.

The conversation ended almost as soon as it had begun because Robert said hardly anything.

But now the phone was lying in front of him, and he screwed up his courage. 'I should also phone Lothar Bisinger.' He was hugely bothered by a tiny detail on his gloves. When he fastened the straps on his wrist there was a very small wrinkle at the top of the glove.

'Give him a call,' Teresa encouraged him.

He described the problem to Bisinger, and as always his glove-man said no problem, he would sort it out immediately.

The conversation didn't even last a minute.

'Great that I've sorted that out,' said Robert in the kitchen. 'That's been bothering me for weeks.'

From such everyday triumphs Teresa drew hope and courage that got her through whole days. There was always something positive to be had. You just had to search for it in the smallest details.

She persuaded him to take a look at the clinic in Bad Zwischenahn. 'Just take a look,' she said.

Dr Ingwersen gave them an appointment on Thursday afternoon, 5 November.

Robert immediately told Teresa he couldn't go, he had training until lunchtime, and they would never get to Bad Zwischenahn in time. It was 150 kilometres to the Ammerland, whose quiet country roads and broad horizon tended to attract cyclists rather than motorists.

'Robbi, tell the coach you've got to leave a bit early. Say we have to take Leila for a special examination and your wife doesn't want to go on her own.'

The psychiatric clinic in Bad Zwischenahn was, like their own house, a converted clinker-brick farmhouse. There was good food, wireless internet and private access to the Zwischenahn Lake. Anyone who didn't look too closely might have thought they had ended up at a five-star country hotel. Robert let them show him everything and explain everything without asking a single question. He would have a think about it, he said to Dr Ingwersen as they left.

When they got back into the car he said, even before he had fastened his seat-belt, 'I'm not going there.'

'Just let the idea sink in for a while.'

'I'm an international goalkeeper. I can't go to a clinic.'

'Robbi, there are lawyers in that clinic, university professors, businessmen! Do you think it was any easier for them to come here? But they did, because sometimes it's the only solution.'

'That's very different from my case. If people find out about them, it's not so bad.'

'If someone's a lawyer or a GP and people in his town are saying "He's a depressive" he has just as much of an existential problem as you do. And they manage to find a life afterwards too!'

Their discussion ended in silence. As always when an argument began between them, eventually they just stopped and tried to forget that they had clashed. This time Robert just went to sleep.

The evenings had already started drawing in fast. Teresa's eyes hurt because she had to concentrate so hard on the gloomy A-road, and all of a sudden she was filled with rage. She looked at him. He looked peaceful, innocent, sleeping there in the passenger seat. 'How can you be furious?' she rebuked herself. 'He's sick.'

As they drove through the moors of Lower Saxony Robert was being talked about once again in the world of professional football. That morning the national coach had announced the squad for two internationals, against Chile and the Ivory Coast, in mid-November, and Robert Enke wasn't on the list. Joachim Löw had noticed that both Robert and René Adler often turned down international games on grounds of injury, so he wanted to test Tim Wiese and Manuel Neuer as possible alternatives. In the world of football, always strictly divided into winners and losers, only a few could see the selection of Wiese and Neuer as a mere test. Many people implied that the coach's decision was a blow for Enke.

As thoughts continued to fire like shots through Robert's head – the clinic isn't the solution, I can't go on like this for much longer, there's only one answer – at the same time, after training on Friday, he was obliged to devote himself with the usual sacred seriousness to addressing the excitements of professional sport. It had been agreed with the national goalkeeping coach that he would stay out of these internationals, he said. He would prefer to do targeted training with Hannover – he had a shortfall to make up. 'I can live with that.'

Because he spoke so monotonously, some sportswriters jumped to the conclusion that he was definitely sad, perhaps even furious at having been disregarded, and just didn't want to show it. If Robert really felt relief at not having to join a training-camp with the national team again, he only let Teresa know.

Now that he had played once, in Cologne, it was quite naturally expected that he would go on playing. A day before the game against Hamburg SV, Jörg travelled to Hanover to be with Robert. He drove him to the final training session. No one mentioned, as they had done a week before, the possibility of feigning a muscle strain. The people closest to Robert wanted to give him the feeling that it was quite natural for him to play on.

On Sunday 8 November at three in the afternoon the flood-lights were already on in preparation for the coming darkness. Since the rebuild for the 2006 World Cup the corridor in front of the dressing rooms looked more like a conference centre than a sports ground; the white walls were freshly painted and halogen ceiling lights gleamed above sparkling linoleum floors. Most of the players were already in position when Robert came out of the dressing room. As he walked past he gave two of his team-mates, Steve Cherundolo and Sérgio Pinto, a slap on the back. Out of the corner of his eye he spotted Hamburg's Piotr Trochowski, a colleague from the national team. Trochowski was about to greet him with a handshake and was surprised by Robert's hug. As if he hadn't seen Trochowski for ages, or wasn't going to see him for ages, he briefly rested his cheek on the other man's shoulder. As in his first Bundesliga game ten years earlier, he was wearing a black jersey, the favourite colour of the great goalkeepers.

It was a derby, and the game was sold out. Forty-nine thousand people filled the stadium; a sea of flags rose from the terraces. When the teams came out, Teresa was shocked. Robert had shaved his hair down to a few millimetres. He must have done it in the dressing room before the game. As if this game needed a fighting haircut.

'White or yellow?' asked the referee. Again Robert won the toss, again he looked frantically behind him. His eye lingered for a few moments on the Hamburg end, as if to estimate how many opponents were there. Then he remembered what was to be done. As always when he had the choice, he played with the Hannover fans behind him in the second half.

The game had a different quality from the Cologne match. Hamburg worked together quickly and imaginatively, and fifteen minutes in they scored after a one-two in the penalty box. Robert threw himself at Marcel Jansen's shot, already aware that no goalkeeper would have had a chance.

At home in Nuremberg, Andreas Köpke sat in front of the

television watching the game. Robert struck him as astonishingly listless. As far as he could tell he wasn't talking to his defenders. Whatever happened on the pitch, his face was emotionless, even when against the flow of play Hannover equalised.

The evening before the game Robert had once again taken psychotropic drugs to calm him down.

The referee whistled for a free kick for Hamburg twenty-five yards out, inside left, and Hannover's players knew this was dangerous: Trochowski could give a free kick a wicked swerve. Trochowski took up his position. Robert was four yards in front of goal – the perfect position; Hannover's wall was eight yards in front of goal, as rehearsed. Trochowski clipped the ball straight into the no-man's-land between keeper and defence. Robert was supposed to run forward, the Hamburg players were already running towards him, he only had a quarter of a second to react. Robert didn't move and Eljero Elia headed into the net.

For a moment Robert irritably waved his hand through the air, and then his face was motionless again. Hanno Balitsch thought to himself, 'I hope that goal isn't going to throw him completely now.'

Teresa tried to keep her calm, or what was left of it, but just ten minutes into the second half she couldn't bear it any more. 'I'm going out,' she said to Jörg. Outside the main stand she walked up and down blowing out cigarette smoke violently. There was no one outside the stadium apart from her. She sensed a great silence. The noises forcing their way out of the stadium seemed to be coming from a long way away. But she couldn't convince herself that they had nothing to do with her.

You know what's happening in a football match when you're standing outside just by listening to the reactions of the crowd: the whistles when the opposition pass back into defence, the surge of outrage when a home team player is fouled, the roaring that suddenly dies when the goalkeeper saves a shot, the silence when a striker is standing over the penalty spot. Teresa didn't hear the distinctive noise that would have told her Robert had let in a third goal.

Just before the game was over, by her calculation, she went back into the stadium. A hostess gave her a smile as if she understood exactly what Teresa was going through. They were still playing. A new shout rose up, rage and joy mingling. Penalty for Hannover. Jiři Stajner scored to make it 2–2, and soon after that the game was over.

Jörg hugged Teresa, and it was a long time before he let her go. Robert had executed two decent reflex saves in the second half.

'That Trochowski free kick was the most difficult ball for a goalkeeper so don't make a big deal about it – the rest was very good,' said Jörg when they met later in the stadium lounge.

'Yeah, sure.' Robert looked in the other direction.

In the stadium car park he said goodbye to Jörg with a quick hug – his face didn't show any particular emotion – and a short 'Good luck'.

On the way home to Cologne – two hours on the Autobahn – Jörg thought 'it was another step forward'. But it was more of a reflex thought than a genuine hope. The past few months hadn't just left Robert exhausted, they'd worn everyone else out too.

Robert got into Uli Wilke's car with Jürgen and Teresa. They all felt that they'd had enough for one day.

'Let's get a few pizzas rather than cook anything.'

The dogs started barking when they walked through the gate. Sabine and Ines had been looking after Leila; Sabine's children were doing their homework at the long dining-table. They opened the cardboard boxes, and the smell of hot cheese filled their nostrils. There was no hotter topic than the game but it was hard to talk about it because they had to be careful not to mention the second Hamburg goal.

Robert made no attempt to conceal the fact that he wasn't following the conversation. 'What?' he snapped every time anyone spoke to him.

They didn't want to stay too long anyway, Sabine said, because of the children. When they took their leave, Robert hugged the women. Then he took the children's faces in his hands and kissed them on the forehead.

Titanic was on television.

'Aren't you going to bed?' Teresa asked with surprise.

'I'll just watch this for a bit,' he said.

He had stretched out on the leather sofa with a cushion under his head. He looked relaxed. He had often lain on the sofa like that in the past, when he came home after a hard day's training, filled with the sort of exhaustion that makes you happy.

Outside, the gate closed gently, with a click. 'Did you see that?' Sabine said to her husband as soon as they were on the road. 'The way Robbi kissed the children? He never does that! And the way he hugged me? Much more intense than usual.'

'Maybe he wanted to say thanks for your help.'

Titanic was over three hours long. He watched the whole film. He hadn't watched a film right to the end for months. It was nearly one when he went to sleep. Lately he had often gone to bed at ten.

The next morning Teresa decided to let him drive to training on his own. There were no rules when it came to striking a balance between control and independence; she had to trust her feelings. Over the past week she had driven him to training almost every day, but yesterday he had got through a game so today seemed like a good day to let him drive on his own. To win back another bit of normality.

The players did some light running that day. As they ran around the Maschsee he and Hanno Balitsch fell a long way behind the others. For the first few minutes Hanno made a few remarks about the previous day's game. The answers he got were sparse, which he took as a hint: Robert didn't feel like talking. Hanno thought this indifference might be a sign of progress. At least there was no expression of self-doubt.

After training Robert said goodbye to the players curtly and impersonally; no one expected anything else. Constant Djakba from the Ivory Coast had been at the club for six months and had taken Michael Tarnat's place next to Robert in the dressing room. He could only assume that the goalkeeper never talked as he had never known him any different.

It had started to rain by the time Robert arrived home. As the raindrops rattled against the window-panes, Teresa started worrying. How could she get through the afternoon with him in this weather?

'Come on, let's go into town,' she said. Even if they just went to Ikea, she thought.

They took Leila with them. Teresa actually did set off in the direction of Ikea as they still weren't sure exactly what they wanted to do. The windscreen wipers flicked incessantly back and forth. When they had almost reached Ikea Teresa spotted the posters near the old Expo 2000 grounds.

'Or shall we go to the exhibition?'

Real Bodies, it said on the posters. *Last few days*. Next to the inscription was a picture of a corpse. Teresa had read about the exhibition in the British Pavilion. Preserved corpses in glass cases, bringing humanity, or perhaps human decay, closer to people.

Before Teresa could stop in front of the pavilion Robert said, 'It's closed.'

'You don't know that.'

'Museums are shut on Mondays.'

'Please, just go and look.'

He sprinted through the rain and came back again. 'It's open. But I've got no cash on me.'

'Then let's go to the hole in the wall.'

She wasn't surprised that he was using every trick in the book to avoid going to the exhibition. In his depression he tried to stonewall every kind of initiative.

A visitor coming out of the pavilion recognised Robert and gave him a spare ticket.

Inside it was cold. The walls and windows were hung with black fabric. The only light came from the glass display cases. Teresa had chosen the exhibition without any ulterior motive. She simply wanted to do something, and art had seemed a better bet than Ikea. She'd entertained no hopes that the horror of the decaying body might distract Robert from suicidal thoughts. Over the past two or three days he'd seemed relatively stable, indifferent rather than desperate.

He walked alone along the glass cases – a smoker's lung, a head and neck with the jugular vein revealed.

Teresa had soon had enough. But she didn't want to drive home with these disturbing impressions in their heads. 'Let's go to Café Kreipe.'

In all the cities they had lived in they'd had *their* places: La Villa in Estoril, the Blues Café in Lisbon, the Reitstall in Sant Cugat. Those places had a magical power for them: as soon as they stepped inside it was as if they were slipping into a warm bath. Café Kreipe was their place in Hanover. Its name had long since been changed to Coffee Time, but for them it had stayed Café Kreipe. On the upper storey there were plain wooden tables on a grey carpet, and a big window afforded a view of the opera house.

Robert ordered a plum strudel with vanilla sauce, she noted happily. He was allowing himself to enjoy something, no longer punishing himself. Take it in small steps. If things continued to go as they had today, he would come back out of it.

Teresa took a photograph of him and Leila. He snapped on his smile as if it cost him nothing.

'How long have we actually known Café Kreipe?' he asked, looking round, as if calling up lots of memories.

They were home before seven. With the lights on the rain now seemed to beat pleasantly, reassuringly on the windows. He offered to put Leila to bed. Teresa turned the television on and watched *The Farmer Wants a Wife*. He came and joined her. 'Please don't tell anyone I like *The Farmer Wants a Wife*,' he had once said to her. Teresa snuggled up to him, and he let her. As he did every day, at nine o'clock he phoned Valentin Markser, his doctor, for the second session of the day.

'Terri, I love you,' he said before they went to sleep.

'I love you too, and we'll get through this.'

* * *

The next day – Tuesday, 10 November 2009 – Teresa went to the doctor's in the afternoon. On the way back she bought fillet steak and figs, which he was always so fond of. He was due back from training around half-past six. On his own initiative he had set up two sessions, even though the team had the day off. He wanted to catch up. Wasn't that a sign that he was motivating himself again?

She called him, wanting to know if he was already on the way home. His mobile phone was switched off. 'Christ, Robbi, don't keep doing this to me!' she called out, alone in the house. Don't get worked up, she thought, he'll be back soon.

Her phone rang. She quickly answered it. It was Jörg. He wanted to talk to Robert about something but his mobile was switched off.

'He isn't home yet. I spoke to him on the phone earlier this afternoon but I'm starting to get worried now.'

'It drives me mad when he goes off on his own. Terri, we can't let him drive alone any more!'

'For now the important thing is to get him home.'

Jörg's nervousness had magnified her own. As soon as she hung up, she called him back.

'Jörg, please give me Colt's phone number, I'd like to find out what's going on.'

It was just after half-past six when she phoned Jörg Sievers, whom they called Colt

'Teresa?' the goalkeeping coach asked in surprise.

'Robbi isn't home yet, so I wanted to hear how you parted after training, and to find out when I can expect him.'

The line fell silent. At last Sievers said, carefully, 'There was no training today.'

After he had hung up, Sievers immediately rang Robert's number. After twenty years in professional football he could think of only one reason for Robert's lie: he was with another woman. Sievers wanted to warn him. It went straight to voicemail.

*　　*　　*

Teresa had Jörg on the phone again.

'Search his room right now, see if you can find a goodbye note.'

She ran up the stairs to the bedroom. The picture book the dog had chewed was on the bedside table, along with some magazines and a thriller. It was the first place she looked. She swept the magazines from the table, and a white sheet fell out. 'Dear Terri, I'm sorry that—'

She read no further. Jörg was still on the phone. He yelled, 'I'm calling the police!'

In the days leading up to their attempted suicides, depressives are often in a better mood. They're relieved that they've finally decided to take what is, in their distorted perception, the only way out. At the same time their improved mood is the façade behind which they hide their plans for death from their loved ones.

That Tuesday, Robert had spent eight hours driving around near Empede. In the afternoon he remembered that there was something else he had to do. At a petrol station he changed the oil in his car. Then he drove to the nearest railway crossing, in Eilvese. Sometimes he travelled by train to his training sessions. An international goalkeeper on public transport? Why not, he thought, the connection was good. He knew the timetable off by heart. He knew, for instance, that the regional express from Bremen came speeding through Eilvese at 6.15 p.m.

The View of the Palace

In the kitchen in Empede there's a new photograph on the wall beside the fridge. The colours in the background are slightly blurred, but in the foreground Robert's smile is clear. It's somewhat cautious, but he looks blissfully happy. Leila is sitting on his lap.

It's the last photograph taken of him.

And so this beautiful photograph is also a disturbing piece of evidence, of the power that he developed to hide his illness behind an innocent face. When he posed with a smile for Teresa's camera in Café Kreipe on Monday 9 November, it would appear that he had already decided to kill himself the following day.

A goalkeeper is trained all his life to give no sign of despair, disappointment or fear. That ability always to appear in control of things helped Robert to live on when depression took hold of him. And that gift became his fate when the illness led him to seek his own death: he concealed his intentions so well that no one could help him any longer.

Afterwards, lots of newspapers mistakenly used the German word *Freitod* – literally, 'free death'. The death of a depressive is never a free decision. The illness narrows perception to the extent that the sufferer no longer knows what it means to die. He thinks it just means getting rid of the illness.

How exactly depression comes about has still not been definitively investigated. The illness is rarely triggered by a single clear cause; sometimes the reason for its arrival remains unexplained. Some people become depressed every winter; many people, like Robert Enke, are affected only occasionally, for brief phases of their lives.

Ewald Lienen, who was closer to Robert than most people in the world of football, rang Jörg Neblung after his death and asked, bewildered, 'Why did I never notice anything?' The simple answer is: because when he was working with Lienen on a daily basis Robert was free of the symptoms of the illness. He suffered from depression twice in his life, in 2003 and 2009. At all other times he was just as we saw him, a warm-hearted person who believed that humility isn't a bad character trait, even for a goalkeeper.

His death hit home to so many people not least because they felt that the values he believed in, such as solidarity and consideration for others, were often denied him in the world of professional football. Robert suffered from this, as do many other footballers who notice that certain coaches – and even more than the coaches, the public – see concern or empathy as a weakness in a footballer. 'I'm not like that, and I don't want to be like that,' shouted Robert when he was wound up once again by the idea that his style of play went unacknowledged because he wasn't a fierce goalkeeper who trod a solitary and reckless path. Clearly too few people were willing to grasp that Robert was something better: a goalkeeper with a powerful jump and uncommon reflexes who didn't make a spectacle of his virtues and who firmly believed that ambition could be realised politely and respectfully.

As so often in November in Empede, the colours of nature looked faded when he was buried. The brownness of the fields and the bare trees looked flat under the grey sky. When the funeral in the little monastery church of Mariensee was over, it started raining. Standing in the cemetery, without a jacket, without an umbrella, dressed only in Benfica's thin club suit, was José Moreira. Rain dripped from his black hair, and turned his light-coloured suit dark grey. The sight of him was a reminder of how unprepared all of us had been, in every respect, for Robert's death.

Confronted with the subject of depression, most people realised that they had at best a vague idea of the illness. So there was much talk of how Robert's tragic fate should be used to strip the illness of its taboos. Because many depressives still don't know they're suffering from the illness. Symptoms like a lack of drive and sleeplessness are often interpreted as purely physical suffering. It would be too much to hope that the illness will be better understood all of a sudden, but perhaps this book will do something to help depressives find more sympathy and understanding.

The last photograph of Robert blurs before my eyes, and so many other images come flooding back.

Robert sitting on the terrace of his holiday home in Portugal. He loved sitting out in the open when night fell and a pleasantly cool feeling settled on the skin after the heat of the day. On the mountain opposite, the Palácio da Pena gleamed in all its glory.

'It's so beautiful, you can only believe it if you say it out loud, over and over again: I'm sitting here on the terrace, looking at the Palácio da Pena.'

Teresa, who had heard this sentence dozens of times, blurted out, 'You're always on about your fantastic Palácio, but in ten years you haven't managed even to go and take a look at it!'

It was July 2009, four months before his death, and he had so relaxed into the happy moment that even Teresa's outburst amused him. He sought her hand. 'We will take a look at the palace,' he said. 'We have our whole lives to do it.'

Notes

Apart from the interviewees quoted in the book, I would like to give cordial thanks to a number of other people who helped me with my work on Robert Enke's biography: Rüdiger Barth, Barbara Baumgartner, Matthias Cleef, Jan Döhling, Lotfi El Bousidi, Christoph Fischer, Max Geis, Rui Gomes, Thomas Häberlein, Karsten Kellermann, Christof Kneer, Birk Meinhardt, Jörg Nabert, Peter Penders, Cordula Reinhardt, Harald Stenger, Josep Miguel Terés, Daniel Valdivieso, Tino Zippel.

One quote from Robert Enke has been taken from interviews with Robert Mucha/*11 Freunde*, Michael Richter/*Kicker*, Matthias Sonnenberg/*Sport-Bild* and Katharina Wolf and Gregor Ruhmöller/*Bild Zeitung*. I have taken two quotes from Victor Valdés from a conversation with Michael Robinson for *Informe Robinson*.

As background literature I found the following useful: Josef Giger-Bütler: *Sie haben es doch gut gemeint. Depression und Familie*, Beltz, 2010; Piet C. Kuiper: *Seelenfinsternis: Die Depression eines Psychiaters*, Fischer, 1995; *Psychologie Heute-compact*: 'Depression. Die Krankheit unserer Zeit verstehen'; Thomas Müller-Rörich et al: *Schattendasein. Das unverstandene Leiden Depression*, Springer, 2007; Ursula Nuber: *Depression. Die verkannte Krankheit*, dtv, 2006.

I had problems with the question of how to deal with Robert Enke's diaries. On the one hand they are a unique insight into the world of a depressive – and one of the intentions of this book is to help people understand what depression really is. On the other hand they are personal notebooks. My only clue lay in Robert's wish that he talk about his illness himself, as well as something that he said to me in Santa Cruz de Tenerife in February 2004: 'I've started taking some notes for our book.'

I've tried to pick individual passages out of his diaries which to my mind provide an impressive description of the illness. I have deliberately excluded passages that I see as too revealing, as well as (with one justified exception) remarks about other people. Which part of his diaries he would have published and which not, I will never know.

Ronald Reng
Barcelona, August 2010